STRATEGIC INDUSTRIAL
MARKETING

STRATEGIC INDUSTRIAL MARKETING

Peter M. Chisnall

Manchester Business School

Prentice/Hall International

Englewood Cliffs, NJ · London · Mexico · New Delhi · Rio de Janeiro
Singapore · Sydney · Tokyo · Toronto · Wellington

British Library Cataloguing in Publication Data

Chisnall, Peter M.
Strategic industrial marketing.
1.   Industrial marketing
I.   Title
658.8   HF5415

ISBN 0-13-851395-3

ISBN 0-13-851395 3

Prentice-Hall, Inc., *Englewood Cliffs, New Jersey*
Prentice-Hall International, UK Ltd, *London*
Prentice-Hall of Australia Pty, Ltd, *Sydney*
Prentice-Hall Canada, Inc., *Toronto*
Prentice-Hall Hispanoamericana, S.A., *Mexico*
Prentice-Hall of India Private Ltd, *New Delhi*
Prentice-Hall of Japan, Inc., *Tokyo*
Prentice-Hall of Southeast Asia Pte, Ltd, *Singapore*
Editora Prentice-Hall do Brasil Ltda, *Rio de Janeiro*
Whitehall Books Ltd, *Wellington, New Zealand*

10   9   8   7   6   5   4   3   2   1

Typeset by Multiplex (medway) ltd, England
Printed by A. Wheaton & Co. Ltd, England

CONTENTS

Chapter Four
MARKET RESEARCH   93

Chapter Five
STRATEGIC PLANNING I   130

Chapter Six
STRATEGIC PLANNING 2   168

Chapter Seven
INNOVATION STRATEGY   206

Chapter Eight
INTERNATIONAL STRATEGY 1   237

Chapter Nine
INTERNATIONAL STRATEGY 2   274

Chapter Ten
COMMUNICATIONS STRATEGY   295

PREFACE

For many years, the techniques of marketing have been successfully applied to consumer products and have become closely associated with those types of products. In some ways this perceived link has discouraged the adoption of marketing as an important management responsibility in industrial, technical and professional activities.

The reluctance to apply marketing techniques more widely is understandable, for some of these seem strangely out of gear with industrial market needs. For example, extensive and expensive advertising campaigns, the razzmatazz of widespread sales promotion, or sophisticated systems of distribution which feature several consumer markets are rejected outright by firms producing capital investment goods, technical components, or professional services.

But marketing, as this text endeavours to show, is not restricted to consumer products; it has an essential role to play in organisations of many kinds: industrial, technical, professional, non-profit motivated services, such as health, education and public welfare, etc. All need clients or customers; all need to communicate effectively with those whom they seek to serve; all need to ensure that the products or services they are offering are those which their present and prospective clients and customers are glad to have.

Technical excellence by itself is not sufficient for success; *every* department of a business should be responsive to customers. Marketing is one of the core management functions which helps to put a cutting edge on a company and keeps it ahead of its competitors.

This book is intended to help management students and also practising managers to get a firm grasp of the essentials of industrial marketing. It shows how research and planning can contribute to effective marketing.

The nature of marketing and its applications to industrial and technical products are introduced in the first chapter. Particular emphasis is placed on the critical interdependence of the various specialised functions of management, and on the need for integrated planning.

Succeeding chapters cover the prime characteristics of industrial markets, the complex nature of buying behaviour, methods of marketing research, and strategic planning. Particular attention is given to innovation which is of paramount importance in industrial as well as customer markets.

The final chapter identifies and discusses strategic challenges which face firms seeking profitable opportunities for their resources.

At the end of each chapter, a summary and list of references are given; these, I hope, will be helpful to readers.

In writing this book I have had the advantage of working in a leading business school where graduate students, researchers, and management from many sectors of industry and the public services develop their expertise. In addition, I have significant personal experience both in marketing and as a consultant to several companies over the past years.

I am grateful to the authors and publishers whose works I have consulted and from which I have quoted. In particular, I acknowledge the cooperative attitude of Longmans who kindly allowed me to build this text on the foundations of an earlier one which I wrote for them on industrial marketing.

I hope that this book will contribute to both a pragmatic and academic understanding of the strategic value of marketing in industrial products and services.

With pleasure, I acknowledge the expert typing of the manuscript by my secretary, Miss Janet Young, and also the professional and friendly assistance of my publishers.

As on several other occasions, I dedicate this book to my wife and family.

Peter M. Chisnall

Chapter One

MARKETING PRINCIPLES AND PRACTICE

INTRODUCTION

Modern communities demand many goods and services; in seeking to satisfy these needs, manufacturers, merchants and professional workers apply their skills and energies. Needs are more than physical; in economies of affluence increasing emphasis tends to be given to satisfying psychological needs. These psychogenic (also known as emotional or psychological) needs reflect the complexity of human behaviour in modern society. As Maslow[1] has pointed out: 'Man ... is a perpetually wanting animal. Ordinarily the satisfaction of these wants is not altogether mutually exclusive, but only tends to be'. Human needs are dynamic: as soon as one is satisfied, yet another replaces it to continue the never-ending spiral of satisfactions.

Needs may originate from personal and domestic consumption, from the factory floor or from the hospital operating theatre. Organisations are of many types, industrial, commercial, public sector services, charities, etc., and their needs range widely, from immense capital investments to relatively low-cost items. (See Chapter 2 for further discussion.)

PRINCIPAL TASKS OF MANAGEMENT

Three tasks face those in charge of organisations, whether they are primarily motivated by profits or by social objectives: (1) decide on the nature and extent of the products and/or services that are to be offered to identified customers/clients; (2) arrange the production of those specific products or services; (3) organise the availability of those products and services (this includes selling and distribution strategies). (Refer to Figure 1.1.)

With the growth of mass markets and more sophisticated patterns of consumption, organisations have become larger and more complex. To control these types of resources, specialised functions of management have developed, covering key responsibilities such as research and development, production, finance and accounting, personnel and marketing.

These tasks are so fundamental to the existence and continuity of any organisation that they demand professional expertise. Sophisticated techniques of management in production, costing, financial control, or personnel are vital, but they cannot by themselves produce success in an environment which is growing increasingly competitive. It is the role of

Figure 1.1   Sequential approach to principal tasks of management.

marketing to interpret and assess the needs, both present and emergent, of specific markets, and to stimulate activities within an organisation to develop relevant products/services.

The prime responsibility of management is to organise corporate resources so that they achieve the objectives which have been agreed by the policy makers. The successful managment of a business calls for entrepreneurial qualities: the function of marketing is to assume the role and responsibilities of the entrepreneur whose traditional role has been to interpret market requirements and relate these to the resources available to him.

The activities of a business, or, indeed, of any type of organisation can be viewed as an input–output model (see Figure 1.2). In the case of commercial companies, inputs into the 'pipeline' will be capital equipment and manufacturing resources such as labour, raw materials, components; these are processed by managerial expertise to result in outputs of saleable products/services. This simple flow diagram illustrates the interdependence of the different sectors of a business which together contribute to either success or failure.

NATURE OF MARKETING

Marketing has two aspects: (1) a business philosophy, and (2) a management function.

Figure 1.2   Simple input–output model of market-directed organisational efforts.

Business Philosophy

As a basic philosophy of business, the marketing concept is simple and as old as the hills. It was cogently expressed by the famous founder[2] of economic theory as follows:

> 'Consumption is the sole end and purpose of all production: and the interests of the product ought to be attended to, only so far as it may be necessary for promoting that of the consumer.
> 'The maxim is so perfectly self-evident that it would be absurd to attempt to prove it.'

In this elegantly phrased sentence, Adam Smith gave the guidelines for business success. The logic and 'self-evidence' of his notable words are deceptively simple: in practice, the rules are far from easy to follow.

When businesses were small and their customers few, there was no need for specialised functions of management. The owners of these enterprises were in almost daily contact with their customers and knew their needs intimately. But as firms became larger and their markets expanded, information about customers was less immediate, and there was the growing danger of distance distorting the view held of customers' needs. In his wisdom, Adam Smith reminded these entrepreneurs of the way to business success: think first of what your customer really wants and then organise your resources to satisfy these particular needs.

There is nothing new or revolutionary in what is termed marketing orientation; it might well be called plain business commonsense. However, commonsense tends not to be so commonly distributed, and even today some organisations seem sadly unaware that their eventual success lies in their customers' hands.

The consumer-goods industries were the first to take note of the marketing concept: that 'market orientation' meant more than mouthing anodyne phrases — it required action. This entailed research, planning and the many other activities now regarded as essential parts of an integrated marketing strategy.

To be able to produce goods was not enough; the new philosophy entailed ensuring that those goods were likely to appeal to certain kinds of customer, identified, perhaps, by social class, age, family life-style, geographical area, etc. As Levitt[3] has remarked: 'A product is something people will buy. If they don't buy it, it's not a product (or a service). It's a museum piece'.

Hence, marketing as a business philosophy is only profitable if it is practised by ensuring that the whole organisation is motivated by recognising its dependence upon clients, customers, patrons (or however else those who buy its 'outputs' are described) for its survival and growth. Peter Drucker[4] commented some years ago: 'If we want to know what a business is we have to start with its purpose ... There is only one valid definition of business purpose: to create a customer ... the customer is the foundation of a business and keeps it in existence.'

Management Function

As a specialised function of management, marketing has a key role to play in generating profitable business. It has far-spanning interests and responsibilities across the whole spectrum of industry, commerce and, indeed, the public services. Marketing is the entrepreneurial force in a company: this may be directed towards the launching of a new product range, a novel type of insurance policy, or a new leisure facility. In small organisations, the owner or general manager will assume these types of responsibilities, but as companies grow larger, the function of marketing becomes more sophisticated and specially trained management is necessary.

Despite the lead given by consumer goods industries, many industrial and service firms have shown a marked reluctance to acknowledge that marketing is a legitimate function of management, relevant to their activities. The view often taken seems to be that marketing is probably very useful for fast-moving consumer goods seen on the shelves of supermarkets, but that its value to technical and industrial firms is distinctly limited. Further, it has no place at all in non-profit motivated organisations such as the public health and welfare services, charities, or cultural organisations.

This blinkered view of the role of marketing was not shared by the Machine Tools Economic Development Committee[5] which initiated a two-year intensive study of the British machine tool industry at manufacturing and distribution levels. It was noted that successful firms were characterised by their total commitment to serving customers' needs. 'Every executive in these companies — from top management down through the entire management structure — was personally oriented towards the customer. Marketing attitudes generated the specific motivation of these successful companies'.[5]

A report in industrial innovation by the Institution of Mechanical Engineers[6] also stated that among the major factors detracting from a higher rate of innovation in the UK was 'a lack of appreciation of marketing techniques in middle and lower engineering management'.

Marketing and Collective Attitudes

Apart from the techniques, marketing involves adopting certain standards which affect behaviour throughout an organisation. 'Marketing covers the collective attitudes of management to markets as well as the operation itself'.[7] This attitudinal orientation should be shared by everyone in the organisation, irrespective of their functional responsibilities. A team spirit should be fostered; a willingness to work at all levels and across all functions of a business in order to win customers and their continued patronage.

In Levitt's[3] words: 'Marketing is not just a business function. It is a consolidating view of the entire business process.' It is more than mechanistic: it goes to the heart of an organisation and should affect everyone who works for it. Successful marketing managers act as catalysts in their businesses, causing attitudinal and behavioural changes in all departments. Selling is not confined by them to products or services: they sell actively *within* their companies and encourage new standards of customer-care to be adopted.

Industrial product manufacturers sometimes seem to suffer mental blocks when introducing their products to customers. Most of their managerial time and energy appears to be expended at the development and production stages; the planning of market entry is often haphazard and distinctly at variance with the professional attention given earlier. Clearly, products should be effectively designed and well made, but the task of management is by no means ended. 'Products must be planned, not just designed. It means that people charged with selling the product must participate in its creation at the outset, not just after they get it from the manufacturing department ... this spells an end to the rigid separation between R&D and marketing, between engineering and marketing, and even between advertising and sales promotion ...'.[3]

Organisations are managed by people. Acting in their various vocational roles, people decide the fate of the organisation to which they belong. 'The enterprise is a community of human beings. Its performance is the performance of human beings'.[4] To be successful, organisations need balanced inputs from the different sectors of management so that wealth-producing resources, in the case of commercial firms, are allocated to achieve organisational goals. In commercial terms, this means securing profitable business by offering customers goods and services which they are willing and able to buy. Individual efforts should be coordinated into team performance, with the goals of the organisation clearly in focus. The health of an organisation, like the human body, depends on the right functioning of its many parts. If sickness or inefficiency occurs in one area, the entire organism may malfunction; the disease may be so contagious and lethal that unless drastic surgery is possible there is little hope of survival.

It is a sad fact that in many organisations corporate resources are never really coordinated effectively. In some cases, the spirit of competition exists more *inside* an organisation than in behaviour towards its market. Managerial energies are sapped and frustrated by corrosive campaigns of internecine warfare waged between different departments. Frequently, hostility is not just covert, and employees have been known to speculate whether they all work for the same organisation. Customers and clients may also become aware of the conflict within the organisation which professes to serve them. It does not inspire them with confidence and may well cause them to look elsewhere for their supplies. Goodwill is largely the willingness which an organisation is perceived to display towards satisfying the needs of its market. Apart from physical products or actual services, the 'constellation of benefits' offered to customers should include the pleasantness of doing business. This behavioural factor may well be the paramount influence, particularly when there is little real or observable difference between products or services of a generic type.

The complex pattern of inputs and outputs in an organisation cannot be left to develop haphazardly. Productive working in all branches of corporate activity rests largely on the articulation of a coherent policy. This calls for vision and leadership from top management, a thorough appreciation of the resources of the organisation, and an awareness of market opportunities. These are exacting criteria; but they are the recipe for effective management of organisations of all types. As Robert Heller has observed with his customary vigour: 'In effect, management is a far more homely business than its would-be scientists suggest, more closely allied to cookery than any other human activity. Like cooking, it rests on a degree of organisation and on adequate resources. But just as no two chefs run their kitchens the same way, so no two managements are the same — even if they all went to the same business (or cookery) school. You can teach the rudiments of cooking, as of management: you cannot make a great cook or a great manager'.[8]

As observed earlier, in most small and in many medium-sized organisations, the function of marketing tends to be closely related to that of general management. Often, the chief executive assumes these dual roles, and as the organisation grows his responsibilities extend into many areas, although, of course, his managerial time is not elastic. Further, his early working years may have been largely spent in specific functions such as production or engineering to which he may continue to pay special attention. As the organisation gets bigger, the problems of production, financing and marketing become more complex and mistakes can have more disastrous effects. As long as the managing director can keep his finger firmly on the pulse of the organisation, he can monitor its progress. Because of his status, he can intervene effectively in day-to-day operations, and a degree of flexibility exists which would be unusual in larger undertakings. Since the foundation of the business, this type of managing director (who displays all the attributes of the textbook entrepreneur) is likely to have built up a cadre of executives who show strong personal loyalty as well as professional commitment in their managerial roles.

This tightly-knit organisation tends to suffer under the strains imposed by expansion beyond the boundaries of the close personal management of its founder or his corporate successor. In particular, the efficiency of the whole organisation may be endangered because the chief executive relinquishes direct managerial responsibility in certain activities such as production or marketing. He is likely to have appointed, perhaps through internal promotion, executives to take some of the load off his back. This new phase of organisation life is critical and requires expert handling if growth is to continue: the seeds of decay may easily be scattered by careless (this may not, of course, be deliberate or malicious) planning and direction. The role of marketing, for instance, may never have been formalised; it rested largely on the personal negotiating style of one man who over the years had acquired considerable insight into the behaviour of 'his' customers. These close personal relationships had resulted in satisfactory business, largely because of the bargaining position of the chief executive in the environment and also within his own organisation.

If the marketing function is now formalised by the appointment of an executive with specific responsibilites in this area, he may well face peculiar difficulties within his company. He will not have the authority of the managing director, yet he will be expected to achieve even greater marketing success. His dilemma may be compounded, if he is a newcomer, by his ignorance of the informal as well as the formal relationships existing between other functional areas of management. That he has been appointed at all, may be perceived by other members of the staff as a threat to their status and career prospects. Unless the role of marketing is understood by everyone in an organisation, misunderstanding is bound to arise. This is particularly likely where the functions of marketing have never been identified separately from those of the general manager.

The transition from 'personalised' marketing to 'professionalised' marketing will not be easy: it will present problems that will challenge managerial stamina. But these problems can be controlled, if not eradicated, by effective communications. It should be explained — and this responsibility rests with the chief executive of the developing organisation — that marketing management is just as vital to the success of a firm (or other corporate organisation) as is production. It is not intended to usurp other managerial roles and certainly not to cause them to disintegrate.

DEFINITION OF MARKETING

The Institute of Marketing has defined marketing as follows: 'Marketing is the management process responsible for identifying, anticipating and satisfying customer requirements profitably'.

This definition emphasises that marketing is concerned with supplying the specific needs of identified target markets at a profit. This is one of the hallmarks of marketing that differentiates it from just selling: the latter can be accomplished and actually result in a loss, whereas marketing focuses on profitable opportunities suitable for the resources of a company.

The essence of the marketing concept is to be responsive to customers and their many needs; this cannot happen unless quite a lot is known about customers (present and prospective) and the types of business they run.

Marketing is involved not just with today or this week, but with planning for tomorrow and next year as well. It seeks to find out, and to understand more about, the factors affecting demand for products and services. Anticipation of needs is another responsibility of marketing management; some needs will be long-standing and overt, others may be latent and as yet undeveloped. The problems (and opportunities) of innovation are discussed at some length in Chapter 7: at this time, it can be said that anticipating what people will buy at some future time is one of the most difficult tasks facing marketing management. If it were otherwise, many manufacturers and distributors would reap rich harvests without undue effort.

Working closely with other functions of management, marketing management has to provide a product or service that will satisfy specific customer needs and whose market value exceeds its cost. Value is, to a considerable extent, subjective, and related to utility and desirability. Successful firms are able to market products of superior value, competitively priced, that will attract business and result in profits. This is the key to corporate survival and growth. Exchange of values is at the heart of all industrial and commercial life: planning profitable exchanges is the particular responsibility of marketing management. To quote Adam Smith again: 'Every man ... lives by exchanging, or becomes in some measure a merchant'.[2]

THREE CRITICAL FACETS OF MARKETING MANAGEMENT

Earlier it was noted that marketing is both a philosophy and an activity. As McCarthy[9] has observed, this relatively innocent-sounding concept is really very powerful if taken seriously because it forces a company to think through what its objectives are and what it is doing to achieve those goals. To do so effectively, marketing management can be viewed as having three special areas of activity; these will overlap in real life but are distinguished here for purposes of discussion: (1) analysis, (2) planning, (3) control.

Analysis

The first function of marketing management relates to finding out about markets in which a company operates at present or which it is planning to enter. Without valid and reliable data, marketing cannot be successful. Through systematic marketing research, present and emergent needs will be identified, analysed and evaluated. This evaluation will cover both quantitative and qualitative assessments related to specific markets and special segments judged to be of value to the business. The interpretation of market needs carries heavy responsibility; it demands, among other managerial qualities, the ability to assess risk and to cope with uncertainty.

Marketing decisions are peculiarly difficult to make; there are so many factors in the environment, such as the level of competitive activity or the effect of fiscal policies, which are almost entirely outside the control of the marketer. The marketing manager is expected to possess entrepreneurial flair and judgement without which he is unlikely to be successful. To rely solely on inspiration would, of course, be totally inadequate; professional marketing calls for a blend of analytical and creative skills, especially in the highly competitive conditions which characterise most markets today. (Detailed consideration of market research techniques is given in Chapter 4.)

Planning

The second facet of marketing management — planning — follows logically from the analytical approach which, in particular, characterises professional marketing. Strategic planning involves choices of markets, development of products and services, devising attractive and effective marketing strategies, organising marketing resources and forecasting levels of demand. These are certainly far-reaching responsibilities which demand expertise of a high order.

The success of many industrial firms rests in the ingenuity of their design and marketing staff in offering feasible solutions to the problems of their customers. By collaborating closely with customers in solving, for example, production bottlenecks, suppliers can build up a store of goodwill which will stand them in good stead in competitive markets. Colt International, the air-conditioning equipment specialists, have explained that: 'We don't look at ourselves as sellers of heating and ventilating equipment. Our marketing approach is to design whole systems to solve a customer's problems. Our task then is to seek solutions. Obviously there is great scope for new approaches'.[10] Colt places particular stress on the contribution which value analysis has made in approaching customers' problems. 'The VA [value analysis] approach has also led to a distinct improvement in inter-departmental relations. Problems are no longer looked at in isolation but in the context of the whole enterprise, beginning with supplies and ending with after-sales service'.[10] (The techniques of value analysis are also referred to in Chapter 11.)

Technological change and planned obsolescence have intruded into industrial markets. It is no longer safe for industrial product manufacturers to assume that the environment in which they seek business is immune from the instability and dynamic activity which often characterises consumer markets. Sometimes managements fall so much in love with the technological beauty of their product that they fail to observe what is happening in the world outside — in the market. Steam locomotive manufacturers, convinced that steam would never lose its prime position, were dismayed to find their 'unchallengeable' market suddenly taken over by diesel electric engines. They had failed to recognise that technological developments had resulted in a more efficient method of rail traction, and that the traditional solution of steam power was no longer acceptable to their customers. The natural law dictates that organisms which fail to adjust to a changing environment, eventually perish. If organisations do not modify their products or their methods of marketing, they run the risk of market extinction. In general, there is no shortage of production capacity in modern economies; there is still plenty of scope for industrial and service organisations to adopt a realistic approach to their markets, based on the principles of marketing which have been proved successful in other product fields.

As the sales director of a large petroleum company observed: 'Whatever product an organistion is marketing — whether it be detergents, ladies' lingerie or motor fuels — all have common problems and often similar marketing objectives. For each there is a constant struggle for optimum profits and market share in a competitive environment, related to supply/demand factors, price, quality and costs. Each is irrevocably linked to the consumer and his changing needs'.[11]

Strategic planning (see Chapters 5–9) is vital: it sets the direction and pace for the whole business — not just for the marketing staff. Decisions about products and services will be formalised in a marketing plan and this can be really successful only if all the other departments of a company are consulted and made aware of the projected market objectives.

Control

The third facet of marketing management — control — is essential to marketing productivity. Standards of performance: territory sales quotas, market share ratios, cost/sales ratios, advertising/sales ratios, new product budgets, etc. provide critical measures of performance. An efficient feedback system should be devised in collaboration with financial colleagues. The entire span of marketing activities must be monitored and made cost-effective. As with production, standards should be drawn up in marketing operations, so that corporate objectives are achieved within given constraints of time and cost.

Other useful marketing control tools will be customer profitability analysis; orders stratified by industry and customer size; the ratio of standard to specially manufactured products, etc.

The discipline of cost-effectiveness can be applied to marketing management with notable success. Large volume orders may be very seductive to salesmen, but to the professional marketing executive their effects on profits could be disastrous. No company can continue to operate for long without a reasonable level of profits; orders of dramatic size may help to fill production lines in the short term and it will be a matter of policy whether or not to accept them, but in the long term, only profitable business will ensure that the business continues to exist.

This brief review of the three competences required for professional marketing will indicate that a well-balanced synthesis of skills makes marketing a far more sophisticated area of management responsibility than selling. Marketing is essentially strategic, whereas selling is tactical. This is not in any way to debase the value of selling — which is an important and vital operation — but rather to emphasise that merely to relabel the sales manager a 'marketing manager' is not necessarily going to guarantee that the far wider responsibilities of marketing will be accepted and the corresponding duties performed.

DUAL ROLES OF MARKETING MANAGEMENT

Marketing managers are obviously busy people who are expected to know what is going on in the many markets in which their companies transact business. Their knowledge must be up-to-date, relevant and reliable, and they must possess analytical talent, creative flair, good social skills and organising ability.

Hence, *two particular roles* have to be fulfilled by marketing managers, in whatever kind of market they operate in. They should act as: (1) *interpreters*, and (2) *integrators*.

Again, these roles are not distinct in actual management; at times, one particular activity will tend to become the focus of attention.

Interpreter

The role of interpreter means that marketing management has to analyse and evaluate market behaviour, and interpret these findings not just to the marketing and sales staff, but to *all* the functions of mangement which contribute to the firm's existence and development. Everyone in the business should know which markets are at present being supplied and which markets it is planned to enter.

The requirements of these markets in terms of quality, price, delivery and after-sales service should also be known.

Integrator

The responsibilities of the marketing manager cover the vital function of integrating the marketing plans with all the other activities of the organisation. Adventurous marketing schemes will fall flat on their faces (and so will the marketing managers involved) if this critical stage of integration is neglected. Not the least important market skill is the ability to work in partnership with other managers and to encourage their whole-hearted cooperation through every stage of the marketing operation. This covers the early stages of innovation when an idea is translated into a feasible product or service, through to production on test plant and finally on to regular production lines. It includes budgeting, financial control and all the associated activities which are routine in modern organisations.

Specific aspects of the interface between marketing management and other areas of an organisation will now be discussed in some detail because the integrative function appears often to be overlooked, if not ignored, in many organisations. It may be thought by some marketing managers that this function is not really in their province; nothing is more erroneous. Who else in the organisation should (or could) assume this responsibility if they do not accept it? Certainly not the financial accountant or the production director or the purchasing director or even the personnel director. The managing director will have the overall responsibility of ensuring the efficiency of the organisation, but he is unlikely, except in a small firm, to have the close personal contact with the various markets in which the organisation operates. The other directors' experience and qualifications are related to different areas of expertise from the marketing man. The responsibility to act both as an interpreter *and* an integrator must be his, and he should develop fully his managerial skills in both directions.

CORPORATE INTERFACES OF MARKETING

Purchasing–Marketing Interface

'The present world energy and UK industrial crises have highlighted the need for purchasing and marketing to be closely integrated. Each must be sensitive to what happens in each other's market place'.[12] This close working will result from the exchange of information between marketing management and purchasing management. The products marketed by many companies, for example motor vehicles or electrical engineering, depend heavily for their reputation and efficiency on the contributions made by component suppliers. Standards of quality and reliability of delivery are major factors in purchasing strategies and eventually affect the success of marketing plans. Apart from components, other bought-in supplies such as packaging can frustrate marketing efforts. It is not an uncommon experience, unfortunately, for ex-factory deliveries of finished products to fall dramatically because of shortage of vital kinds of packaging. Dual-sourcing — alternative supply sources — has tended to become widely adopted in an effort to overcome the danger of relying exclusively on one supplier whose own production and distribution arrangements may be upset by economic or industrial difficulties.

In the planning of new products, purchasing and marketing should cooperate closely; some novel products may have component parts which place rigorous demands on supplying firms because of new types of raw material or finishing processes. The level of stocks to be held and the anticipated rate of deliveries are critical matters to be discussed between production, purchasing, finance and marketing. Supplies must be assured *before* new products are introduced into the regular manufacturing and selling lists. One large pharmaceutical chemical company, because of restricted storage at one of its factories, holds a working-stock of a vital material sufficient for only one week's production. But they have taken great care to ensure that supplies of this material are regularly shipped to them on a tightly controlled delivery schedule.

Another valuable contribution which can be made by purchasing management relates to the expert evaluation of trends in, for instance, world commodity markets which are likely to affect sources of raw materials. Production and marketing plans may have to be modified drastically unless adequate buffer stocks have been built up. The soaring costs of some basic materials and the consequent increase in the replacement values of manufacturing stocks are matters which also demand the attention of financial experts in the organisation.

From time to time, suppliers will develop new materials or improve the design of the components which are bought-in. If close links are established between marketing, production and purchasing departments, these improvements and innovations can be fully explored. Recognition of the interdependence of the various functional areas of management in modern organisations should help to break down the barriers of professional chauvinism that still tend, regrettably, to feature managerial behaviour. Innovation is difficult enough without its risks being intensified by the lack of constructive communications between functional areas of management.

Hakansson[13] has noted that some industrial companies encourage an extensive exchange of technical information with suppliers. One strategy, termed 'follow-my-leader', involves buying from the leading supplier in order to obtain early knowledge of technical developments. The other strategy — 'open house' — encourages several suppliers to have ready access to the customer's factory to help in solving technical problems and to develop appropriate products. Suppliers are used, in effect, as extensions of the customer's own technical skills, and if this joint development occurs then both parties are likely to benefit significantly.

Two further strategies adopted by some firms' buying departments are: 'market orientation' — continuous monitoring of different sources of supply through close cooperation with several suppliers, and 'environmental anchoring' which involves intensive commercial interaction with one important supplier.

Purchasing management in collaboration with production management may need to investigate the alternatives of make-or-buy; the economies require careful assessment by the financial and costing experts. The security of continued supplies of critical components should not be overlooked. Multiple-sourcing is a favoured buying strategy in order to protect a firm's own markets. In these discussions, the marketing side of the organisation should be consulted so that an overall view of the implications of the proposed new buying strategy could be objectively taken.

Marketing management have the responsibility of advising purchasing departments of the trends in sales of the various products marketed. Maximum/minimum stock levels and ordering quantities of dependent components may have to be adjusted to avoid stock losses and tying up capital in abnormally high stocks.

Production–Marketing Interface

'While marketing is the essential background for business policy, not all of the decisions governed by policy are marketing decisions ... Many decisions about the management of company resources can be defined as problems of plant layout, materials handling, inventory control, quality control, labour relations, or administrative organisation'.[14]

Marketing efforts need the firm back-up given by an efficient and cooperative production management. Likewise, production is not an end in itself: its functions are to supply products and services which have been designed and made to meet the specified needs of customers, as interpreted by marketing management. As with purchasing, production and marketing efficiency cannot, realistically, be viewed separately. There must necessarily be a spin-off between these sections of an organisation which affects the roots of policy.

If, for instance, marketing management plan to enter a higher quality market, where customers are likely to be more experienced and sophisticated in their buying behaviour, one of the first steps to take is to ensure that production people are fully aware of the need to upgrade the quality of some product ranges. Higher prices will no doubt be charged, so greater added-value should be contributed to products, or the whole marketing operation will prove to be a disastrous flop. It may be necessary to use higher grades of raw materials, to redesign some products, to adopt different manufacturing techniques, and to arrange for stricter standards of quality at every stage of production. Marketing and production efforts should be synchronised; only by sharing the responsibilities of meeting customers' needs are inconsistencies in marketing and production policies to be avoided. Expensive promotional campaigns are wasteful and counterproductive if the goods fail to give satisfaction, or if they are not available to inspect and buy. Companies still fall into the trap of publicising their products on a national scale before ensuring that production resources are adequate to meet the anticipated demand, and that the logistics of distribution have been carefully planned well in advance.

Marketing management should allocate part of their time to discussing problems with their production colleagues. As with purchasing, the likely levels of demand for specific products should be fully explored. Limitations in immediate production capacity may mean that the introduction of new products should be carefully phased, perhaps on a regional basis. Essentially, an equilibrium should be established between production and marketing efforts.

Blois[15] has stated that the marketing and manufacturing parts of a business have the same ultimate goal which is the welfare of the enterprise; this depends on the enterprise's ability to create value. Conflict arises between these functional areas of management because of their 'compartmentalisation', the fact that measures of efficiency are related to departmental and not overall effort, and disagreement as to whether marketing or manufacturing is the most cost-effective way of producing value. The first two problems are said to be well known, but the third is little discussed, despite its critical nature.

The most specialised manufacturing becomes, the more restricted are the end-use markets of the resultant products; marketers most appreciate that such relatively narrow markets can be catered for only if profitable prices are obtainable. An equally important way in which marketing and manufacturing can work well together is for marketing to identify new applications for existing products so that full profit potential is achieved through exploiting experience in production.

It is valuable from time to time for production and marketing management to check manufacturing lists together; stock levels should be compared with sales achieved over certain time periods. One manufacturer once discovered that stocks of a component which was still on their active manufacturing list were sufficient, at present rate of sales, to last for at least 40 years.

By working closely with production colleagues, marketing managers not only break down prejudices and suspicions (the 'them and us' syndrome), but they will also develop a deeper understanding of the whole operation of their organisations. This fuller knowledge will help them in negotiation with customers, and will enable them to suggest feasible solutions to customers' problems which lie within the resources of their firms. Marketing recommendations about product development, for instance, are more likely to attract production management's interest if they take into account the realities of manufacturing, including the constraints under which all firms inevitably have to operate.

Associated closely with production are the research and development activities of companies, particularly those in science-based and technically advanced industries. The critical role of successful new products as a source of corporate development underlines the need for marketing management to keep closely in touch with their R&D colleagues. (Chapter 7 discusses the management of innovation.) Marketing managers should appreciate the problems and processes involved in the development of new products from the idea stage to test-plant production and eventually, perhaps, to commercialisation. It is no use grousing about the nature or rate of new product development if no real interest has been displayed by marketing management in the inevitable frustrations and problems of this exacting task. Marketing knowledge of the needs of particular types of customers, should be shared fully with the R&D people so that they have some useful guidelines in their work. They should also know of the contribution which marketing research could make in the evaluation of new products. Sharing of knowledge by the commercial and technical managers involved in new products would reduce the risks which are an inseperable part of an enterprising product strategy.

To quote again from the report of the Institution of Mechanical Engineers to the Advisory Council for Applied Research and Development: 'To define a saleable product requires contact between designer and purchaser. In too many cases these two extremes of the production process fail to meet. Engineers responsible for design should, ideally, have marketing experience. Failing that, they should be in day-to-day contact with the sales force to ensure that essential requirements are not overlooked or lost in transmission'.[6]

Personnel–Marketing Interface

This aspect of a marketing manager's general interest in the efficiency of his organisation should not be regarded as being of little importance in providing customers with acceptable goods and services. As was observed earlier, people make up organisations and their actions decide the destinies of these firms or other types of corporate undertakings.

Marketing managers are clearly interested in the methods of selecting, training and motivating personnel who work directly in the marketing function. Personnel managers need to be briefed about the nature of the tasks involved in marketing at different levels so that the right kind of staff can be recruited. But apart from this direct influence on personnel policies, marketing management may be able to contribute to the staff training programmes to ensure that a consistent corporate image is reflected to the environment. The telephone operator and receptionist, for example, occupy immensely important links in the chain of corporate communications; often, regrettably, these tend to be the weakest links. Marketing and personnel managers might well tackle this kind or problem, because unless they do so it is unlikely that other functional areas of management will regard it as their responsibility.

Finance–Marketing Interface

Marketing has been defined as profit-generating activity as distinct from selling which is primarily concerned with sales volume. Since marketing management are motivated by profit, it necessarily follows that they should have a professional interest in efficient methods of budgetary control and costing. The inter-relationships between costs, sales volume and profits require to be clearly understood. The impact of marginal analysis on pricing requires to be appreciated, while thorough knowledge of the mechanics of cash-flow needs to be acquired.

Marketing managers should encourage financial executives to take part in drawing up marketing strategies. A regular flow of financial information related to market performance should prove to be of immense benefit in directing marketing activities. Financial and marketing men have a great deal in common: the profitable exploitation of corporate resources. Much greater efficiency could result in most organisations from the mutual exchange of knowledge in these vital functions in management.

Pricing policies, for example, while based on accurate systems of costing, are also subject to expert evaluation of market trends. Experts in both financial and marketing areas need to understand the nature and limitations of the inputs which they can contribute to the final policy decisions. (See Chapters 2 and 5 for further discussions of price.)

Marketing involves expenses, sometimes, in the case of advertising campaigns, involving large sums of money. Marketing management should accept the primary discipline of managerial accountability and cooperate in a system of budgetary control. The responsibility of management is to use corporate resources efficiently. Because marketing inputs are often extremely difficult to measure for their effectiveness, particular care is needed to control expenditure in this area of management.

The short-term and long-term costs of entering new markets call for several skills in evaluating likely success. Market shares, for example, may be increased quite remarkably, but overall profitability may decline. In dynamic marketing conditions, management expertise should be subscribed from many specialities; that marketing management and financial management are able to offer complementary knowledge and skills should be acknowledged by practical managerial involvement.

Coordinating and Integrating Marketing

By discussing the interface relationships of marketing, an attempt has been made to widen the traditional perspective of its responsibilities and to emphasise the need for the various managerial disciplines to cooperate actively in pursuit of the declared objectives, *viz*. policy, of an organisation. (Refer to Figure 1.3.)

The parochial activities which tend to drive wedges between areas of management cannot be tolerated. Marketing management should not be viewed as hatching some kind of sinister takeover scheme for their organisations. All organisations must serve their publics or eventually they will fail in economic terms as well as in the social benefits they plan to confer. To be successful, organisations should keep in touch with the environment; this is the specific task of marketing, particularly in large organisations which have lost the personal antennae with which the small business can so usefully check its sphere of operations.

At a given period in the life of an organisation, certain constraints are the principal limiting factors. In the case of industrial concerns, these could relate to production capacity or skilled labour, or the availability of specific qualities of raw materials. The immediately available corporate resources must be used to greatest advantage, while in the long-term, production and marketing plans are devised which will ensure the growth and prosperity of the organisation. Stability must be ensured, before expansion is feasible. Objective analysis of market opportunities will give management guides as to where the organisation can 'plug into' the market.

Figure 1.3   Corporate interface of marketing.

Marketing strategies rarely succeed in isolation; marketing managers should not regard themselves as solo performers in the environmental area. They need the professional expertise and personal support of other departmental executives. It is time that managers were educated in the art and science of intra-organisational negotiations.

To summarise, the marketer is viewed by Kotler as 'a professional whose basic interest and skill lies in regulating the level, timing and character of demand for a product, service, place or idea'.[16] The strategy he adopts will depend on the resources of the organisation and the needs of the market-place; to some extent there has to be a trade-off between the ideal and what is feasible.

CORPORATE PERFORMANCE: VITAL INPUTS AND RELATIONSHIPS

In this chapter, the nature of marketing, its range of responsibilities and specific functions have been discussed. Further, the interdependence of the specialised areas of management expertise have been described in some detail.

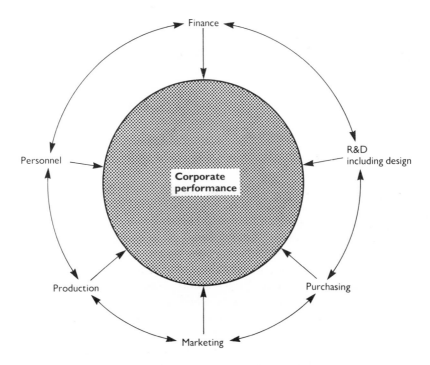

Figure 1.4   Vital inputs to corporate performance.

These vital managerial inputs and relationships are shown in Figure 1.4: these six principal areas of management expertise make distinctive contributions to corporate performance. Together they form a coherent and balanced set of specialised skills; one weak performer in this 'circle of competences' can frustrate overall performance and even result in corporate losses being incurred.

Management specialists are inevitable in complex organisations; each functional area of mangement can make its own unique contribution to the general prosperity of an organisation. Marketing expertise is a necessary but not sufficient condition for success in competitive environments. The whole-hearted enthusiastic backing from *all* managers and staff is critical for significant corporate performance. Linkages between management specialisms should be actively forged and encouraged to develop.

APPLICATIONS OF ORGANISATIONAL MARKETING

Marketing expertise can be applied in a diverse range of organisations. In Chapter 2, the UK economy is described as a service economy and this phenomenon is explored at some length.

In the language of economics, both goods and services provide 'utilities' which possess value-in-exchange. The production of tangible goods dominated the earlier years of industrialisation and provided the main source of employment in the UK and other developed countries. Although manufacturing industry is still a significant part of the UK economy, the tertiary or service section of the economy has achieved prominence both as a source of employment and as a major contributor to the national income. It is, therefore, very relevant to consider marketing in its relationship to the service industries.

MARKETING OF SERVICES RELATIVELY NEGLECTED

The role of marketing in the service industries has tended to be neglected; management literature has largely confined marketing theory and applications to products, the majority of which have been concerned with consumer markets. Discussion of how marketing techniques can be useful in the service sector has largely been limited to banking over the past decade or so. Now it is advisable to extend the discussion to a much wider range of services because of the importance they have assumed in modern economics. It will be useful to lead this enlarged discussion by a brief look at the nature of services and some of the ways in which they could be defined and helped by marketing action.

In 1964, Robert C. Judd,[17] writing in the *Journal of Marketing*, deplored that 'the dollar volume of marketing services continues to increase, yet the definition of what constitutes a service remains imprecise'. His article was followed about two years later by another American marketing professor who noted: 'The marketing discipline has a strong 'goods' orientation. In academic courses in marketing, tangible goods are considered, but rarely services to any extent. Yet services represent an area of economic activity that accounts for 30–40% of consumer dollar expenditures'.[18] Today, of course, the contribution of services to modern economies such as the US has risen very significantly.

Aubrey Wilson,[19] in 1972, presented the case for adapting and applying marketing techniques to achieve greater efficiency in professional services such as banking, consultancy, architecture or accountancy, to which he confined his constructive text. Apart from the wide spectrum of professional services there are, of course, many other non-tangible inputs into the national economy. Further, Wilson's definition of professional services: 'A professional service is one purchased by industry and institutions from individuals and organisations ... '[19] appeared to overlook that professional services (such as legal services) are used by individuals as well as by corporate undertakings. Moreover, the nature and extent of the services which attract the label 'professional' is not at all clear. After protracted study, the Monopolies Commission report on professional services' activities could only go so far as to comment: 'We have not found it possible to define them precisely or to establish a definitive list of professions. We do not in any case think such a definition necessary'.[20]

TYPES OF SERVICE

Services may be classified in two broad areas: commercial services (corporate clients) and consumer services (private clients); these are not mutually exclusive.

Commercial services are provided to organisations to enable them to achieve their corporate objectives which, in the case of industrial and commercial companies, generally relate to profit targets. However, services are consumed by non-profit organistions, because the entire economic system requires services of many kinds to keep it viable. Financial, insurance, legal, transport, security and communications services typify those which are indispensable to organisations, whether profit-motivated or not. Organisational buyers in the public service and in industry may differ in their prime motivation, but they share the same responsibilities: to procure goods and services for use in their organisations as opposed to personal consumption.

Consumer services, on the other hand, are those provided direct to satisfy personal needs; these are of many kinds — legal, financial, medical, technical, insurance, hairdressing, etc. Expenditure on services, as noted earlier, has increased significantly over the past 30 years or so. (See Chapter 2 for further discussion.)

Some kinds of service, e.g. legal, are, of course, used for both personal and organisational benefit, although for different tasks.

Services may also be viewed along a continuum from complex to simple. At one extreme, there are services such as air-conditioning or airlines; at the other pole, the delivery of domestic milk or newspapers. It is suggested that services often tend to devolve from complex to relatively simple projects. Domestic central heating installations, for example, have been simplified by automatic boiler equipment and small-bore piping. Air transport has been simplified ('air-shuttle' operations) and there is, therefore, a move across the continuum. Computer installations, although intrinsically complex, can offer a wide variety of data services, from relatively simple analyses to highly complex statistical manipulations. Programs may, therefore, range across the whole continuum.

Services could also be typified according to the time they are administered; several commercial and consumer services could be rendered: pre-sales → during sales → post sales. Pre-sales services would include advertising, point of purchase displays, demonstrations, exhibitions and related activities. Also included would be the provision of technical data, submission of quotations and specimen products. The intermediate services cover negotiations — which may be a lengthy and involved series of discussions — leading to the booking of acceptable business. After-sales service is a vital element of the product–service mix. Many products require efficient after-sales services. 'In several industrial product markets, "package deals" involving the supply, installation and servicing of equipment help to overcome buyers' legitimate anxieties and confirm their judgement in selecting particular suppliers'.[21] Dissonance reduction should be one of the main objectives of a planned system of servicing.

Levitt[22] points out that prospective buyers of services are generally forced to depend on surrogates to assess what they are likely to get. For instance, they can gaze at glossy brochures depicting distant holiday locations; they can consult current users of a certain software program about its performance; or they can ask existing clients of solicitors or management consultants of their level of satisfaction with the services provided. Whereas tangible products can often be directly handled and even tested in advance of commitment to purchase, it is usually difficult, if not impossible, to do the same with intangible products. It may be possible, of course, as with hotels, to book a weekend stay as a preliminary to a longer holiday, and this may test the facilities.

The complexity of some services may inhibit their diffusion; sometimes there are too many variables to consider before a decision can be taken. The popularity of package-deal holidays supports the argument for simplifying the adoption processes in services. The method of acquiring several other services could be simplified with advantage; for example, life assurance. The growth of credit usage in Britain in recent years has been greatly influenced by the introduction of bank credit cards. This credit service offers customers a relatively easy method of acquiring a financial loan to purchase goods at stores and other outlets which are parties to the credit card franchise. This is a decidedly more flexible approach by the banks to customers seeking credit than the rather cumbersome enquiries which, at one time, characterised the granting of an overdraft.

MARKETING TECHNIQUES FOR SERVICES

As with products, the markets for services are dynamic, and so services should be designed to keep abreast of changing needs. Hence, marketing research should be undertaken to analyse and evaluate market behaviour. This systematic and analytical approach uses the same methodologies as applied for many years in researching product markets. Whether products are tangible or intangible, buying motivations, for example, should be identified before attempting to influence people or organisations to acquire them. (See Chapter 4.)

Some American researchers[23] were interested in determining the degree of market orientation by service firms in the US. It was believed that, generally, service firms lagged behind manufacturing firms in market orientation. From a mail survey of 1000 service firms randomly chosen from the 1982 edition of Dun and Bradstreet's *Million Dollar Directory*, an effective sample of 323 firms from a variety of service industries was obtained. Firms were asked to rate on a five-point scale nine statements which were chosen as indicators of marketing orientation; for example: 'When a customer is dissatisfied with our service, we perform the service again at no charge'. The findings of this study showed that service firms 'are quite heterogeneous with respect to their degree of marketing orientation'. Local firms were significantly less marketing orientated than non-local firms; so also were consumer service firms compared with firms which 'had above average competitive positions'.

The researchers concluded that service firms which neglect marketing principles are 'exceedingly vulnerable in the 1980s'. The combined impact of a low-growth economy and deregulation — which has centred on service industries — is resulting in intensified intra-type and inter-type competition'. In virtually all service activities, new entrants are threatening established firms: 'everyone, it seems, is getting into everyone else's business'. Borg Warner recently diversified into armoured car transport and retail inventory financing. Sears has ambitions to be America's largest department store of financial services; with their immense merchandising experience, they pose a distinct threat to traditional banking operations.

Service industries cannot neglect marketing expertise and expect to survive in the free-for-all that now characterises their markets, as well as tangible goods markets.

After using marketing research, the next marketing technique that can be applied to the service industries is strategic planning (see Chapters 5–9).

Planning, whether of tangible or intangible products, is the foundation of an effective marketing strategy. Again, the principles are the same across diverse markets; the 'marketing mix' or combination of marketing inputs, may well vary, according to the nature of specific services and market environments.

Market planning entails the design and development of services aimed to satisfy the needs of particular kinds of clients, as identified through market research.

Strategic planning should be done thoroughly: it includes the setting of objectives, market target figures, promotional policies, distributive arrangements (e.g. branch network related to market potential), tactical selling operations (this may involve sales training programmes), etc. The planning stage should include the development of new services: innovation in the service industries is as vital as in product markets. Over recent years, many new services have become available to industrial and private users: containerised shipments, roll-on/roll-off loaders, cash dispensing machines, launderettes, private health insurance, abolition or rationalisation of bank charges, option mortgages, barge-aboard catamarans and special banking arrangements for students. Marketers of services should monitor their markets and be prepared to innovate by offering new or improved services.

At the planning stage, the communications policy has to be worked out: from this will develop the corporate image upon which a bank, building society, or technical service's future success will largely depend. (See Chapter 10.)

An effective communications strategy makes full use of the varied forms of publicity available in modern communities. These include media advertising, editorial comment and public relations activities or various kinds. With financial services in particular, the location and appearance of offices is important in building an acceptable corporate image. The joint stock banks have adopted corporate symbols which clearly distinguish their branch offices and given psychological reassurance to clients.

In the past, the joint stock banks have tended to ignore the marketing concept, they have not responded quickly enough to the more critical expectations of their clients, both corporate and personal. Efforts to attract customers have been sporadic and not very well organised. The phenomenal growth of American banks in Britain and the development of other financial houses indicate the dynamic, competitive nature of modern financial services markets. The rapid growth of unit trusts in the UK was largely due to highly trained and motivated salesmen who were able to communicate effectively with target audiences.

Two essential marketing techniques — research and planning — have been discussed relative to service industries. A third technique — marketing control — is applicable; an organised feedback system is necessary to evaluate the performance of marketing strategies. In dynamic market conditions, strategic targets and tactical operations should be under continuous appraisal so that an organisation retains the initiative in its markets. Strategy links the needs of the client with the objectives of the organisation to achieve the optimum allocation of corporate resources. While it is obviously necessary to formulate plans covering activities some time ahead, rigidity should be guarded against; the development of alternative strategies ensures that management has a flexible approach to changes in the environment.

The marketing information system referred to earlier should incorporate control data to ensure that marketing efforts are effectively deployed.

SERVICE INDUSTRIES AND THE 'MIXED' ECONOMY

In the UK, the private sector and the public sector are closely meshed and form what is termed the 'mixed economy'. (See Chapter 2 for further discussion.) The public services of health, welfare, education, and communications, and the nationalised energy industries form an indispensable part of the infrastructure of a sophisticated community.

Private sector businesses and public sector undertakings differ in their philosophies and market behaviour, but they are all concerned with meeting specific needs at both corporate and personal levels. The efficient allocation of scarce resources should be a matter of concern for all management, wherever they may exercise their responsibilities.

It has been argued elsewhere[24] that government and social planners should make far greater use of marketing research in the design of the public services. Many of these, such as health care, intimately affect the minds, bodies and lives of people of all ages and social groups. Such vital services should not be designed without objective enquiry about patients' health and social needs, life styles, expectations, etc. Good intentions are no substitute for decisions which have been based on systematic research.

In the United States, where the organisation of the health services is different from the UK, marketing research is quite widely used to assess market needs. Since the roots of marketing research in the UK lie deep in social investigations by such pioneers as Booth, Bowley and Rowntree, application of market research to the areas of health and the other public services should certainly not be regarded as unacceptabloe.

Objective survey enquiries have helped in the development of services for the disabled[25] by identifying the nature and extent of certain kinds of disablement and the ways in which people of various ages are able to cope with the ordinary tasks of living in their own household. There are many other areas of human activity where marketing research can be most usefully applied to give insight and guidance to policy makers and professional workers. Vast programmes of public health and social welfare should not be undertaken without systematic research at both national and regional levels.

The publicly administered services are not subject to the management discipline of generating profit. Standards of efficiency should be drawn up, therefore, related to the expectations and needs of the specific communities catered for by these services.

Clearly, the provision of services in response to the needs of modern society should not be undertaken without heed to the costs involved; this particularly applies to service monopolies which are not primarily affected by commercial constraints.

In planning services, whether these are associated with commercial activities or with the public sector, more attention should be given to input/output measurement. Otherwise, there is a very real danger that services may become over-elaborated and wastefully administered, devouring resources out of proportion to their contribution to the efficiency of an organisation or to the welfare of a community.

The public and private sectors in the UK are in tandem, and are substantially interdependent. Managers in both sectors should establish mutual respect and understanding of their individual roles in the economy: partnership is preferable to partisanship.

Later discussion in this text highlights the critical dependency of several private sector industries in the public sector. In addition, political factors may intervene and largely determine the fates of certain industries or even companies.

Government intervention in industrial activities is no longer unique. Regional policies have been developed to influence, both directly and through various incentives, the location of new factories, in an attempt to balance the decline of some of the UK's traditional industries such as coal mining, textiles and shipbuilding.

The complexity of the public sector, which frequently endures internal conflict between commercial viability and social policies, places particular stresses on the management of undertakings such as the electricity, gas and coal boards. Until recently, pricing policies have tended to be strongly affected by 'non-economic' considerations, substantially inspired by political direction and pressures. In the UK, a more realistic commercial policy is now in evidence, and the pricing of public services has reflected this changed orientation.

Private sector suppliers to these public undertakings may experience a harsher style of negotiation now that government policy has indicated that the public utility services should stand on their own financial feet.

MARKETING IN A POST-INDUSTRIAL SOCIETY

The wealth of a nation is built up from the contributions made by its productive resources. In a developed country like Britain, these resources are many and complex. Radical changes have affected the structure of the industrial and commercial base; the older industries of steel, coal, shipbuilding and textiles have shrunk while newer industries based, for example, on electronics, computer technology, or sophisticated technical and advisory services have become significant contributors to the national wealth.

From being once the 'Workshop of the World', Britain, in common with the other developed economies of the western world, is experiencing competition in manufactured products from the new industrialised countries. (See Chapter 2 for extended discussion.)

In this competitive, dynamic environment, British industry and commerce should use all the talents and energies of her workforce. Production resources relate to both tangible and intangible products; to the public sector and to the private sector industries; to goods and services marketed for profit, and to those provided by national and regional administrations. Various management disciplines have evolved to handle efficiently the production and exchange of goods and services. Marketing is one of these vital managerial functions necessary to ensure that organisations across the whole spectrum of economic and social activity, provide people in industry and elsewhere with acceptable products and services.

SUMMARY

Marketing is a specialised function of management which is not restricted to consumer products: it has a vital role in many types of organisation, e.g. industrial, commercial, public sector services, charities, etc. The techniques of marketing cover three areas of activity: analysis, planning and control; these tend to overlap in real life. The analytical approach involves marketing research and interpretation of data; the planning factor follows logically, and involves choices of markets, development of products and services, organising effective marketing strategies and tactics, etc.; the control element is essential for marketing productivity: setting of performance standards–market share ratios, territory sales quotas, etc.

Marketing management has two roles: (1) interpreter, and (2) integrator. The first role concerns analysis and evaluation of markets and communicating findings in terms of quality, price, service, etc., so that the whole business is responsive to customers' needs. The second role covers the important task of integrating marketing plans with all the other activities of the business. The corporate interfaces of marketing necessitate close relationships with other specialised functions of management, such as purchasing, finance, personnel, production, R&D and design. All these specialised skills contribute to corporate performance; a balanced team is imperative for success.

Apart from physical products, marketing has valuable applications in service industries, and its techniques, such as marketing research, can be applied to improve market knowledge and in the preparation of strategic plans. There is immense scope for effective marketing in modern service economies. As well as profit-motivated services, the public sector services of health, education and social welfare can improve their efficiency and offer more relevant benefits through using, for example, market and social research to guide the design of patient-care programmes.

REFERENCES

1. Maslow, A.H., 'A Theory of Human Motivation', *Psychological Review*, Vol. 50, 1943.
2. Smith, Adam, *Wealth of Nations*, Rawdon House Inc., New York, 1937.
3. Levitt, Theodore, *Marketing for Business Growth*, McGraw-Hill, New York, 1974.
4. Drucker, Peter F., *The Practice of Management*, Heinemann, London, 1961.
5. Machine Tools Economic Development Committee, *A Handbook for Marketing Machinery*, HMSO, London, October, 1970.
6. 'Industrial Innovation: A Submission to the Advisory Council for Applied Research and Development', The Institution of Mechanical Engineers, 24 October 1979.

7. National Economic Development Office, 'The Plastics Industry and its Prospects'. A Report of the Plastics Working Party of the Chemicals EDC, HMSO, London, July 1971.

8. Heller, Robert, *The Naked Manager*, Barrie & Jenkins, London, 1971.

9. McCarthy, E. Jerome, *Basic Marketing*, Richard D. Irwin, Homewood, Illinois, 1975.

10. Tavernier, Gerard, 'Where Value Analysis is a Way of Life', *International Management*, February 1975.

11. Smolden, Wilfred, 'Increasing Penetration in Consumer Markets', in *Long Range Planning for Marketing and Diversification*, Wills, G. and Taylor, B. (eds), Bradford U.P./Lockwood, 1971.

12. Davies, Owen, 'The Marketing Approach to Selling', *Long Range Planning*, Vol. 7, No. 3, June 1974.

13. Hakansson, Hakan (ed.), *International Marketing and Purchasing of Industrial Goods: An Interaction Approach*, Wiley, Chichester, 1983.

14. Alderson, Wroe, *Marketing Behaviour and Executive Action*, Richard D. Irwin, Homewood, Illinois, 1957.

15. Blois, K.J., 'The Manufacturing/Marketing Orientation and Its Information Needs', *European Journal of Marketing*, Vol. 14, No. 5/6, 1980.

16. Kotler, Philip, 'The Major Tasks of Marketing Management', *Journal of Marketing*, Vol. 37, October 1973.

17. Judd, Robert C., 'The Case of Redefining Services', *Journal of Marketing*, Vol. 28, January 1964.

18. Rathmell, John M., 'What is Meant by Services?', *Journal of Marketing*, Vol. 30, October 1966.

19. Wilson, Aubrey, *The Marketing of Professional Services*, McGraw-Hill, Maidenhead, 1972.

20. Monopolies Commission, 'A report on the General Effect on the Public Interest of Certain Restrictive Practices so far as they Prevail in Relation to the Supply of Professional Services, Part 1, HMSO, 1970.

21. Chisnall, Peter M., *Marketing: A Behavioural Analysis*, 2nd edn, McGraw-Hill, Maidenhead, 1985.

22. Levitt, Theodore, 'Marketing Intangible Products and Product Intangibles', *Harvard Business Review*, Vol. 59, No. 3, May/June 1981.

23. Parasuraman, A., Berry, Leonard L. and Zeithaml, Valarie A., 'Service Firms Need Marketing Skills', *Business Horizons*, Vol. 26, No. 6, November/December 1983.

24. Chisnall, Peter M., 'Market Research' in *Management for Health Service Administrators*, Allen, D. and Hughes, J.G. (eds.), Pitman Medical, London, 1983.

25. Chisnall, Peter M., 'Market Research Applied to Health and Social Welfare: A Study of Health and Disability in a UK Metropolitan Borough', ESOMAR, Barcelona, August/September 1983.

Chapter Two
INDUSTRIAL/ORGANISATIONAL MARKETS

CLASSICAL ANALYSIS OF INDUSTRIAL ACTIVITIES

Economists have traditionally divided the activities of working populations into three main groups: primary, secondary and tertiary. The primary or extractive sector covers agriculture, mining, forestry and fishing, which are particularly significant occupations in relatively mature economies. The secondary or manufacturing sector refers to the manufacturing and construction industries which, as a country's industrial development evolves, competes with and finally supplants the primary sector as the major source of economic wealth. The tertiary sector relates to the service and distributive trades; to those employed in what have been termed 'incorporeal production'.

The shift from growing products to making products and then to offering services, often closely associated with specific types of products, characterises all advanced economies. In what has been termed the post-industrial society, the tertiary sector of the economy has become the major source of new employment. Increasingly, the service sector has focussed on knowledge-related services for professional and business needs.

BIRTH OF SERVICE ECONOMY

As already noted in Chapter 1, a service economy reflects a relatively wealthy society which has the major proportion of its employment in the tertiary sector. Sophisticated products, such as those based on chemicals and electronics, advance while the older industrial activities, like coal-mining and textile manufacture, assume less importance to the overall national economy. The industrial revolution has been reactivated by far-reaching technological changes, automation, and improvements in managerial systems of administration and control which have profoundly changed industrial and commercial life. With improved standards of health, education, welfare, conditions of employment, rising levels, in general, of real incomes, a new industrial society has been created. 'In a poor society, there is insufficient wealth to provide capital for social services, scientific and industrial research, and the many opportunities of an advanced economy'.[1]

Obviously, the increasing dependence of modern economies on the efficiency of the service industries is a matter of particular interest to marketing executives. Service industries will increasingly absorb more spending power, while being responsible for a greater proportion of the national economic progress.

Over 40 years ago, Colin Clark[2] drew attention to the trends in service employment: 'careful generalisation of available fact shows ... the most important concomitant of economic progress to be the movement of the working population from agriculture to manufacture, and from manufacture to commerce and services'.

The United States, by virtue of its trends in employment and economic activities, claims to be the first nation to have a 'service economy'.

A NEDO[3] publication noted that: 'If transport is included in the service sector, by 1966 the UK just about qualified for admission to the exclusive club of service economies, since services claimed, for the first time, half the labour force. Reckoned on the basis of full-time equivalents, the proportion of the labour force in services was slightly less than half; this reflected the sector's disproportionate reliance on part-time workers'.

DISTINCTION BETWEEN GOODS AND SERVICES

It is perhaps unfortunate that economic activity has been traditionally, and rather arbitrarily, divided by professional economists into the goods and service sectors. This dichotomy is not altogether satisfactory, and NEDO[3] pointed out: '... no criterion is likely to provide a clear cut distinction between the two sectors'. This view is shared by the American National Bureau of Economic Research: 'The boundary between service and goods production is very difficult to draw, and probably no division based on industrial classifications would be completely satisfactory ...'.[4] Judd[5] has defined services as 'market transactions where the object of the exchange is something other than the transfer of a tangible commodity'. Such transactions involve the provision of transport systems, cash security and transfer (banks), public utility undertakings, etc.

Service industries tend to be labour intensive, employing, in particular, large numbers of female and part-time workers. Services have been traditionally described as being perishable in nature, ('unstockable'), intangible, having close relationship to consumers, etc. But these characteristics do not satisfactorily delineate services; it is often difficult — if not impossible — to separate the contribution of a service from the satisfaction given by the ownership of a particular product. Service is frequently an intrinsic part of the package of benefits offered to the customer. So interrelated are the benefits derived from some products and their surrounding or dependent services, that it would be futile to attempt to differentiate between the value of the goods provided and the services rendered. For instance, 'retailing the goods sold, or legal services and the house acquired'; or the service rendered may be reflected in the tangible product — 'teeth fabricated by a dentist'.[3] The growing trend towards the leasing of equipment illustrates how difficult it becomes to differentiate satisfactorily between goods and services. To benefit from the use of such equipment, the customer does not have to become the owner.

Increasingly, customers expect an efficient servicing back-up with the products they buy. These services, such as arrangement of finance, or after-sales maintenance, provide a constellation of benefits which attract business. Service becomes an essential element in the marketing mix; attractive complementary service helps to differentiate products and wins customers.

DEPENDENCE OF ADVANCED ECONOMIES ON SERVICE INDUSTRIES

That an advanced economy depends increasingly on the contribution of the service industries is clearly evident from this discussion. Without an efficient system of transport or effective methods of communication, or the availability of adequate power supplies, the whole economy would grind to a catastrophic halt. In addition, the health, education and welfare services add immeasurably to the well-being and also the efficiency of the population. The public sector with far-reaching responsibilities in town planning, slum clearance, recreational facilities and related welfare services, contributes the major part of the services in the United States and in Britain. The mixed economy of modern industrialised communities seems, in fact, to depend on an essential equilibrium being maintained between the production of tangible goods by industry and the provision of complementary services by public sector organisations.

Table 2.1 shows the enormous sums disbursed by the public sector of the British economy. Over the period 1970/1 to 1981/2 given in Table 2.4, total current and capital expenditure can be seen to have increased over six-fold.

Table 2.1 Summary of public expenditure on social services and housing (UK) (£ million)

	1970/71	1974/75	1979/80	1981/82
Education*	2,638	5,528	10,511	13,873
National Health Service	2,071	4,095	9,195	13,274
National Social Services	274	768	1,951	2,689
Social Security Benefits	3,927	7,171	19,415	28,699
Housing	1,339	4,480	6,676	5,198
Welfare foods	176	9	29	44
	10,425	22,051	47,777	63,777

* Includes school meals and milk from 1974/75.
Source: Central Statistical Office.

The public sector is particularly significant in capital expenditure on plant and equipment, accounting for over 40% of all investment in fixed assets. Central and local government authorities finance about 60% of capital expenditure on new building and construction apart from private housing.

The expenditure of local authorities on goods and services for consumption, as given in Table 2.2, shows the strategic importance of this area of the public sector in the UK economy. Vast purchasing power is, moreover, concentrated in a relatively small number of large regional authorities.

Table 2.2 Local authorities (UK): current account expenditure

	£ millions	
1971	1975	1980
4,078	9,698	19,244

Source: National Income and Expenditure, 1982.

The public sector industries occupy a key position in the British labour market. Public sector employees (see Table 2.3) totalled over seven million in 1981, and represented almost 30% of all those in employment compared with just under 24% in 1961.

Table 2.3 Public sector employees

	Millions		
	1961	1971	1981
Local authorities (General)	1.9	2.7	3.0
Central government (General)	1.8	1.9	2.4
Nationalised industries including Post Office	2.2	2.0	1.9
Total: Public sector	5.9	6.6	7.3
Private sector	18.6	17.8	17.0
	24.5	24.4	24.3

Source: Economic Trends (Annual Supplement), 1984.

Disruption of the entire economy would inevitably follow from prolonged stoppages or breakdowns in the basic services listed in Table 2.3.

The influence of the public sector is widespread in industry. Contracts for supplies and equipment for the steel, coal, gas, electricity and public transport services are responsible for a substantial proportion of the total economic activity in the private sector of the economy. Some industries, although not actually in the public sector, are virtually dependent on business from public undertakings. Motorway construction, sewers, bridge building and telecommunication equipment are examples of 'dependent' industries.

For instance, the public sector demand, mostly from the Ministry of Defence and British Telecom, represents over 50% of total demand and also funds half of the total electronics research and development.

The near-monopoly of BT has resulted in the three leading telecom equipment suppliers (GEC, Plessey and STC) being almost totally dependent on one buyer in the UK.[6] Some degree of competitive activity is likely to follow from the Stock Exchange flotation of B.T.

IMPORTANCE OF SERVICES IN BALANCE OF PAYMENTS

Traditionally, services have rendered invaluable assistance to Britain's export performance. Without the contribution of invisible exports such as insurance, banking, merchanting and brokerage, the balance of payments would have been even more precarious. Invisible exports have consistently shown a surplus over invisible imports — see Table 2.4, which gives figures over the eleven years 1973–1982.

The consistently favourable pattern of invisibles should be compared with visible trade balances over the same period of time, which, until 1980, were in debit. Oil revenues have fundamentally changed the long-term pattern of visible.

The data given in Table 2.4 are clear evidence of the immense importance of the service industries to the overall trading activities of the UK. Far from being 'non-productive', the financial services, for example, play a dynamic role in the economy with astonishing verve and consistency.

OVERALL TRENDS IN PRODUCTION

It has already been observed that since the early years of this century, the relative importance of the primary industries in the national economy has consistently declined while greater emphasis has been placed on the contribution of the service industries. It is also significant to observe that the secondary industries, from the late 1960s, have been overtaken by the tertiary sector which is now the major contributor to the national product.

From Table 2.5, percentage trends in GDP for the period 1960–1980, indicate that radical changes have taken place. Agriculture, fishery and forestry and also the distributive trades have declined as contributors to the national income; while mining and quarrying showed decline for most of this period, they increased later in relative importance, largely because of North Sea Oil. However, the most significant trend relates to manufacturing industry where the share of GDP fell from 41.8% (1960) to 31.2% (1980).

NATURE OF ORGANISATIONAL PRODUCTS

In the opening chapter it was observed that organisations are of many kinds, some with commercial objectives while others, for example, may be primarily concerned with health and social needs.

Market behaviour affecting the demand for organisational products and services is, in general, very different from that experienced with consumer

Table 2.4 Balance of Payments (UK)

						£Million					
	1972	1973	1974	1975	1976	1977	1978	1979	1980	1981	1982
Current account											
Visible trade											
Export (fob)	9,437	11,937	16,394	19,330	25,191	31,728	35,063	40,687	47,415	50,977	55,546
Imports (fob)	10,185	14,523	21,745	22,663	29,120	34,012	36,605	44,136	46,182	47,696	53,427
Visible balance	−748	−2,586	−5,351	−3,333	−3,929	−2,284	−1,542	−3,449	+1,233	+3,008	+2,119
Invisibles											
Credits	6,300	8,506	10,503	11,457	15,039	16,847	19,130	23,804	25,943	29,760	26,221
Debits	5,329	6,899	8,430	9,637	11,946	14,509	16,430	21,008	23,941	26,221	28,415
Invisible balance	+971	+1,607	+2,073	+1,820	+3,093	+2,338	+2,700	+2,796	+2,002	+3,539	+3,309
of which:											
Services balance	+701	+786	+1,075	+1,515	+2,503	+3,338	+3,816	+4,071	+4,267	+4,249	+3,844
Interest profits and dividends balance	+538	+1,257	+1,415	+773	+1,365	+116	+661	+990	−186	+1,257	+1,577
Transfers balance	−268	−436	−417	−468	−775	−1,116	−1,777	−2,265	−2,079	−1,967	−2,112
Current balance	+223	−979	−3,278	−1,513	−836	+54	+1,158	−653	+3,235	+6,547	+5,428

Source: Annual Abstracts, 1984.

Table 2.5 Percentage distribution of GDP by industry 1960–1980

	1960	1965	*Percentage* 1970	1975	1980
Agriculture, forestry and fishing	4.7	3.7	3.4	3.5	2.8
Mining and quarrying	3.4	2.6	1.9	2.0	7.1
Manufacturing	41.8	38.6	38.0	37.0	31.2
Construction	7.0	7.8	7.5	9.2	8.5
Gas, electricity and water	3.1	3.7	3.8	3.7	3.8
Transport and communications	9.8	9.6	10.1	7.1	10.0
Distributive trades	14.0	13.1	12.0	13.2	12.6
Insurance and banking	3.3	7.6	9.2	9.9	11.9
Other	12.9	13.3	14.0	10.7	12.1
	100.0	100.0	100.0	100.0	100.0
Production and trade as % GDP	87.8	88.3	82.8	74.8	74.9

Source: Channon.[10] Reprinted by permission of Pergamon Press Ltd.

supplies. There are basic differences which directly influence strategic and tactical operations. These fundamental characteristics relate to factors such as demand, supply, pricing, concentration ratios and special trading policies. In this section the significance of these special features will be outlined and discussed, so that a useful foundation will be laid for the subsequent study of buying behaviour.

Compared with many consumer supplies, organisational supplies tend to be complex and sophisticated, e.g. computer installations, power stations or automated processing plants. This particularly applies to capital equipment which is also characterised as having relatively high durability. Such products tend to be bought fairly infrequently by any one organisation; furthermore, they are distinctly different from high-frequency purchases of consumer products such as food, in that purchase can often be postponed for long periods of time. Admittedly, this may eventually lead to problems in industrial efficiency, but in the short term, at least, buyers of industrial equipment are able to exercise their prerogative as to *when* they buy specific equipment. Industrial markets are, therefore, subject to policy decisions on investment which may be affected by many factors, e.g. political, outside the control of market suppliers.

Within particular industrial markets, the complexity and costs of products vary considerably; some suppliers may be limited to low-cost products like components, while other specialise in complete package deals, such as the design and building of a major institution like a hospital or airport — these are usually referred to as turnkey contracts.

Technological advances and the rate of innovation vary across industrial markets. Lead time has been cut drastically and, in general, industrial products are now sharing some of the dynamic character traditionally associated with consumer products. Over twenty years ago, the president of Du Pont acknowledged: 'Lead time is gone. There is no company so outstanding technically today that it can expect a long lead in a new discovery'.[11] When Du Pont invented nylon in the 1930s, it experienced a virtual monopoly for years, but when it introduced Delrin in 1960, it was only a year before Celanese marketed a rival product. Today the pace of change is remorseless, as particularly evidenced in the electronics field. (The problems of innovation are considered in some detail in Chapter 7.)

TYPES OF INDUSTRIAL PRODUCTS

It is difficult to classify organisational goods definitively; there are bound to be borderline cases so that mutually exclusive groupings are virtually impossible. One approach would be to start at the fundamental point of basic raw materials and then to proceed through semi-processed products, components and eventually to completely finished equipment. This was the foundation of the classifications adopted by the Industrial Marketing Research Association[12] and applied to analyses[13] of the functions of marketing research in industrial markets. Three categories of products (and services) were noted: (1) capital goods: 'sold as an inherent whole to further production, in machines, accessories or components', (2) primary products: 'basic materials like steel, chemicals, or aluminium bars sold to manufacturers', and (3) intermediate products: 'such as tubes, castings or building materials which have to undergo some major change of form'.

Other researchers have adopted various criteria for classifying industrial products. For example, Kotler,[14] who refers to the 'producer market (also called industrial market)' as 'the market consisting of individuals and organisations who acquire goods and services to be used in the production of further products and services for sale or rental to others', has three main methods of classifying goods:

I   *Goods entering the product completely — materials and parts*
   A. Raw materials
      1. farm products (wheat, etc.)
      2. natural products (fish, crude petroleum, iron ore)
   B. Manufactured materials and parts
      1. component materials (e.g. steel, cement, wire, textiles)
      2. component parts (small motors, tyres, castings)

II *Goods entering product partly — capital items*
  A. Installations
    1. buildings and land rights (factories, offices)
    2. fixed equipment (generators, computers, elevators)
  B. Accessory equipment
    1. portable or light factory equipment and tools (hand tools, lift trucks)
    2. office equipment (typewriters, desks)

III *Goods not entering the product — supplies and services*
  A. Supplies
    1. operating supplies (lubricants, typing paper)
    2. maintenance and repair items (paint, nails, brooms)
  B. Business services
    1. maintenance and repair services (window cleaning, typewriter repairs)
    2. business advisory services (legal, management consulting, advertising)

Stanton[15] states that industrial goods are differentiated from consumer goods because of their ultimate use. 'Industrial goods are those intended for use in making other products, or for rendering a service in the operation of a business or institutional enterprise'. He classifies industrial products as follows:

1. raw materials
2. fabricating materials and parts
3. installations
4. accessory equipment
5. operating supplies

These five categories are based on the broad uses of products in contrast to the classification of consumer products on basis of buying habits.

1. Raw materials: 'industrial goods which will become part of another physical product and which have received no processing at all, other than that necessary for economy or protection in physical handling',[14] e.g. (a) minerals, land; (b) wheat, cotton, tobacco, fruit and vegetables, livestock, and animal products such as eggs and raw milk.

2. Fabricating materials and parts: become actual part of finished product: already processed to some extent. Fabricating *materials*, e.g. pig iron, yarn, will undergo further processing. Fabricating *parts* will be assembled with no further change in form, e.g. spark plugs, fan belts, buttons.

3. Installations: manufactured industrial products — the long-lived expensive major equipment of an industrial user, e.g. large generators, factory building, jet aeroplanes for airline. 'The differentiation characteristic of installations is that they set the scale of operation in a firm.[14]

4. Accessory equipment: used to aid production operations of an industrial user, but it does not have a significant influence on the scale of operations in a firm; does not become actual part of finished product. Life is shorter than installations (3) and longer than operating supplies (5). E.g. office equipment, small power tools, forklift trucks.

5. Operating supplies: 'convenience goods' of industrial field. Short-lived, low-priced items usually purchased with minimum of effort. Help firm's operations but do not become part of finished product. E.g. lubricating oils, stationery, heating fuel.

Marrian[16] classifies industrial goods as those commodities (goods and services) purchased, hired or leased for use either directly (in the production of) other goods and services destined for either the industrial or ultimate consumer markets (domestic and export) or for rendering services to organisations engaged in serving the industrial or ultimate consumer markets. She makes four 'broad' distinctions in industrial goods: (1) industrial equipment (buildings; installation equipment; necessary equipment: operating equipment; tools and instruments; furnishing and fittings); (2) industrial materials (new materials, processed materials; fabricated materials; fabricating materials); (3) industrial supplies (packaging; operating supplies; spares and replacements), and (4) industrial services (equipment services; facilitating services; advisory and consultative services).

Marrian also characterises industrial buyers as those who buy on behalf of commercial, professional and institutional organisations; they act to further organisational rather than personal goals. Within organisational buying, three main divisions are made: industrial, institutional and intermediate buyers. These are briefly as follows:

Industrial buyers are those 'buying goods and services for some tangible productive and commercially significant purpose', e.g. manufacturers, primary (extractive) producers, agricultural, forestry, fishery and horticultural producers.

Institutional buyers are those buying goods and services for institutional (in the sense of providing a service which is often intangible) and not necessarily commercially significant purposes, e.g. schools, hospitals, local government, professions, hotels.

Intermediate buyers are those buying goods and services for resale or for facilitating the resale of other goods, in the industrial or ultimate consumer markets, for commercial purposes, e.g. distributors, dealers, wholesalers, retailers, service trades.

McCarthy's[17] typology of industrial goods has six categories; the first two closely comparable to Kotler's 'category two'; the third and fourth can be readily related to Kotler's 'category one', while the fifth and sixth compare with Kotler's third category, as follows:

Categories of industrial goods   *cf Kotler*

1. Installations
2. Accessory equipment   } II
3. Raw materials
4. Component parts and materials }   I
5. Supplies
6. Services   } III

McCarthy states that while consumer goods classification 'is tentative and perhaps arbitrary, the industrial goods classification is keyed directly to the way industrial purchasing departments and accounting control systems operate day by day. Buyers, for example, often specialise by product categories'.[15]

Hill *et al.*[18] offer the following 'general classifications' of industrial products which can be usefully compared with McCarthy's and Kotler's typologies:

	cf: McCarthy	*Kotler*
1. Major equipment	1	II
2. Accessory equipment	2	
3. Fabricating or component parts	4	I
4. Process material	5	III
5. Operating supplies	6	
6. Raw materials	3	I

These researchers further differentiate these categories of industrial products, e.g. major equipment is of two general types: multi-purpose or standard machines, and special or single-purpose machines (e.g. McCarthy's: custom-built; standard).

These various systems of industrial product classification have much in common, as can be noted from this brief review.

Products are viewed in different ways according to their function in diverse industries. The use to which a product is put biases it towards a particular classification. Car accessories supplied as original equipment would attract a different classification from 'replacement' sales to fleet-owners or distributors.

NATURE OF DEMAND FOR ORGANISATIONAL PRODUCTS

Vertical Demand vs Horizontal Demand

The demand for organisational products will be significantly affected by their end-use. Analysis of the end-uses of such products leads to the development of effective methods of market segmentation. Some products have many applications in industry and commerce; others have distinctly limited market opportunities. Vertical demand applies where a product has virtually only one market; for example, manufacturers of telecommunication equipment or coal-mining machinery must obtain most of their business in the UK from the public sector. Less extreme instances relate to steel-making equipment and supplies where, in the UK, the market is largely represented by the British Steel Corporation; or to potters' clay which has few buyers in the UK and of which two groups account for almost 60% of the tableware section of the ceramic industry.

Vehicle component manufacturers have distinctly limited outlets for their production. In general, the greater the concentration of demand for a particular product, the more likely is the demand in that market to be vertical. Suppliers who experience only limited markets for their products should weigh up their business opportunities very carefully: the old adage of 'too many eggs in one basket' suggests that such firms should actively seek new uses for their products and also develop new types of product within their manufacturing competences.

Other products experience horizontal demand and have applications over many markets in different industries, e.g. weighing machines, first-aid kits, steel, fork-lift trucks, chemicals such as ethano-lamines, etc.

In addition, there are 'vertical' segments within horizontal markets, as occurs with fire protection products. These are sold to practically every industry, but some specific items, such as fire engines, are limited to relatively few buyers who are almost entirely in the public sector. (See Chapter 6: Product Portfolio and Market Segmentation Strategies.)

Variety of Uses for Product

Marketers of products enjoying horizontal demand may advantageously plan to apportion their sales over market sectors to minimise trading risks and the effect of cyclical or other trend phenomena. China clay, for example, originally experienced a vertical demand from the pottery industry, but the pattern of demand is now horizontal because of the many uses of this mineral in modern industry. These include paper, pharmaceuticals, paint, rubber, plastics, agricultural chemicals, etc. The paper industry is, in fact, the major user of china clay, accounting for about three-quarters of total market sales.

Another product with diverse applications is carbon dioxide, which is 'used as a carbonating agent in the brewing industry, as a refrigerant in food processing, as an inert atmosphere in oil refineries, and for welding in the engineering industries'.[19] Each of these market segments has its own distinctive pattern of demand and buying behaviour.

To market carbon dioxide successfully, it is important to acquire knowledge about user industries, e.g. specific rates of growth and the diverse structures which will affect negotiation. 'You do not have the same type of marketing problem in selling to, say, the brewing industry, as you do with, say electronics'.[20] Not only are the structures of the industries different, but the whole pattern of buying behaviour also varies, as also do the specialist media of advertising.

The Plastics Division of ICI manufacturers a very wide range of plastics which are based on very different technologies and are used in a very great number of industries in the manufacture of their products. (See Table 2.6.)

Table 2.6 Consumption of plastics by industry sector

Sector	Percentage of total consumption
Packaging	21.7
Building	20.9
Electrical	7.8
Automotive	4.3
Housewares	4.1
Other transport	3.5
Furniture	3.5
Clothing (including footwear)	3.0
Toys, fancy goods, etc.	3.0
Mechanical engineering	2.8
Consumer durables	2.0
Agriculture	1.6
Miscellaneous and unidentified	21.8
	100.0

Source: See Owen.[19]

ICI consider that their business 'can be and is regarded as a number of separate businesses at the vital marketing stage, although further back there are a number of common functions which gather considerable strength from being part of a large organisation'.[19]

Derived Demand

With many industrial products, demand is directly dependent upon the rate of usage which may be several stages from the initial purchaser. Companies may contribute part of the finished product or, perhaps, only the packaging. The demand for capital equipment, for example, is largely dependent on the prospective demand for the goods (industrial or consumer) which this plant will be capable of producing. This will be likely to refer not only to short-term demand patterns but also to estimates of demand extending over twenty years or even longer. Associated with these problems are the lead times necessary to design, develop and produce new capital equipment. In general, industrial products have longer manufacturing cycles than consumer goods.

Similarly, the demand for the materials and components used in the manufacture of capital goods will depend heavily on the rate of sales in the equipment market.

The demand for extinguishant gases, such as Halon, is directly dependent on the number of free protection appliances sold to users.

Sheet metal demand is generated by the demand for products which are made from it; the demand for safety-belt webbing will derive from the sales of car safety belts which, in turn, are now almost entirely dependent on the level of demand for new cars.

The impact of derived demand on the chemical industry is given in Figure 2.1.

Figure 2.1   Chemical industry's pattern of derived demand.

Source: See Eugster. [21]

Inevitably, the dependency of derived-demand products on factors outside the control of those marketing such products, indicates that such companies should become acquainted with trends in markets beyond the one in which they are directly active. Clearly, there is a great amount of inter-dependence between industrial firms; sometimes, unfortunately, there is a danger that component manufacturers degenerate into 'captive suppliers' to large assembly plants. On the other hand, industrial buyers tend to become heavily dependent on the performance of their suppliers: the ability to adhere to strict standards of quality and scheduled deliveries becomes of vital importance in allocating available business.

It is important that industrial marketers understand the uses to which their products are applied in various markets. As Hakansson and his co-researchers[22] have observed: 'The firm has to be both an expert in its product as a component as well as the function of that component in the larger product'. Product and process knowledge are critical to success in competitive markets. In the industrial detergents market, it was found that the technical advice of suppliers is a pronounced marketing input. Also, the production and technical staff of customers are much more heavily involved in the product selection stage than with many other products.

Companies marketing products which experience derived demand may actively intervene lower down the 'demand chain' in order to stimulate demand for their products. Fibre manufacturers such as Courtaulds or ICI Fibres undertake systematic marketing research at several levels of the fashion industry, and they also advertise directly to consumers with the objective of gaining insight into trends in demand and of influencing, to some degree, the derived demand for synthetic yarns. This type of market intervention is termed 'back pressure' selling, or 'reverse' selling.

Packaging manufacturers, for instance, cooperate closely with food processors in the development of improved types of materials, closures, etc. Technical advisory services are an essential part of the marketing effort of industrial marketers, and through this type of cooperation, goodwill is built up over the years of personal involvement in customers' problems. Research could usefully identify areas in which suppliers may offer technical assistance to promote business.

Some companies, e.g. Coats Patons, the large diversified group which originated in the production of yarns and threads, have developed vertically integrated structures which may be effective in increasing their influence on the pattern of demand at several stages of production and distribution. Horizontal integration, adopted by other companies, is designed to reduce competition at the manufacturing stage in specific industrial markets by rationalising production methods, product ranges, and lowering overall costs. Research should endeavour to trace the organisational pattern of particular companies and evaluate the extent of influence exercised on demand.

Elasticity of Demand

Classical economic theory postulates that as price falls, demand tends to rise, and vice versa; the extent of this movement is termed the elasticity of demand and is graphicaly indicated by a downward sloping curve. (Refer to Figure 2.2.)

In effect, a demand curve is a considered estimate of the likely outcome of the demand for a product at different levels of price. Certain assumptions about buying behaviour are necessarily incorporated.

Figure 2.2   Simplified model of elastic demand.

The alternative model of demand refers to those buying situations where only relatively small changes in demand follow from price alterations. (Refer to Figure 2.3.)

Figure 2.3   Simplified model of inelastic demand.

In consumer markets, price reductions are designed to attract an immediate response (e.g. washing machines, cookers or colour television sets), but market behaviour in industrial products is different, and although lower prices may suggest, for instance, that certain kinds of equipment are now feasible, spontaneous ordering would be unlikely because of the more complicated decision-making processes involved, and the need to plan a series of dependent events.

In general, industrial products with derived demand characteristics do not benefit from relatively small price reductions. The demand for several industrial products tends to show a reverse elasticity in the short term; hence, industrial marketers are seldom able to expand demand significantly merely by reducing price.

In expectation of further price reductions, industrial buyers may be able to delay purchasing if they hold adequate stocks of certain materials or components. A price increase, on the other hand, may lead to increased demand from buyers anxious, and able, to stock up, since they believe that prices may suddenly start to soar in the near future.

This behaviour contrasts sharply with the general behaviour of demand in consumer product markets, where price variations tend to affect inversely levels of consumption. The relative freedom of competitive consumer product manufacturers to increase market share through price reductions is largely not the experience of industrial marketers.

However, as Stacey and Wilson[23] emphasise, it is important to distinguish between the price elasticity of an industry and that of an individual manufacturer who may hope to increase his turnover, if only for the time being, by reducing his prices below current market levels.

Because of the dependent nature of derived demand, it is possible for reductions in the prices of a particular supplier to be accompanied by reduced sales if the general level of demand experienced by the industrial customer is falling.

Where the product being supplied represents only a minor element in the total cost structure of the finished product, reductions in price are not likely to increase demand; when components represent a major cost factor, price will, of course, be far more critical. If, for example, the price of stainless steel fell appreciably, new or extended applications could result which would increase overall market demand.

Substitution may also affect the level of demand for certain products at existing prices. Synthetic yarns have been instrumental in capturing a large share of the traditional carpet market, and have also expanded overall demand considerably. Leather upholstery in cars has largely been replaced by synthetic coverings. In many areas of industrial activity, the by-products of the petrochemical industries have dramatically changed traditional buying preferences. Shortages of some natural raw materials, emphasised by price rises, have accelerated the rate of substitution.

Elasticity of demand refers, therefore, to sales volume in specific segments of the total market for a product, and it follows that different elasticities may operate in various sectors. Market segments, and individual customers within them, should be analysed and rated for their likely sensitivity to price changes. For example, aluminium has many applications, such as airframes, saucepans, kettles and cooking foil. In airframe construction, aluminium offers unique advantages (light weight related to strength, ductility and anti-corrosion properties), so that at even higher prices it would still be in great demand. (Refer to Figure 2.3.) However, aluminium foil is in competition with other types of wrapping (waxed paper, cellulose film, etc.), and unless it can establish unique advantages (as with cooking), price levels are likely to influence market growth.

The latitude with which an individual supplier may vary his price will relate, as far as the buyer is concerned, to his market position (major, average, or marginal supplier), the degree of essentiality of his product/service, the general level of competition in a specific market, and the extent to which he may be able to differentiate his product. (See Chapters 5 and 6 for further discussion of price.)

The interaction of demand and supply, and hence price, will be affected by the intensity of demand at various stages, in many cases, of the demand chain (refer to 'Derived Demand' discussion on p.41).

As noted, the trading structure of an industry affects the bargaining power of individual suppliers. Conditions can vary from those approximating a perfect market, as theorised by economists, to a situation of virtual monopoly. In the first case, many firms of about the same size may be active in a market which has minimal barriers to entry; in the second case, one or two very large firms may dominate an industry and make entry to that market extremely difficult. In practice, the majority of industries tend to be characterised by a mixture of large, medium and small firms and price competition is significantly affected by the balance which exists between the various firms of a particular size. The more equitably market shares are distributed within an industry, the more marked will be the tendency for price competition to be active. (See Chapter 5 — Porter's analytical model.)

Industrial buyers may be sensitive to other factors in the marketing mix apart from price. The reputation of a supplier, the availability of efficient servicing, acceptable delivery dates, design leadership, etc., are non-price factors which research should identify as being significant in certain markets.

In the short term, supplies of many industrial goods and services are relatively fixed; price competition may, therefore, be inhibited. However, new methods of production, improved technology, or better designed products may enable industrial marketers to challenge the existing price structure in a market. Marketers should take note of the nature and level of competition, including the pace of technological innovation in specific industrial markets.

Trends in Demand

The nature and extent of trends in demand functions of particular organisational product and service markets require careful evaluation. Trend analyses are concerned with isolating and identifying market movements so that a better understanding of market behaviour may be obtained.

It may be possible to establish the causes of significant market movements; these may be attributable to technological, fiscal, financial, economic, political, cultural or demographic changes. One particularly dramatic category of long-term trend has become known as the Kondratieff cycle.

In 1925, Nicolai Dimitriyevich Kondratieff, after some years of research into long-term trends in selected economic indicators, stated that 50-year-long cycles existed; his findings, published in Germany, were translated into English in 1935.

Sahal[24] notes that in 1913, Van Gelderen, followed by Kondratieff about a decade later, advanced the thesis that economic development occurred in the form of long waves of about half-a-century consisting of 'spring-tides' of prosperity and 'ebb-tides' of relative scarcity. Schumpeter, he says, contended that the origin of such long waves (Kondratieff cycles) lay in the clustering of fundamental innovations over certain periods of time.

The first Kondratieff cycle (1787–1842) sprang mainly from innovations resulting from the development of steam power; the second (1843–1897) from innovations focussed around railroads; and the third (1898–1953) through the development of electric power and the internal combustion engine.

Sahal adds that the importance of Schumpeter's pioneering work cannot be over-emphasised, but it requires further verification. This view is supported by Ray,[25] who also observes that neither Kondratieff nor Schumpeter lived long enough to witness the peak of the upswing in the 1960s, which was '... probably attributable to a combination of major innovations in the chemical industries (catalytic cracking, synthetic materials and fibres, antibiotics); in aircraft (jet engine, helicopters); in the electrical/electronics industry (TV, computers); and perhaps even in the peaceful application of nuclear power'. He speculates that the next great innovatory cycle will centre on the microprocessor.

A sharp critic of the Kondratieff cycle is Mathias,[26] who states that its existence in more than price terms is 'far from proven'. Further, there is certainly no agreement about the variables used in the research. 'The inherent periodicity and replicability of the Kondratieff long-swing has been challenged no less than its characteristics and structural units. This being so, in the present state of research, it is wise to refrain from interpreting trends in the British economy between 1873 and 1896 as the structural dynamics of the downswing phase of a Kondratieff cycle'.

Even though Kondratieff's theory may be held in some dispute, it is a fact that during certain periods of time, innovations had profound effect on technologies and the direction and pace of industrial activities were fundamentally affected. (The impact of innovation on marketing strategies is discussed at some length in a later chapter.)

Four general categories of demand trend have been noted: secular (or 'normal'), seasonal, cyclical and erratic. Expert marketing research will help in providing data over time which will guide management on investment policy, marketing strategy, etc.

In all markets there is a typical demand trend — this is described as the secular or normal trend and refers to the smooth or regular movement of a series of data observed over a fairly long period of time. Some industrial products, e.g. machine tools, are subject to relatively violent changes in demand over a period of years ranging from five to twenty. This trend is typified as cyclical; certain industries tend to 'lead' a general upswing in economic activity and are also likely to be the first to experience a downturn in demand. The wavelike movements observable in cyclical variations involve periods of prosperity, recession, depression and recovery, and are caused by factors other than the weather or cultural or social behaviour. Cyclical fluctuations may be manifested at several levels, *viz.* national economy, industries or sectors of industries, and individual firms. Many explanations — some ingenious — have been offered of business cycles: these range over real, psychological and monetary theories. No simple explanation is really possible; there is not just *one* type of cycle. Individual business cycles require separate evaluations, although the anticipation of these strong movements remains exceedingly difficult.

The significance of seasonal trends also needs careful appreciation; peak demand may have to be met from buffer stocks, but since these tie up capital, a reliable assessment of the level and duration of demand is obviously desirable. 'Seasonal' variation is not necessarily related to seasons of the year, but refers to any kind of variation of a recurrent nature where the period of time involved is not longer than one year. Sales of fertilisers, wines, paint, heating fuels and holiday travel are typical.

The last category of demand trend — erratic — is not predictable from marketing research. Experience and sensitive observation of market behaviour may suggest, however, that some unusual trend is likely to occur. Irregular trends could be triggered off by some unusual natural disaster or economic event, e.g. blizzards, droughts, wars, strikes, etc. Opec, for instance, has had immense impact on the economics of the whole of the western world. This cataclysmic event shattered the developed world and triggered off the so-called energy crisis. Yet, it was early in 1970 that the US Cabinet Task Force on Oil commented that they did not predict a substantial price rise in world oil markets over the next ten years.

NATURE OF SUPPLY FOR ORGANISATIONAL PRODUCTS

Categories of organisational products have been discussed earlier, when it was seen that these range from complex, sophisticated and costly equipment to relatively simple, low-cost components or routine supplies. In some cases, repeat purchases are regular features of the market, e.g. lubricating oils, while in other instances, one-off deals, such as the installation of a major industrial plant, are the order of the day.

Custom Built Products

Custom built or specially designed products tend to be more evident in industrial than in consumer markets. Often, these types of products involve considerable development time and costs, e.g. designing and building a new passenger liner or a major process plant, or opening up a new ore mine. Suppliers require expert skills related to particular user-industries, and so are able to build customer loyalty because their products often become so closely integrated with the businesses of their customers that a high degree of mutual dependency arises. Food manufacturers, for example, rely heavily on the efficiency of food-processing machines for the profitability of their operations. Some of these machines may, of course, be standard designs, although in some cases, considerable modifications may have rendered them virtually custom built.

Standard Products

Standard products are, generally speaking, more open to competitive activities. They may be generic in nature, so differentiation across alternative sources of supply is not particularly marked. In cases like this, supplies are almost at the level of 'commodity products', with the resultant disadvantages for marketers. Often, industrial products are from standard ranges; research could usefully identify the optimum width of the product range of specific types of goods. Customers' specifications could be related to standard products and an acceptable degree of product rationalisation should be attempted.

Industrial inventory policies are critical factors in the successful operation of businesses. The problem of maintaining adequate stocks has already been alluded to; another aspect refers to the sensitive relationship between changes in the stocks held by customers and those of their suppliers. If customers change radically their consumption patterns because of increased sales, component suppliers may suddenly be faced with heavily increased demands both to satisfy the immediate production needs of their customers and to build up larger working stocks. This is also likely to escalate stock holdings at the supplying firm in the expectation of future increased business.

If a market decline sets in, the impact on component suppliers will probably be immediate and severe, as customers run down their heavy stocks before reordering.

The importance of a carefully articulated inventory policy is an important factor which contributes to the success of a business undertaking. Since most industrial production is in anticipation of demand, management has to accept the responsibility of balancing supply with demand, and endeavour to eliminate, as far as possible, tying up capital in abnormal stocks while at the same time avoiding loss of orders because of inability to deliver in an acceptable time.

Expectations of buyers' demands will be helped by closely studying the trends of user-industries, noting the impact of new technologies on their products and of new markets that their customers may be developing. As noted earlier, derived demand is a typical characteristic of industrial markets, so it will pay industrial suppliers to be aware of what is happening in consumer products markets; new tastes may cause significant changes in some industrial supplies.

Industrial products are frequently made to BSS or other accepted standards, so that, superficially at least, there is little to choose between competitive suppliers. In such instances, the astute marketer builds into his product other reasons why people should buy *his* version against those offered by his competititors. This approach will be considered in the next section (Augmented Product).

Augmented Products

The augmented product concept is a particularly valuable one for industrial marketers. Simply stated, it is that a product or service is more than just a simple transaction: it provides not merely the physical benefits inherent in its use but can be designed to give a cluster of benefits that are attractive to specific kinds of buyers. The application of this concept can help suppliers of basic commodity-type products to differentiate their market offerings, and so win business through a positive strategy of adding new values to their deals with customers. In other words, they offer a package deal, as against trying to compete with a product that is virtually identical to that sold by several other firms; moreover, often relying solely on sharp pricing to attract orders.

Of course, many shrewd suppliers of basic products already ensure that their customers receive good back-up service and regular supplies of essential raw materials. But this concept of the augmented product could be used far more widely in industrial markets, particularly because, in several product fields, competition is not just from home-based suppliers but from many ambitious overseas firms which are able to provide products of comparable technical quality.

Kotler[14] has distinguished three levels of product (see Figure 2.4): the core product, the formal product, and the augmented product.

These categories correspond closely to those offered by Levitt,[27] who added a fourth dimension: (1) the generic product; (2) the expected product; (3) the augmented product, and (4) the potential product.

Basically, these two well known writers are projecting the same message: competing products may be physically identical but one can be more acceptable than the other because of some additional reason or reasons which motivate customers to buy. One large chemical company found, for example, that their excellent technical data provided with the product frequently contributed to their marketing success.

Taking the various 'levels' of a product further, the core product or service refers to the basic or minimum benefit provided, such as transportation by a car, the facility to deposit or withdraw money at a bank, or the ability of a screwdriver to fit certain sizes of screws. These are the fundamental qualities of products or services that are largely taken for granted and are available from many sources.

At the next level, a product is designed to offer additional benefits, such as branding (which helps to control risk in buying), convenient packaging

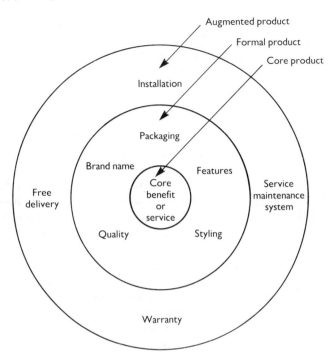

Figure 2.4   Three levels of product.

Source: See Kotler.[14]

(which may protect a product from accidental damage or give it prolonged life), or distinctive styling (which may make a product aesthetically more pleasing, or ergonomically designed to give better value in use). Price competition is now being diluted by adding attractive new benefits to appeal to certain market segments.

The augmented level of a product adds extra values, such as delivery and installation services, well designed maintenance systems, first-class warranties, etc.

Cunningham and Roberts[28] have shown the importance of service in the valve and pump industry; they classified service as (1) convenience, and (2) reliability; these related to what are usually described as before- and after-sales service. The former refers to features such as technical advice in selecting the right product for a particular task, credit facilities, reliable delivery information, etc. The latter helps to reduce the uncertainty attached to a buying decision, through offering, for example, user training courses, good repair facilities and technical back-up, after the product is bought.

These researchers[28] found that 'buyers were not only prepared to pay for a more reliable service but also were reluctant to change suppliers for a reduction in price of less than 5%.' This led them to believe either that the market may be 'service-elastic', in that the better the quality of the service, the greater the likelihood of business, that the customer may be able to impose certain standards of service on his most important suppliers.

This UK study was followed up by Banting[29] who conducted a similar study of Canadian pump and valve manufacturers. Delivery, reliability, prompt quotation and provision of technical advice were found to be the most important aspects of service which suppliers of forgings and castings could offer pump and valve makers.

Both the UK and Canadian surveys found that delivery reliability ranked first with this industrial sector; in second ranking for the UK was technical advice, compared with prompt quotation for the Canadian industry; test facilities achieved third ranking in the UK, and technical advice in Canada; fourth ranking in the UK was given to replacement guarantee and, in Canada, to discounts. Overall, some divergent values were apparent: 'much more than minor shuffling is manifested', and further research would be advisable, particularly in view of the fairly low response (21%) to the Canadian survey. However, there is evidence that Canadian pump and valve manufacturers can be segmented according to service expectations: valve makers are more concerned about the provision of technical advice, ease of contact with suppliers, and replacement guarantees, and are more generally satisfied with their metals suppliers, whereas pump manufacturers are most interested in discounts and after-sales service.

Product augmentation offers many opportunities to industrial marketers; the 'added benefit' should be based on adequate market research to identify and evaluate customers' behaviour in relation to specific supplies. Buyers' expectations are dynamic in competitive markets, so information should be up-to-date. Creative marketing strategies can lift a product out of the rut of being a commonplace, basic good, and reposition it so that it is perceived by buyers to be a more useful product. This enhanced product will give the supplier greater negotiating advantages, and may lead to systems-selling.

Systems Selling

This concept is closely related to that of the augmented product; a complete package of products and/or services is designed and offered to identified target customers. This differentiation strategy may involve, for example, the design, installation and servicing of a complex production facility; or a combination of hardware and software computer services, including the training of personnel.

Levitt[30] has described how the term 'systems selling' actually originated with the buyer and not the seller. The US federal military contracts office 'developed the practice of buying major weapons and communications packages through a single prime contractor'; this simplified the placing of contracts. In practice, however, this method of buying had been used for some time in public works contracts, although not formally described as 'systems selling'.

Increasingly, the complexity of many industrial products has meant that their efficiency depends on expert servicing and so 'package deals' have grown substantially over the past few years. Customers are seeking comprehensive solutions to their problems and the reduction of risk and uncertainty.

The service aspect of selling products has, therefore, become far more important in the strategies of organisational market suppliers. From being considered as a rather secondary business activity, servicing has now attracted special attention because it can be a most effective marketing tool.

Distribution

With consumer products, a sophisticated network of distributive trades channels the goods from manufacturers to consumers. These intermediaries are frequently highly specialised, e.g. food, fashion clothing, household furniture, etc., and serve the needs of a vast population spread over the whole country.

The efficiency of 'traditional' methods of supplying certain industrial markets also deserves attention. Some companies have experimented, successfully, with alternative marketing operations, e.g. franchise deals, telephone selling, etc.

In industrial markets, the channels of distribution are generally direct, apart from functions such as steel stockholding, builders' merchants or agricultural machinery distributors. Selling is mainly by direct contact between manufacturers and their customers, and often demands considerable technical knowledge. Orders are likely to be of large volume and entail commitments over a fairly long period of time.

Distribution decisions in industrial markets may take years to develop; management should, therefore, give adequate thought to this important factor in successful marketing. Steel stockholders, for example, fulfil a vital role in stocking a wide range of steel for quick delivery to diverse industries. The tasks involved in the physical flow of products from manufacturers through to end-users are sometimes referred to as the logistics of supply. In some very large organisations, this responsibility has developed into a specialist function of management. (Further discussion of industrial distributive strategies occurs in Chapter 5.)

CONCENTRATION FACTORS

On the whole, transactions covering the supply of organisational goods and services are more complicated than in consumer markets. Also, the actual number of buyers for specific products is smaller, and there tend to be greater differences between buyers.

The range of buying extends from virtually monopsonistic (single buyer) power to many buying points, where no individual buyer is able to dictate terms of business. The nature of price competition is related to the degree of concentration of buying power, and the structure of the supplying industry. (See Chapter 5: Market Bargaining Factors.)

Geographical Concentration

Industries may be clustered geographically, and a few large firms dominate the total output, as, for example, in the British pottery industry centred around Stoke on Trent, where two large groups, Wedgwood and Royal Doulton account for about 60% of total sales of tableware. Industrial clustering of cutlery manufacturing occurs in Sheffield, and of motor vehicle production in the Birmingham and Coventry areas. However, some other important industries, e.g. electronics, manmade fibres and pharmaceuticals are not clustered geographically.

Ancillary Industry Clustering

Industrial concentrations related to specific types of products tend to attract localised ancillary or service industries. These related industries add to the density of specialised industrial activities, and are a significant factor in planning industrial marketing strategies.

US Research into Industrial Concentration

For some years, the professional sales journal *Sales and Marketing Management*,[31] has conducted valuable surveys into the marketing and business environment in the United States.

The extent of manufacturing concentration is shown in Table 2.7, which indicates that the ten states accounted for practically 57% of all US shipments in 1982.

The SMM survey identifies 409 industries — almost 50% of the 850 representing the private sector — 'that have a degree of regional concentration which makes them attractive sales targets'. Marketing executives can, therefore, focus on specific areas which have significant volumes of consumption. For instance, five counties accounted for 77% of total US shipments of iron ore in 1982. Nearly 40% was concentrated in St Louis, with 96% of shipments from plants employing more than 100 employees. Suppliers of equipment to this industry could target, therefore, the 69 plants classified as iron ore mines in the five leading counties.

Regional concentration patterns influence at least half of the industries making up the American economic structure. SMM note that the reasons vary according to the type of industry, but the following three categories appear to account for this phenomenon. (1) *Resource concentration* — as, for

Table 2.7 Top ten manufacturing US states in shipments (1982)

State	Total plants	Large plants	1982 Shipments ($millions)	Approx. % of US
California	11,817	3,456	174,424.6	7.79
Texas	7,341	2,206	163,307.0	7.30
Illinois	9,621	2,929	151,300.5	6.76
Ohio	8,949	2,690	146,331.7	6.54
Pennsylvania	8,835	2,958	142,717.0	6.38
Michigan	7,483	1,727	138,042.1	6.17
New York	10,459	2,849	122,556.6	5.48
New Jersey	7,172	1,843	93,224.9	4.16
Indiana	4,049	1,363	77,644.7	3.47
North Carolina	4,678	1,922	65,921.8	2.94
				56.99%

Total plants are all manufacturing establishments with 20 or more employees. Large plants are those with 100 or more employees.

Source: *Sales and Marketing Management's* 1983 Survey of Industrial and Commercial Buying Power.[31] © July 26, 1982, Survey of Buying Power.

example, natural resources underlying the concentration patterns of the mining industries, or for the bulk of oil and gas output. Intellectual resources, such as advanced university facilities, have led to the concentrated manufacture of computers and advanced electronics in, for example, Silicon Valley in California. (2) *Market concentration* — many goods and services (e.g. milk, bread, banking or hospitals) tend to be located close to the source of demand. Large metropolitan populations are obvious clusters of high buying propensity. (3) *Capital concentration* — location decisions in some industries, such as automotive, steel and chemicals, are often a compromise between proximity to sources of supply and market demand. Ancillary industries are attracted by the presence of major firms specialising in specific industrial activities. The SMM survey showed, for instance, that a single county, Monroe, NY, with 13 establishments and a total of 30,000 employees, accounted for 35% of the national output of SIC 3861 photographic equipment and supplies. Following the Eastman Kodak Co., other manufacturers, e.g. Xerox, Bausch and Lamb, and Rochester Film, moved to Monroe County, causing it to become a centre of technology for cameras, lenses and related photographic equipment.

SMM list the six industries given in Table 2.8 as having the highest concentrations.

The highly concentrated industries are much larger than those having least industrial concentration. It will also be observed that within these groupings there are distinct differences in ranges; for example, in the most concentrated industries, guided missiles account for shipments of $9,979 million compared with shipments of over $75,000 million for motor vehicles and car bodies; however, in the least concentrated industrial grouping, there is far less distinction between the top and bottom values. Further, the least concentrated industries are made up of many more establishments with a much smaller proportion of large plants.

This sophisticated and detailed analysis of industrial markets in the US is clearly of great benefit in developing marketing strategies, including the effective allocation of advertising expenditure on media likely to achieve maximum impact in targeted markets. The degree of concentration will also affect the planning of sales territories as well as the recruitment of salesmen skilled in negotiating with large corporations.

Table 2.8 Six most concentrated industries (US) 1982

SIC	Industry	Total Estab.	Large Estab.	Shipments/receipts ($millions)	% in leading countries
2111	Cigarettes	10	10	10,885.8	97.99
4511	Certificated air transportation	280	98	21,656.8	95.93
3711	Motor vehicle and car bodies	179	110	75,270.6	95.46
3721	Aircraft	123	79	29,418.6	95.14
3761	Guided missiles and space vehicles	72	42	9,079.1	93.07
3312	Blast furnaces and steel mills	357	211	38,264.0	90.58

Source: See Sales and Marketing Managment.[31] © July 26, 1982, Survey of Buying power.

Table 2.9 Five least concentrated industries (US) 1982

SIC	Industry	Total Estab.	Large Estab.	Shipments/receipts ($millions)	% in leading countries
2951	Paint mixtures and blocks	633	108	2,284.9	2.65
2452	Prefabricated wood buildings	324	87	1,744.4	3.99
2035	Pickles, sauces and salad dressings	204	72	3,820.9	4.38
2434	Wood kitchen cabinets	429	77	2,154.0	4.44
3362	Brass, bronze and copper foundries	295	57	629.9	4.64

Source: See Sales and Marketing Managment.[31] © July 26, 1982, Survey of Buying Power.

Concentration Ratios by Size of Firms

Industries tend to be populated by many relatively small-scale producers and to be described as having low levels of concentration, such as furniture, leather goods or timber; or they are characterised by mass production, e.g. vehicles, and heavy capital-intensive production plants, such as chemicals. In these cases, high levels of concentration are said to be present.

Channon's[10] research on UK industrial concentrations over the period 1970–1978, revealed an overall trend towards higher concentration (see Table 2.10). By 1978, 55 (35.2%) of 156 industry segments had a 5-firm concentration ratio greater than 60%. (This ratio refers to the percentage of net output for the industry segment represented by the five largest enterprises.)

Table 2.10 Five-firm industry concentration ratios

Concentration ratio %	1970		Industry segments 1970 cumulative		1978		1978 cumulative	
	No.	%	No.	%	No.	%	No.	%
0–9	1	0.7	1	0.7	2	1.3	2	1.3
10–19	13	8.7	14	9.4	15	9.6	17	10.9
20–29	21	14.1	35	23.5	13	8.3	30	19.2
30–39	22	14.8	57	38.3	23	14.8	53	34.0
40–49	31	20.8	88	59.1	28	8.0	81	52.0
50–59	17	11.4	105	70.5	20	12.8	101	64.8
60–69	11⎫	7.4	116	77.9	13⎫	8.3	114	73.1
70–79	9⎬44	6.0	125	83.9	15⎬55	9.6	129	82.7
80–89	15⎨	10.1	140	94.0	17⎨	10.9	146	93.6
90–100	9⎭	6.0	149	100	10⎭	6.4	156	100
	149	100			156	100		

* 1978 — no data given for sugar industry.

Source: See Channon.[10] Reprinted by permission of Pergamon Press Ltd.

Since the early 1960s, concentration has gradually increased until the mid 1970s when the pace accelerated somewhat.

Taking account earlier research data[32] into the concentration ratios of British industry, there was a decided swing during the period 1958–1963 (see Table 2.11). Of the 209 industries listed, which accounted for approximately half of all sales by manufacturing industries between 1958 and 1963, five firms made over 50% of the total sales in 120 industries, but in 1963 this figure had increased to 127 industries.

Concentration again increased over the period 1963–1968: five firms covered 75% and over of total sales in 99 industries in 1963, whereas in 1968 this figure jumped to 127 industries.

The above data, and others given by these researchers[32] are viewed as 'almost certainly an underestimate of the true position, since they do not (and

Table 2.11 Distribution of five-firm ratios (based on sales), 1958–1963

Concentration ratio %	1958 No. of industries	Sales %	1963 No. of industries	Sales %
under 25	30	16.5	16	8.4
25–50	59	25.3	66	28.3
50–75	66	33.3	67	35.4
75+	54	24.9	60	27.9
	209	100.0	209	100.0

Concentration	Changes 1958–1963 Number of industries	Share of sales 1958 %	1963 %
Increased	128	69.0	67.7
No change	25	10.1	11.4
Decreased	56	20.9	20.9
	209	100.0	100.0

Source: See Aaronovitch and Sawyer.[32]

cannot) take account of the fact that one firm may operate in several industries, and so a large firm may dominate a number of industries'. Since 1935, the shares of the largest firms of both net output and of employment have grown very significantly. The dramatic increase in British industry concentration is of particular interest to marketing management and, of course, economic and social policies in general.

Earlier, it was noted that industrial markets are often dominated by a relatively limited number of enterprises with aggregate sales accounting for the bulk of industry sales in specific markets, a trend accentuated over recent years by industrial mergers in many industries, e.g. brewing, shipbuilding, carpet production, electronic engineering, etc. Buyers in these large firms wield considerable power in purchasing a wide range of products and services. The 80/20 rule has increasingly become evident in industrial markets. For instance, over 80% of the capital products turnover of the UK-owned electronics companies is accounted for by five indigenous manufacturers, *viz.*: GEC, Plessey, Racal, Ferranti and ICL.

Some industries, however, remain considerably fragmented, e.g. house building, or road haulage in which, as a survey revealed, 55% of total turnover was accounted for by the 150 largest companies, the balance being covered by 18,000 enterprises.

'High concentration of buying power inevitably leads to demands for special terms, priority in deliveries, and other preferential treatment from suppliers to these large organisations. There is a substantial danger, of course, that, for example, component manufacturers, as noted earlier, may become "captive suppliers" to their very big customers; marketing strategists should carefully evaluate the risks of accepting contracts for very high proportions of their total outputs'.[11]

Fewer sources of supply will be open to buyers of several types of products or services. This might encourage some finished product manufacturers to acquire suppliers of strategic components in order to safeguard their own production lines, or it could accelerate the noticeable trend in some industries to scan world markets for suitable sources of supply. This global-scanning approach to buying may extend as 'traditional' customers become more concerned about their lines of supply, and has been referred to as 'multiple sourcing'.

Industrial clustering has wide repercussions. It may foster new styles of negotiation between supplier and customer which recognise their interdependence, and the fact that 'bargaining is not the same as fighting, because suppliers made weak by systematic, unfairly based contracts represent a real danger to the long-term profitability of the firms they do business with'.[11]

Hakansson,[22] whose interaction model of industrial buying is discussed in Chapter 3, has referred to the power-dependence relationship. Both parties hold expectations; the business environment is dynamic, and buyer and seller interact and establish distinctive patterns of behaviour. Among the establishment and development of mutually satisfactory trading relationships, buyers whose firms represent significant proportions of an industry's total production, may exert considerable bargaining powers against their suppliers, both prospective and present. Skilful negotiation is clearly imperative in industrial marketing; cultivation of the right 'atmosphere' ensures that bargaining does not deteriorate into bickering.

CHARTING CONCENTRATION RATIOS

A useful method of representing the degree of specific concentration ratios is by the use of what is termed the Lorenz Curve. (Refer to Figure 2.5.) If all firms in an industry were of equal size, they would be represented by the diagonal which is described as the line of absolute equality. The extent to which the Lorenz Curve deviates from this line indictes the relative concentration; the area between the Lorenz Curve and the diagonal is generally termed the area of concentration. The flatter the Lorenz Curve, the less is the degree of concentration, i.e. the more equitably the total production of a specific industry is distributed over various sizes of firms.

The construction of a Lorenz Curve conveys graphically the actual structure of a given industry.

PUBLIC SECTOR MARKETING

Earlier in this chapter, the growing importance of the public sector in modern 'mixed economies' was discussed; marketing management needs to know more about these important sources of business and the methods of negotiation involved.

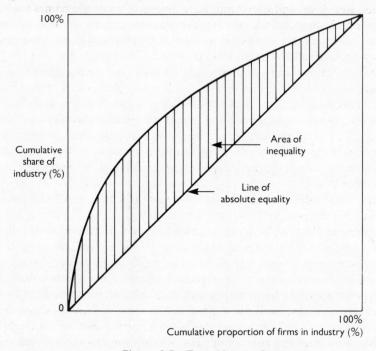

Figure 2.5   Typical Lorenz Curve.

Public corporations in the fuel and power industries (NCB, British Gas, Electricity Council and Boards), in iron and steel production, in housing (new town corporations), in transport and communication services (British Rail, British Airways, the Post Office, the BBC) and local government services are disbursing vast funds in the purchase of supplies and services of many kinds. The main government services covering military defence, the national health service, education, etc., are also responsible for the expenditure of ever-increasing funds on a gargantuan scale.

From 1 April 1974, a National Water Council was set up to administer water supplies in England; in Wales, a Welsh National Devlopment Authority operates. Nine new regional water authorities — North West, Northumbrian, Yorkshire, Anglia, Southern, Wessex, Thames, Severn/Trent and South West, are now responsible for conservation, water supply and distribution, land drainage, sewage disposal, recreation and amenities. This far-spanning range of fundamental services includes, it will be noted, recreational facilities, and replaces the administration formerly undertaken by a multitude of local authorities and water supply boards.

Local government in England and Wales was reorganised as from 1 April 1974; the most drastic restructuring since 1888. Replacing 1385 local councils by just over 450 greatly increased financial and administrative responsibilities. County boundaries have also been altered; some new counties, like Avon and Cleveland, have emerged, while old names such as Westmorland disappeared. Within the county structures, new 'district councils' took over the duties of city corporations, county and non-county boroughs and urban and rural districts.

In May 1975, reorganisation of local authorities in Scotland reduced their number from 431 to 65, distributed as follows: 9 Regions; 53 Districts; 3 Island Areas.

The total industrial demand generated by local authorities and now controlled by a small number of large councils, demands professional marketing efforts by suppliers. Standards of negotiation are likely to improve as local authorities increasingly acquire more expertise in bulk buying of goods related to their diverse responsibilities in education, social services, housing, street lighting, leisure activities, refuse collection, etc. (Bid pricing is considered in Chapter 5.)

The sensitivity of public administration to political and economic factors deserves some reflection by industrial marketing management. Road construction programmes, for instance, may be suddenly curtailed, with serious repercussions on private industrial planning and profitability. The interdependence of the public sector and the private sector is discussed in the next chapter, and the need for much closer sharing of forward planning is stressed. Because of the magnitude of spending by public sector, and the reverberations this has throughout the whole economy, policy decisions should be made much more carefully than, unfortunately, sometimes appears to be the case. Managements in both sectors of the economy are working under constraints which, multiplying in their complexity and effects, emphasise the need for an objective approach to the management of resources. On mutual understanding and cooperation rests the fragile structure and future of the economic system in which the public sector and private sector are in permanent partnership.

SPECIAL TRADING PRACTICES

Reciprocal Trading

Reciprocal trading (reciprocity) is a factor which influences some industrial markets. Similar to bilateral trading agreements between countries, reciprocal business agreements between firms occur when, as far as practicable, intertrading takes place in certain defined products. Pressure may be exerted by the more dominant 'trading partner' so that equitable reciprocal business is not, in practice, transacted, and there may be occasions when firms could buy more advantageously from an 'outside' supplier. Reciprocity may inhibit buying practices, rendering it diffcult for new suppliers to enter some markets.

An oligopolistic market situation (where there are only a few producers or sources of supply of a particular commodity) favours reciprocal trading, because the options open to buyers are limited.

A type of reciprocity may occur involving a third party. A firm may suggest or designate where one of its suppliers should obtain specific materials or components to be used in the manufacture of goods on order.

Intergroup trading is practised in some industrial organisations with diverse manufacturing activities. This tends to occur with companies which are organised in some form of vertical integration. *Joint ventures* usually involve large industrial and commercial organisations which pool their substantial combined resources to attain specific objectives, such as infiltration into a highly competitive overseas market. (These activities are discussed in more detail in Chapter 8.)

Volvo BM, the farming, earthmoving and forestry equipment subsidiary of Volvo set up a joint venture with Poclain, the French manufacturer of hydraulic excavators and mobile cranes, to market their products, with the exception of farm machinery. The managing director of Volvo BM was reported as saying that this strategy was 'intended to meet competition from the US companies which dominated in the field ... Poclain will distribute Volvo BM products in France, while Volvo BM take over Poclain's Swedish subsidiary and the marketing of the French company's products in Sweden ... In addition, Poclain's West German subsidiary, Deutsche Poclain, will market Volvo BM products in West Germany and a new subsidiary is to be found in Austria, in which Volvo will have the majority'.[33] These companies will now be able to market complementary ranges of equipment.

The terms of joint ventures should be specific and agreed by both parties; one company may be responsible for the bulk of finance, while the other provides technological or marketing expertise. Joint buying arrangements may sometimes be effected.

Consortia

In certain markets, particularly related to the construction industries, a number of companies may form a consortium or voluntary association for a limited time period to secure large contracts, the demands of which would be outside the limits of individual resources. Specialised skills can be fully deployed, while capital commitment and risk are shared, presumably, in equitable proportions. Such consortia may exercise very considerable buying influence. Consortia may be restricted to nationally-based companies or membership could be extended to include foreign companies which may have special access to certain overseas markets, as in civil engineering contracts.

Leasing of Equipment

Most industrial equipment is sold outright to the customer, but over recent years there has been a growing tendency to offer certain kinds of machinery on a rental basis. Some particular types of equipment, e.g. Rank Xerox copying machines or shoe machinery, were once only available through leasing agreements, although Xerox's market policy has been modified over recent years.

Where equipment entails considerable capital costs and it may be used only intermittently, users may benefit substantially from leasing. Leasing also allows entrepreneurs to enter markets which would not otherwise be open to them. The construction industry, for example, uses leased equipment on a fairly wide scale, thus reducing fixed investment.

Some leasing agreements allow customers to exercise an option to lease or buy after a stipulated period of time.

Leased equipment is occasionally supplied on the understanding that supplies of materials or parts are ordered exclusively from the leasor. This is usually ensured by designing equipment which will operate only with specific branded supplies. In many cases, equipment is provided at nominal cost in order to stimulate sales of dependent materials.

Dynamic examples of leasing which have enabled one company to build a profitable new business, the other to get back on to its feet, and also result in the earning of substantial export revenues, relate to two airline carriers: Tempair International Airlines and British Midland Airways. These companies 'wet lease' aircraft, i.e. supply other carriers with jet aircraft plus the aircrews and the supporting ground staff.

Tempair originated in the mid-1960s as a brokerage service dealing in the sale and lease of secondhand airliners. As developing nations progressed they aspired to operate long-range international air services, but lacked the expertise to do so. Wet leasing of jet aircraft was an attractive proposition to countries such as Burma, Bangladesh and Indonesia; it enabled them to test the market without incurring heavy capital investment. As countries develop, leases can gradually be 'dried out', so that the deal no longer includes the supply of trained personnel.

British Midland Airways were forced to look for new opportunities when they were 'left with two unmarketable Boeing 707s on their hands'[34] following the severe setback in 1972 of the North Atlantic charter market. They decided to repaint the aircraft in neutral colours and enter the wet leasing buiness, and secured a contract with Sudan Airways. Since 1973, British Midland have earned $22 million from this package deal activity 'without having to spend a penny on operating costs which are borne by the client airlines'.[34]

British Midland hires its own fleet by a dry lease method and pays on an hourly utilisation basis, thus eliminating capital repayment costs.

Project Management (Turnkey Operations)

With large capital investment projects, often overseas, marketing strategies tend to become highly specialised. A large power station or hospital will entail the application of many skills over a long period of time. Design could take two years and construction a further three or four years. Professional expertise and diverse manufacturing facilities contribute to these multi-million pound contracts; these resources have to be coordinated so that projects are completed satisfactorily.

The essence of project management is handling complexity over a period of limited duration. Often, a 'turnkey contractor' is appointed who has total responsibility for both design and construction. This strategy offers new opportunities for contractors to develop project management skills and to market this type of expertise related to specific kinds of capital projects. STC[35] were successful in obtaining a very large project because they had anticipated the buyer's needs and over some years had undertaken preparatory studies which enabled them to be well placed to win the contract. Their long-term planning typifies the strategic approach necessary to secure these highly valuable contracts.

On a rather different scale, Perkins Engines view the marketing of their diesel engines as having 'a large element of project management'.[36] In selling to original equipment manufacturers — such as vehicle builders, agricultural and mechanical handling equipment manufacturers, and producers of generating sets and compressors — a great deal of coordination is necessary.

Licensing and Joint Ventures

These methods of operation are discussed in Chapters 7 and 8, in connection with innovation strategies and international marketing strategies.

SUMMARY

Classical economic theory has traditionally divided industrial activities into three main groups: primary, secondary and tertiary. The tertiary or service sector grows in importance in developed economies.

It is difficult to distinguish satisfactorily between goods and services; there is significant interdependence.

Many methods of classifying industrial products have been promulgated: with all, border line cases are inevitable. A basic approach starts with raw materials, through to manufactured products and then related services. Products can be viewed differently according to their functions in diverse industries.

The nature of demand for industrial products is derived, i.e. it is significantly affected by end-use. Hence, the need to research end-use markets and understand trends right down the demand chain.

Products may be custom built ('specials') or standard; the latter are more prone to competitive pressures. The 'augmented product' concept offers valuable opportunities to industrial marketers to differentiate their products, even if they are basically 'commodities'.

Concentration factors complicate industrial markets: geographic; size of firm within industries. Bargaining power may be increased because of high concentration.

Public sector organisations exercise very significant patronage in some industries, e.g. civil engineering and building supplies.

Special trading practices, such as reciprocal trading, consortia, leasing, project management, licensing and joint ventures also characterise industrial markets.

REFERENCES

1. Reader, K.S., *The Modern British Economy in Historical Perspective*, Longmans, London, 1969.
2. Clark, Colin, *The Conditions of Economic Progress*, Macmillan & Co., London, 1940.
3. Smith, Anthony D., *The Measurement and Interpretation of Service Output Changes*, National Economic Development Office, London, 1972.
4. Fuchs, Victor R., 'The Growing Importance of the Service Industries', Occasional Paper, No. 96, National Bureau of Economic Research, New York, 1965.
5. Judd, Robert C., 'The Case for Redefining Services', *Journal of Marketing*, Vol. 28, January 1964.
6. 'The UK Electronics Industry', *Barclays Bank Review*, Vol. LVIII, No. 3, August 1983.
7. Checkland, S.G., *The Rise of Industrial Society in England, 1815–1885*, Longmans, London, 1966.
8. Gabor, Dennis, *The Mature Society*, Secker and Warburg, London, 1972.
9. Breach, R.W. and Hartwell, R.M., *British Economy and Society 1870–1970*, Oxford University Press, 1972.
10. Channon, Derek, 'Industrial Structure', *Long Range Planning*, Vol. 15, No. 5, 1982.
11. Pessemier, Edgar A., *New Product Decisions*, McGraw-Hill, New York, 1966.
12. Industrial Marketing Research Association (IMRA), *Regulations*, Lichfield, 1969.
13. Pearce, F.T., *The Parameters of Research*, IMRA, Lichfield, 1966.
14. Kotler, Philip, *Marketing Management, Analysis and Control*, Prentice-Hall, Englewood Cliffs, No. 9, 1980.
15. Stanton, William J., *Fundamentals of Marketing*, McGraw-Hill, Kogakusha, 1978.
16. Marrian, Jacqueline, 'Marketing Characteristics of Industrial Goods and Buyers', in *The Marketing of Industrial Products*, Wilson, Aubrey (ed.), Hutchinson, London, 1968.
17. McCarthy, E. Jerome, *Basic Marketing*, Richard D. Irwin, Homewood, Illinois, 1975.
18. Hill, Richard, M., Alexander, Ralph S. and Cross, James S., *Industrial Marketing*, Richard D. Irwin, Homewood, Illinois, 1975.

19. Owen, Douglas,' 'Organising' for Profit and Growth', in *Long Range Planning for Marketing and Diversification*, Taylor, Bernard and Wills, Gordon (eds.), Bradford U.P./Crosby/Lockwood, London, 1971.

20. MacLean, I., 'Structural Classifications — Structure and Development', *IMRA Journal*, Vol. 7, No. 4, November 1971.

21. Eugster, Carl, 'Growth Planning', in *Long Range Planning for Marketing and Diversification*, Taylor, Bernard and Wills, Gordon (eds.), Bradford U.P./Crosby/Lockwood, London, 1971.

22. Hakansson, Hakan (ed.), *International Marketing and Purchasing of Industrial Goods: An Interaction Approach*, Wiley, Chichester, 1983.

23. Stacey, Nicholas A. and Wilson, Aubrey, *Industrial Marketing Research*, Hutchinson, London, 1963.

24. Sahal, Devendra, 'Invention, Innovation and Economic Evolution', *Technological Forecasting and Social Change*, Vol. 23, 1983.

25. Ray, George, 'Innovation in the Long-Cycle', *Lloyds Bank Review*, No. 135, January 1980.

26. Mathias, Peter, *The First Industrial Nation: An Economic History of Britain 1700–1914*, Methuen, London, 1983.

27. Levitt, Theodore M., 'Marketing Success Through Differentiation — Of Anything!', *Harvard Business Review*, Jan./Feb. 1980.

28. Cunningham, M.T. and Roberts, D.A., 'The Role of Customer Service in Industrial Marketing', *European Journal of Marketing*, Spring 1974.

29. Banting, Peter M., 'Customer Service in Industrial Marketing: A Comparative Study', *European Journal of Marketing*, Vol. 10, No. 3, 1976.

30. Levitt, Theodore, *Marketing for Business Growth*, McGraw-Hill, New York, 1974.

31. Gould, Jay and Paykin, Bentley, 'SMM's Survey Moves into the Post-Industrial Era', *Sales and Marketing Management*, 25 April 1983.

32. Aaronovitch, Sam and Sawyer, Malcolm C., 'The Concentration of British Manufacturing', *Lloyds Bank Review*, No. 114, October 1974.

33. Dullforce, William, 'Volvo BM and Poclain Agree Joint Marketing Venture', *Financial Times*, 2 July 1975.

34. Green, David, 'Rent-An-Airline Scoops in Earnings Abroad', *Telegraph*, 24 June 1976.

35. 'The Marketing of a Major Contract', *Industrial Marketing Digest*, Vol. 6, No. 2, 1981.

36. Reed, John, 'How Perkins Changed Gear', *Marketing*, 27 October 1983.

Chapter Three
BUYING BEHAVIOUR

The effectiveness of marketing management does not depend solely on being able to offer competitive ranges of products and services, backed up, perhaps, by extensive publicity campaigns.

More than this is necessary for success: knowledge of the many influences which affect buying preferences is called for. This insight into factors which affect purchasing decisions should be comprehensive. Apart from technical and economic factors which, of course, are important, 'non-economic' inputs are also significant. These latter factors are based on some of the concepts of sociology and psychology; their influence is often subtle and not easily identified. But this does not mean that they should be ignored or left largely to trial-and-error learning, with all its associated shortcomings.

In business negotiations, the interaction between buying and selling companies is at both corporate and individual levels. At the former level, contractual obligations are arranged, while at the latter level, personal contacts are made and individual relationships established. This interaction[1] continues if both buyer and seller consider that they benefit from it; the relationship is essentially mutual and dynamic; conflict may arise from time to time, but most industrial markets tend to have stable and long-established relationships.[2]

As observed in Chapter 1, business enterprises have three levels of activity: the physical level covering plant, tools and materials; the economic level reflecting the activities of making and distributing products; and the human level relating to the activities of individuals within organisations. The policy and tactics adopted by enterprises depend on the decisions made by individuals in their various professional roles.

Human behaviour is complex; that strange, mythical figure 'Economic Man', completely motivated by rationality, who had access to perfect knowledge about market conditions and who could buy freely, clearly does not relate closely to actual buying behaviour in organisations.

The case for acquiring systematic knowledge of the social, psychological and cultural factors affecting buying behaviour has been argued elsewhere.[3]

The fundamental psychological factors of cognitions, learning processes, interpersonal traits, attitudes, motivation and personality theories should be related to particular market situations. 'The interaction of these individual factors and the ways in which they affect buying behaviour in both personal and organisational areas deemed careful study. People are members of society; they form cultures and subcultures. Market enquiries should be extended to include assessment of these environmental factors. Organisational buyers do not live like hermits; they are influenced by the personal behaviour of their colleagues, by the trading practices of other enterprises, and by the standards of the society to which they belong.

It is unrealistic, therefore, to approach the study of buying behaviour — personal or organisational — without an appreciation of the multiplexity of buying motivations. A balanced view is necessary; explanations of buying behaviour should not go from the one extreme of regarding 'rational' economic factors as solely responsible, to the equally extreme view that emotional or 'irrational' influences entirely account for the purchase of products and services.

Organisational Buying Motivations

The products and services bought by organisational buyers are related to the objectives and needs of their organisations: thus, their buying behaviour will be influenced by these constraints. In industrial and commercial transactions, products and services will be acquired primarily because they will be expected to contribute to the overall profitability of an enterprise, enabling, for example, production to be carried out more efficiently or methods of office adminstration to be made more cost-effective. In many cases, the products and services bought for industrial and commercial consumption will be similar to those purchased by consumers; for example, paint, stationery, heating fuels or cars, but the *reasons* for purchase will be different, and so buying criteria may also be distinctive.

As already observed, in addition to industrial and commercial undertakings which form the private sector of the economy, a great deal of buying activity is undertaken by purchasing agents acting for the public corporations such as the gas, electricity and coal boards, public transport, health and welfare authorities, local authorities and various government departments. The constraints on buying behaviour, although not, in most cases, related to profit generation, will reflect the objectives of these organisations.

Apart from profit, companies may also be motivated by social or legal obligations, particularly related to safety and welfare provisions for their workforce. In some cases, certain costs may be incurred by companies in order to promote favourable attitudes towards them; for example, buying sports facilities, endowing scholarships, or providing special facilities for staff.

Although the primary motivation of commercial buyers and those in non-profit-making organisations may differ, they have identical responsibilities: to acquire goods and services for use in their organisations as distinct from personal consumption.

CONFLICT OF MOTIVATIONS

A buyer's professional activities may be tempered by the fundamental instinct he has for survival and for enhancing his career. This powerful motivation for self-preservation and improvement reflects the philosphy of Thomas Hobbes[4] (1588–1679) who held that man is 'instinctively' orientated towards preserving his own well-being. Buying decisions involving considerable risk are likely to be influenced by personal attitudes; as David MacClelland[5] has observed: 'A great part of the efforts of business executives is directed towards minimising uncertainties'. Cyert and March[6] in their behavioural theory of the firm, identified four classifications of buying determinants: individual, social (interpersonal), organisational (formal) and environmental. Within these four types of determinants, these researchers discussed the interaction of 'task' and 'non-task' variables. The former related to the so-called rational factors which affect buying decisions, e.g. price, quality, delivery, etc. — typified as 'hard date' in marketing research. Non-task variables referred to factors such as motivation, personal values or political, social and cultural activities which may intrude in certain buying decisions. These influences are generally described as 'soft data'. Although task factors are of paramount importance in organisational buying, the influence of 'non-economic' factors should never be ignored. Research by Wilson[7] has suggested that the personality traits of purchasing agents may significantly affect their style of decision making.

The organisational buyer is exposed to the complex interplay of economic and non-economic factors; he is also vulnerable to some element of conflict between organisational demands and personal needs; and he has to function as part of the management team, mediating between suppliers and users of a wide range of goods and services.

COMPLEXITY OF DECISION MAKING

As experienced marketers know well, organisational buying processes are generally complex and involve several people, frequently from different departments. Over the years, several studies have been made of typical buying situations and the numbers of people involved in them. A pioneer study, in 1958, by Dun and Bradstreet (see Alexander et al.[8]) revealed that in the average firm no fewer than nine people influenced the buying decision.

Research by Alexander, Cross and Cunningham[8] revealed that in 106 industrial firms, three or more persons influenced buying processes in over 75% of the companies studied. In a special investigation of British engineering firms, McGraw-Hill[9] found that there were more than five buying influences in companies with 400–1000 employees, and in companies employing over 1000, more than six people were involved in buying decisions. There is general agreement by these and other researchers that organisational buying almost always involves more than one individual. In some very large and complex contracts, buying negotiations are likely to be sophisticated; special committees may be set up to consider suitable sources of supply. 'Approved' suppliers may be invited to tender for specific goods and services, and the general tendency is for 'arms length' dealing. Long-term agreements for the supply of capital equipment, for example, will be dealt with at top-management level, where the advice of specialist managers and consultants will be carefully evaluated before commitments are made.

Industrial production techniques are also often complex and demand expert knowledge; these skills may contribute to sophisticated buying procedures in which the role of the actual buyer is considerably diminished.

THE BUYING CENTRE/DECISION MAKING UNIT

In 1950, the journal *Scientific American*, made a notable study of the various influences on purchasing decisions over eleven major industries including chemicals. Their enquiries centred on the journal's readership which is largely made up of scientific and technical staff, many of them employed in large companies. This research was updated in 1970, and expanded by Erickson[10] in 1978 when, however, the study was restricted to the chemical industry. There was generally a very good agreement between the 1970 and 1978 survey findings which indicated the influence of various departments in buying decisions.

The purchasing department continues to play a key role in buying materials, components and equipment, especially when it comes to taking advantage of new price differentials, tracking new sources of supply and choosing suppliers.

The earlier studies conducted by *Scientific American* led, in 1967, to the introduction of the term 'Decision Making Unit' to British marketing literature. *How British Industry Buys*[11] was sponsored jointly by the Institute of Marketing and Industrial Market Research Ltd and gave a wealth of data about the buying procedures of over 900 companies. This enquiry, conducted by Hugh Buckner, revealed the inadequacy of some marketing strategies because communication was not being made with the people in organisations who really made the decisions to buy specific types of products or services.

This important British pioneering research indicated that industrial purchasing was essentially a team effort involving 'groups of specialists each with a definite delegated task'.[11] Actual routines varied according to the types of products and the nature of the organisations concerned.

Gordon Brand[12] in 1972, added valuable new data which showed how decision making units reached their purchasing decisions.

A further step forward was taken in 1974 with the publication of 'How British Industry Buys, 1974'[13], which was sponsored by the *Financial Times* and based on research undertaken by Industrial Market Research Ltd. This updated the earlier research and also extended it into two new areas — industrial buying of private cars and commercial vehicles. Also covered are plant and equipment, materials and component parts; there is, in addition, a special study of the British construction industry's purchasing routines.

The findings of this survey confirmed that industrial purchasing is a complex operation with the nature of products and the amount of expenditure largely controlling the levels of management involved.

In 1983 the *Financial Times* commissioned the Cranfield School of Management to undertake further research into British industrial buying practices. The following sectors were studied: plant and equipment, commercial vehicles and trailers, company cars, materials, component parts, office equipment including microcomputers, and mainframe and/or minicomputers. A stratified random sample of 2963 companies was drawn from Dun and Bradstreet's computerised list of Key British Enterprises, and a pilot study of 300 firms in the early part of 1983 was followed by the main survey over the period May to September 1983.

Questionnaires divided the decision making process into four basic stages: initiation of a purchase; specification; commercial evaluation; and monitoring performance. For each of these stages in the buying process, executives were asked to indicate whether decisions were collective, individual, departmental, or external.

Table 3.1 shows the dispersion of financial responsibility within the companies surveyed.

Table 3.1 The structure of financial responsibility within companies

Final authority to approve rests with:	Board (collectively)	Individual director	Departmental manager	Lower management/ clerical
For expenditure up to:	%	%	%	%
£ 500	4	31	52	14
£ 2500	18	54	24	4
£ 5000	29	55	14	2
£50,000	70	25	4	1
Over £50,000	88	11	2	—

Source: 'How British Industry Buys, 1983'.[14] Reprinted with permission.

It will be observed that few companies authorise staff below departmental manager status (apart from routine reordering procedures) to make significant financial commitments. Above £2500, the majority of companies required specific director approval, and board sanction tends to be required for larger sums with ultimate authority for expenditure in the range of £50,000 and above.

The responsibility for buying expenditures over £50,000 by size of firms is given in Table 3.2.

Table 3.2 Buying expenditure, over £50,000: responsibility by size of firm (employees)

No. of employees	Board (collectively) %	Individual director %	Departmental manager %	Lower management/ clerical %
Under 100	88	11	–	–
100–499	92	7	1	–
500–999	87	11	2	–
Over 1000	80	14	6	–

Source: 'How British Industry Buys, 1983'.[14] Reprinted with permission.

From Table 3.2 it will be noted that, as may be expected, major buying propositions are decided at board level, although individual directors exercise fairly significant influence in small firms and in those employing from 500 upwards.

Purchasing policy in companies with several establishments was also surveyed. Table 3.3 reveals some distinct variations in buying policies; for example, capital equipment is more likely to be bought centrally than products of relatively continuous consumption such as materials and component parts. The research indicated, however, that very few companies admit to having no clearly defined buying policy related to specific products.

Table 3.3 Policy on purchasing in multiple establishment companies

	Plant equipment %	Materials %	Components %	Office equipment %	Commercial vehicles %	Private cars %	Computers %
Centralised purchasing policy	68	56	48	57	81	86	87
Decentra- lised purchasing policy	27	40	47	38	17	12	11
No firm policy	5	4	5	5	2	2	2

Source: How British Industry Buys, 1983'.[14] Reprinted with permission.

These researches indicate the importance of understanding the complex nature of organisations and their needs. In the case of plant and equipment, 'How British Industry Buys, 1983'[14] showed that the production manager played a vital role in initiating the decision to expand existing capacity. This was particularly evident in larger companies. In smaller companies, the managing director was significantly involved at this buying stage, and in companies having between 100 and 499 employees, other directors were active. This detailed report[14] includes 'buying clout charts' which indicate the buying responsibilities assumed by various members of the DMU; these data are also analysed by size and type of industry.

FIVE ROLES IN THE BUYING PROCESS

Five roles in the buying process have been identified as: gatekeeper; user; influencer; buyer; decider — they form what has been termed the 'buying centre'.[15] At times, these roles may be undertaken by the same person; often, however, different people are active in these various roles in specific buying situations. The influence of individual members of the buying team will also be likely to change according to the nature of the purchaser under consideration, as the surveys into British industry revealed.

'Users' in some organisations may have particular influence on the type of product and the origin of supply, especially with some technical supplies. Their recommendations may be considered as vital inputs in the buying process. Users of products may be groups of individuals, perhaps laboratory research teams whose expert knowledge and practical skill will be likely to weigh more heavily than considerations relating to price, discount terms, etc.

In one research,[16] it was found that the works manager may want a product to have long life, the safety officer, on the other hand, may want one that carries no risk, while the buyer may be looking for the cheapest product. In such cases, there is a resultant clash of objectives; the shrewd marketer will segment his promotional campaign so that different appeals are made to the various specialists taking part in the purchase of his products.

'Influencers' may not be readily identified. Communication within organisations is likely to be informal as well as formal. The informal and personal influence may be significant in suppliers. Personal influence in consumer buying behaviour has been researched at some length, based on Katz and Lazarsfeld's[17] sociological research. In industrial markets, a survey of 58 purchasing agents and other executives involved in buying was undertaken by Professor Frederick E. Webster[18] of Dartmouth College, US. His findings supported beliefs which already were widely held about industrial buying behaviour.

Table 3.4 details the relative importance of sources of information available to the organisational buyers surveyed.

Webster found that informal communication in industrial markets may be much less frequent than in consumer markets. Buyers may occasionally telephone their counterparts in other firms to check urgently *where* to buy certain supplies, but seldom *what* to buy. The general reaction was to avoid giving information about newly purchased products which gave particular companies some competitive advantage. The well known tendency of consumers to reduce post-purchase anxiety by discussing their purchases with other users appears to be absent from industrial markets.

Table 3.4 Percentage of respondents finding each source important, by stage in
buying process

	Awareness	Interest	Evaluation	Trial	Adoption
Manufacturer's salesman	84	90	64	70	56
Trade journals	90	38	22	16	8
Buyers in other companies	18	22	28	16	8
Engineers in other companies	26	34	44	20	18
Trade associates	42	24	14	4	8
Trade shows	76	38	16	12	4

Notes

1. Respondents were asked to indicate any source that was useful to them at each stage of
   buying process.
2. No requirements were placed on the number of sources — it was possible for a respondent
   to indicate that all sources were important at all stages or that none was useful at any
   stage.
3. Out of a possible 30 responses (6 sources × 5 stages), the average respondent indicated
   10.

Source: Webster, Frederick E. Jnr.[18]

Another important finding related to the role of the manufacturer's
salesman who was regarded as a source of highly useful and reliable
information. (See Table 3.4.) His influence was felt throughout the various
stages of purchasing. His 'flexibility' as a communicator was regarded as
particularly important; the right kind and amount of information could be
provided by an experienced technical representative who was highly trusted
by purchasing agents.

The vital role played by industrial sales forces is also confirmed by later
research[1], which stresses that 'personal contacts are at the heart of the
interaction between organisations and, in industrial markets in particular,
serve as the medium through which communications in buying and selling
take place'. Multiple tasks are performed during the interactions between the
negotiating parties: information exchange, assessment, negotiation, crisis
insurance, social and ego enhancement.

Opinion leadership — another marked factor affecting consumer buying
— seemed to be largely ineffective with organisational supplies. Webster[18]
found that, in general, companies felt that the specific nature of their
problems precluded the probability of other manufacturers having exactly
the same experience, and, therefore, these would be unlikely to be useful
guides. The two respondent companies which acknowledged the value of

opinion leadership shared similar views: that companies who were looked upon as 'opinion' leaders were of large size, were committed to planned programmes of new product development, were financially successful and were characterised as 'growth' companies.

Table 3.4 shows that at the 'awareness' stage, trade journals were marginally more important than salesmen.

Webster concluded that informal or word-of-mouth communication from *external* sources does not appear to be significant in the industries he researched; the key figure was the supplier's salesman. It should be noted that Webster focussed on *inter-firm* dimensions of informal communications; he did not study *intra-firm* relationships. This aspect was researched by John A. Martilla[19] whose studies in three industrial markets showed that 'word-of-mouth communication *within* firms is an important influence in the later stages of the adoption process. Opinion leaders were found to be more heavily exposed to impersonal sources of information than other buying influences in the firm'.[19]

Martilla's researches led him to state that contrary to Webster's general findings, 'buying influentials' in the paper converting markets also reported that they sought 'information and opinions about paper from persons in competing firms, in much the same way as within the firm'.[18] Generalisations about buying behaviour — industrial or consumer — appear to be unwise; the nature of cooperation which exists even among competitors varies from industry to industry. 'Some industries are characterised by their attitude of friendly collaboration with competitors at trade federation level and through personal contacts at senior level'.[19]

He suggested that if this pattern of impersonal communication applied to other industrial supplies, substantial advertising campaigns may be advisable to bring to the attention of buying influentials, who had no direct contact with suppliers' salesmen, new ranges of products and services.

The functions of buyer and decider are sometimes undertaken by the same executive. The specifier or decider may only be discovered after considerable research. A firm supplying components for air filtration equipment found that the vital link in the buying chain was, in certain cases, the section leader of the team of design draughtsmen who actually nominated the suppliers of specific components.

Firms generally prefer to draw their suppliers from companies which have established a reputation for quality and reliability. Professional judgement of the suitability of some prospective suppliers may well hinge on the estimation of, for example, the production engineer. The power of the buyer is therefore subject to considerable constraints in selecting some suppliers. (This aspect of buying power will be discussed later — p.77.)

The gatekeeper in the buying team deserves special consideration by organisational suppliers. His identity, also, may not be easily discovered. In some cases, he may be a junior executive who collects data sheets on equipment and sends out routine enquiries for standard supplies. With more expensive and infrequently purchased items, the gatekeeper's role may be filled by a senior technical expert. It is of tactical importance to know *who* the specific gatekeeper is and the extent of his influence in purchasing particular types of goods.

In the purchase of a computer system, Pettigrew[20] noted that internal politics were important influences; in particular he observed how the 'gatekeeper' can structure the outcome of buying processes by filtering and amending the flow of information to suit his own objectives.

Johnston and Bonoma[21] have attempted to evaluate the dimensions of interactivity within the buying centre in research based on sixty instances of buying involving capital equipment and services. They examined the following dimensions:

1. lateral involvement; number of departments involved
2. vertical involvement; how many levels were involved
3. extensivity; total number of individuals involved
4. connectedness; degree to which members of the buying centre are communicating
5. centrality; of the purchasing managers

They noted that the mean process time was about 6 months, with the longest extending over several years. They also noted that in the search of a supplier of services the prime concern was the reputation of the vendor.

For equipment sales, bids are often called as a basis for negotiation and much effort was necessary before a contract could be agreed. It was concluded that what is important to the seller company is:

1. the degree of lateral involvement, because it indicates the potential diversity of opinion within the buying centre
2. the centrality, because it indicates the power of the purchasing manager

Research should aim to identify members of the 'buying centre' and to evaluate their relative contributions to the decisions to buy particular types of products and services. The more insight which can be obtained into the buying procedures of an organisation, the more effectively can marketing strategies be developed. Market knowledge includes the acquisition of up-to-date information about the 'mechanics' of buying within prospective customers' organisations.

A more sophisticated planning operation is needed by organisational supply firms; the responsibilities of individual executives concerned with purchasing routines in specific organisations require expert valuation. Salesmen should not be left without adequate guidance in the critical task of locating those who are likely to contribute to particular buying decisions. Collective, departmental individual areas of responsibility need to be identified, and the marketing programme should include a variety of tactical communications — personal and through advertising media — which will ensure that *all* who are likely to be of importance within customers' organisations are aware of the supplying companies' products and services and of the benefits which they offer.

It will readily be seen that organisational buying procedures which relate to particular supplies are complex, and that the interaction of the individuals concerned in the buying process compounds this complexity. Further, the scale of purchase is substantial and the repercussions on an organisation from purchasing particular quantities of some products may be far-reaching. Investment programmes involving the purchase of capital equipment will have, for instance, significant effects on the financial and production policies with the objective of increasing efficiency and giving a manufacturing company special competitive advantages in their markets. Social costs may also result from improvements in technological efficiency; the installation of modern equipment may result in problems in labour utilisation. These effects of organisational purchases are, therefore, widely diffused and often go to the heart of a business.

CHALLENGE TO BUYER'S AUTHORITY

The role and status of the buyer in large organisations are, to some extent, adversely affected by the influence of technological specialists who may have more real power in nominating suppliers than he is able to exercise. Specialist buyers, such as steel or packaging, are appointed in certain instances where the volume of business transacted and the responsibilities of ensuring adequate supplies are very significant. In such instances the general buyer is able to exercise considerably more influence at senior management level than if he had to rely heavily on the advice and guidance from managers in other departments.

To maintain his status in the organisation, which some buyers may feel to be endangered, the professional buyer may seek to reassert his authority through adopting, as George Strauss[22] has shown, a variety of techniques ranging from rigidly enforcing routine procedures to persuasive and cooperative tactics, with the object of retaining the initiative in buying decisions.

Strauss identified five techniques:

1. rule-orientated tactics
2. rule-evading tactics
3. personal–political tactics
4. persuasion–educational tactics
5. organisational–interactional tactics

Buyers who were characterised as 'expansionists' aimed to influence work-flow patterns by a flexible mixture of informal and formal tactics. They aimed to influence buying considerations at an early stage, so that they retained control of the operations. Success seemed to be governed by these factors: (1) the technology of an industry (complexity offered the greatest opportunities), (2) management philosophy (where relationships were unformed because of new management, particular benefits accrued to the buyer), (3) education (this enabled greater use to be made of informal approaches and assisted in committee discussions).

EVALUATING THE RISK FACTOR IN ORGANISATIONAL BUYING

The rapid growth of new technologies and the marked development apparent in many industries have added to the complexities and difficulties of purchasing goods and services.

In the packaging industry, for example, progress has been accelerated by the exponential growth of chemical- and petroleum-based plastics which have spawned a rich vocabulary of highly specialised descriptions far beyond the traditional and readily understood specifications of paper packaging. To add to this bewildering array of technical terminology, many new laminates incorporating paper and plastic are also offered to buyers of packaging.

Similarly, textiles buyers are confronted with an intimidating list of new fibres and materials sprung from the creative genius of textile laboratories and presented with all the panache of modern merchandising. The breathless pace of the manmade fibre industry has imposed on buyers of synthetic fabrics completely new standards of quality. By comparison, the pre-War buyer who dealt almost exclusively in natural fibres must have had an idyllic existence.

Information about new types and ranges of raw materials, products and methods has cascaded on to the desks of industrial buyers over the past decade. Advertisements and editorial comment in trade journals provide a rich diet of data relating to new technologies and products. Technical representatives also add to the flow of knowledge, eager to give personally the latest information on their products.

Business executives are directly concerned with decision making under conditions of uncertainty. This involves risk of varying degrees, and buyers, in particular, will evaluate the type and extent of the risk associated with specific products and services. The ability to tolerate risk has been seen as related to the firm's size and liquidity, and the degree of self-confidence of its management. These firms are generally able to absorb the risk of innovation, and to profit from exploiting the market opportunities. Pilkingtons have scored worldwide success with the float-glass process, but only after vast expenditure in research and development which was continued despite early disappointments.

Bauer[23] proposed the concept of 'perceived risk' in buying decisions, i.e. that risk is assessed differently according to the perceptions of individual buyers. Although Bauer's original research applied to consumer behaviour, the perceived risk model may usefully be related to industrial buying. Suppliers can help in reducing 'perceived risk' by the exchange of technical and other information with their customers and prospective buyers and thus improve their credibility.[24] Cunningham and White,[25] in research of buying processes in the UK machine tools industry, found that 60% of all machine purchases surveyed, went to suppliers of whom the buyer had previous experience; in the case of very large companies, this 'high inertia' was 80%, but fell to as low as 17% with the smallest companies.

Knowledge and experience gained over the years help, of course, in reducing the element of risk in many buying situations. It is frequently possible to draw up 'decision rules', which will be useful when evaluating competitive offers. Decisions rules economise on management time and effort and reduce overall costs of administration. They also help to control the level of risk in buying. Bauer[23] hypothesised that consumers adopted risk-reducing strategies with certain products and tended to buy only well known or advertised lines. In the industrial area, there is evidence that buyers tend to display similar characteristics when faced with buying decisions involving significant risk.

Where essential raw materials or component parts are bought in, the influence of risk and uncertainty will be considerable factors in industrial buying decisions. Acceptable standards of quality, service and price will be carefully drawn up and discussed with potential suppliers. It has already been noted that organisational buyers become heavily dependent on the efficiency of their suppliers. Levitt[26] has observed that the whole process of bargaining in industrial negotiation becomes increasingly sophisticated: 'Price will be an enormously important consideration but it will hardly exhaust the proposition. Ability to perform the logistics of tightly scheduled delivery will become fully as salient an issue as price ... the thing people and companies buy is not just a tangible product, but a whole cluster of related benefits, services and values'.

Professional buyers recognise that the true value of products is made up of many parts. The relative importance of these qualities should be assessed in relation to the needs of the organisation.

Seven critical factors were found to influence buyers in the British valve and pump industry in the choice of their suppliers of raw materials.[27] These factors were; delivery reliability, technical advice, test facilities, replacement guarantee, prompt quotation, ease of contact and willingness to supply range. These attributes helped to reduce the risk element in purchase decisions. A 'favourable impression' of suppliers resulted from their ability to satisfy buyers on 'quality, service and price in that order'.[27]

Buyers, as was observed earlier, may seek to reduce delivery risks by distributing their business over several suppliers, so that in the event of a local strike or some other unexpected event, their own production lines are not seriously in danger. 'Multiple sourcing' is now standard practice in many large firms. This strategic buying policy is paralleled in the marketing side of the business by ensuring that the output of the factory is not wholly dependent upon a few large customers continuing to place their orders regularly.

The element of risk in buying decisions could be considered along a continuum ranging from routine (low risk) purchases at one extreme to novel (high risk) purchases at the other end of the scale. In the centre would fall many industrial transactions where the hazards could reasonably be calculated sufficiently to allow decisions of tolerable risk to be made. The situation may be seen as:

Little or no risk	*'Reasonable' risk*	*High risk*
Routine purchases	Occasional purchases	Novel purchases

So-called 'occasional' purchases would include those where the buyer had sufficient knowledge of product specifications and market conditions which would enable him to place business with tolerable risk. Although these types of products may not be bought very regularly, and therefore not qualify to be classified as routine purchases, buyers will have gathered valuable experience and information over time which contribute towards keeping risk at a minimal level.

The 'high risk' purchases include innovations in goods and services which may be radically different from established supplies. Innovation may relate to the intrinsic nature of a product, to its overall appearance and design, to the type of packaging used, or, perhaps, to some new method of distribution. Even more fundamental innovation may be created by new technology, as in high duty special alloys, electronic components, or ballistic missiles.

The technological and entrepreneurial qualities required for successful innovation need the practical support of official commercial organisations which are able and willing to place firm orders. In many cases this means that those who buy these types of products first are exposed to relatively high risk. Few firms would be willing to expose their production lines to this sort of risk by adopting new techniques or components without prolonged trial and evaluation. Only then will they be willing to go further, provided that the innovation offers them the firm prospect of improved profitability. The increasing competitiveness of modern industry is forcing managers to demand, however, even higher standards of performance before it is worthwhile disrupting existing production methods by changing suppliers or adopting new versions of products.

The industrial buyer is, to some extent, in a dilemma regarding innovating products. He will not wish to retard the development of his own organisation but, at the same time, he will be reluctant to accept unduly heavy risk. Yet he will be conscious of his status within the management hierarchy and of the opportunities which he should use to enhance his career. It has been seen that progressive buyers typified by Strauss[22] as 'expansionists' deliberately involved technical managers in discussions and decisions regarding supplies, and were skilled in using formal and informal approaches. In this way the corporate or organisation man aims to steer a careful course between satisfying his personal need for status and security and the development of his company as a progressive organisation.

Mansfield's[28] research into the rate of diffusion of new products and the impact of risk which affected their adoption is noted in Chapter 7 on Innovation Strategy. As experience and information about an innovation accumulate, the risks associated with its introduction grow fewer and competitive pressures mount. Moreover, in cases where the profitability of an innovation is difficult to assess, the mere fact that a large proportion of a firm's competitors have adopted the innovation may act as a spur to that firm. Suppliers should obviously try to reduce the element of risk, as perceived by buyers, through imaginative marketing strategies, particularly where new products are being introduced. (Further consideration of risk occurs in Chapters 5 and 6.)

Post-decisional Dissonance

After it has been decided to purchase some product carrying above-average risk, buyers may experience a feeling of dissonance or discomfort about the wisdom of their action. This post-purchase evaluation takes place when selection had to be made from several alternatives. On later reflection, buyers may recall the strong points of the rejected alternative products and, at the same time, become more aware of some disadvantages of the product chosen. For example, equipment bought may have high productive potential but spares may not be as readily available as some competitive model with lower output. The 'negative' feature of the product which has now been ordered may begin to cause nagging doubts giving rise to post-decisional dissonance. This psychological tension will tend to be particularly intrusive where a major investment has been made and the commitment is likely to result in the acquisition of relatively permanent assets, such as machine tools.

The concept of post-decisional dissonance emanates from the Theory of Cognitive Dissonance propounded by Leon Festinger,[29] Professor of Psychology at Stanford, USA. The theory rests on two hypotheses:

1. The existence of dissonance, being psychologically uncomfortable, will motivate people to attempt to reduce the dissonance (disharmony; conflict) and to achieve consonance (agreement; equilibrium)
2. When dissonance occurs, people not only try to reduce it but also avoid situations and information which would be likely to increase dissonance.

An individual strives towards consistency (consonance; agreement; equilibrium) within his cognitive structure (set of beliefs about people, products, events, etc.) and endeavours to reduce tension so as to make life pleasant. Dissonance (disharmony; frustration) is a state of psychological tension which may result from purchasing a product, particularly if it is an expensive one. 'The magnitude of post-decision dissonance is an increasing function of the general importance of the decision and of the relative attractiveness of the unchosen alternatives'.[29]

Although published studies refer almost exclusively to consumer products, the concept of dissonance would appear to have some significance in industrial buying behaviour. It is closely concerned with the risk factor in buying situations.

According to Festinger's theory, a buyer will tend to seek reassurance in many instances *after* purchase decisions are taken. He may endeavour to reassure himself by seeking information in support of his decision, and will avoid sources of information which could result in loss of confidence. He may even actively seek information which reflects disadvantageously on the alternative products. Because it is generally recognised that perception is selective, people tend to collect information congruent with their existing beliefs and attitudes. They constantly receive stimulus information which is interpreted personally in order to achieve internal harmony. Conflict causes tension; this results in psychological discomfort which people dissipate by searching for evidence to confirm their earlier behaviour.

> 'A great deal of advertising, contrary to what one might expect, is read after rather than before the car is bought, and serves to persuade the reader that he has been wise and practical. Cadillac is well aware of this and its advertisements constantly pat the owner on the back for his good taste and rationality'.[30]

It is well known, of course, that people become more aware of advertisements (and other owners) when they have recently bought an important new product. But this phenomenon does not fully explain the decided interest which new buyers have in reading advertisements featuring their chosen product. (See Chapter 9 related to corporate personality and risk.)

Buyers of office equipment, industrial plant and machinery, etc., do not shed their fundamental human characteristics when exercising their professional skills. It would be reasonable to surmise that dissonance theory could be applied to some aspects of organisational buying behaviour. As noted in Chapter 2, 'package deals' involving the supply, installation and servicing of commercial and industrial equipment may be taken as evidence that buyers are interested in controlling risks and in reducing post-decisional dissonance doubts.

MODELS OF ORGANISATIONAL BUYER BEHAVIOUR

In attempting to understand the complexity of buying behaviour in organisational supplies, theoretical constructions of phenomena which are considered to be interrelated and significant in specific market situations are formed by researchers. These conceptual frameworks are termed models.

A model is, therefore, 'a set of assumptions about the factors which are relevant to a given situation and the relationships which exist between them. The term model is normally taken to mean a formal developed model in which the assumptions are stated explicitly and relevant conclusions have been drawn by formal deductive (usually mathematical) methods. Hopefully, the model has also been tested in various ways by adducing evidence in favour of the original assumptions or by testing conclusions drawn from the model'.[31]

The purpose of a model is to clarify the relationships between the inputs, such as advertising, competitors' activities, or the various motivations which influence purchase behaviour, and the outcomes or outputs (adoption or rejection of a specific product or service from a particular supply source).

In the process of analytical and creative thought that is involved in the development of a theoretical model, variables may be identified and tested for their relevance to a particular business problem, such as the marketing of a technical product or service to certain types of customers.

Buying models should be helpful in understanding current purchasing practices and in giving clues as to likely future behaviour. Because of the acknowledged complexity of industrial buying behaviour, simplistic models are clearly not valid, while, at the same time, it is obviously unrealistic to make positive projections based on very limited data. Yet some attempts must be made to understand how a market works; what makes buyers 'tick'; and what the likely trends in a market are going to mean for specific products. Based on valuable experience over years, most businessmen carry in their heads a fairly sound appreciation of the factors affecting demand for their products; setting these variables down more formally is a valuable step towards more sophisticated and profitable understanding of market behaviour.

Because trading conditions change — sometimes quite drastically, as most firms have found over the past decade or so — models need to be updated from time to time. A static model of a dynamic market environment is worse than no model at all.

Industrial buying behaviour models have been rather sparse; those that have been available have largely focussed on various theories of motivation, which have been considerably influenced by consumer empirical research.

In the study of consumer supplies, theoretical models have been developed which fall into three broad classifications:

1. subjective verbal or descriptive models
2. decision-process or logical flow models
3. behavioural models

Verbal (Descriptive) Models

The first category of model is the simplest and probably the most subjective, but it can be useful in giving researchers a general picture of the way in which buyers typically approach problems of purchasing certain supplies. In freestyle interviews, buyers would be asked to describe their routine behaviour which will probably be strongly influenced by personal knowledge and experience over several years. Their general buying behaviour may give an insight into how best to communicate with them: are trade journals regularly consulted?; what kind of discussion takes place inside an organisation before certain supplies are ordered? These enquiries are often useful in the early stages of designing marketing research strategies.

Logical Flow (Decision Process) Models

Logical flow (decision process) models project buying behaviour as a series of steps which lead to either purchase or final rejection of the supplies offered to some prospective customers. These stages start with recognition of a problem (i.e. a need), progress through a phase of search activities for solutions to the problem, to the next stage of evalution of alternative solutions (comparing competitive offers), through to the processes of buying (selection and nomination of supplier) and so to the last phase of post-purchase evaluation.

This relatively simple buying model can be elaborated at each of the stages outlined, and the rate of movement through these phases will vary according to the nature of the supplies under consideration.

In this connection, it may be helpful to recall the three broad areas of buying which were discussed in the section dealing with the impact of risk on buying behaviour. With routine stores, decision rules are likely to have been drawn up — formally or otherwise — which enable progress through the various buying phases to be fairly speedy. With high-cost equipment, or supplies novel to the purchasing organisation, more deliberation is likely, and so it will take longer for buying decisions to be taken.

The Marketing Science Institute (MSI) model, devised by Robinson, Faris and Wind[32] is an example of a logical-flow model related to industrial supplies. (Refer to Figure 3.1.) The model analyses buying situations into three 'Buyclasses' and eight 'Buyphases'.

The 'Buyphases' (numbered 1–8) follow a sequential flow which is applicable to the purchase of a wide variety of supplies. These phases are set against three alternative 'Buyclasses' which are likely to modify considerably buying practices. At different points in the buying sequence, inputs into the decision process may be made, as observed earlier, from several areas of functional management.

The activities of the decision making unit/buying centre, discussed earlier in this chapter, could be related to the MSI model. The last phase, clearly, is associated with the impact of post-decisional dissonance, and underlines the necessity for sales staff to accept, as part of their regular duties, the responsibility of reassuring customers who have committed themselves to purchasing certain supplies. Post-purchase evaluation, particularly of expensive equipment, will be thorough, and the likelihood of further business

BUYCLASSES

		New Task	Modified Rebuy	Straight Rebuy
B	1. Anticipation or recognition of a problem (need) and a general solution			
U	2. Determination of characteristics and quantity of needed item			
Y P	3. Description of characteristics and quantity of needed item			
H	4. Search for a qualification of potential sources			
A S	5. Acquisition and analysis of proposals			
E	6. Evaluation of proposals and selection of supplier(s)			
S	7. Selection of an order routine			
	8. Performance feedback and evaluation			

Notes

1. The most complex buying situations occur in the upper left portion of the BUYGRID matrix, when the largest number of decision makers and buying influences are involved. Thus, a New Task in its initial phase of problem recognition generally represents the greatest difficulty for management.
2. Clearly, a New Task may entail policy questions and special studies, whereas a Modified Rebuy may be more routine, and a Straight Rebuy essentially automatic.
3. As Buyphases are completed, moving from phase 1 through phase 8, the process of 'creeping commitment' occurs, and there is diminishing likelihood of new vendors gaining access to the buying situations.

Figure 3.1 The Buygrid analytic framework for industrial buying situations.

Source: See Robinson, Faris and Wind.[32]

will depend on product performance and on the committed interest of a supplier in satisfying customers' needs. The provision of efficient technical advice and servicing arrangements should be viewed as critical inputs into the general marketing strategy. An excellent sales-service network is a powerful addition to the marketing mix, and may be the deciding factor when alternative suppliers are being evaluated (Buyphase 6).

The various phases of buying outlined in Figure 3.1 are unlikely to be self-contained; some degree of spill-over will be most likely. The model is, after all, a theoretical concept and guide which should be interpreted in the light of a particular buying situation. The MSI model is not fully acceptable, however, because it fails to acknowledge the multiplexity of behavioural factors which may influence the inputs made by various executives to specific buying decisions. It could be assumed that such inputs are solely affected by economic considerations; clues are given as to the nature of the other inputs — social, psychological and cultural — but the extent of their influence is not assessed. For this reason, the MSI model is more of a skeletal framework of buying behaviour than a fully integrated and completed model of the decision processes in organisational buying.

Behavioural Models

The third type of buying model, *viz.* behavioural, recognises and seeks to formalise the many inputs (economic and behavioural) which at times make buying a complicated and difficult process. The actual nature of these various inputs and their relative importance should, of course, be identified from systematic marketing research.

In consumer buying, the Howard–Sheth model is a highly developed theoretical explanation which takes into account social, psychological, cultural and economic factors and relates them to the buying habits connected with particular kinds of products. This model is discussed in some detail in consumer marketing literature.[3]

Based on the general design and methodology of the Howard–Sheth consumer buying model, Sheth has developed a model[33] in industrial buying behaviour in which he has attempted to integrate the multiple factors involved in buying goods and services for organisations as distinct from personal consumption. His integrated model is shown in Figure 3.2, from which it will be noted that three aspects of buying behaviour are clearly identified: (1) 'the psychological world of the individuals involved in organisational buying decisions; (2) the conditions which precipitate joint decisions among these individuals' and (3) 'the process of joint decision making with the inevitable conflict among the decision makers and its resolution by resorting to a variety of tactics'.[27]

Sheth's model describes many of the factors of organisational buying and articulates the complexity of decision making; these relationships are reflected in this integrated framework. As with the Howard–Sheth consumer model, this industrial buying model requires systematic testing over a range of supplies and with particular kinds of organisations.

The theorised relationships which are believed to affect buying procedures may be considerably modified in practice. Sheth's model is not intended to be definitive; it is valuable in offering a framework which, first of all, draws attention to the multiplex nature of organisational buying influences and, secondly, presents these factors in a systematic way. How far they relate to actual buying situations in particular organisations is a matter for objective investigation.

Interaction Model

This new approach to industrial marketing and purchasing underlines the interaction which takes place during negotiations, and is based on research by

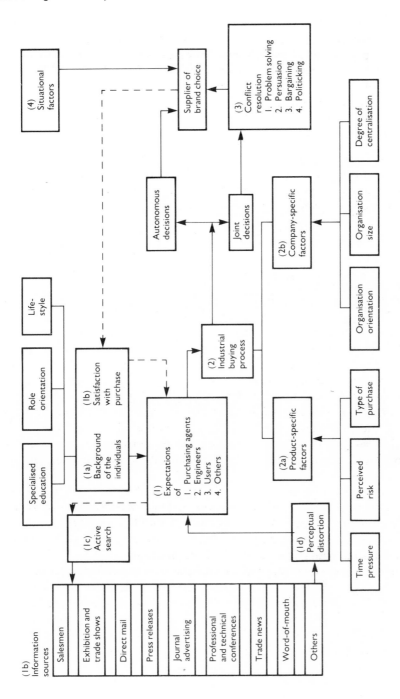

Figure 3.2 An integrative model of industrial buyer behaviour.

Source: See Sheth, Jagdish N.[27]

Hakansson and others who formed the IMP Project Group.[34] The research project studied industrial buying and selling behaviour in five European countries: France, Italy, Sweden, West Germany and the UK. Six research institutes were involved; in the UK UMIST and the University of Bath. Both qualitative and quantitative data were collected from 900 'operative interviews'.

The theoretical base underlying the Interaction Model is derived from two sources: interorganisational theory and the new institutional economic theory. In addition, it is said to be directly related to evolutions in the literature of marketing, and particularly to the emphasis on intercompany relationships.

The marketing and purchasing of industrial goods and services is viewed as a process in which both parties take active roles within a certain environment. Four basic elements contribute to the interaction between buyers and sellers: (1) the interaction process; (2) the participants in the process; (3) the interaction environment, and (4) the atmosphere created by the interaction. The researchers believe that industrial marketing can 'only properly be analysed by examining both the buying and selling process'; 23 cases studies are included in their detailed text [34] to illustrate the central thesis.

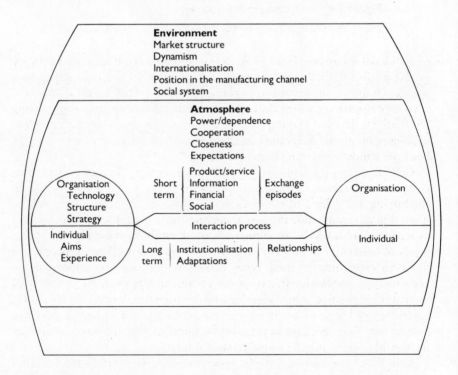

Figure 3.3   The Interaction Model of industrial marketing and purchasing.

Source: See Hakansson.[34] Reprinted by permission of John Wiley & Sons, Ltd.

The four sets of variables mentioned earlier are shown in Figure 3.3. It will be seen that there are several subdivisions of these basic elements. For example, in the interaction process there are what is termed 'episodes' which may be 'individual' and refer to the placing or delivering of a particular order or to long-term relationships developed through contacts over time which lend to expectations of behaviour by both parties. These expectations eventually become institutionalised and may have much in common with the traditional behaviour which is observable in a particular industry.

The interaction process is governed by relationships and by episodes, as shown in Figure 3.4.

Relationships

		Limited	Extensive
Episodes	Simple	I	III
	Complex	II	IV

Figure 3.4 Interaction process typology.

Source: See Hakansson.[34] Reprinted by permission of John Wiley & Sons, Ltd.

Cell I of the matrix in Figure 3.4 refers to situations characterised by simple problems and limited previous relationships between the two parties to a business transaction. According to Hakansson[34] this is the 'classical' model of exchange situations, where the buyer can quite freely choose among existing alternatives; decision making is relatively simple because of the nature of the problems involved. Marketers in these situations have very limited scope because 'almost everything is standardised'.[34]

Cell II (complex episodes/limited relationships) occurs where two companies are about to transact business for the first time. For example, in the buying and selling of major capital equipment, the relationship will be limited in duration while the actual negotiation is complex. Routine buying procedures are unlikely, so companies must establish mutually acceptable levels of behaviour at an early stage in the negotiations. Several people are likely to contribute to these types of negotiation, so it is important for suppliers to coordinate effectively the various inputs made by members of their staff. A positive 'atmosphere' can be developed over time, but it requires careful nurturing to ensure that, once established, it is maintained. This will benefit suppliers, because buyers will be loath to switch sources once they have established mutually sound relationships.

Cell III of the matrix (simple episodes/extensive relationships) occurs frequently in business transactions; firms will have established routines for solving problems which they do not need to resolve in detail, since they can rely on well trusted relationships with their suppliers. In such situations, both parties need to be sensitive to changed circumstances that may result in 'episodes' becoming more complex than hitherto.

Cell IV (complex episodes/extensive relationships) may arise from a crisis or need for change in an established relationship. The need may have technical or commercial origins; as, for example, in product development or in changes of ownership.

The interaction approach towards buying and selling projects the relationship as formed by the actions of both parties '... in contrast to the more traditional view of marketing which analyses the *reaction* of an aggregate market to a seller's offering'. Hence, it is claimed that industrial marketing and purchasing can properly be described as the 'management of buyer–seller relationships'. That business negotiation is essentially a dynamic process will hardly surprise experienced executives who, although they may not be able to articulate the theory, know full well the complexities involved in successful business deals. The interdependence of buyers and sellers in industrial product and service markets is well recognised in practice, although even long-established relationships and loyalties may be vulnerable to new levels of competition from, for instance, the newly industrialised countries.

Hakansson's theory is helpful in drawing attention to the need for executives — both in purchasing and marketing — to develop negotiating skills appropriate to specific products and market conditions. Both formal and informal contacts contribute to the establishment of relationships that can result in mutually satisfactory business transactions. Since the research enquiries were over several countries, it is, perhaps, not surprising that attitudes towards participation and authority were found to be 'quite different' in France and Germany compared with Sweden, although it was considered that more extensive research would be needed before this cultural phenomenon could definitely be established.

SUMMARY

Organisational buying behaviour is complex: motivations are mixed and often conflict; decision making is frequently shared, sometimes as many as six people are involved. The DMU identifies five roles: gatekeeper, user, influencer, buyer and decider.

Risk is inevitable in buying; the evaluation and control of risk are important to successful buying. Dissonance is often felt after buying commitments are made.

Various models of organisational buying have been developed: subjective verbal (descriptive); decision process (logical flow); and behavioural. Sheth's model is complicated and offers a systematic framework; this model requires objective testing. Hakansson *et al.* have produced an Interaction Model which emphasises the important role and processes of negotiation between buyers and sellers.

REFERENCES

1. Cunningham, Malcolm T. and Turnbull, Peter W., 'Interorganisational Personal Contact Patterns', in *Industrial Marketing and Purchasing of Industrial Goods: An Interaction Approach*, Hakansson, Hakan (ed.), Wiley, Chichester, 1983.
2. Drucker, Peter F., The Practice of Management, Heinemann, London, 1961.
3. Chisnall, Peter M., *Marketing — A Behavioural Analysis*, 2nd edn, McGraw-Hill, Maidenhead, 1985.
4. Hobbes, Thomas, *Leviathan*, Routledge, London, 1887.
5. McClelland, D.C., *The Achieving Society*, The Free Press, New York, 1961.
6. Cyert, Richard M. and March, James G., *A Behavioural Theory of the Firm*, Prentice-Hall, New Jersey, 1973.
7. Wilson, David T., 'Industrial Buyers' Decision-Making Styles', *Journal of Marketing Research*, Vol. VIII, No. 4, November 1971.
8. Alexander, R.S., Cross, J.S. and Cunningham, R.M., *Industrial Marketing*, Richard D. Irwin, Illinois, 1961.
9. McGraw-Hill 'Special Report on the Buying and Selling Techniques in British Engineering Industry', McGraw-Hill, London, 1963.
10. Erickson, Robert A., 'How Industry Buys — An Update', in *The Challenge of the Eighties*, Esomar, Brussels, September 1979.
11. Buckner, Hugh, *How British Industry Buys*, Hutchinson, London, 1967.
12. Brand, Gordon, *The Industrial Buying Decision*, Cassell, London, 1972.
13. 'How British Industry Buys, 1974', *Financial Times*, November 1974.
14. 'How British Industry Buys, 1983', *Financial Times*, January 1984.
15. Webster, Frederick E. Jnr. and Wind, Yoram, *Organisation Buying Behaviour*, Prentice-Hall, New Jersey, 1972.
16. Fletcher, W., 'The Diversity with the DMU', *Marketing*, December 1978.
17. Katz, Elihu and Lazarsfeld, P.F., *Personal Influence*, The Free Press of Glencoe, 1955.
18. Webster, Frederick E. Jnr., 'Informal Communications in Industrial Markets', *Journal of Marketing Research*, Vol. VII, No. 2, May 1970.
19. Martilla, John C., 'Word-of-Mouth Communication in the Industrial Adoption Process', *Journal of Marketing Research*, Vol. VIII, No. 2, May 1971.
20. Pettigrew, A.W. Industrial Purchasing as a Political Process', *European Journal of Marketing*, Vol. 9, No. 1, 1975.
21. Johnston, W.J. and Bonoma, T.V., 'Purchase Process for Capital Equipment and Purchases', *Industrial Marketing Management*, Vol. 10, 1981.
22. Strauss, George, 'Tactics of Lateral Relationship: The Purchasing Agent', *Administrative Quarterly*, Cornell, September 1962.
23. Bauer, Raymond A., 'Consumer Behaviour as Risk Taking', in *Dynamic Marketing for a Changing World*, Hancock, R.S. (ed.), A.M.A., Chicago, 1960.
24. Cunningham, Malcolm T. and Homse, Elling, 'An Interaction Approach to Marketing Strategy' in *Industrial Marketing and Purchasing of Industrial Goods: An Interaction Approach*, Hakansson, Hakan (ed.), Wiley, Chichester, 1983.
25. Cunningham, M.T. and White, J.G., 'The Behaviour of Industrial Buyers in the Search for Suppliers of Machine Tools', *Journal of Management Studies*, May 1974.
26. Levitt, Theodore, 'The New Markets — Think Before You Leap', *The Harvard Business Review*, May/June 1969.
27. Cunningham, M.T. and Roberts, D.A., 'The Role of Customer Service in Industrial Marketing', *European Journal of Marketing*, Vol. 8, No. 1, 1974.
28. Mansfield, Edwin, *Industrial Research and Technological Innovation*, W.W. Norton, New York, 1968.

29. Festinger, Leon, *A Theory of Cognitive Dissonance*, Stanford University Press, 1957.
30. Riesman, David and Larrabee, Eric, 'Autos in America', in *Consumer Behaviour*, Clark, Lincoln H. (ed.), Harper, New York, 1958.
31. Rothman, James, *Consumer Research Handbook*, Worcester, Robert (ed.), McGraw-Hill, Maidenhead, 1972.
32. Robinson, Patrick J., Faris, Charles W. and Wind, Yoram, *Industrial Buying and Creative Marketing*, Allyn and Bacon, Boston, 1967.
33. Sheth, Jagdish N., 'A Model of Industrial Buyer Behaviour', *Journal of Marketing*, Vol. 37, No. 4, October 1973.
34. Hakansson, Hakan, *International Marketing and Purchasing of Industrial Goods: An Interaction Approach* (IMP Project Group), Wiley, Chichester, 1983.

Chapter Four
MARKET RESEARCH

MARKET DECISIONS

One of the principal functions of management is to make decisions. Drucker has actuely observed: 'Whatever a manager does he does through making decisions ... management is always a decision-making process ... the important and difficult job is never to find the right answer, it is to find the right question. For there are few things as useless — if not dangerous — as the right to answer to the wrong question ... nor is it enough to find the right answer, more important and more difficult is it to make effective the course of action decided upon. Management is not concerned with knowledge for its own sake; it is concerned with performance.[1]

Marketing management has to accept responsibility for making complex decisions; these cover factors such as the nature of products, product mix, pricing policy, distribution strategy, promotional activities, etc. In order to make decisions that are likely to lead to successful business, marketers need to:

1. assess the extent of their existing information about specific markets;
2. relate this store of knowledge to the types of dcisions they have to make;
3. specify the nature of additional information they will need before particular decisions could be made within an acceptable degree of risk.

Robert Schlaifer has described marketing as 'the place where the most money is risked on the least information'.[2] Admittedly, a substantial amount of advertising appears to be undertaken with more optimism than actual knowledge or reasoned argument about the likely pay-offs. In the majority of marketing problems it is usually possible to collect data that will enable decisions to be based rather more firmly on fact. Information is the raw material of management productivity; marketing management should be alert to the need to acquire and use intelligently, information about the markets in which they are operating or plan to enter.

NEED FOR DISCIPLINE IN DATA COLLECTION

Management information should not be gathered indiscriminately or viewed merely as a 'play safe' strategy. Russell Ackoff[3] has pointed out that many people demand more and more information when, in fact, they already have more paper coming into their offices than they can possibly read effectively. As the result of carefully analysing the type of decisions which executives had to make, Ackoff found a that a great number of these could have been taken quite reasonably with more limited and selective information. Yet, paradoxically, there are occasions when executives are badly served with information: the symptoms shown are of malnutrition rather than of over-indulgence. The right kind of information is not always to hand at the time it is wanted; it needs to be available not only in adequate quantity, but it should also be relevant to the decisions under consideration.

Before seeking information, marketing management should first of all define the nature of the problem facing them. This disciplined approach will help to clarify information needs, and avoid wasteful use of management and other resources in acquiring data which may not be really relevant to the problem in hand. Too frequently managers seem to be seeking solutions to problems, the nature of which they have never taken the trouble to identify and analyse. 'Instant solutions' are demanded for problems which themselves are never actually clarified. (The stages of market planning are discussed in the next chapter.)

Only by defining the problem can the constraints in certain marketing situations, for example, be known and research directed to these specific areas. 'Rolls Royce used for years to congratulate itself because it had half the world market for civil airliner engines. But this true fact concealed the vital information: What was the company's share of new business? The answer wasn't a half or even a quarter: Pratt and Witney had been clobbering Rolls Royce all over the airways, and failure to recognise that fact was as fatal to the company as deadly nightshade'.[4]

CATEGORIES OF INFORMATION NEEDS

Information for marketing decision making could be usefully classified in three broad categories:

1. Information for strategic decisions (e.g. whether to enter a particular overseas market; or to diversify into new markets)
2. Information for tactical decisions (e.g. planning of sales territories)
3. Information to provide a 'data bank'; this will require periodic updating to ensure that it retains its usefulness (e.g. details of competitive products, market share analyses, VAT requirements, etc.)

Collection of information in any of these categories should be undertaken systematically and according to the nature of individual companies and the types of commercial or industrial activity in which they are engaged. As companies develop, new needs for information will tend to arise; hence, data should be reviewed from time to time and evaluated for its contribution towards the specific decisions now being undertaken by management. Some data may require to be improved in quality, e.g. markets may have become highly segmented and relatively superficial market assessment may be of little value as more sophisticated competition emerges.

IMPACT OF DYNAMIC ENVIRONMENT

The dynamic nature of many markets underlines the need for managers to keep their information up-to-date. Marketing information interprets the changing environment and its needs so that the right kind of decisions can be taken affecting production and marketing policies. As Kotler has pointed out: 'The relevant environment includes the *microenvironment*, specifically the economy, technology, law and culture, and the *task environment*, specifically buyers, channels, competitors and suppliers ... A major task of an effective marketing information system is to provide speedy, accurate, and interpretive information to its decision makers'.[5]

TWO-WAY FLOW OF INFORMATION SYSTEMS

Marketing management information flows are two-way: from the organisation to the environment and from the environment or market to the organisation which seeks to service specific needs in that market. (Refer to Figure 4.1.)

Marketing information should be gathered methodically, both from within the marketing organisation, using the accounting and financial control system, as well as from market sources. Many firms do not coordinate the information which is in the accounting department with the data needs of marketing management. At a relatively small extra cost, invoices and other financial records could be designed so that they provide useful analyses of sales by product type, region or territory.

In defining information needs, marketing management should not fall into the trap of demanding unlimited data. Levitt[6] has stressed the difference between data and information. 'The enormous prodigality of the computer has so accelerated the process of data accumulation that we often actually know less than we did before. Great masses of data are disgorged ... what is

Figure 4.1   Two-way flow of marketing information system.

needed is discrimination in the case of data, not its sheer abundance'. Data are useful only if relevant.

DANGEROUS DATA

There is no shortage of information in many organisations; the trouble is that it is often the wrong kind of information, excessive, irrelevant and incompatible, apart from being outdated. Robert Heller[4] vigorously comments: 'Managers are to information as alcoholics are to booze. They consume enormous amounts, constantly crave more, but have great difficulty in digesting their existing intake'.

Mr Harold Macmillan's (as he then was) famous observation about the value of official statistics to management of the British economy — that using them was like planning a train journey with last year's Bradshaw guide — could equally apply to the value of outdated management statistics. Inevitably, statistical and other data are historic, but with effective planning the time intervals between collection and presentation can be shortened.

To be really useful, marketing information does not necessarily have to be sophisticated or expensive to produce. Relatively simple but up-to-date information is preferable to sophisticated information which has lost most of its value because of the long time taken to collect and present it.

Misleading Impressions of the Research Function

Robert Buzzell,[7] in an article some years ago in the *Harvard Business Review*, expressed concern that 'the term "research" ever came to be used to describe the activities of most marketing research staff units'. He suggested that a much more appropriate designation would be 'marketing intelligence', since its function was analogous to military intelligence in warfare. 'Military intelligence personnel are not expected to develop a science of warfare. Their mission instead, is to obtain complete, accurate and current information'.[7] (Discussion of the particular responsibilities of researchers in marketing strategy recommendations occurs later in this chapter.)

It could be argued, of course, that the label is of little consequence, that it is the function that matters. On the other hand, misleading descriptions can put people off products. Research may suggest to some management, esoteric enquiries undertaken in the cloistered calm of an academic institution far removed from the hurly-burly of commercial life. This view is enhanced by the academic aura which surrounds the function of learned research.

Marketing research has a very practical purpose: to provide reliable knowledge about specific aspects of marketing. It is nearer to the function of field intelligence than of the research laboratory. But its function is not just to provide intelligence or information, but to *interpret* data. To be of value, research into marketing should be objective; the opinions of executives and representatives may be based on years of experience in a particular industry, but they tend to be subjective views. Marketing research is scientific enquiry ... 'science may be at least partly defined in terms of the attitude of disinterest and impersonality one must take towards the outcome of scientific investigation ... science deals with the unembroidered fact rather than with opinion and belief'.[8]

Marketing research can make a real contribution to the marketing of organisational supplies. By their training, scientists, engineers and technicians demand objective facts which are subjected to close scrutiny and analysis. This objective approach should not end at the laboratory or factory door: it should be extended to include objective analysis and interpretation of all those factors which are likely to affect the profitable marketing of industrial products. This is the key role of marketing research — and it can be applied to companies of all sizes.

Optimising Internal Records

The incompatibility of data originating from various departments of an organisation may be frustrating. For example, if weekly or monthly statistics are kept by production, marketing and financial sections of a business, do they relate to the same bases? Some companies have special accounting periods which may not coincide with the records kept by the production management or by the marketing people. Personnel investigations with the Department of Trade were, in a particular instance, considerably frustrated 'because half the figures relating to staff were collected on a calendar month basis and the other half on a four week basis'.[9] A similar problem has been experienced with sales statistics and the financial records kept by a manufacturing firm.

In Chapter 1, the interface relationships of marketing management were discussed at some length. The collection and dissemination of information for managerial guidance should be designed so that full value can be derived from departmental statistics. Marketing management should become acquainted with the various statistical returns made, for example, by the production controller to the financial department. Stock records should be compared against market targets and actual sales performance. The profitability of an organisation may be increased if managers in all functional areas are more willing to exchange information and to perceive that a parochial use of statistics is a short-sighted policy which could damage general efficiency. It was suggested earlier than an audit of information available within an organisation would be a worthwhile management exercise. It might reveal (and often has) that records of very similar nature are being kept by different sections; that duplication of this nature has grown up from either ignorance or managerial competitiveness; and that some of the information assiduously collected serves no real function. It may have been demanded some years ago when markets were different, but no one in authority had issued instructions to stop this routine production of data. From time to time, therefore, organisations might usefully check the application of the data which, at today's staffing costs, entail considerable expense. Inadequacies may be discovered in the existing data because of changes in the environment and which may require additional analyses; for example, expansion in overseas markets, formerly analysed by broad regional breakdown, may now require the collection of more elaborate data. Essentially, a marketing information system should be flexible to retain its value. Special data may be necessary to supplement routine information so that specific marketing problems can be approached objectively.

DEFINITION OF MARKETING RESEARCH

Several attempts have been made to define marketing research in formal terms. At one time, 'market research' and 'marketing research' tended to be used to describe particular activities; the former referring merely to enquiries into market size and related statistics, whereas 'marketing research' covered a far fuller area of enquiry involving, for example, behavioural factors and advertising strategy, as well as measurement of market demand. This pedantic distinction is now largely discarded, and nowadays the terms are used indiscriminately.

The American Marketing Association (AMA),[10] in 1961, defined marketing research as:

> 'The systematic gathering, recording and analysing of data about problems relating to the marketing of goods and services.'

In 1962, the British Institute of Management (BIM)[11] followed closely the AMA's definition:

> 'The objective gathering, recording and analysing of all facts about problems relating to the transfer and sales of goods and services from producer to consumer or user.'

Kotler[5] has drawn attention to marketing research's role as 'systematic problem analysis, model building and fact-finding for the purposes of improved decision-making and control in the marketing of goods and services.' This definition emphasises the end-purposes of marketing research activities.

The fact that market research has a strongly pragmatic value — to aid decision making — should make it especially attractive to industrialists. The reduction of uncertainty and the avoidance of potentially 'wrong' decisions are two very good reasons for using it. At the same time, and as two American researchers[12] have emphasised, there is no point in doing research if the person who receives the resultant data is not in a position to do anything differently. 'Marketing research is committed to the principle of utility. In general, if research is not going to have an effect on decisions, it is an exercise in futility.'

Marketing research related to industrial products has been defined by the Industrial Marketing Research Association (IMRA)[13] as:

'The systematic, objective and exhaustive search for and study of facts relevant to any problem in the field of industrial marketing'.

These various definitions emphasise that marketing research involves objective analysis and fact-finding for marketing effectiveness related to supplies, either for consumption by individuals or to be used in production of other goods.

Far from being theoretical, marketing research applies in real-life conditions some of the techniques of scientific analysis to provide management with up-to-date marketing knowledge. It forms, therefore, the cornerstone of a successful marketing strategy; applying marketing research does not guarantee success, but it *will* narrow the field of uncertainty surrounding many marketing decisions. Marketing research is not an end in itself: it is not some kind of expensive peripheral activity which only organisations with substantial resources can indulge in. Decisions have to be made in organisations of all sizes; if they are based on accurate knowledge it is reasonable to surmise that they are more likely to be sound than if they rely solely on managerial experience and inspiration, or what a salesman said when he last visited the works. Marketing research should not be regarded as a luxury service but as an essential method of acquiring facts which were not available beforehand.

Since market research has, therefore, the prime function of reducing risks in decision making related to the marketing of goods and services, the greater are those risks, the more justification exists for investing in objective information. Small-scale, low risk decisions obviously do not warrant the costs and time involved in extensive research, but strategic options that may have highly uncertain outcomes and result in the commitment of significant resources, call for professional research enquiries. Figure 4.2 shows a typical relationship between investment in market information and the risk characteristics of the decision associated with different levels of information. After a time, the typical curve flattens out, indicating that beyond a certain limit it would no longer be advantageous to spend more money on research activities.

APPLICATIONS OF ORGANISATIONAL MARKET RESEARCH

In the past, market research has tended to be closely associated with consumer products. Studies of the effectiveness of research techniques have normally been confined to markets other than industrial, and the impression may have been formed that the field of marketing research is limited to products which can be bought in supermarkets and other retail outlets. But

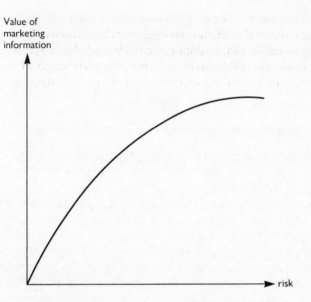

Figure 4.2   Typical relationship of market research information and risk in decision making.

this is to underestimate the value of marketing research to industrial markets. The problems of marketing industrial and technical products are certainly no less complex than those faced when devising the launch of a new soap powder or soft drink. Many industrial managers would say quite strongly that they face far more difficult problems which demand considerable technical knowledge, apart from commercial acumen and experience.

The diversity and complexity of industrial marketing decisions demand better knowledge. Information needs, it has been noted, fall into three broad classes: strategic, tactical and 'data bank'.

In organisational markets, technical and scientific factors add to the web of influences affecting buying preferences. The time scales of consumer and industrial markets are, in general, vastly different.

Marketing management is responsible for identifying customers for its products and services, of evaluating their present needs, and predicting their likely future needs. Marketers largely control the destinies of their companies, and it is no longer defensible that their decisions should be based on inspired guesswork or hunches. Objective, systematic research into market opportunities should become the first step in forming the marketing plan. Research should include economic and business analyses, technological evaluations, assessment of competitors' activities, analyses of political, social and other environmental factors — particularly where overseas trading is concerned — and an overall appreciation obtained of the factors affecting or likely to affect a company's market.

Some of the fundamental knowledge needed for the development of effective industrial marketing strategies has been discussed in Chapter 2. This basic information will, no doubt, need to be added to before specific decisions can be made. As will be indicated later, the early stages of market research will be centred around the identification of available data.

Information for Service Industries

As well as physical products, industry and commerce are concerned with the marketing of services. These 'intangible' goods require expert marketing no less than tangible products.

As with products, the markets for services are dynamic, and so services should be designed to keep abreast of changing market needs. This entails market research to analyse and evaluate industrial and commercial trends. Research could indicate, for example, that specific markets for some services are relatively poorly catered for by present suppliers. It may suggest new areas for profitable marketing, or indicate where resources could be most usefully deployed. For example, there is greater potential for home improvement loans in districts where there is a high rate of home-ownership. Research should enable profiles to be developed of typical customers. With financial sources such as banks, clients may, in fact, have two profiles, one as a borrower and the other as a lender of funds.

It will be advantageous for service industries to identify, through research, key accounts and to devise strategies to win this business by offering specialised services. With low-volume customers, 'package deals' may be designed that will satisfy their needs and keep the costs of servicing them at acceptable levels. 'The case of a large European banks shows what can happen when individualised products are offered in the mass market, or poorly planned standard products introduced to a market that may not even recognise or appreciate its expensive features. A detailed analysis of the bank's economics uncovered differences in the cost–revenue structures of two important market segments: small individual customers accounted for 6% of all revenue and 14% of all costs, while small commercial customers accounted for 39% of all revenue and only 15% of all costs'.[14]

Apart from feedback of 'hard data', service industries would benefit from a general appreciation of the service rendered (attitudes of staff, quality of service, accuracy of information, etc.). Some American banks are reported[15] to use 'professional shoppers' who are existing customers and also report anonymously to their bank on their perception of the overall standard of service. User-panels are not, of course, new to product marketing; perhaps service industries also could benefit from regular feedback from their clients.

Market research can also be useful in designing effective methods of market communication, including media advertising. With financial services in particular, the location and appearance of offices is important in building an acceptable corporate image. The joint-stock banks have adopted corporate symbols which clearly distinguish their premises and give reassurance to clients, especially if they are away from their home town. Banks need to project an image of security, reliability, confidentiality, accessibility, financial expertise, etc.: hence the plan of corporate communications deserves special attention. In the past, joint-stock banks have tended to ignore marketing research or to use it in distinctly limited ways. The greater level of competition now evident in the financial sector of the economy suggests that banks, building societies and insurance companies should make more use of a well established marketing tool. These enquiries should be comprehensive — not just limited to economic data — and cover psychological, social and cultural trends; these have been discussed in some depth in a specialist text.[16]

Public Sector Services

Marketing research techniques can also be applied productively in the planning of non-profit making activites such as the social services, public transport, education, health services, etc. Unless reliable information is used at the design stage of these services, it is clear that public resources may be unwisely committed. To serve people's needs it is advisable to identify these as closely as possible; mere conjectures are not good enough. Objective research will also be of value in assessing the effectiveness of existing services and may identify new areas which could legitimately be the concern of public authorities. Far greater use of marketing research could, therefore, result in better utilisation of scarce resources and improved benefits to the community. In some directions, services may have become over-elaborated when simpler services may be adequate to meet the needs of particular sections of the community. There may be need for new types of public services where a district is changing its character because of industrialisation or the arrival of immigrant populations.

That marketing research techniques used by profit-orientated firms are of use in the public sector, where primary motivations tend to be different, should not be regarded as a bizarre proposal. 'Research techniques by which profit making firms measure the market ability of their products, and improve the effectiveness of their services, distribution and communications, are applicable to projects concerned with education, culture, health, environments and energy supply. New standards may thus evolve to help measure the effectiveness of such non-profit organisations in achieving goals that do not pertain directly to such economic goals as sales and profits'.[17]

The needs of people deserve objective analysis; managerial accountability for the effective use of corporate resources applies equally in both sectors of the economy.

Planning is accepted as an important element of public administration. Marketing research is not confined to commercial investigations; it evolved, in fact, a substantial part of its methodology from the pioneer social investigations made, for example, by Bowley *et al.*[18] in the early part of this century. Since that time, techniques have been refined and extended, and the strong link between marketing research practitioners and social investigation continues with several research agencies specialising in medical and social welfare investigations.

High Technology Products

The trend in manufacturing in the UK is, as observed earlier, in the direction of the newer, high technology products (with their related services), and so it is relevant to consider how marketing research can help in the development of this important sector of the economy.

Particularly useful examples of this application of market research are given in a paper by Cowell and Blois.[19] This has an interesting account of three cases of technologically advanced products and their marketing problems.

In a research institute a new technique had been developed that was able to detect minute vibrations in objects. An outside body was considering finance for the further development of this project, but before committing themselves, they demanded that a survey should be conducted to ascertain (1) the potential markets for the applications of this technique, and (2) the outline specification of equipment acceptable to the markets identified in (1). Following systematic market enquiries, the level of market interest and the necessary guidelines for development of the technique were established.

In another case, a research institute was interested in buying some equipment that made it possible to examine complex molecular structures. Initial enquiries by a member of the scientific staff revealed that this specialised machine would have only limited use throughout the year by the institute but that there was a 'large' market for its use by other organisations. As the result of an attractive offer by a potential supplier, the institute instructed its marketing manager to (1) check the validity of the physicist's market enquiries, and (2) collect some more information about the commercial viability of the potential purchase. Within the tight limitations of time and cost, this survey was able to establish that (1) the physicist's estimate of outsiders usage of the equipment was too high, and (2) the type of service offered to potential users would cost more than originally believed because of the need for advisory services. In addition, the machine would rarely be fully loaded; any delay in filling the machine to achieve economic operation would clash with the market need which was primarily for a 36-hour sample analysis service.

The third case concerned a company making a wide range of equipment for the engineering industry, which was offered the opportunity of making a new design of a solid/solid batch separator. So far, only prototypes of this separator had been made and used by the designer.

The company wished to extend its product range, and so asked consultants to investigate the market potential for this product. Estimates were needed of

(1) potential industries and users of the separator; (2) present and potential UK market in terms of units and value in these specific industries, and (3) state of competition.

The market researchers were provided with enough technical data to enable them to undertake the survey. The resultant research indicated that (1) criteria listed by a group of chemical engineers with known expertise in the use of separators did in practice influence the choice of separators; (2) some aggregate value of market size was obtained, but it was evident that purchases fluctuated quite violently, and (3) the costs of market entry would be extremely high and involve concentrated efforts over a long time period to provide acceptable proof of the separator's capabilities under operating conditions.

PLANNING MARKET RESEARCH

Marketing research can be conveniently divided into five steps which lead logically to the final survey report. These phases apply irrespective of the nature of the market — consumer, industrial or public service. Professional skill is needed at every stage of the research programme to ensure that the findings of the survey are based on objective data which have been obtained from representative samples of a specific population. (Refer to Figure 4.3.)

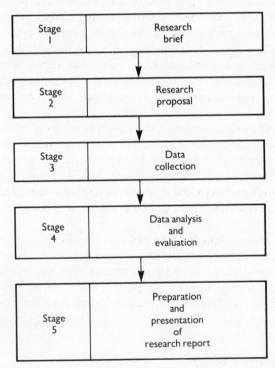

Figure 4.3   Five sequential stages of marketing research.

Stage 1: Research Brief

This initial and crucial stage will decide the nature and direction of the entire research. It entails defining clearly and specifically the marketing problem to be investigated. With industrial products, market research objectives may be focussed on the needs of particular customers for machines of special capacity or for specific formulations of chemicals. The extent of the product range, the likely demand for spares (and the resulting stock levels needed), the nature of sales-service support expected by some industries, or the type and level of competition, are a few of the problems which industrial marketing researchers continually tackle.

Before clear definition of the marketing problem is feasible, it may be necessary to make some exploratory enquiries in certain areas of the organisation, e.g. selling arrangements, publicity methods, pricing structure, etc. This preliminary work should gain researchers valuable background knowledge, and may, in fact, point to the real problem which has to be investigated. The marketing problem may relate closely, for example, to production methods and some degree of integrated research may be necessary.

At this critical briefing stage, both management and researchers should endeavour to obtain clear agreement on the objectives of the research. Management should be prepared to take researchers into their confidence and present them with an unvarnished picture of their organisation and the kind of marketing problems which face them. Marketing researchers have the duty to probe and ensure that they have been given adequate information on which to base a research strategy. The relationship between client and researcher is similar to that of a barrister and his professional client. Unless the briefing is thorough, misunderstandings and even catastrophe could result.

If the proposition put forward by a client seems unrealistic, a reputable marketing researcher will point out the constraints which, inevitably, govern the nature of research activities. Like all products and services, research costs money; it involves time and professional skills. Before a research brief is accepted, both parties should agree on the level of accuracy required, the date by which the research report will be available, and the approximate price to be paid.

A great deal of thought, time and care should be given, therefore, to the marketing research brief. Clients and researchers should be prepared to spend some time on defining the precise terms of reference which will guide the research programme. Slip-shod thinking at this initial phase will set the whole research off course, and probably cause deep annoyance to both parties later on.

Stage 2: Research Proposal

At this stage, a research proposal or work plan should be developed which, by means of a simple model of the problem, will specify the data to be collected and the methodology to be adopted. It is important to check that the proposed research strategy will satisfy the objectives set out in phase one. These objectives should be developed and refined into one or a series of working hypotheses which can be tested during the research programme. These hypotheses 'arise as a result of a prior thinking about the subject, preliminary investigation of available data and material (including related studies), or advice and counsel of experts or interested parties. Like the fomulation of the problem, such hypotheses are most useful when expressed in precise, clearly defined terms'.[20]

A research schedule should be drawn up giving timing for the various operations. This will take account of the methodology to be used — specific techniques of marketing research will be covered in the next chapter — and the time constraints imposed by the client.

Stage 3: Collection of Data

The research programme having been agreed, the next stage is likely to occupy a considerable amount of time. The relative efficiencies of collecting data by alternative methods will have to be checked. Complementary data may be desirable in some types of market investigation. Sampling procedures need to be thoroughly planned to avoid some of the biases which make research such a precarious profession.

Stage 4: Analysis and Evaluation of Data

Every stage of the research programme is interrelated. It is no use applying sophisticated techniques of analysis and statistical tests of data at this stage, if the original research design did not ensure that, for example, the sample methodology was soundly based.

Data are the raw material of the research programme; they have to be refined by means of tabulation, analysis and interpretation. During these processes, significant relationships between variables may be discovered; these require objective discussions and evaluation related to the problems which the survey has undertaken to study.

Systems of data storage and retrieval may also be incorporated in this stage of the research. Provision should be made to update information so that market knowledge on critical factors in buying behaviour retain their value for management decision making. New competitors may, for example, enter the home or an overseas market. Different distribution strategies may radically alter the nature of competition. A comparatively low-ranked competitor may be taken over by a large industrial group which is prepared to invest substantial funds in an aggressive bid for a larger market share.

Computers have revolutionised data processing which, in a short period, has progressed from hand analysis to systems of mechanical tabulation, eventually to arrive at the speed, flexibility and diversity of modern computerised systems. The attractions of such a flexible and speedy system may contain dangers: a careful check is needed to avoid the GIGO effect (garbage in-garbage out).

Questionnaires can now be read mechanically and at great speed. Sophisticated analytical techniques such as factor analysis are no longer fairly tedious (if not prohibitive) methods of analysing certain kinds of data.

These improvements in the technical efficiency of research data processing are of direct benefit to clients. Speedier and more elaborate surveys are possible and at very economic cost.

Stage 5: Preparation and Presentation of Research Report

This stage completes the research programme; it deserves professional attention because faulty communication can undo a lot of the good work done earlier.

Researchers should develop their managerial expertise in presenting the findings of research surveys so that they are fully understood by clients. 'Interpretation of survey findings is a matter on which experts express strongly conflicting views. Some would have researchers give their own interpretation of the findings of surveys, while others, equally dogmatic, believe that researchers should limit themselves to reporting the facts discovered through the survey'.[21]

The question of interpretation should be discussed at the time the research brief is agreed. Clients as well as researchers may have different views, so some clearly agreed policy is desirable. To discourage researchers from exercising their professional knowledge in the interpretation of a survey's findings would seem to be a rather short-sighted policy. They may be able to suggest alternative marketing strategies as a result of approaching problems with professional objectivity. For several months, the client's problems will have become the focus of intense commitment: it would be unproductive not to exploit this valuable source of creative managerial inputs.

In preparing a survey report, researchers 'should keep in mind those who will read it'.[21] Both content and style should be designed to satisfy the needs of particular readers. Clear, grammatical language should be used with data shown attractively in tables and diagrams. The format, printing and binding are factors that can help considerably in making the contents of a report intelligible and acceptable.

Some industrial marketing research reports include substantial technical data which, in detail, may not be required by commercial management. In such cases, it is often advisable to prepare two editions. One to be read exclusively by technical specialists and which contains a detailed technological assessment; the other intended principally for commercial management would cover technology in less depth and would concentrate more on commercial implications of the marketing developments studied. Where separate reports are not desirable, care must be exercised to ensure that any technical terms are defined so that the report would be understood without undue trouble.

Because delays may occur in production of the main report, clients may find it helpful to have a preliminary report which distils the research findings. In addition to the final written report, some clients invite researchers to discuss the survey findings, preferably after all involved have carefully studied it.

TECHNIQUES OF MARKET RESEARCH

An important part of research activity is to decide on the research strategy, the second step of the sequential stages shown in Figure 4.3. Research strategy covers the selection of suitable methods of survey, the nature of the research instruments, the sampling design, types of data to be collected (quantitative or qualitative or, ideally, both).

Data for marketing research can be obtained by several methods and from various sources. An effective research design 'is the overall operational pattern or framework of the project that stipulates what information is to be collected, from which sources, and by what procedures. If it is a good design, it will insure that the information obtained is relevant to the research problem and that it was collected by objective and economical procedures'.[22]

Sources of Data

Marketing research data are derived from two main sources:

1. *Primary data* — these originate from field research which may use either one or a mixture of techniques such as: observation, experimentation and questionnaires.
2. *Secondary data* — result from existing information which may be available from internal records or from external sources.

Secondary data

Secondary data will be discussed first because, as PEP observed some years ago: 'The answers to many problems often lie within the files of an organisation or in published material'.[23] This level of research, often known as desk research, has many advantages: it is economical, comparatively speedy and can be undertaken with complete confidentiality. Desk research should always be made full use of in any type of marketing research problem; it may well provide adequate information for the decision which has to be taken. Only rarely is there no relevant information which can be culled fairly readily from internal records or from published sources.

The advantages of harnessing routine accounting and production records for marketing analyses were discussed earlier. There are many opportunities for making better use of internal records to give, for example, sales analysed by area, type of customer, or industry. Much greater 'mileage' should be extracted from company delivery notes, invoices and other departmental records.

Where companies are selling products or services direct to users, as with most industrial marketing, it is possible to develop a fairly simple method of collecting market data which experienced representatives can operate successfully.

Kodak were reported[24] to use a system of 'customer indexes' which are based on survey cards filled in by representatives giving basic information such as industry of a customer, particular application of supplies purchased, size of organisation, extent of use of competitive products, etc. This 'customer profile' is completed for every call made by a representative. A follow-up card is also designed to ensure that records are kept up-to-date. At the end of a 'journey cycle', representatives return survey cards, with the latest data recorded, to the sales office for incorporation in a master data file. These customer index cards are subsequently returned to representatives who will, as necessary, complete follow-up cards recording any changes in the customer profile and send these to head office so that the master records can be amended. Most of these records are fully computerised which enables overall analyses of the current position of industrial sales to be made very quickly.

These customer indexes are also useful in designing territories, promotional activities, forecasting etc. The great advantage of this method lies in its simplicity of collection and the fact that it is constantly being up-dated.

With a little ingenuity and cooperation from staff in various sections of an organisation, many internal records could provide data of value to the marketing department.

External secondary data are available from many sources: statistics and reports issued by governments, trade associations, academic institutions etc. In the UK, the Central Statistical Office (CSO) acts as a coordinating organisation in guiding researchers to the appropriate source of statistics issued by individual government departments. The Business Statistics Office (BSO), Cardiff Road, Newport, Gwent, deals specifically with industrial and commercial data. Two very useful official publications: *Guide to Official Statistics* (HMSO) and *Regional Statistics* (HMSO) provide valuable guides to sources of statistical data for particular products and services.

All continental European countries operate central statistical offices which collect and annually publish statistics relating to those countries. Monthly statistics may be available and also data dealing with specific industries.

Extra data, so far unpublished, may be obtainable on payment of a fee.

Some examples of principal official sources of general reference for industrial marketing research are listed below:

Annual Abstract of Statistics: provided information on population, housing, manufactured goods, etc.

Monthly Digest of Statistics: similar to the AA but published at monthly intervals.

Abstract of Regional Statistics

Scottish Abstracts of Statistics

Digest of Welsh Statistics

Digest of UK Energy Statistics: published annually and gives details of production and demand for various energy fields in the UK. Reports of the nationalised energy industries provide additional statistical. analyses.

Overseas Trade Statistics of the UK: published monthly and gives detailed analyses of overseas trade statistics. Special analyses obtainable from HM Customs and Excise.

Housing and Construction Statistics: published quarterly by the Department of the Environment.

Local Housing Statistics: also published each quarter by Department of the Environment.

Agricultural Statistics

Financial Statistics (key monetary data)

Passenger Transport in Great Britain: published annually by Department of the Environment.

Highway Statistics: annual publication emanating from the Department of the Environment.

Social Trends: valuable collection of key social statistics published annually.

Annual Report of the Department of Health and Social Security

Economic Trends: monthly review of the British economic situation. Quartlery data on the national income and balance of payments are also included.

Census of Population: gives detailed analyses of the UK population, which may be particularly useful in some derived demand markets.

Census of Distribution: gives basic information on the structure of retail distribution. Last taken in 1971 but superseded by annual sample enquiries from 1976.

Census of Production: one of the most important sources of desk research for industrial marketers. The first Census of Production in the UK was taken in 1908 in respect of 1907. It originated from the controversy over tariffs: one of its main objectives was to ascertain the quantity and value of different kinds of manufacturing output. Originally planned on a quinquennial basis, although this time interval was distorted by the two World Wars, the Census has now been replaced by an annual one, the first of which occurred in 1970. The new system of censuses offers similar information to the old quinquennial enquiries but by means of quarterly enquiries into sales coupled with a summary Census of Production each year. These quarterly enquiries will be supplemented by monthly enquiries, and detailed enquiries may also be extended into purchases of materials at three-year intervals. Summary findings are published in the journal *British Business*.

The Census covers production which is defined as 'industrial production, including construction, gas, electricity and water supply and mines and quarries'. Full details were required only from firms with over 25 employees; smaller firms provide summaries of their activities. From 1973 certain modifications were made to comply with the statistical requirements of the Statistical Office of the European Communities.

The first change affected the coverage of the Census. Previously, Census returns had to be submitted, as noted above, by establishments employing 25 or more people except that in 13 industries, where small firms made an important contribution to total output, the coverage was extended to establishments with 11 or more employees. In the 1975 Census, all establishments employing 20 or more were asked to complete a questionnaire.

For those establishments employing 20–99 people, the 1973 Census questions were little different from those used in the Census for 1971 and 1972. New questions covered payments for outworkers and the cost of goods bought for merchanting; questions on transport costs were discontinued apart from a few industries.

Establishments with 100 or more employees were also asked these new questions, and also questioned on Value Added Tax and the cost of non-industrial services.

To avoid identification of individual firms, Census report figures are sometimes amalgamated.

Department of Employment Gazette: monthly publication giving details of employment in Britain.

British Business: (formerly known as the *Trade and Industry Journal*) weekly publication by the Department of Trade and Industry which gives valuable data on industrial and commercial trends, both home and overseas. Publishes industry reviews, trade fair guides, etc.

Bill of Entry: Customs and Excise data.

National Economic Development Office (NEDO): published reports on a range of industries.

Business Monitors: give detailed information about many important industries. The P (production) series covers a wide sector of industrial activities. The SD (Service and Distribution) series covers shops, catering trades and instalment credit business of finance houses and retailers. The CA (Civil Aviation) series deals with airports, passengers, freight and airlines. Seven M (Miscellaneous) monitors include motor and vehicle registrations, cinemas, company finance and acquisitions and mergers.

Non-governmental sources of published data in Britain are plentiful: some of the principal sources are detailed below:

CBI Overseas Reports: issued quarterly by the Confederation of British Industries.

Yearbooks: Kelly's Directory of Manufactuers and Merchants; Kompass Register (company-based, hence establishments are not listed, only head offices being recorded); Dunn and Bradstreet's directories: *Guide to Key British Enterprises; International Market Guide; British Middle Market Directory* (major drawback of Dunn and Bradstreet registers is that they are based on companies, not establishments; hence, branch offices are omitted, and subsidiary companies are not always recorded).

Extel Group: published, as a subscription service, details of British and European companies.

Keynotes Reports: give valuable data over many industries.

ICC: publishes specific information related to ratios of corporate efficiency.

The Economist Group: partly under the name of The Economist Intelligence Unit (EIU) publishes, on a regular basis, reports on certain industrial sectors, such as the automotive industry, as well as special reports on topics of current interest.

As the result of a management buy-out in 1984, the *Corporate Intelligence Group* was set up. This publishes *ad hoc* surveys for clients, as well as continuing surveys on off-highway equipment and industries markets in North America and West Europe.

Euromonitor: publishes *Market Research Great Britain* each month.

BLA Group: publishes, bi-monthly, *Market Assessment* which covers many industrial product markets.

Mintel reports cover mostly consumer products and are available on subscription.

The Press: The Economist; Financial Times; The Times; The Daily Telegraph; The Guardian; The Sunday Times; The Observer; The Sunday Telegraph, etc.

Times Top 1000: lists major British-based companies.

Gower Press: publishes a valuable series of economic survey reports which relate to specific industries and markets both home and overseas.

The Association for Information Management (formerly Aslib:

Association of Special Libraries and Information Bureaux), 26–27 Boswell Street, London WC1: authoritative British source of diverse range of information.

Other professional institutions also offer information on special aspects of industrial markets:

British Institute of Management (BIM), London WC2.

Industrial Marketing Research Association, 28 Bore Street, Lichfield, Staffordshire.

Institute of Marketing, Moor Hall, Cookham, Berkshire.

Market Research Society, 15 Belgrave Square, London W1.

National Institute of Economic and Social Research, 2 Dean Trench Street, London SW1.

Institute of Practitioners in Advertising (IPA).

Chambers of Commerce: some of the larger organisations, for example, London, Birmingham or Manchester, are able to provide very useful guidance in locating industrial firms.

The Financial Times Business Information Service: provides, for a fee, specific information on markets for a wide range of products and services.

Specialist Libraries such as The City Business Library, London EC2, the libraries of London Business School and Manchester Business School, the Science Reference Library, 25 Southampton Row, London WC2, are significant sources of published data.

TV Audience Research Reports: available from individual television contractors and also from specialist research agencies.

In addition to official data guides there are several commercially published guides to market data such as: *Sources of UK Marketing Information* by Elizabeth Tupper and Gordon Wills (Benn, 1975), *Principal Sources of Marketing Information* by Christine Hull (Times Newspapers), and *Where to Find Business Information* (John Wiley, 1979). Also, it may be useful to approach professional and trade journals, whose editorial staff may be willing to give valuable insights into the specific industries covered by them.

From this listing of sources of published data, it will be appreciated that study of some of these may well result in enough information without extending research into field enquiries. Moreover, this stage of desk research will be very useful in developing the methodology of research, because of the structural knowledge of particular industries which results from this intensive search.

Official Industry Classification

Before considering primary sources of data, it will be advantageous to describe in general terms the basis of industry classification which is used in official statistics such as the Census of Production.

In Britain, the basic framework for analysing industrial activities is the Standard Industrial Classification (SIC).

The SIC was first issued in 1948 to encourage uniformity in preparation of the UK official statistics for industry; as the result of experience in use and reflecting changes in the structure of British industry, the SIC was revised in 1958, in 1968 and again in 1980. This edition is the present-day system of classification based on industries. This revision has tended to restrict the usefulness of some of the past data when analyses have been concerned with examining trends in certain industries over a fairly long period of time. The Central Statistical Office acknowledges that it has to face the problem of keeping a balance between the need to be up-to-date against the loss in comparability with past data. They believe that change in industrial classification once in ten years is about right.

The SIC has been described by the chief statistician of the Central Statistical Office as an empirical classification which is 'not derived in any way from theoretical ideas on how activities should be grouped or should necessarily be combined because products or processes are similar, or other notions. It does try to reflect the way in which economic activities are found to exist in the UK'.[25]

Until the 1980 revision, SICs were divided into Minimum List Headings (MLHs) which progressively narrowed down industrial activities for the purposes of classification and measurement. However, while these breakdowns were often useful, specific products tended to be subsumed under fairly broad headings. In some cases, it may be possible to obtain more relevant information from the Business Statistics Office.

The 1980 revision of the SIC was primarily designed to bring it more into line with the European Communities' Statistical Office's activity classification, Nomenclature Générale des Activités Economiques dans les Communautés Européenes' (NACE), and so enable statistical data across EEC countries to be more readily compared, as well as providing for analysis of UK industry and commerce.

Unlike previous SICs, the 1980 edition has a decimal structure. The full range of industrial activities is first divided into 10 broad divisions (indicated by single digits), which are then subdivided into 60 classes (two digits), further divided into 222 groups (three digits) and then into 334 activities (four digits). The full range of potential subdivisions is not necessarily followed in all cases; it depends on the diversity of the activities covered by a specific classification.

The general effect will be to provide more detailed classification of economic activities, since there are 334 activity headings compared with 181 MLHs. For example, a distinction is drawn, wherever possible, between principals and agents in the distributive trades. Also, in the financial area, a distinction is made between the insurance companies and insurance brokers or agents and between banks, building societies or investment companies and services such as stockbroking or foreign exchange dealing.

The CSO plans to publish reconciliations between the revised SIC and the 1968 edition (and vice versa), between the revised SIC and NACE and between the revised SIC and ISIC (International Standard Industrial Classification).

Full details of the revised SIC are available from CSO.

Problems of unit of classification

Although the SIC is valuable, this basis for analysis may result in the total production of some important firms being included under one classification, whereas they may in fact, produce considerable quantities of some other products which are important in those particular markets but represent only a relatively small proportion of their total output. Factory canteens run by companies would, for instance, be included in the turnover of the 'establishment'. However, there are exceptions to this 'blanket' measurement; where, at a particular address, two or more departments have distinctly different types of activities and completely separate records are available, each department may be treated as a separate establishment for purposes of official analysis. The unit of classification is the 'establishment', *viz.* the whole of the production at a particular address of a farm, mine, factory or shop, classified according to their main products on the basis of the Standard Industrial Classification (SIC). Care is needed in interpreting data from sources using the SIC; for example, establishments concerned chiefly with merchandising, broking, importing and exporting are analysed under distributive trades, and not under the product classification to which their activities relate. Repairers of radio and television sets, watches and clocks, furniture, etc., are classified under distributive trades, whereas establishments concerned with repairing ships, locomotives, aircraft and most kinds of plant and machinery are entered under the respective manufacturing activity.

As noted already, statistical breakdowns by the SIC often tend to be too wide for specific industrial analyses. There is, for example, 'a tremendous difference between harvesting machinery and barn machinery. To classify these two as the same industry is quite unrealistic in many ways. They are influenced by totally different considerations; they require totally different production techniques; and they require totally different materials and components'.[26]

Researchers frequently encounter other examples of official classifications which do not contain homogeneous industrial activities.

The International Standard Industrial Classifications (ISIC) was drawn up by the United Nations in 1948, in an attempt at standardisation of statistics between nations so that comparisons could be facilitated. It is 'a compromise of the classifications of a number of countries';[4] like the SIC, which it closely resembles, it was revised later. The ISIC is a valuable source of data for export marketers. The Standard Industrial Classification (SIC) and the Nomenclature Générale des Activités Economiques dans les Communautés Européenes (NACE) were derived from ISIC, principally by extending the analyses to further subdivisions and sectors. The 1980 revision of the SIC applies NACE as closely as possible to the structure of British industry, as already noted.

The United Nations has published lists of principal products under each ISIC industry and also an international classification of goods and services, known as ICGS, which classifies into subgroups the products of each industry group. NACE is supported by the Nomenclature Commune des Produits Industriels (NIPRO); this gives detailed lists of products under each industry but only for that section of NACE covering manufacturing industry.

United States SIC
The SIC system was developed by the federal government of the US to facilitate the collection and analysis of industrial data. Each major area of activity, known as 'divisions', is assigned a two-digit classification code. Each division is divided into 'major groups' which, in turn, are subdivided into more than 150 three-digit 'industry groups'. At the next level of analysis, they are further separated into four-digit 'specific industries'.

The basic reporting unit of the American SIC system, like the British, is the Establishment. Also, as with the other SIC systems, drawbacks occur, such as assigning the entire output of a multi-product establishment to a single four-digit manufacturing industry, and so inflating returns for that industry as well as understating those of secondary industries to which part of a firm's output may contribute.

Need to Distinguish Between Trade Classifications and Industry Classifications

Trade classifications are used mainly by Customs and Excise to classify goods by the materials from which they are made. Industrial classifications, on the other hand, relate to the production processes which result in certain types of goods.

Trade classifications
The need for greater comparability of trade statistics resulted in a League of Nations Committee of Statistical Experts in 1938, which drew up a Minimum List of Commodities for International Trade Statistics. This list was revised in 1950 by the United Nations Standard International Trade Classification (SITC), and by 1960 about 80% of world trade was classified on a trade-by-commodity basis.

UK statistics of overseas trade are collected by HM Customs and Excise within the framework of the Customs Cooperation Council Nomenclature (CCCN), which, prior to 1976, was an internationally agreed classification for Customs purposes; since 1976 it has been known as the Brussels Tariff Nomenclature (BTN).

The Department of Trade publishes UK overseas trade statistics according to the United Nations' Standard International Trade Classification (SITC). From 1960 to 1977, these figures were based on the SITC (Revised) or SITC(R), but from January 1978, the headings are those of the enlarged and revised SITC (Revision 2) or SITC(R2) published by the United Nations in 1975. The headings of both of these classifications correlate with those of the CCCN but are in a different order.

Directories of business

The BSO maintains registers of production firms for the purpose of conducting statistical enquiries which may be of significant value to industrial marketing researchers.

The Classified List of Manufacturing Businesses has been compiled from the BSO's register of UK manufacturing businesses. Contributors to the Census of Production from 1970, were asked if they were willing to have the name and address of their business included in an official classified list of businesses. The resultant list gives these details for each manufacturing local unit belonging to an establishment covered in the annual census. In cases where a company has more than one manufacturing local unit, separate entries are made. Non-manufacturing units, in particular units which are offices, are omitted; hence, the head office of a firm may not be listed.

The lists are arranged alphabetically within each MLH of the SIC; the complete list contains about 27,000 business addresses and covers approximately two-thirds of the employment in the UK manufacturing sector of the economy. The Classified List of Manufacturing Businesses is published in ten parts as *Business Monitor PO 1007;* these are separately available; a magnetic tape is also obtainable. Special regional and alphabetical analyses as computer printouts may be had from the BSO at reasonable cost.

Overcoming Statistical Shortcomings

One ingenious method of overcoming statistical shortcomings is to 'derive market size by utilising other information. For instance, by developing a consumption factor for the product based on employment ... The principle is quite straightforward: if there is a homogeneous industry classification then employment, for example, does become an extremely good measure of the importance of an industry because you are able to develop a relationship between employment and the use of your product in that industry'.[26]

Oxygen consumption per employee in constructional steel work for example, is 200 cubic feet per man, but in agricultural machinery it is only 10 cubic feet per man. This method could be used to calculate regional usage rates, and the relative impact of technical change on demand could be forecast. Other basic indicators of industrial activity could relate to power consumption, floor area, etc. The output of the British car industry affects the demand, for example, for machine tools, steel, petrol and many other commodities.

Statistical demand analysis attempts to discover the size and importance of real factors which affect demand for a product. Many industries make use of 'each other's forecasts in deriving their own. Thus, forward estimates for the production of steel, coal, cement, alkali and sulphuric acid are often taken as general predictors of a country's overall economic progress'.[26] Sales of one product may be closely related (as with derived demand) to the sales pattern of other products; for instance with the demand for f.h.p. motors and sales of washing machines, dishwashers, refrigerators, etc. 'Sometimes a "double tie" can be identified ... for example, if a company manufacturing metal cans identifies a specific end-product market it may forecast the sales of its own product by using the tied indicator of the demand for tinned peas. But also the forecast of the market for the sales of cans for that specific product could be ascertained by considering the acreage of peas which are contracted for sowing by the leading canning companies'.[27]

The effect of lead/lag indicators should be appreciated: 'changes in one variable do not necessarily have an immediate effect on the other: one may lead and the other lag'.[27] The number of cars sold affects the demand for steel, but this demand is lagged by about 18 months, hence providing an indicator of future activity in the steel industry. The wholesale price index generally leads the cost of living index by about three months.

It is sometimes possible to construct a model of market behaviour which assists market analyses and forecasting. Movements in demand may be correlated with economic indicators, but great care is needed to avoid spurious deductions. Total consumer disposable income, increases in birth rates, distribution of age groups in the population, etc., are useful in predicting likely trends in consumer product markets. In some industrial markets, Gross Domestic Fixed Capital Formulation (GDFCF) could be a useful indicator in forecasting demand, for example, for air-conditioning equipment.

Monsanto, one of America's three largest fibre producers, was reported[28] to have developed a mathematical model for the US tyre market which is analysed by motor trade sectors (car original equipment, car replacement, truck) and further subdivided by type of tyre (cross-ply, belted cross-ply, radial). By this method, Monsanto 'are able to quantify the volume of fibre or steel used and so arrive at the expected future demand for each type of fibre'.[28] In addition, Monsanto staff 'every quarter, and sometimes more frequently visit the five leading tyre manufacturers'[28] to present their latest market predictions and obtain the views of these tyre executives who are encouraged to take an active part in the discussions by supplying Monsanto with their own market predictions. These various inputs are fed into the computer and result in consensus forecasts.

Gordon Bolt[29] has described the effect of chain reaction in specific industrial products, portable compressors, which have basically four market segments: government departments, local authority and service authorities, contractors and plant hire. In times of economic stringency, the first market affected will be that of government departments, and within a few months local and service authorities will curb their purchasing; contractors will be affected within 6–9 months, as new projects are cut or postponed. But because some activities must continue, the plant hire segment tends to experience a considerable increase in business from three months after a national credit squeeze has been imposed.

A European steel firm[30] used a mathematical model based on sales statistics to forecast market trends; inputs cover products, customers, factories and sales agents.

A cement firm in Europe studied several correlations between the consumption of its products and the total national investment, both governmental and private sector. 'It found a close correlation exists between the demand for cement and the demand for electricity'.[30]

For several years, the American Can Company has forecast beer-can demand by correlating sales to 'income levels, number of drinking establishments per thousand persons, and age distribution of the population. Armour and Company has found that it can accurately predict the number of cattle to be slaughtered in future months by using such explanatory variables as range-grass conditions and steer–corn price ratios'.[30]

In attempting to relate lead/lag indicators or correlation factors, either simple or multiple, market analysts should proceed cautiously.

While model-building 'is essential as a means of learning more about the relationship between economic variables ... the complexity and scale of such an exercise limits the possibility of research to academic or government agencies'[31] ... or possibly also to large commercial organisations which can afford to invest funds in management ventures. There is, as Jones and Morrell pointed out, 'always a temptation for those who are skilled in statistical and economic techniques to try to wring more out of their raw material than it is capable of producing', and to become more absorbed in the elegance 'of their techniques than the validity of their conclusions'.[32]

This brief review of the alternative ways of analysing and estimating the demand for industrial products will show that marketing research requires an imaginative approach to sources of market data as well as judgement in selection and expertise in handling the resultant statistics.

Primary data

This refers to data which is unique in the sense that it has to be specially generated because of the inadequacy or, indeed, absence of secondary data.

Three main methods of collecting primary data, which are common to all types of market surveys, are: observation, experimentation and questionnaires.

Observational techniques may provide valuable marketing information. As a technique of marketing research, observation has been borrowed from anthropology which has distrusted people's ability to verbalise their feelings or experiences accurately or completely. In studies of the pub-going and drinking habits of an industrial town in Lancashire in 1943, Mass-Observation (the firm founded by Tom Harrison, a pioneer in observational research methods) 'used personal interviews, observations and diaries kept by volunteer observers'.[33]

In industrial situations, observational techniques could be useful in checking the types of equipment used by different kinds of customers (origin of manufacture, capacity, etc.), or customary working behaviour could be studied to assist in the design, for instance, of safety factors in hand tools and workshop equipment. One large petrol company checked consumers' reactions to 'talking' petrol pumps (self-serve) by a team of 'spies' who watched, from a discreet observation post, the behaviour of motorists to the printed and broadcast instructions. As a result, they 'found it necessary to simplify both the equipment and instructions'.[34]

Observation, like other methods of survey, is prone to bias. 'In making observations we each select, organise and interpret visual stimuli into a picture that is as meaningful and as coherent to us as we can make it. Which stimuli are selected and how they are organised and interpreted are highly dependent upon both the backgrounds and frames of reference of the observer'.[22] This technique is not, therefore, to be used indiscriminately: trained, professional observers are likely to perceive factors which an untrained naïve observer could easily overlook. But there is also a danger that a trained technician acting as an observer will see only factors which relate directly to technology; he may not appreciate that other influences, perhaps personal, may well account for the behaviour he is observing. Observers should be briefed on all aspects of the action or event they are to observe.

Experimentation, in the strict scientific sense, refers to controlled experiments in constant environmental conditions, so that the effects of a particular variable or factor may be carefully studied and evaluated. This ideal testing environment is the very antithesis of the conditions which are experienced in the actual marketing of goods and services. Commercial transactions are complex and subject to many variables, several of which lie outside the control of the marketer. In consumer markets, considerable attempts have been made to gauge the likely reactions of consumers to new products, advertising campaigns, etc. through so-called laboratory tests and by phased marketing involving, usually, test-marketing campaigns. Experiments have also been undertaken in pricing, packaging and methods of distribution.

While the highly organised systems of test-marketing cannot apply to industrial supplies, there is some value in being prepared to evaluate alternative methods of approaching customers. In one sector of a market, for example, a different distribution policy using franchises might be adopted and carefully checked over a period of time. Pricing policies could be tested out in distinctive market areas, bearing in mind the level of competitive activity. Promotional campaigns could be varied in different market sectors and advertising media assessed for their effectiveness. From 'experimentation' of this nature, useful information may be acquired, although the dangers of broad generalisations should be avoided.

Questionnaires are widely used in marketing surveys of all kinds; they can be administered by telephone, mail or through personal interviewing.

Constructing a questionnaire is an expert task which sould be undertaken with great care. 'The type of questionnaire obviously depends on the method of survey, and this will be dependent on the nature of the problem being investigated, the kind of population sampled, and the sample size'.[21]

Industrial marketing surveys frequently use technical terms; it is important that these are correctly used because technical experts will soon grow tired of responding to badly drafted survey enquiries. It is also important that the questions asked are not likely to be misunderstood and so attract biased answers. Questions should be drafted and pilot-tested to ensure that their meanings are clear. As noted earlier, it is sometimes advisable to divide research enquiries into specific question areas relating to technical or financial aspects so that specialists can give replies to these questions more readily.

Interviewing in industrial surveys is a particularly vital function of success. It demands considerable skill in locating the right person (or persons) who can give valid and reliable information, and it also calls for a flexible approach to individual respondents who may range from the managing director down to factory charge-hands or operatives. (Refer to Decision Making Unit: Chapter 2.)

Interviewers should have expert knowledge of the industries which are being covered by the survey, or the intellectual ability to acquire sufficient information in a short period of intensive training.

Some organisations tend to rely on their sales staff to provide market information. It is argued that surveys are better undertaken by people who have an intimate knowledge of the product and the industry. But the fact remains that a hopeful seller is rarely able to adopt a completely objective view of the market in which he is active. Industrial research interviewing should not be regarded merely as an alternative occupation for members of the salesforce; the problem of bias is too serious.

Professional interviewing skills are necessarily the most important factor in survey work; technical knowledge of a particular industry alone does not ensure successful interviews.

Telephone surveys, although of limited value, may be particularly useful in the early stages of designing a sample to establish, for example, whether a particular kind of machine was being used in the case of a 'user survey'. Some fairly simple questionnaires may also be suitable for this type of approach, but spontaneous answers could not be expected to highly technical enquiries. On the other hand, with skilful research staff, some extremely valuable survey work can be satisfactorily undertaken by telephone. It is particularly important to organise efficiently such surveys; for example, a list of areas of questioning should be prepared beforehand so that the interviewer covers adequately the topic under survey. Some telephone contacts may well be selected, with their agreement, for personal extended interviews if their telephone responses indicate that they have unusually good information to provide for a specific research project. One of the most difficult aspects of telephone interviewing is, of course, ensuring that the right person is being approached. Some degree of tactful probing may be necessary to check that a willing talker on the telephone is, in fact, able to give valid and reliable information.

Other factors affecting the quality and efficiency of telephone surveying relate to the personal style of the interviewer. Without the added advantage of personal contact and, therefore, of being able to assess the likely reactions and behaviour of respondents, telephone interviewers need to develop their communication skills so that they can almost 'feel' the atmosphere of an interview and guide it to a successful outcome. A few people develop such skills to great effect; others can improve through good training.

Obviously, lists of representative firms or other oganisations would have to be prepared in advance of telephoning; every care should be taken to make contacts which will result in a reliable sample of the specific population under survey. Stratifications will assist in this important task.

Mail surveys are superficially attractive in terms of economy and speed. But realistic cost appraisal should be based on *all* the costs involved (printing, stationery, postage — including pre-paid arrangements — and administration), and also related to the number of *effective* replies received. The valid reply rate may well double or treble the original crude estimate, apart from the problems of bias from non-reply and the doubts about the representativeness of those who have responded. If questionnaires are mailed, every care should be taken with presentation. Clearly designed questionnaires with simple instructions to guide respondents should be accompanied by reply-paid facilities and a covering letter inviting cooperation in the survey. At least two follow-up shots will be advisable, but it should be borne in mind that, inevitably, these tend to extend the period of the survey. Some cut-off point will need to be established or the client will never receive his report.

Since an interviewer will not be present to assist in interpreting survey questions (a useful though risky intervention because of possible bias), mail questionnaires require particularly careful drafting. Questions should be free of ambiguity, capable of being answered without excessive trouble, and reasonable in the type of information they request.

Response rates tend to be low with mail surveys, unless the subject of enquiry is of vital professional interest. It may be possible to weight the answers from various sectors of a market and so overcome to some degree the handicap of low response. This will depend largely on adequate knowledge of the pattern of industrial structuring in a market, and this very information may, of course, depend on the outcome of the survey.

Some method of following up non-respondents is to be recommended, and it may also be possible to check reasons for non-response either by telephone or personal enquiries. In some cases, a simple version of the original questionnaire may be accepted for completion.

Group discussions. Consumer marketing researchers often organise discussions between, for example, a group of housewives about their shopping habits. People tend to be influenced by the psychological atmosphere generated by a group, and their feelings may be expressed quite strongly. 'In the atmosphere of a group, individuals react to one another and the way in which they influence personal attitudes can be studied. Sharp criticism of individual beliefs is frequently aroused, and the discussion generated among the group by their shared interests tends to become extremely frank'.[21] It has been reported,[35] for example, that physicians, 'who are often difficult to interview alone, seem to be considerably more garrulous, frank, and at times argumentative when in a group with other physicians'.

In industrial market research, group discussions may be useful in obtaining the views of a body of professional buyers or users. British Oxygen adopt this technique in order:

1. to get a better understanding of markets
2. to solve problems
3. to get action from management

'In technical markets, a group discussion amongst, say, engineers can bring out areas of interest that you did not know even existed ... A greater understanding of attitudes and opinions is also obtained as members of the group are defending their views with people of an equal level and experience'.[36]

This process of material and frank exchange of ideas and experience should be initiated and guided by a group or discussion leader, who should not impose his own views but encourage discussion and keep it flowing in relevant channels. The proceedings could be tape-recorded (with the approval of group members) or noted by an objective observer; preferably both methods should be used.

The qualitative data from this kind of research should be expertly evaluated. They will add depth to more formal investigations, and also could most effectively indicate the real reasons why certain products or services have not been successful. The 'Freudian slip' in group discussions may offer a most valuable clue to market behaviour.

There is clearly scope for developing this branch of survey methodology in researching organisational supplies. Recruitment of representative groups is an important factor, and the actual place and time of meetings should be carefully planned.

Continuous research. Most marketing research tends to be *ad hoc*; specific problems are the trigger for market investigation. This 'one-off' attitude to surveys overlooks the benefits of monitoring the market so as to spot emerging trends or changes in the overall structure of competition.

Some years ago British Gas[37] undertook continuous research on fuel prices over sectors of industry. Industrial fuel users, selected by stratified random sample to be representative of industrial activities by region, were contacted each month to obtain data and current fuel prices, negotiations, and 'offers'. Approximately 170 companies covering about 240 fuel contracts relating to about 1600 industrial establishments were surveyed.

Cooperation was encouraged by offering, without charge, price data in respect of the fuel for which respondents provide price information. Competitive fuel prices with the respondent's own pricing data are supplied.

British Gas use this research data to construct their contract prices which are market-orientated. Marketing research showed that three possible situations of price/demand relationships apply whenever an industrial fuel is bought. These were classified as:

1. load retention — price/demand relationship in which a customer using a fuel at present will remain using it
2. new business — when new equipment is being installed involving a choice of fuel
3. change-over — point at which a customer using one fuel will change to another fuel

From detailed analyses of these marketing relationships, British Gas designed a differential pricing scheme for these distinct market segments.

Expert informants. It is frequently valuable to identify and contact recognised experts in the particular industries under survey; they are not necessarily in the largest firms. From a series of free-discussion interviews, an extremely good insight may be obtained on the structure and problems of a particular industry. Reed Paper Group were reported[38] to approach marketing research by subdividing the market into homogeneous sectors and to commence enquiries in each sector with the best informed sources known. The sample size is not predetermined; successive firms are interviewed until a stable answer pattern emerges.

Integrated Research Strategy

An effective research strategy is not necessarily confined to one method of enquiry. 'It is not so much a question of which *method* is best, as which *set* of methods is likely to result in an objective research programme ... Some leading American social scientists, who are particularly concerned with the limitations of research, have made a strong plea for "triangulation" of research methods in order to reduce the effects of bias, especially reactive measurement errors'.[39] Reactive measurement effects may arise from respondents' personal reactions to being surveyed or from the nature of the investigator.

The basic methods of questionnaire and interviewing will remain generally popular, but researchers should be willing to consider alternative and complementary methodological strategies. This more creative approach will assist in reducing bias, and also add a new dimension to survey findings.

Problems of Sampling

In organisational markets, the universe or population researched is usually comparatively small ranging from, perhaps, twenty organisations to a few hundred. Consumer samples may extend to several thousand. Typically, an organisational market supplier deals with a very restricted number of customers, several of whom are likely to represent a substantial proportion of total turnover. (The incidence of the 80/20 rule in organisational markets will be recalled from the discussion in Chapter2.)

Where this skewed distribution of customers applies, it would clearly be incorrect to choose a random sampling technique because the survey findings would be unreliable if one or more of the major organisations were to be omitted in the sample selected.

In forming a sample design for an organisational market, some general knowledge of the structure of the market is required. Hence the usefulness of preliminary discussions with knowledgeable people connected with that market and supported by intensive desk research.

Sampling frames (sources from which potential informants can be raised) may be developed from some of the sources listed earlier under 'secondary data' (p.107). As with the research strategy, more than one source will be needed to build up an adequate sampling frame. This can be a tedious job, but it is important that it is well done. Every aspect of the research programme contributes to the value of the eventual survey report.

Strict random sampling is unusual in researching organisational markets; some type of quota sampling is generally adopted: 'many industrial researchers do not pay much attention to sampling, preferring to fill their information gaps by a process of sequential interviewing until they are satisfied that they have obtained a reasonably representative view of the market'.[40] (For further definition of sampling techniques see reference 35.)

By stratifying an organisational market a sample can gradually be designed which will result in adequate coverage of the population under survey. Survey findings could then be weighted according to the known or estimated sizes of strata.

A sample is a microcosm which can only be accepted as accurate within certain limits. With random samples, it is possible to estimate by statistical tests of significance the degree of accurancy of specific samples from a given population. With non-random samples, it is not legitimate to use statistical tests of significance. Since many marketing research surveys in organisational supply markets are not based on random samples, their findings cannot, unfortunately, be subjected to rigorous testing.

Industrial Marketing Research Association Study

The Industrial Marketing Research Association, the professional British organisation of researchers specialising in this branch of market research, published[41] the results of enquiries conducted to identify the principal characteristics of industrial firms using marketing research and the reasons they did so.

General interest in marketing research was found to extend over several industries, but the following, ranked by importance, were the major users:

chemicals and allied industries
vehicles
engineering and electrical goods
construction
food, drink and tobacco
metal manufacture

Companies using marketing research tended to be characterised more by financial and capital intensity than by number of employees.

The principal ten functions of marketing research in those industries surveyed were 'positively identified' as indicated in Table 4.1.

Table 4.1 Top ten functions of industrial marketing research

Functions	% regularly carrying out
Sales forecasting	76
Analysis of market size	70
Trends in market size	61
Estimating demand for new products	51
Competitive position of comparing products	48
Determining characteristics of markets	43
Determining present uses of existing products	41
Studying economic factors affecting sales volume	38
General business forecasting	30
Evaluation proposed new products and services	30

Source: See Pearce, F.T.[41]

This pattern of research functions 'turns out to be similar to that of United States marketing research in general, although US firms practise research more consistently.[41]

Table 4.1 reveals that there is little general interest in researching into the promotional effectiveness, or in the psychological investigation of buying behaviour.

The relative importance of desk research is reflected in Table 4.2.

Table 4.2 Survey information-gathering and evaluation methods

Method	% using method	% ranking top
Desk research	88	38
Expert informants	77	23
Own staff and records	79	22
Sample surveys	59	16
Other methods	25	1

Source: See Pearce, F.T.[41]

With desk research, the most important source was stated to be the Census of Production.

Sampling frames tended to be raised internally and were used by about three-quarters of respondents. Sampling methods tended to be stratified; 'formal probability sampling is the exception'.[41] Larger companies were much more likely to adopt a flexible approach to sampling; the report suggested that this relaxed attitude was feasible because they were likely already to possess considerable knowledge about their markets because of their high market shares. They were, therefore, prepared to let a picture gradually emerge as the fieldwork progressed.

Summing Up

Systematic marketing research has been slow in developing in the marketing of non-consumer products and services. There is clearly plenty of scope for this vital tool of marketing management in the dynamic and competitive market environment where reliable information is more than ever necessary for success.

Many years ago it was said that: 'Some British industries do not make sufficient use of market research; they thus suffer from a removable uncertainty'.[42]

Unfortunately, much the same could be said today, although there are growing numbers of industrial firms interested in knowing more about the benefits that market research could bring them.

SUMMARY

Effective marketing is based on sound market information: this is obtained through objective marketing research.

Markets are dynamic and information needs to be kept up-to-date. Organisations of all kinds can benefit from using marketing research; it helps to reduce the uncertainty or risk related to specific management decisions.

Five sequential stages in marketing research have been identified: brief, proposal, data collection, data analysis and evaluation, and preparation and presentation of final report. At all stages, professional objectivity must be maintained.

Two types of data, primary and secondary, are generally used in marketing research. Sources of secondary data should be identified and used before embarking on expensive field research (primary data collection).

Industrial and trade classifications assist in analysing market behaviour.

Specific research techniques include personal, postal, telephone, group and panel research. A carefully devised, integrated research design is important.

REFERENCES

1. Drucker, Peter, F., *The Practice of Management*, Heinemann, London, 1955.
2. Schlaifer, Robert, *Probability and Statistics for Business Decisions*, McGraw-Hill, New York, 1959.
3. Ackoff, Russell L., 'Management Misinformation Systems', *Management Science*, 14 December 1967.
4. Heller, Robert, 'Why Facts Need Figuring Out', *Observer*, 20 April 1975.
5. Kotler, Philip, *Marketing Management: Analysis, Planning and Control*, Prentice-Hall, New Jersey, 1980.
6. Levitt, Theodore, *Marketing for Business Growth*, McGraw-Hill, New York, 1974.
7. Buzzell, Robert D., 'Is Marketing a Science?', *Harvard Business Review*, January/February 1963.
8 Geldard, Frank A., *Fundamentals of Psychology*, Wiley, New York, 1963.
9. Easterfield, T.E., 'Operational Research Studies', in *Accelerating Innovation*, Aslib. 1975.
10. American Marketing Association, 'Report of the Definitions Committee', AMA Chicago, 1961.
11. British Institute of Management, 'Survey of Marketing Research in Great Britain', *Information Summary No. 97*, BIM, London, January 1962.
12. Aaker, David A. and Day, George S., 'Increasing the Effectiveness of Market Research', *California Management Review*, Vol. XXIII, No. 2, 1980.
13. Industrial Marketing Research Association, *Regulations*, IMRA, Lichfield, 1969.
14. Rosier, Jacques A., 'The Coming Crisis in Bank Management II', *The Bankers' Magazine*, August 1973.
15. Gaulton, John, 'Marketing and All That', *Journal of the Institute of Bankers*, December 1973.
16. Chisnall, Peter M., *Marketing — A Behavioural Analysis*, 2nd edn, McGraw-Hill, Maidenhead, 1985.
17. Horne, Annette, Morgan, Judith and Page, Joanna, 'Where Do We Go From Here?', *Journal of the Market Research Society*, Vol. 16, No. 3, 1974.
18. Bowley, A.L. and Barnett-Hurst, A.R., *Livelihood and Poverty: A Study in the Economic Conditions of Working Class Households in Northampton, Warrington, Stanley and Reading*, Bell, London, 1915.

19. Cowell, D.W. and Blois, K.J., 'Conducting Market Research for High Technology Products', *Industrial Marketing Management*, Vol. 6, No. 2, 1977.

20. Ferber, Robert and Verdoorn, P.J., *Research Methods in Economics and Business*, The MacMillan Company, Toronto, 1969.

21. Chisnall, Peter M., *Marketing Research: Analysis and Measurement*, McGraw-Hill, Maidenhead, 1981.

22. Green, Paul E. and Tull, Donald S., *Research for Marketing Decisions*, Prentice-Hall, New Jersey, 1975.

23. Political and Economic Planning, 'Sample Surveys — Part One', PEP Report No. 313, Vol. XVI PEP, London, May 1950.

24. Anderson, P.G., 'The Industrial User and His Marketing Research Needs', in *The Effective Use of Market Research*, Aucamp, Johan (ed.), Staples Press, London, 1971.

25. Green, R.W., 'Statistical Classifications — Structure and Development: The Government's Viewpoint' *IMRA Journal*, Vol. 7, No. 4, November 1971.

26. MacLean, I., 'Statistical Classification — Structure and Development: An Industrial Marketing Research Viewpoint', *IMRA Journal*, Vol. 7, No. 4, November 1971.

27. Battersby, Albert, *Mathematics in Management*, Penguin, Harmondsworth, 1971.

28. Trafford, John, 'Monsanto's Model for the Tyre Market', *Financial Times*, 16 May 1972.

29. Bolt, Gordon J., *Marketing and Sales Forecasting — A Total Approach*, Kegan Paul, London, 1971.

30. Teresi, S., 'Sales Forecasting', *Management International Review*, Vol. 6, No. 2, 1966.

31. Parker, George G.C. and Segura, Edilberto, L., 'How to Get a Better Forecast', *Harvard Business Review*, March/April 1971.

32. Jones, E.O. and Morrell, J.G., Environmental Forecasting in British Industry, *Journal of Management Studies*, Vol. 3, 1966.

33. MacFarlane-Smith, Joan, *Interviewing in Market and Social Research*, Routledge and Kegan Paul, London, 1972.

34. Courtenay, Edward, 'Talking Pumps', *Sunday Telegraph*, 23 April 1972.

35. Goldman, Alfred E., 'The Group Depth Interview', *Journal of Marketing*, Vol. 26, July 1962.

36. Ansell, A.E., 'The Group Depth Interview', *Journal of Marketing*, Vol. 26, July 1962.

37. Johnson, F.J., *Market Segmentation and Pricing Research in an Industrial Market*, Esomar, Hamburg, 1974.

Chapter Five
STRATEGIC PLANNING I

THE NEED FOR A METHODICAL APPROACH TO PROBLEMS

Management is essentially concerned with problem solving, decision making and organising finite resources to achieve identified objectives.

Being methodical implies adopting and following an effective method; it involves a disciplined and well coordinated effort. A methodical approach concentrates mental and physical energies; haphazard and erratic actions dissipate and eventually destroy these vital forces. Of course, the blind following of a routine, no matter how methodical, may sometimes result in failure and frustration. But this may be because the problem was wrongly diagnosed or an inappropriate method of dealing with it was devised. Clear, objective thinking is necessary at the diagnostic stage and throughout the planning process.

Adopting a methodical approach does not mean that the same path is the way to success with different kinds of problems. What *is* important is a methodical *and* flexible approach, so that feasible solutions are offered for specific problems. One of the salient characterstics of a first class manager is the flexibility of his reactions to problems.

As the operating environment becomes less stable and more difficult to predict, organisations should ensure that their strategies are adaptive to the changes which are taking place both inside and outside their businesses. From time to time, all organisations should review their basic operations to make sure that they are attuned to the changing environment and opportunities.

For example, the operating environment of the British Post Office Corporation has become increasingly competitive over the past decade or so. The 1969 Post Office Act transformed the Post Office from a Department of State into a State Corporation that had to achieve a predetermined level of profits. Later, the establishment of a Marketing Department in 1972, added to the keen commercial awareness and new professional skills which were needed to tackle, for instance, the fast growing and aggressive competition in parcels traffic from several new market suppliers.

ROLE OF PLANNING

Planning attempts to control the factors which affect the outcome of decisions; actions are guided so that success is more likely to be achieved. 'To plan is to decide what to do before doing it. Like methods, plans can be specially made to fit circumstances or they can be ready-made for regular use in recurrent and familiar situations'.[1] In other words, a methodical approach can be custom-built, or ready-made, according to the nature of the problem involved.

As discussed earlier in this text, most organisations — whether they are primarily motivated by profits or by, for example, social welfare policies — are today immersed in dynamic environments. The whole fabric of society has changed so radically, bringing new expectations and demands with it, that organisations of all kinds can continue to be useful only if they react to the changing needs of their markets. In the specialised managerial function of marketing, flexibility is essential. Strategic planning is concerned with allocating the resources of an organisation in the most effective pattern of reaction to the identified needs of those whom it professes to serve.

Plans must be regularly assessed for their effectiveness, and systematic updating should be an accepted management discipline. Simmons[2] has drawn attention to the fact that in their early days Communist planners made some of their greatest mistakes by not realising their plans had to be subject to change if they were to continue to be relevant and effective. 'They tried to impose a fixed 5 year plan on changing conditions. Unfortunately, some American businesses are still making this mistake ... Frequently, a well-constructed plan only six months old will be found to be very much out-of-date. Someone may claim it could not have been a good plan. In fact, it may have been the best possible plan. It is serving its purpose. Because of the plan, management now know what changes are necessary to improve future business'.[2]

Export markets in particular, as discussed in Chapter 8, require careful planning some long time ahead of actual entry operations. The time lag is affected by the product type, its manufacturing complexities and the methods of distribution adopted. Exporting cannot be jumped into at the last moment; strategic planning should map the route along which companies travel to secure profitable overseas business. The contributions of marketing research, product design and development have been covered in earlier chapters. The integration of production and marketing plans, etc., are matters requiring adequate study before final decisions are made to enter particular markets.

Managers of successful companies have frequently pursued strategies of one kind or another without consciously analysing their actions. However, there is increasing evidence to support the development of formal strategic plans. This becomes particularly important when the tasks of operational management are delegated from the policy-forming centre and as businesses acquire wider interests. Kotler[3] points out that the development of strategies has two main benefits: (1) they facilitate the achievement of objectives, and (2) the formulation of strategies requires people to come together. This produces better understanding and awareness and a 'shared sense of opportunity, direction, significance and achievement'.

This identification of shared objectives is also stressed by another researcher[4] who states that the need for an explicit strategy stems from two key attributes of an organisation: that success hinges on people working together thus mutually reinforcing corporate inputs, and that these efforts have to be done in rapidly changing conditions.

CHARACTERISTICS OF AN EFFECTIVE PLAN

Over 25 years ago a leading management scientist[5] listed four general features of an effective plan: unity, continuity, flexibility and precision. These characteristics are, of course, interdependent. Unity means that only one organisational plan should be operating at any one time; if more than one plan is put into action, confusion will result, and organisational resources will be used inefficiently. Continuity refers to the linking of successive strategies over time so that long-term objectives are finally attained. Flexibility has been discussed in the preceding paragraph; in a dynamic environment it is courting disaster to adopt a static strategy. Precision demands disciplined methods of market measurement and forecasting. Without reliable data, plans cannot be formulated with reasonable chances of success. Measurability is also a link between planning and control; plans should be monitored for their tactical effectiveness.

Drucker[6] has identified three elements in business planning which 'is a continuous process of making present entrepreneurial decisions systematically and with best possible knowledge of their futurity, organising systematically the effort needed to carry out these decisions against expectations through organised feedback'. This definition was observed by Ansoff[7] to contain three elements: making decisions systematically; preparing programmes for their implementation; measuring actual performance against the programmes. Management planning requires, therefore, method, sustained effort, precise standards by which to evaluate performance and continuous monitoring to ensure that resources are being optimised. Without planning, chaos takes over and soon reduces any kind of organisation to a miserable shambles.

RELATIONSHIP BETWEEN MARKETING PLANS AND CORPORATE PLANS

Strategic planning is based on two concepts: market environment and strategic fit, i.e. the way in which a company organises its resources in order to secure an effective relationship with the markets in which it operates.

Kotler[3] feels that where a firm is marketing orientated, its entire organisation is welded together in one unified, coherent system which is directed towards a well defined set of objectives. Unless an organisation has devised an effective strategy, it is open to buffeting from its competitors. As pithily expressed by Howard Perlmutter: 'Without a strategy, the organisation is like a ship without a rudder, going around in circles'.[8]

The relationship between marketing planning and corporate planning has been emphasised, although it is accepted that the value of integrated planning is 'more observed in theory than in practice[9].' According to an experienced American senior executive,[10] marketing planning is the starting point for all corporate planning. Businesses exist because customers are willing to buy the goods and services offered to them, so planning for those markets is the basis for the extent and direction of all other corporate decisions.

The survival and growth of an organisation depends heavily on the quality of management planning. Some die-hard businessmen despise planning, preferring a 'seat-of-the-pants' approach to problem solving. Sometimes they are spectacularly successful, but, more frequently, their disorganised efforts have led to catastrophe. 'General Eisenhower was reputed to have said, "In preparing for battle I have always found that plans are useless, but planning is indispensable"'.[1]

SYSTEMATIC PLANNING

It would, of course, be naïve to believe that planning can ever be perfect: it is an art as well as a technique. However, it is useful to consider it as a series of integrated events that lead sequentially from stated objectives. These steps in the planning process are as shown in Figure 5.1.

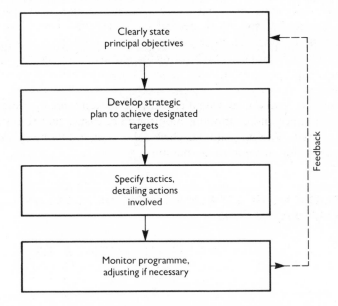

Figure 5.1 Four sequential stages of planning.

These main stages of planning will now be considered in more detail, so that the various elements which contribute to successful operations can be identified and assessed. Planning should not be viewed as a sterile exercise; if it is thought to be so, then this may be a reflection of a deteriorated management philosophy. Managers are not just men of action: they need to think ahead and to do so clearly. Planning clarifies the processes of thought, because the very act of writing down proposed courses of action is a powerful mental discipline which leads to more effective behaviour.

PLANNING STAGE 1: STATING CLEAR OBJECTIVES

The setting up of goals or objectives is the first step in the planning process. This foundation step should be carefully designed so that an effective structural plan develops. To guide efforts, objectives should be stated in specific terms related to the fundamental philosphies and policies of a particular organisation. 'Vague or undefined objectives lead to vague, undefined and uncoordinated plans, and to decisions taken under pressure of circumstances leading to actions which are often incompatible'.[11]

Economists generally assume that firms aim to maximise profits. However, another view which is attracting support is that modern, large corporations, managed by professionals, may well pursue other objectives, such as organic growth. As a result, the traditional view of profit maximisation as a prime objective may be challenged by the behaviour of corporate management in certain firms. Risk-aversion policies, for instance, may well discourage professional managers from pursuing profit maximisation at all costs.

Bearing in mind these observations, two main types of organisational objectives can be identified: primary and secondary.

As just mentioned, the traditional view was that the primary objective of a business could be presumed to be the generation of profit. However, other objectives may be desirable and affect profit-earning activities. These secondary objectives — which as Ansoff[7] has observed, are not in any way inferior to the primary objective — are necessary if a company is to plan effectively for its future progress. In the short term, for instance, a profit maximisation policy may be affected by changes in economic conditions which demand some restructuring of corporate resources to meet new levels of competition. Survival or market share defence, may, in fact, become primary objectives.

Quantified objectives set standards of performance against which progress can be measured; these can be one or more of the following typical marketing criteria: percentage share of defined market; ratio of profit on sales; total sales (home; export); contribution ratios, etc.

With refreshing directness, Drucker[12] has reminded top management that their first responsibility is to ask top management the question '"What is our business?" and to make sure that it is carefully studied and correctly answered ... That the question is so rarely asked — at least in a clear and sharp form — and so rarely given adequate study and thought, is perhaps the most important single cause of business failure'. The definition of a business (or non-profit-making organisation) should be derived from an examination of customers' needs, because through satisfying customers (or clients), organisations survive and prosper.

Organisations should set realistic objectives; these should be related both to short-term and long-term goals. Since marketing is concerned with the efficient use of corporate resources to meet specific market needs, these targets — short- or long-term — should be based on budgets which are tied in with levels of forecasted demand.

Firms may be broadly classified as either reactive or proactive; the former receive stimuli from their markets and respond in some way — a largely passive posture in which entrepreneurial energy is at low ebb; the latter adopt a positive attitude to their markets, searching actively for new business opportunities, monitoring market trends and energetically pursuing likely business opportunities. These entrepreneurial firms aim to shape the environment to fit their resources. These contrasting business styles will obviously affect the objectives set down by such firms and, of course, their overall trading performance.

Situation Analysis

A logical starting point in setting corporate objectives would be an objective audit of resources, identifying strengths and weaknesses of existing skills: technological, production, financial, administrative, marketing, etc.

Ansoff[7] has observed that a large majority of corporate decisions have to be made within the framework of a limited total resource, no matter what size the organisation may be. There are alternative uses for scarce resources, and the objective 'is to produce a resource-allocation pattern which will offer the best potential for meeting the firm's objectives'.[7]

Financial audits are standard features of organisations of all types: with similar professional objectivity companies should carefully check the various factors that contribute to their marketing efficiency.

Marketing audits are seen[3] to have three diagnostic steps: (1) marketing environment review, (2) marketing system review, and (3) detailed marketing activity review. The first stage establishes the current and expected marketing environment of the organisation. The second stage reviews the internal marketing system as to its suitability for the emerging marketing environment, while at the third stage, a review is made of the main components of the specific marketing mix (see later discussion).

One way in which a marketing audit can benefit a business may derive from an internal audit of customers' accounts. For example, one company found that small orders represented 62% of total orders received, but only 17% of total value; by contrast, the biggest customers made up 10% in value of total sales, although representing only 1% of total orders. Clearly, changes were advisable to the direction of marketing efforts.

Companies may, for example, stipulate that orders should be of certain minimum size for direct shipment; smaller orders may be diverted to distributors. Standards may be laid down related to the frequency of salesmen's visits to specific types of customers, rated for new potential profitability; quantity discounts may be introduced to encourage the placing of larger orders at one time. Indiscriminate selling is not likely to result in maximum profitability; planned operations are necessary in today's highly competitive conditions.

It may sometimes be advisable to prune or rationalise product lines in order to increase marketing productivity. Most companies tend to list some products which do not really pay for their keep.

Sevin[13], who has undertaken notable research into marketing productivity analysis, has categorically stated: 'Manufacturers and wholesalers generally do not know reasonably accurately the dollar marketing costs and the dollar profit (or loss) contribution of each of their products, customers, sales territories and other segments of their business'. As the result of controlled market experiments a company was able to eliminate 592 out of 635 unprofitable products, many of which, it was discerned, were viewed by their customers as not being substantially different from standard and profitable items in the product line. As the result of this rationalisation programme, Sevin reported that: 'long run sales volume was increased and marketing costs were reduced substantially, while the dollar net profit contribution was increased by almost 24%'.[13]

The systematic analysis of product ranges by ranking the profit contribution of individual products or main types of products is a very useful exercise for marketing management in conjunction with financial colleagues.

Evaluating products by the contribution which they made to overheads and profitability is a realistic approach which acknowledges that it is frequently difficult, if not impossible, to allocate scientifically overheads over individual products in a multi-product firm. As a result, overhead charges tend to be distributed more or less arbitrarily; different methods of allocation are likely to affect significantly the net profit ranking of individual products. Table 5.1 lists main product groups by monthly sales volume, sales revenue and direct profit (defined as net selling price minus total variable costs). The last column on the right gives the cumulative gross contribution to profits. It will be observed that 80% of the total contribution to profits is generated by about 46% of the product groups. Further examination of this ranked list of product performance will reveal the very marginal value to the business of some product groups: one third of the product range renders only 5% of the total profit contribution. Clearly, questions will have to be asked about the reason for continuing to sell certain product groups.

Table 5.1 Analysis of profit contribution ranked by product groups

Product group units	Sales vol. £	Sales revenue £	Direct profit £	% cumulative gross contribution
A	108	9,900	4,844	13.5
B	454	10,229	3,734	23.9
C	308	7,937	2,887	32.0
D	144	6,614	2,757	39.7
E	420	6,934	2,621	47.0
F	51	4,952	2,455	53.9
G	28	4,088	2,356	60.4
H	351	5,520	2,204	66.6
I	325	4,262	1,751	71.5
J	59	4,226	1,731	76.3
K	182	3,825	1,360	80.1
L	78	3,117	1,236	83.5
M	132	2,617	1,053	86.5
N	29	2,083	946	89.1
O	140	2,354	940	91.8
P	76	1,895	657	93.6
Q	11	1,174	570	95.2
R	19	1,354	537	96.7
S	60	1,068	427	97.9
T	38	984	281	98.6
U	2	278	146	99.0
V	23	530	143	99.4
W	2	278	135	99.8
X	9	177	63	100.0
Total	£3,409	£86,426	£35,834	

Source: 'Planning the Product Range', Muir, Andrew.[14]

In some cases, it may be possible for customers to accept substitutes from the main range, which may have been introduced since they were supplied with 'specials'. There may be valid reasons for leaving some of these 'marginal' products in the selling list; they may attract other, and more profitable business, or it may be feasible to increase prices to offset their general low level of contribution. In some cases it may be more advantageous to buy-in certain products for which a firm experiences limited demand. This will enable it to maintain the attraction to customers of a comprehensive range of products without incurring diseconomies. There can be no hard-and-fast rules which generally apply. In the end analysis, marketing managements have the responsibility of ensuring the profitability of their companies, and at the same time, of satisfying, as far as reasonably possible, customers' needs. The temptation to be the world's supplier must, of course, be resisted.

The data in Table 5.1 are graphically represented by the asymptotic curve shown in Figure 5.2.

Imbalance can exist between sales and profits over various product ranges; one company discovered that almost 50% of total profits were generated from just under 38% of total turnover represented by one product group. Another product group accounted for 7.5% of total sales, but contributed only about 3% of profits; while home market sales were nearly 43% of total business, they contributed just under 30% of operating profit. New marketing strategies were designed to remedy this potentially dangerous corporate situation.

Linking Marketing Audit and Marketing Research

Marketing research, as indicated in Chapter 4, provides objective and relevant data for marketing decision making. The characteristics of demand, market shares, buying behaviour, competitive activities and related factors will be collected from systematic market research, and assist in developing strategic objectives.

Significant Corporate Influences

Before attempting to fix corporate objectives, management should identify and evaluate likely obstacles or constraints which may exist in their

Figure 5.2 Cumulative gross profit contribution by product groups (Tables 5.1).

Source: See 'Planning the Product Range', Muir, Andrew.[14]

organisations. Some of these may be overcome eventually, but in the short term, at least, they are likely to inhibit management objectives. It is advisable, therefore, to classify the nature of the constraints and to consider how, for instance, a phased programme within the scope of developing resources could be designed to attain specific corporate objectives.

Two specific factors are likely to be particularly influential in strategic planning: (1) the principle of the limiting factor, and (2) leverage.

The principle of the limiting factor

Even the largest organisations do not have unlimited resources: and one will show itself to be more critical than the others when, at a particular time, corporate opportunities are being considered.

Chester Barnard, an influential American management theorist and highly successful business executive, has referred to the principle of the limiting factor in solving corporate problems: 'The limiting factor is the one whose control, in the right form, at the right place and time, will establish a new system or set of conditions which meets the purpose'.[15]

Finance is, of course, always limited, but there may be occasions when finance is available but other factors inhibit its effective application. All organisations tend to have significant factors that influence their development; the identification and appreciation of these dominant planning components may reveal, for instance, unexpected competitive disadvantages. In marketing terms, the immediate limiting factor could relate to the level of distribution which may be inadequate for national coverage, or, perhaps, to the technical knowledge of salesmen who may be expected to sell more sophisticated products. The existing design resources within a firm may be inadequate to meet new competition which has eaten its way into the market share held by the company.

A few years ago, the British Oxygen Company recognised that its limiting factor was the nature of demand for its products: this was essentially reactive and dependent on industrial activity. In addition, BOC products could not economically be transported more than 150–200 miles from the point of production.

The invasion of the British market by Air Products faced BOC with an entirely new competitive situation; for years they had enjoyed a virtual monopoly situation in the British gas market. BOC, in the words[16] of the chairman of their industrial and medical cases group, were forced to start marketing gases: a task for which they were ill prepared. The defensive posture adopted against Air Products aggressive marketing in the late 1960s was abandoned and BOC sought to regain ground by positive marketing not only of gases but of the technological expertise and advice which they could offer to customers.

Another outcome of the changed market environment was that BOC vigorously pursued a policy of diversification, so that its activities now range across welding products, vacuum engineering, medical equipment, refrigeration equipment and frozen food retailing and specialised food distribution.

Leverage

In addition to limited resources, including, probably, one particularly influential limiting factor, organisations have — or should aim to have — distinctive competences which give them significant market advantages. McKinsey[9] studied the management practices of 37 companies. Among other findings, they concluded that the distinguishing characteristic shared by these companies was that they did one particular thing well. They have developed significant strength in one feature of their businesses which gave them a comparative advantage over their competitors. As Blois[17] observes, this concept is well known and understood, but one of the problems of applying it is that the features which result in this competence change over time in line with environmental changes. Hence, leverage should be viewed as a dynamic factor, particularly in volatile market conditions.

This concept of comparative advantage could be linked, perhaps, to the early nineteenth century classical economic theory of international trade. The principle of comparative cost or advantage advanced by David Ricardo and others, stressed that specialisation of production in which a country had special proficiency would be more beneficial to its economy.

Manufacturers (and distributors) should deliberately seek to develop recognised, distinctive abilities which are attractive to their customers. There are many ways in which 'leverage' can be developed; it may, for instance, relate to specific patents, or to superb after-sales service, or to efficient distribution arrangements, including acceptable delivery times. Even in commodity product markets, leverage can be built into the deal — it is, perhaps even more important for this to be done, because of the nature of supply in these markets. (In Chapter 2, the concept of the augmented product was mentioned, particularly with reference to commodity products.)

Market dynamics

Porter[18] has stated that: 'The essence of formulating competitive strategy is relating a company to its environment'. Since companies operate within distinctive market conditions of supply and demand, it is vital to study the dynamics of market behaviour before attempting to devise a market strategy. 'Every industry has an underlying structure or set of fundamental economic and technical characteristics ... the strategist must learn what makes the environment tick'.

Obviously it is not always easy to define an industry absolutely; Porter[18] takes a 'working definition' of an industry as a group of firms that are making products (or supplying services) that are close substitutes for each other.

He also observes that competition in an industry continually operates to drive down the rate of return on investment towards the 'competitive floor rate of return', or to that which would be earned in the classical 'perfectly competitive' industry. This approximates to the yield on long-term government securities adjusted upwards for risk-bearing.

Many experienced managers will already know a good deal about their industries, but even they can benefit from systematically updating their knowledge by objectively considering the five basic forces which determine the dynamics of demand and supply in their particular industrial and commercial sectors. This will lead to a thorough grasp of the relative strengths and weaknesses of their respective businesses.

These five market forces are briefly:

1. threat of new entrants
2. bargaining power of buyers
3. bargaining power of suppliers
4. threat of substitute products/services
5. rivalry among exisiting firms

(see Figure 5.3).

The nature of these various influences and their effects on market behaviour will now be considered. Both product and service markets can be evaluated across the five basic factors listed above.

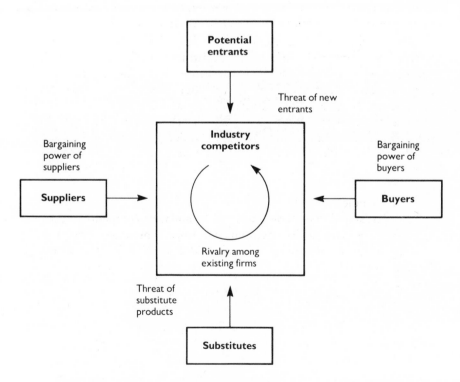

Figure 5.3 Forces driving industry competition.

Source: See Porter, E.[18] Reprinted by permission of Macmillan Publishing Company.

1. *Threat of entry*

A prospective new supplier brings an alternative source of supply to the market which may threaten existing suppliers shares and profitability. Depending upon the corporate resources of the market entrant and the state of the market at that time, the overall profitability of the industry may be imperilled. If formidable barriers to entry exist and present suppliers are well managed, a newcomer will not pose a serious threat. The seriousness of the new market competition will depend on six major barriers to entry:

(a) *Economies of scale* which refer to declines in unit costs of production (or other functions associated with a company's activities) as the absolute volume increases over a given period of time. If economies of scale exist within an industry, they will act as barriers to entry by forcing a new firm to enter on a large scale (in order to reap comparative benefits) and thus risk retaliation from the existing large-scale suppliers, or, alternatively, to enter as a small-scale producer and accept the inherent cost disadvantages. Porter[18] notes that scale economies may be generally applicable over a business, or they may be highly specific. For instance, scale economies in production, research, marketing and service are probably the key barriers to entry in the mainframe computer industry, as Xerox and GE discovered to their cost; whereas, in television production, significant scale economies are limited to the manufacture of colour tubes and do not apply to the same extent to cabinets. Multi-product businesses may be able to enjoy economies of scale by applying certain components across several types of product ranges, or by sharing selling and distribution costs.

(b) *Product differentiation* acts as an important barrier to entry because of brand identification and loyalty, built up from extensive advertising, customer service, unique design — perhaps patented, etc. Consumer product companies have aimed to develop particularly strong loyalty to their highly promoted brands. Industrial products do not have the same general market visibility, although in their market sectors, industrial and commercial firms should be able to develop strong customer allegiance through consistent attention to factors like quality and service. 'Image' building, discussd in Chapter 9, may be very beneficial in attracting orders across a range of products offered by a multi-product firm.

Products can be differentiated intrinsically, i.e. by functional design, or they may be perceived to be different because of better appearance ('applied' design) or because of higher standards of sales-service. Industrial as well as consumer goods and services should be assessed creatively for opportunities to differentiate them from the general run of goods on offer.

(c) *Capital requirements* may be significant barriers to entry if extensive investment in, for example, production, stocks, research and development is necessary in order to challenge existing suppliers. In capital intensive industries, in particular, investment costs and the nature of risks, may be distinctly limiting. Xerox chose to rent copiers rather than sell them outright, thus creating a formidable capital barrier to entry in this product market.

(d) *Access to distribution channels* — products of all types must be readily available to customers. Established firms are likely to have well defined channels of distribution with which they may have particularly strong links because of efficient servicing. In other cases, a widesprad network of exclusive distributors may prove very difficult for a newcomer to challenge or build up from scratch. Perhaps a non-traditional channel of distribution may offer new entrants an opportunity to develop his business.

(e) *Cost disadvantages independent of scale* — established firms may enjoy certain cost advantages that are not available to potential competitors, irrespective of their size and attainable economies of scale. Such advantages may derive from: (i) proprietary product technology; (ii) favourable access to raw materials such as mineral deposits; (iii) favourable locations; government subsidies applicable to existing firms and (iv) learning or experience curve (Porter[18] refers to the latter as a 'first cousin' of the former). In some businesses, there is an observed tendency for unit costs to decline as experience in, for example, producing or marketing a product increases. (This concept will be discussed later in this chapter.)

(f) *Government policy* which may limit or even prohibit entry to certain industries by imposing regulations related to the extraction of raw materials, safety and pollution standards, or by licensing and other controls related to particular activities, such as airline operations, banking, medical and nursing establishments.

Porter[18] stresses two important additional points about the threat of entry: (1) It changes as market conditions change; for example, the expiry of patents (as occurred with Polaroid and led to Kodak's sudden challenge in the instant photography market). On the other hand, the vastly increased economies of scale in the automobile industry have virtually prohibited new entry; (2) strategic decisions involving a large segment of an industry can significantly affect the threat of entry as, for example, when the American recreational vehicle industry adopted vertical integration in order to lower costs.

2. Bargaining power of buyers
This requires very careful consideration in evaluating market behaviour. Buying power can be influenced by one or more of the following factors:

- relative buying power — large volume buyers are particularly powerful where an industry has fixed costs, as in chemicals (aspects of buying concentration have already been discussed in Chapter 2)
- where the product being bought represents a high proportion of an industry's costs (as with capital goods) and 'shopping-around' is therefore likely
- where products are largely undifferentiated, so alternative sources of supply can be easily to hand and switching costs are insignificant
- where buyers may be able to threaten backward integration, as has happened in the automobile industry. 'Tapered integration' — producing a proportion of their component needs themselves and

buying the balance from outside suppliers — not only gives these manufacturers a very strong bargaining advantage but also provides them with detailed knowledge of costs of producing these components

- where the product supplied is an important element of the end product, buyers tend to be less price sensitive as, for example, in components for oil field equipment or medical instruments, where malfunction can have disastrous consequences.

Sellers may be able to improve their strategic bargaining position by selecting particular types of firms whose buyers exercise reduced power in the market for a specific product or service. Selective targeting of customers has been successfully adopted by two American firms — National Can and Crown Cork and Seal — which focus on segments of the can industry where they are able to offer differentiated products, minimise the threat of backward integration, 'and otherwise mitigate the awesome power of their customers'.[18]

3. Bargaining power of suppliers

This arises by the threat to increase prices or reduce the quality of goods and services, thus squeezing maximum profitability from a particular industry, as happened when the chemical companies raised their prices to contract aerosol packagers.

The following conditions contribute to the power of suppliers in a given market:

- when a supplier industry is dominated by a few companies (oligopoly) and is more concentrated than the industry it is selling to
- the product being supplied is unique or at least differentiated, or if it has significant switching costs (buyers would be faced with considerable difficulties if they attempted to change suppliers)
- a supplying industry does not have to cope with alternative products offered to a specific industry, as for example, when steel suppliers and aluminium suppliers competing for the same industry inhibit their respective bargaining powers
- when suppliers may be able to threaten forward integration into their customers' industry
- when an industry is not a relatively important customer of the supplier group — otherwise, supplying companies' fortunes will be closely linked with that industry and strong cooperation will be actively encouraged to ensure the continuity of customers' businesses; this may be reflected in reasonable pricing policies, assistance with R&D, etc.

4. Threat of substitute products/services

This limits the potential profits of an industry by imposing price ceilings which can be avoided by upgrading the product or differentiating it in some way so that it is distanced from potential substitutes. Suppliers of a specific product compete not only among themselves but also against suppliers of acceptable substitutes. Natural fibres have experienced crushing competition from synthetic fibres; sugar producers have had to face large-scale production of high fructose corn syrup; banks are facing increasing competition from building societies; life assurance sellers are also competing with unit trust marketers; plastics increasingly replace timber in window frames and doors; concrete roofing tiles decimated the clay roof tile industry, etc.

Substitute products that merit particular strategic attention are: those able to develop increasingly attractive price/performance characteristics relative to an industry's 'traditional' purchase; or those produced by industries earning high profits, when substitutes are rapidly adopted 'if some development increases competition in their industries and causes price reduction or performance improvement'.[18] Supplier firms in an industry may act jointly to counter the effects of substitutes, as, for example, the famous 'Woolmark' promotion has done for several years.

5. Rivalry among existing firms

This becomes more marked as an industry matures and little real growth is apparent. Rivalry among suppliers intensifies as profits are threatened and weaker companies go to the wall. Competitive tactics such as price cutting, increased promotional expenditure, and product variations are widely practised in the fight for market share. Such activities will soon be noted by rival firms which are likely to retaliate.

Where high fixed costs operate in an industry, suppliers may deliberately shave prices in order to keep production at economic levels. Lack of product differentiation — virtually 'commodity products' — is likely to result in low customer loyalty, price sensitivity and fierce competition.

High exit barriers arising, for example, from specialised assets, may oblige supplier firms to 'dig in' and grimly fight for survival in the hope that demand conditions will improve in the near future.

In some industries, for example chemicals or paper production, capacity is usually increased by large increments which, for the time being, often result in severe imbalance in the supply–demand position.

From time to time, the nature and extent of rivalry in an industry will vary, hence individual firms should be flexible in their product strategies so that they maintain a competitively attractive position.

From this evaluation of the structure of the industry in which a company operates and of the market or markets it supplies, a corporate planner should be able to identify his firm's relative strengths and weaknesses. His next responsibility is to design effective plans of action so that his company can most effectively use its resources to achieve the agreed corporate objectives. Before this step is taken, however, it is necessary to incorporate the planned objectives into specific time periods.

Time horizons in forecasting and planning

The nature of an organisation will affect the time horizons of its objectives. A component manufacturer will not have the same degree of forward planning as a supplier of petro-chemical installations. In general, heavy industry and capital intensive industries have long-term planning horizons and the life of the capital assets involved also tends to be longer than in many consumer product industries. It is usual to distinguish between short-range (3 months – 1 year), medium-range (1–5 years) and long-range forecasts (5–25 years). Short-term forecasting provides information to guide 'day-to-day operations within the limits of the resources currently available. It usually needs to be accompanied by estimates of the random fluctuations which the tactical decisions aim to reduce'.[19] Short-term forecasts are primarily concerned, therefore, with tactical planning. Medium-term forecasting acts as a check point indicating whether progress is being maintained along long-term trend lines. Medium-term forecasts are valuable in checking on the optimum use of corporate resources. The third category of forecast, i.e. long-term, 'provides information for major strategic decisions: it is concerned with extending or reducing the limits of the resources' [19] mainly affecting capital expenditure. Clearly, the longer the time period, the greater the probability that new environmental facts will arise. 'For the generality of industries 5 years is the basic period forecast and in nearly every case a short-term view of from 1 to 2 years is incorporated in the forecast ... in most cases the forecast forms part of an annual business plan, sometimes being subject to revision during the course of the year'.[20] (The incidence of lead/lag indicators on industrial suppliers was discussed in Chapter 6.)

Some discrimination should be exercised in using the expressions 'short-term', 'medium-term' and 'long-term', because perceptions will be influenced by the nature of particular industries. Battersby[19] has pointed out that the Post Office looks 40 years ahead; ship-builders' short-term forecasts would be very different in the period covered from a consumer products manufacturer, whose market changes much more rapidly. Capital goods are not subject to the violent swings that often characterise consumer products such as fashion clothing. Lead time will also vary considerably across industries; specially skilled labour may require a training period extending over several months and even years, adding further to the complexity and uncertainty of long-term forecasting and planning.

Fundamental Questions for Corporate Planners

This initial phase of corporate planning should, if done thoroughly, include answers to the following fundamental questions:

What kind of organisation are we managing?
Why does our organisation exist?
What kind of customers/clients do we aim to serve?
What kinds of products/services do these customers need?
What are we particularly good at doing?
How does this strength relate to market needs?
What are our competitors doing?

What makes us different from our competitors?
What should we do to improve our market position in the:
(a) short term?
(b) long term?
What should we do to achieve these targets?

PLANNING STAGE 2: DEVELOPMENT OF STRATEGIC PLAN

In stage 1, the objectives of the organisation will have been clearly stated in relation to its corporate resources. These objectives may be diverse, ranging from improved market performance leading to profitability (in the stringent economic environment of today, this may be secondary to corporate survival dependent upon adequate cash flows) to, as in the case of the public sector education and welfare activities, more effective allocation of available services.

The concept of strategy has its origins in military operations; over the past two decades or so this impressive term has been used increasingly in management literature, first occurring in 1948 when Von Neumann and Morgenstern presented their now well known business games theory. Antony Jay,[21] in his stimulating text, *Management and Machiavelli*, has suggested: 'The first transference you have to make when studying political history in management terms is to read "economic conflict" for "military conflict". — The difference between killing and selling may, objectively, be rather more than superficial, but not in the qualities they demand of those planning and executing the campaign'.

Military metaphors have been further pursued by Kotler and Singh[22] who comment that Clausewitz saw war as a necessary means to pursue national self-interest; its objective being to vanquish the enemy by achieving unconditional surrender. On the other hand, Liddell Hart, the greatest twentieth century military theorist, saw the objective of war to be a better state of peace and was severely critical of Clausewitz's theory of total annihilation.

In business terms, cut-throat competition can lead to ultimate defeat, so modern competitors rarely adopt the Clausewitzian objective. In the US, this type of competition is inhibited by the anti-trust laws, apart from the generally unacceptable outcome of forcing utter defeat on competitors. Liddell Hart's doctrine may be a more appropriate guide for businessmen. Giant firms may well compromise on market shares, at least in the short term.

Peaceful coexistence may indeed be present in some markets and encourage firms to seek niches or segments where they can exercise comparative advantage. Market segmentation strategies will be discussed in the next chapter.

Attack strategies, based on the military model, should make use of the 'principle of mass', *viz.* that superior contact power must be concentrated at the critical time and place for decisive action. Five possible strategies are identified as: frontal, flanking, encirclement, bypass, and guerilla.

For pure frontal attack to succeed, an aggressor needs to have strength over competitors. Military dogma asserts that for frontal attack to be successful against a well-entrenched opponent or one controlling the 'high ground', the attacking force must deploy a 3:1 advantage in fire power.

A modified form of frontal attack is commonly used, such as to cut prices related to those of other suppliers. This could be effective provided the market leader does not retaliate, and also that customers perceive good value in the cut-price product and are willing to buy it. Texas Instruments are quoted as being brilliantly successful in using the price weapon strategically; they invested heavily in R&D and moved very rapidly down the experience curve. (See Chapter 6.)

Flanking attacks concentrate on weak spots; an aggressor may act as if he will attack the strong side to tie up defenders' troops, but actually launch an attack at the side or rear. His limited resources limit an aggressor's use of force, so he uses subterfuge.

Encirclement — also called 'envelopment' — involves launching a grand offensive on several fronts so that the enemy must protect his front, sides and rear simultaneously. However, for this strategy to succeed, the aggressor must have superior forces.

Bypass attack is analogous to peace-time political warfare ('cold war'). This might be reflected in commercial terms by diversifying into unrelated products; and into new geographical markets for existing products. In these ways, the main enemy is avoided and easier target markets are attacked which enable the business base to be broadened. In the US, Colgate had traditionally fought against Proctor and Gamble, until it was recognised that head-on battle was futile. The new strategy involved maintaining Colgate's lead abroad and bypassing Proctor and Gamble in America by diversifying into markets where there was no Proctor and Gamble presence. Several acquisitions in textiles, hospital products, cosmetics, sporting and food goods enabled Colgate to re-establish its business strength: in 1971, Colgate was underdog to Proctor and Gamble in about half of its business, but by 1976 in 75% of its business it was either comfortably placed or faced no competition at all from Proctor and Gamble.

Guerilla warfare consists of making small, intermittent attacks on different territories held by an opponent, with the aim of harassing and demoralising him and eventually securing concessions. In business terms, this might be achieved, for example, through selective price cuts, intense bursts of promotional activity, 'assorted legal actions against the opponent'[22] related to possible violations of anti-trust law, trademark infringement and deceptive trade practices. This pin-pricking strategy, although normally practised by a smaller firm against a larger one, and less expensive than the other strategies outlined, is not necessarily cheap in terms of resources. In the end, it has to be backed by a stronger attack, if the opponent is to be beaten.

Six defence strategies modelled on military engagements have been identified as: position defence ('fortified front line'); mobile defence ('defence in depth'); pre-emptive defence ('offensive defence'); 'flank-positioning' defences; 'counter-offensive' in defence; 'hedgehog' defence ('strategic withdrawal').

Position defence is tied to a psychology of 'fortification', for example, the French Maginot Line, or the German Siegfried Line, the twentieth century versions of the medieval fortresses, suggesting impregnability; but all failed in time.

In the business world, static defence is marketing myopia: the myth of the invincible product. Like frontal attack, it is one of the riskiest military strategies. 'Henry Ford's myopia about his Model T brought an enviable healthy company to the brink of financial ruin'.[22]

Mobile defence occurs when a firm attempts to stretch its domain over new territories that can serve as future centres for defence or counter-attack. Market expansion would be carefully controlled to avoid wasted efforts.

Pre-emptive defence ('offensive defence') assumes that prevention is better than cure; war not peace is considered to be the natural state of business. All the various attack strategies could be used in pre-emptive defence, the aim being to keep the competition always on the defensive.

'Flank positioning' defence occurs when a firm establishes a flanking 'position' as a hedge against some probable but uncertain event, or as a defensive corner overlooking a weak front. As in the military sphere, this strategy is of little value if it is so lightly held that it could easily be frustrated by a small force, while the main force passes by unmolested.

'Counter-offensive' in defence strategy is when the defender can respond to an attack by mobilising reserves and counter-attacking vigorously, by either head-on, flanking, or pincer movement strategies. To do this effectively, a defender should identify a chink in the attacker's armour, *viz.* a segment gap.

'Hedgehog' defence, or strategic withdrawal, occurs when a firm decides to consolidate its competitive strength and to concentrate resources at strategic points for counter-attack. This may involve rationalisation of product ranges, and strategic withdrawal from fragmented market segments.

The various attack and defence strategies which have been outlined indicate some of the alternatives open to business planners. Since companies frequently borrow from the military strategists in describing their market behaviour, knowledge of certain martial theories may help in constructing marketing plans.

As observed earlier, managers, like the proverbial prose-speaker, frequently adopt a business strategy of some kind without being consciously aware of its theoretical origin. With relatively small enterprises where personal ownership and management are not separate functions, strategy is not formalised; the policy maker is also responsible for the tasks of management. However, as the organisation develops, managerial responsibilities tend to become divorced from ownership, and specific aspects of management, such as marketing strategy, are delegated. The need for an explicit strategy then becomes apparent. This working plan coordinates the activities of individuals in an organisation, and it also endeavours to direct their efforts so that the organisational goals are achieved.

Strategy is concerned with the broader aspects of organisational performance; it maps out the roads to be traversed — alternative routes will require to be studied — to reach the planned destination. The vehicles to be used are a tactical choice (the third phase of planning).

Two schools of thought in the development of a strategic plan have been identified[23] as occupying different positions on a continuum; at one end is the 'rational-comprehensive method' while at the other end is the 'process of disjointed incrementalism'.

The first method makes three basic assumptions: (1) that the goals and objectives of a company can be clearly identified and agreed upon; (2) that the strategic planner has access to complete information and (3) that the selected strategy is rationally chosen by all members of the organisation.

The other method — disjointed incrementalism — directly challenges the views held by the 'rational-comprehensive' approach. It proposes instead that it is virtually impossible for either an individual or an organisation to deal adequately with the complexity and conflict confronting them; it recognises that data, both internal and external, are frequently not available; and it accepts that individual members of an organisation tend to have different goals and objectives that cannot be dealt with adequately by a single set of decisions.

This alternative approach to the development of corporate strategy involves a continuous process of choice between policies that differ only marginally from the status quo. Objectives are more implied than explicit, and gradually, through a series of decisions, a strategy appears.

Not surprisingly perhaps, the researchers[23] agree that strategy, in most cases, is formed by a combination of the two contrasting approaches. 'Broad strategic decisions are based on partially formulated objectives and incomplete estimates of external and internal affairs'. These broad strategies are then put into effect in a stepwise manner, and modified from time to time in response to new information and pressures from members of the organisation.

Porter[18] perceives competitive strategy as taking offensive or defensive action in order to create a *defendable* position relative to the five competitive forces enumerated earlier in this chapter. This involves several potential approaches: (1) positioning the firm strongly against competitors; (2) influencing the balance of power by strategic moves, such as product innovation, or large-scale capital investment and (3) anticipating changes in market behaviour and adopting a pro-active strategy.

Whatever strategic plan is devised, it is essential that marketing information is up-to-date and objective. (See Chapter 4.)

Facets of Marketing Strategy

Marketing strategy has several aspects: product range strategy; pricing; promotional activities; selling and distribution, etc. These various marketing inputs are customarily referred to as the 'marketing mix' (see Figure 5.4); combinations of these inputs are needed to secure particular marketing objectives.

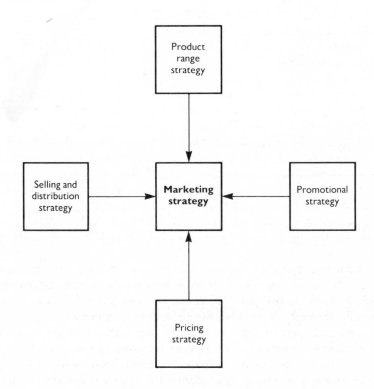

Figure 5.4   Facets of marketing strategy.

Product or service planning is strategic because the growth of an organisation depends largely on the development of new products or services, the elimination of outmoded or unprofitable lines, and the improvement of existing products/services to give better satisfaction to customers or clients. (In Chapter 7 the innovation of products is discussed in some detail.)

Over 25 years ago, Ansoff projected a useful matrix (see Figure 5.5) to enable companies to assess their market efforts and growth opportunities. This basic matrix has since been developed and freely used by many researchers.

Products

		Existing	New
Markets	Existing	1	3
	New	2	4

Figure 5.5 Product/market matrix

Source: See Ansoff.[24] Reprinted by permission of the *Harvard Business Review.*

Option 1: Market penetration is based on existing products in existing markets with the objective of increasing business through more effective marketing. Three courses are feasible: (1) stimulate consumption of products; (2) take business from competitors, and (3) attract non-users to buy the product. Where markets are experiencing zero growth and purchasing frequency cannot be increased, a desperate fight for market shares will be evident.

Option 2: Market development focusses on selling existing products in new markets or market segments. This can be achieved by (1) opening up additional geographical markets (home or overseas), or (2) developing alternative versions of existing products to appeal to defined market segments not presently served.

Option 3: Product development produces a policy of product innovation for sale in current markets. This may involve intrinsically new types of products derived from technological inventions, or product adaptations and improvements.

Option 4: Diversification entails both new products and new markets and is the most radical of the options outlined. This enterprising strategy compounds the risks to which a firm is likely to be exposed when it seeks to grow by a mix of both new products and new markets.

Kotler[3] outlines three broad types of diversification: concentric, horizontal, and conglomerate.

Concentric diversification occurs when a company adds new products or services that have technological and/or marketing synergies with current products, and, generally, will appeal to new customer groups.

Horizontal diversification occurs when a company adds new products, that are technologically unrelated to current products, but which could appeal to current customers.

Conglomerate diversification occurs when a company markets new products, that are unrelated to current experience, but which could appeal to new classes of customers.

Businesses are most likely to have products and markets at various stages of development, and it is important that they should know of the relative distribution of sales and profits over these sectors. Innovation, as discussed later, is crucial to corporate development. At the same time, risk is a significant factor in decisions regarding new products and new market ventures, particularly those where a company lacks significant technological or marketing experience.

A creative product strategy aims to build a balanced product range which optimises productive efficiency and marketing effectiveness. The product or service mix should be wide enough to attract and retain customers' interest; at the same time, firms should not aspire to be universal providers in these days of high-cost operations.

As recommended earlier in this chapter, marketing management should devote some of their energies and time to product range analysis. Thus the function of marketing tends to be viewed as rather humdrum, but it should not be shirked because overall profitability can be seriously eroded if this task is neglected.

Product Positioning

Product (or brand) positioning is a very useful concept in assessing marketing opportunities; it refers to the place occupied by a particular product in a given market. This evaluation should be comparative and assessed by measuring customers' (or consumers') perceptions and preferences for all products (or brands) of a type available in a specific market.

Hence, as discussed earlier, products should be developed which have characteristics readily distinguishable by buyers and which are relative to their needs. Marketers should appreciate that perception is rarely entirely objective, even in technological markets. Company image may, for example, play an important part in the position occupied by a firm in the specific product market. (See Chapter 10.)

Positioning, therefore, may relate to one or more features such as intrinsic design, suitability for special uses (e.g. underwater), well known firm or brand name, industry track record, established name for technological innovation, etc. In a study of the UK car market, relative positioning of the principal suppliers indicated quite distinctive market segments. (See Figure 5.6).

Product positioning analysis enables marketing management to understand better the nature of competition relative to certain types of

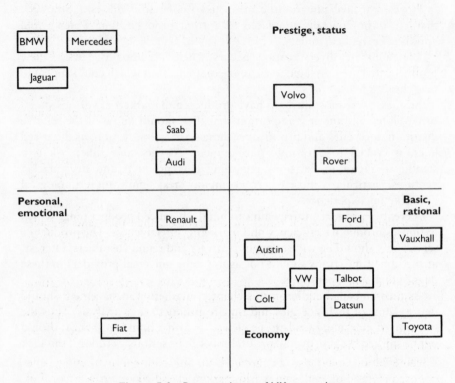

Figure 5.6   Perceptual map of UK car market.

products and markets. This comparative evaluation may give clues as to how products might be developed to coincide more closely with customers' perceived needs, and to give suppliers a competitive edge. In some instances, it may be feasible to re-position a product through more skilful promotion, by design modifications, or by new channels of distribution. Strategic repositioning of products and/or services may be desirable from time to time, as technological and other changes affect market demand.

Product Portfolio

The portfolio method of market planning adopts the analytical approach of financial investment which has the objective of spreading risk and the opportunities of profit across a balanced range of investments. Like an investment portfolio, different combinations of products and markets may be devised by companies according to their objectives, experience and resources. The product/market grid shown in Figure 5.5 can be further elaborated by developing profit projections for each of the cells in which a company is operating or planning to enter.

More attention will be given to portfolio planning in the next chapter;

now, it might be enlightening to recall Levitt's reflection that most companies have products which can be classified in one of the following categories:

1. 'Yesterday's winners — products, at one time profitable, which, because of declining demand or intensifying competition, now contribute little, if anything, to corporate earnings.
2. 'Today's providers' — these products are the backbone of corporate profitability ... 'the milk cows on which all else feeds',
3. 'Tomorrow's hopefuls' — these products are being developed or have been recently launched. As yet, they are not self-supporting but their sales performance so far suggests that they may become 'the milk cows of the future'.

An even more pungent classification described a typical product range as: (1) killers (2) fillers, and (3) thrillers. On reflection, most companies would agree that, on a contribution basis, their products qualify for inclusion in one of these categories.

Critical Role of Pricing in Marketing Strategy

Pricing is a critical element in the overall marketing strategy: it is one of the most difficult tasks facing management. Price is only one of the variables which contribute to the marketing mix: it is interrelated with the other factors affecting buying decisions, such as product design, after-sales service, promotional efforts, etc. Pricing cannot, therefore, be considered in isolation: it certainly should not be determined without a thorough appraisal of the contributions made by the other elements in the marketing strategy.

Pricing can be projected as an active, dynamic part of marketing strategy, planned to achieve certain corporate objectives or it may play merely a subservient role in the marketing of goods and services. Some specific pricing objectives may relate to attracting quick cash flow without profit maximisation; keen pricing may be pursued in order to enhance market share; prices may be set to achieve minimum levels of return on investment; there may be cases where unusually high prices can be charged because of relative scarcity, product patents, technological supremacy, etc.

Firms tend to have pricing strategies relative to specific market environments.

The problem of industrial pricing was the focus of a survey, *How British Industry Prices*,[26] published in 1975. In most industrial companies, pricing appeared to be cost-dominated and little influenced by marketing policy. There was little variation in pricing behaviour over the three types of industrial markets covered, *viz.* capital goods, components and materials. The vast majority of companies reported that prices were fixed in relation to costs either by adding a customary percentage to costs or by establishing a required gross profit margin. Only about one-fifth of respondent companies said that selling prices for at least some of their products were primarily affected by factors other than costs, but even they tended to adopt mainly a defensive pricing posture and follow the general level of prices set by competitors.

The survey also found little evidence that discounts were used effectively to promote marketing objectives; the most common basis of discounts was customer classification rather than more directly sales-related factors such as quantity per order or volume bought over an agreed period. It seemed that the granting of discounts has degenerated into a routine activity which has little relevance to the actual volume of business transacted.

Only about one-third of the companies surveyed carried out any kind of formal investigation of price acceptability before setting prices. Likewise, the result of pricing decisions were hardly ever investigated apart from a few relatively elementary enquries. In general, systematic marketing research involving pricing policies was rarely used.

Interaction of demand and supply on prices

Specific markets (or segments) have particular pricing problems; many influences operate but it is possible to isolate some general factors. One, which is significant, refers to the relevant demand–supply position. The interaction of demand and supply and its impact on prices should be considered at three levels: (1) raw materials and bought-in component parts; (2) the nature of the demand for the industrial goods produced from these supplies and (3) the nature of the demand for the products which are made from the industrial goods in (2).

From Chapter 2, it will be recalled that some of the principal factors affecting levels of demand (and prices) in organisational supplies were outlined. Of particular importance is the fact that organisational buyers may be more sensitive to other factors in the marketing mix than merely price. Price is an indicator of quality as well as an economic label: the concept of value is subjective. Buckner's[27] researches showed that price reductions below 1% of existing market suppliers' prices caused virtually no change in choice of supplier. But price reductions of 1–9% resulted in significant switching of supply sources; approximately 40% of buyers said they would be prepared to change suppliers. Where price reductions were over 10%, 14% of buyers were reported to be willing to accept new suppliers; this indicates that if prices are reduced too much, suspicions about quality, for instance, tend to be aroused. Fewer sales may, in fact, result for the firm which attempts to expand its market share by severe price cutting.

Demand factors are usually responsible for setting price ceilings; cost factors form a floor (or several floors) for pricing in a market. But neither floor nor ceiling are necessarily static: they may be changed by promotional activities (lifting demand) or by a different allocation of costs (raising or lowering the floor). Competitive activities, technological developments, etc., may also intrude to affect pricing.

Trading structure and pricing strategy

Another important factor which influences prices relates to the trading structure in particular industries. In Chapter 2 the incidence of concentration factors was observed to affect buying behaviour and, particularly, bargaining power. Trading structures range from where many firms of approximately the same size are active in a market which has minimal barriers to entry to a monopolistic (or near monopolistic) market situation where one or two very large firms dominate supply and entry to the market is extremely difficult. The majority of industries are characterised by a mixture of large, medium and small firms. Price competition is affected significantly by the balance which exists between the various sizes of firms. The more suppliers which exist within an industry with an equitable distribution of market shares, the more marked will be the tendency for price competition to be active.

Pricing decisions are complex and should be considered, therefore, against the following factors:

1. nature and extent of demand
2. competitors' activities (influenced by the trading structure)
3. costs of production and marketing
4. pricing objectives (business policy)
5. product life cycle (discussed in next chapter)

Effect on pricing policy of horizontal and vertical integration

Some companies have developed vertically integrated organisations in an effort to exercise some measure of control on market demand at several levels of production and distribution. Horizontal integration is aimed at reducing the level of competition at a specific level, for example, manufacturing, with the objective of reducing costs and achieving higher profits through economies of scale, rationalisation of production, etc. The degree of integration and the level of price competition in an industry tend to be closely linked.

In a study of 1649 manufacturing processing units in the US, Buzzell[28] found that because vertical integration requires managers to invest considerable capital into new operations, the strategy may not be productive from a cost savings viewpoint. However, he also observed that integration strategies are often successful, both in terms of profitability and greater production innovation, especially for firms enjoying strong market positions.

Bid pricing

Public sector organisations are subject to statutory controls; these are likely to stipulate that certain supplies must be obtained as the result of competitive tendering. Firms are invited, by advertisement, to quote for specific contracts, for example, road construction, and 'sealed bids' are deposited with the buying authority. It is customary for the lowest bid to be accepted, but in some cases a company which has made an attractive, though not necessarily the lowest, offer may be invited to negotiate further.

Sealed-bid pricing, as Kotler[3] observes, is a prime example of pricing based on expectations of how competitors will price rather than on a fixed ratio to a firm's costs or to demand. While a firm may be very interested in securing a particular contract, its bid cannot be less than marginal cost without damaging its business position. However, the higher its price is raised above marginal cost, the less likelihood there is that it will be successful in attracting the desired business.

Firms need to consider the probability of getting a contract at a particular bid price against the potential profit. A series of calculations at various price levels will indicate the expected profits and guide the final bid price. (Potential Profit × Probability = Expected Profit.)

Price collusion
Companies may seek to reduce price competition and establish some control over markets by some form of collusion, generally unofficial. Legal sanctions usually apply against such trading practices.

Important to identify nature of costs
An efficient system of costing is vital for management pricing decisions. These costs should be clearly identified so that the nature of their impact is understood. Costs are the foundation of prices. Basically, costs are usually divided into two general categories — fixed and variable. Fixed costs do not vary significantly with volume of output over a stated period of time. (Rent, salaries, insurance, etc.) Variable costs, as the name suggests, vary, often proportionately, according to changes in the volume of output. (Labour, power, raw materials, etc.) The critical factor is the relationship in the overall cost structure between these two main types of costs.

Another way of looking at costs is to classify them as either incremental or full. Incremental costs refer to the direct costs of labour, materials and supervision incurred if a particular order is taken and which would not arise otherwise. Full costs include the direct costs and also the apportioned overheads, such as administration and depreciation, which, of course, apply whether or not a specific order is booked.

When a business operates below capacity, the general tendency is to accept orders that will cover incremental costs and make a *contribution* to overheads. In the short term, this policy is often sound, but it could be dangerous if it became extended indefinitely.

In the crisis conditions of world markets where prices of raw materials are subject to violent changes, up-to-date costing information is clearly more important than ever. Pricing in times of chronic inflation is a nightmare exercise for which no really satisfactory guidelines have yet emerged.

Consistency of pricing in product range
Indiscriminate price reductions may adversely affect the total sales of a product range. Price reduction of a 'quality' product may shift sales from 'standard' lines of similar characteristics. The impact of price variations on sales of the total product range, and on its overall profitability, require careful

assessment. Pricing is, therefore, strategic in directing the profitable development of businesses.

Major factors affecting export pricing

Three major factors affect pricing in export trading: (1) changes in exchange rates; (2) changes in import duties; (3) changes in transport, including insurance charges.

The heavy fall in the trading value of the pound and the general uncertainty of current movements experienced by British exporters in the mid-1970s raised new issues for export pricing strategies. A trend developed towards the pricing of longer-term contracts in foreign currency rather than in sterling which has been the traditional pricing base for generations.

Exchange rate fluctuations have serious repercussions on profitability, especially where long-term trading commitments are involved, such as in the supply of specially designed equipment or major contracts for the installation of textile or steel mills which take several years to complete. The country of destination and the strength of its currency clearly influence pricing decisions because it is less risky for an exporter to negotiate business in terms of a strong currency than the other way round.

Traditionally, British export business has been transacted in sterling which was widely accepted as a dependable international currency. However, major British companies are now restructuring their export price lists.

Overall, there are indications that sterling as a pricing base for British exporters, particularly those engaged in long-run businesses, is being abandoned in favour of quoting in currencies like the US dollar, the West German Deutschmark or the Swiss franc.

The risks and actual costs involved in export business require objective analysis. There is a need, therefore, for systematic research into specific overseas markets to establish the nature of competition, the nature and level of demand and the other important factors which are discussed in Chapter 8 dealing with international marketing. (The complexities of export pricing demand special and lengthy discussion which is outside the scope of this text.) Essentially, management information for pricing to win overseas business should be developed methodically, and, over time, regularly updated because of the complexity and dynamic nature of international markets.

Promotional Input to Marketing Strategy

Two facets of marketing strategy — product range and pricing — have been reviewed; the third input to the overall strategic plan relates to promotion. In Chapter 10 particular attention will be directed to the problems of corporate communications, including the promotion of organisational supplies and services. This chapter, which concentrates on strategic planning, is concerned with underlining the interdependence of the various inputs. Unfortunately, the promotional inputs to the overall strategic plan tend, in some firms, to be developed in relative isolation from the other contributory factors. In organisational markets, promotional inputs to marketing strategy are often underrated and demoted to an inferior role. As a result, advertising agencies may be badly briefed, so that the resultant advertising campaigns do not seem to have direct relevance to overall marketing objectives. This myopic view of advertising is reflected in the low quality of a great deal of technical advertising, although over the past decade or so some industrial suppliers have greatly improved their standards of advertising. The leading management and professional journals now feature advertisements which are often extremely well designed — a refreshing distance from the flat-footed approach which generally stigmatised industrial, technical and professional promotional efforts.

Marketers of organisational supplies and services should be prepared to spend time and effort in planning promotional inputs that will reinforce the overall marketing strategy. A fully integrated plan is just as necessary in non-consumer markets as it is with chocolates, cosmetics or washing machines. (The logistics of planning advertising campaigns are discussed in Chapter 10.) Promotional strategies themselves depend on the effective linking of several variables: media, timing, intensity, etc. These demand professional skills which may partly be available within an organisation; more usually, however, they are drawn from the services of specialist advertising agencies. But as noted earlier, the essential point is for marketing management to ensure that promotional specialists work closely within the general marketing plan. While creative flair should not be stifled, marketing management have the final responsibility for developing an integrated and coherent marketing plan in which the various inputs are balanced effectively.

Of course, promotional activities are not solely concerned with tangible products. In the service industries (refer to Chapter 2), promotional policies play an important part in developing market demand. Not only in industrial services but also in the public sector, promotional activities have been most effective. There are several notable examples in the health and welfare services, e.g. the extremely successful 'immunisation' campaign which has played a large part in influencing parents to have their children safeguarded against diptheria and other infectious diseases.

Selling and Distribution Input to Marketing Strategy

This fourth main input to the overall marketing strategic plan is particularly important in organisational markets. In Chapter 2 the logistics of supply affecting consumer and industrial products were compared. Selling is mainly affected by direct contact between manufacturers and their customers, many of whom are likely to be of considerable size. Channels of distribution, unlike most consumer products, are, therefore, relatively simple. Many products sold to organisational buyers are designed to meet their specific needs, and involve complicated technical specifications. The critical role of the industrial salesman was noted in Chapter 3 to be particularly effective at the various stages of the sophisticated buying routines which characterise organisational markets.

Although direct selling is prevalent in industrial markets, industrial distributors, such as steel stockholders or builders' merchants, play important roles in certain product markets. IBM sells its computer systems direct to users, while Dow Chemicals use a distributor–fabricator channel for their polyethylene foam.

Distribution systems can be characterised generally as intensive, or exclusive. The first category results in widespread availability of a product, such as basic raw materials. The second category deliberately limits distribution of specific products, as with appointed regional distributors of farm implements, etc. Between these two extreme distributive policies, selective distribution may be adopted; this gives adequate access to a market without the high costs of intensive distribution and also allows the marketer more control over the final selling arrangements for his product.

Selling may be one of the many tasks of a salesman whose responsibilities, according to Kotler,[3] may be analysed across six activities: prospecting, communicating, selling, servicing, information gathering and allocating. The actual mix of tasks will vary with the purchase decision process, company marketing strategy and the market conditions.

Of the various tasks listed, those of servicing, selling and prospecting are likely to be core responsibilities. With many industrial products, servicing may involve consultation on customers' problems in manufacture of their own goods, technical advice, arrangement of finance and expediting delivery.

Prospecting covers the search for new business which, in some firms, may be supported by advertising to act as an introduction to the sales force (see Chapter 10). Other valuable support could be rendered by the sales office, and market research manager, who might be able to prepare lists of target customers for the salesman to concentrate on. By these kinds of back-up, the salesman would be able to increase his productivity and give more time to his principal task, *viz.* selling.

Selling is a vital element of the marketing strategy and demands professional commitment, product knowledge, integrity and good organising ability. Levitt,[29] whose well known article 'Marketing Myopia', published in the *Harvard Business Review* during 1960, stirred up debate about the function of marketing, later reviewed the impact of his missionary zeal. He felt that his astringent views had particularly influenced firms in 'the more technical industrial products and services' and had shown the need for clearly communicating product and service characteristics through face-to-face selling. However, precisely because these products are so complex, 'the situation produces salesmen who know the product more than they know the customer, who are more adept at explaining what they have and what it can do than learning what the customer's needs and problems are'. As a result, a narrow product orientation has developed instead of really trying to understand a customer's problems and offering him feasible solutions within the capacity of the products or services marketed, salesmen tend 'to look in the mirror rather than out of the window'. Only their own production-orientated biases are reflected; what they should be looking at are customers' problems. (Also see Chapters 2 and 10.)

In Chapter 3, research studies on the complexity of industrial buying practices were noted: the DMU (Decision Making Unit) was seen to be significant factor in the buying practices of industrial and economical organisations. In 1976, a research publication 'How British Industry Sells,'[30] focused on the *marketing* behaviour of industrial suppliers. Among its findings are the following useful insights:

- many companies might well profit from developing the consumer goods concept of key account salesmen
- industrial salesmen might well be centred where business is, rather than nursing traditional territories
- wide variations in selling costs (1–10%) suggest that better use might be made of salesmen's time. Although the average salesman makes three or four calls a day, there is no correlation between the frequency of calls and orders placed — the reverse, in fact seems to apply
- only in about 20% of companies was the salesforce under the direct control of the marketing director
- 26% of companies do not set sales targets
- selection and training procedures seem generally inadequate

From the above, there appears to be plenty of scope for introducing higher standards of professional selling in industrial markets, particularly in view of the greatly increased competition and soaring costs since the date of this report.

Hakansson's researches[23] emphasised that industrial selling behaviour is concerned with establishing positive interaction between the two negotiating firms, and that this is not just the responsibility of the salesman. 'Personal contacts between buyers and the technical and general management personnel were rated as highly as sales representatives as channels of communication'. Teamwork is clearly involved in both successful buying and selling.

Industrial selling is, therefore, a complex activity: products and services are often highly technical and involve long-term contractual obligations; industries are frequently dominated by powerful firms, sometimes multinational in ownership and operations; technological developments in some fields, like electronics, are dynamic; available sources of business in the home market may be few: industrial restructuring has had widespread effects on suppliers to the older industries; and imported manufactured goods are more evident in the UK than ever before. These are a selective list of factors which contribute to the sophisticated nature of the industrial salesman's job.

The various stategic inputs which make up the overall strategic plan should be well integrated. For instance, selling efforts should be synchronised with advertising campaigns; advertising copy should reflect some of the principal features of the sales presentation. Media, for example, technical journals, should be carefully chosen for their effective coverage of specific types of industrial and other organisational sources of business.

The impact of effective distribution was experienced some years ago by a British firm of crane makers, whose sales engineers used to sell pulley blocks singly. These blocks were subsequently packaged and distributed through merchants, thus eliminating wasteful use of salesmen's time. The cost of one call by a sales engineer wiped out completely the profit on a pulley block. Export marketing of standard overhead travelling cranes was also reorganised. Because these cranes consist substantially of structural steel, which is bulky and costly to transport, export crane kits are made up of motors, winches, etc. From these components, cranes are expertly constructed in overseas markets.

Just as in consumer markets, industrial products and services will profit from creative ideas in marketing. Technical excellence supported by professional marketing lends to survival and growth, even in slow or no-growth markets.

PLANNING STAGE 3: SPECIFYING TACTICS

This third phase of the planning process spells out the tactical operations by means of which the strategic objectives are to be achieved. The precise boundaries of strategic and tactical decisions and operations tend to become rather blurred. Short-term goals and the related activities to achieve them, are sometimes referred to as tactical, while the term 'strategic' is used to describe long-term corporate objectives and planned activities. In general, it may be said that tactics are subservient to strategy; tactics are the tools which implement the strategic policies.

Tactical operations should detail the specific actions which it is considered will result in the target objectives being attained. These may refer to profit or to some other measure of efficiency, such as more effective allocation of public services. Areas of personal responsibility should be explicitly mapped out together with detailed schedules showing the time periods involved. The tactical programme should be divided into a series of phases with individual subsidiary goals. This will aid management in checking progress and will also be effective in motivating staff to attain goals that do not appear to be so remote as to lose their immediate appeal.

Marketing tactics (and their related targets) could be divided into four main phases: infiltration, consolidation, expansion and domination. This systematic phasing would enable marketing management to allocate responsibilities for opening up, for example, key accounts in particular areas or industries. As a foothold is gained in a market, new tactics may be necessary to build up business and expand market share. Undoubtedly, competitive reactions are likely to become tougher and market growth will become increasingly difficult. The final phase — domination — may not, in fact, be feasible or even desirable. Although not dominating the total market, some suppliers may develop particularly profitable market sectors in which they are able to specialise, and where they become major sources of supply. (See later discussion on market segmentation.)

PLANNING STAGE 4: MONITORING PLANNING PROGRAMMES

The last stage of planning is concerned with monitoring the tactical efficiencies of an organisation marketing plan. Beforehand, measures of performance will, of course, have been drawn up. Systematic reporting is an essential constituent of corporate planning. (See Chapter 1: 'Control' Factor in Marketing Management.)

Evaluating market trends and the relative performances of competitors will provide guidelines for the strategic repositioning of products and services. Regular checks on corporate image are also valuable in relationships with suppliers, customers, financial institutions and the trade unions.

In the introductory chapter of this book, the three functions of marketing management were identified as analysis, planning and control. The analytical function was specifically covered in subsequent chapters; this chapter has concentrated on the planning and control functions. Professionalism in marketing demands that attention should be given to all of these responsibilities. Like any other business activity, marketing incurs costs; hence the importance of control mechanisms to ensure that expenditure is productive in terms of the corporate objectives stated in the first phase of planning.

ITT operate a highly developed planning system throughout their diversified group of companies with particular emphasis being given to effective monitoring of actual results. Any deviations from planned results are immediately investigated and corrective action is taken. ITT's annual planning cycle[31] consists of the following phases which are related to specific time periods:

Steps	Timing
Update long-range plans	Continuous
Establish objectives	January–March
Develop full plans	April–July
Screen and consolidate plans	August–September
Review and approve plans	October
Modify plans	October–November
Establish monthly budgets	November–December
Approve budgets	December
Measure results	Monthly

SUMMARY

Strategic planning is vital for successful marketing; corporate resources are limited and should be effectively used. Market environment and strategic fit underlie strategic planning. Marketing planning is the starting point for all corporate planning.

Four steps in the planning processes are identified as: state objectives; develop relevant plan; specify tactics; establish monitoring system.

Situation analysis involves market audit which has three diagnostic steps: (1) marketing environment review; (2) marketing system review, and (3) detailed marketing activity review.

Significant corporate influences are: limiting factor, and leverage.

Porter's model of market dynamics notes five forces: (1) threat of new entrants; (2) bargaining power of buyers; (3) bargaining power of suppliers; (4) threat of substitute products/services, and (5) rivalry among existing suppliers. From careful evaluation of these factors, a company can develop an effective marketing strategy.

Time horizons should be built into plans: the intervals involved will depend significantly on types of industry.

Four facets of marketing strategy (4-Ps) have been identified as: product, promotion, price and place (distribution).

Product/market matrix is useful in analysing market behaviour; four options are open: market penetration, market development, product development, and diversification.

Product (or brand) positioning refers to the place occupied by a particular product in a given market; this comparative evaluation should be based on research.

Product protfolio planning aims to spread risks and opportunities of profit across a balanced range of products and markets.

Pricing is a critical input to marketing strategy and should be interrelated with the other inputs, so that it contributes creatively to the total marketing effort.

Promotion — discussed further in Chapter 10 — is often badly handled in organisational markets: it deserves expert attention.

Selling and distribution — together forming the fourth element of overall marketing strategy — are significant factors for success. Selling in organisational markets is usually direct and often involves considerable technical knowledge and complex negotiation. Research-based information about customers' needs and buying behaviour is imperative.

The final stage of planning entails monitoring the tactical efficiencies of the marketing plan. Standards of performance (quotas, targets, etc.) should be devised. Professional marketing, as outlined in the first chapter, has three responsibilities: analysis, planning and control. All three functions demand attention.

REFERENCES

1. Jackson, K.F., *The Art of Solving Problems*, Heinemann, London, 1975.
2. Simmons, W.W., 'Practical Planning', *Long Range Planning*, Vol. 5, No. 2, June 1972.
3. Kotler, Philip, *Marketing Management: Analysis, Planning and Control*, Prentice-Hall, Englewood Cliffs, N.J., 1980.
4. Tilles, S., 'Making Strategy Explicit', in *Business Strategy*, Ansoff, H. Igor (ed.), Pelican, London 1972.
5. Fayol, Henri, *General and Industrial Administation*, Pitman, New York, 1949.
6. Drucker, Peter, F., 'Long-Range Planning: Challenge to Management Science', *Management Science*, Vol. 5, No. 3, April 1959.
7. Ansoff, H. Igor, *Corporate Strategy*, Penguin, Harmondsworth, 1968.
8. Perlmutter, Howard, 'The Tortuous Evolution of the Multinational Corporation', *Columbia Journal of World Business*, Vol. IV, January 1969.
9. Leontiades, Milton, 'The Importance of Integrating Marketing Planning with Corporate Planning', *Journal of Business Research*, Vol. 11, November/December 1983.
10. Davidson, J.H., Foreword to *Offensive Marketing or How to Make Your Competitors Followers*, Cassell, London, 1972.
11. Hill, Colin, 'Introduction to Planning and Forecasting', *Management Accounting*, Vol. 45, May 1967.
12. Drucker, Peter F., *The Practice of Management*, Heinemann, London, 1955.
13. Sevin, Charles H., *Marketing Productivity Analysis*, McGraw-Hill, New York, 1965.
14. Muir, Andrew, 'Planning the Product Range', in *Long Range Planning for Marketing and Diversification*, Taylor, Bernard and Wills, Gordon (eds), Bradford U.P./Crosby Lockwood, London, 1971.
15. Barnard, Chester, *Functions of the Executive*, Harvard U.P., Boston, 1938.
16. Leslie, Nicholas, 'The Open Society at BOC', Ensor, James, (ed.), *Financial Times*, 18 November 1975.
17. Blois, K.J., 'The Manufacturing/Marketing Orientation and its Information Needs', *European Journal of Marketing*, Vol. 14, No. 5/6, 1980.
18. Porter, M.E., *Competitive Strategy*, Macmillan, New York, 1980.
19. Battersby, Albert, *Sales Forecasting*, Pelican, London, 1971.
20. Jones, E.O. and Morrell, J.G., 'Environmental Forecasting in British Industry', *Journal of Management Studies*, Vol. 3, 1966.
21. Jay, Antony, *Management and Machiavelli*, Penguin, Harmondsworth, 1967.
22. Kotler, Philip and Singh, Ravi, 'Marketing Warfare in the 1980's', *Journal of Business Strategy*, Vol. 1, No. 3, 1981.
23. Hakansson, Hakan (ed.), *International Marketing and Purchasing of Industrial Goods*, Wiley, Chichester, 1982.
24. Ansoff, H. Igor, 'Strategies for Diversification', *Harvard Business Review*, Sept./Oct. 1957.
25. Levitt, Theodore, 'Ideas for Action', *Harvard Business Review*, Nov./Dec. 1974.
26. Atkin, B. and Skinner, R.N., *How British Industry Prices*, Industrial Market Research Co., London, 1975.
27. Buckner, Hugh, *How British Industry Buys*, Hutchinson, London, 1967.
28. Buzzell, Robert D., 'Is Vertical Integration profitable?', *Harvard Business Review*, Jan./Feb. 1983.
29. Levitt, Theodore, 'Marketing Myopia: Retrospective Commentary', *Harvard Business Review*, Sept./Oct. 1975.
30. *How British Industry Sells*, Industrial Market Research Co., London, 1976.

31. Simons, Gerhard, 'Developing a Product Market Strategy as Part of the Formal Corporate Planning Process – ITT', in *Long Range Planning for Marketing and Diversification*, Taylor, Bernard and Willis, Gordon (eds), Bradford U.P. in association with Crosby Lockwood, 1971.

Chapter Six
STRATEGIC PLANNING 2

In this second chapter on strategic planning, discussion will focus on specific features such as market segmentation, product life cycle analysis, and the marketing portfolio approach. These aspects of market planning are more popularly related to consumer product markets, but in organisational markets — public as well as private sector — these concepts also have useful applications.

MARKET SEGMENTATION STRATEGIES

Nearly every market can be divided into several submarkets which have significant characteristics affecting demand and supply. Often, the trend in the macro or global market is different from that observed in the micro or submarkets. The growth of specialised market segments has encouraged firms to make and supply goods and services which are closely related to the needs of particular kinds of customers. Instead of treating all customers the same, i.e. offering identical ranges of products and levels of service, objective market research enables groups or clusters of customers to be identified, whose needs can be more adequately met through specific marketing attention.

A business executive should 'stop thinking of his customers as part of some massively homogeneous market. He must start thinking of them as numerous small islands of distinctiveness, each of which requires its own unique strategies in product policy, in promotional strategy, in pricing, in distribution methods, and in direct-selling techniques'.[1]

Market segmentation, as Wendell R. Smith[2] noted in 1956, has a disaggregative affect because it recognises several demand schedules for the supply of particular commodities or services. These differential responses are the *raison d'etre* of market segmentation strategies.

Segmentation encourages the development of specialist firms which can cater for the needs of relatively small markets. Unlike the big manufacturer who has invested heavily in volume-production equipment designed to make a restricted range of products, enterprising small manufacturers can avoid headlong collision by concentrating on those sectors of the global market demand which are relatively insignificant to the large-scale producer.

In cases where a market is markedly fragmented, a new entrant, particularly if only limited resources are available, would be advised to focus on a relatively small segment. Kotler[3] terms this a 'niching strategy', and states that an ideal niche should have: (1) sufficient size to be potentially profitable; (2) growth potential; (3) opportunities for an entrant company to exercise its superior competences (refer to 'Leverage' in preceding chapter); and (4) customer goodwill. Other characteristics favouring 'niching' would be patents and a measure of channel control.

As a practical example of successful market 'niching', *Fortune* magazine[4] reported that for years 3M's strategy has been to avoid domination of a product market. Instead, they try to find 'crevices' that others have missed and fill them in. 'We're a nickels-and-dimes company. We don't have many big ticket items'.

Dynamic segmentation has resulted in the British transport undertaking, BRS,[5] growing in real terms despite the general fall off in demand for trucking in the UK. BRS have spearheaded their marketing efforts over the following closely-identified segments: rental (short term, from one day upwards); contract hire (customer's livery is used even though BRS may supply driver, maintenance, finance and even management for an entire fleet); haulage (now only 10% of BRS turnover); service (maintenance, rescue, etc.); and Transcard (charge card for transport operators). Selling and promotional efforts are specially tailored for these segments.

The fastest growing segment is contract hire, so BRS are focusing one-third of their total sales and marketing expenditure on advertising impact in promotional activities, and only two-thirds on its new sales force. This concentrated marketing expenditure is expected to have significant impact in an industry which has traditionally restricted its total marketing and sales costs to less than 5% of turnover.

Factors Affecting Feasibility of Market Segmentation

Four principal factors influence the opportunities for effectively segmenting markets: identification; measurability; accessibility and appropriateness.

The first factor — identification — is in the province of marketing research (see Chapters 4 and 5). As a result of objective enquiries, knowledge of market consumption behaviour should enable specific subsectors to be identified.

The second factor — measurability — relates to the estimation of subsector patterns of consumption. With some technical products, any accurate measurement of demand may be difficult because of the lack of specificity in published data. However, reasonable estimates may often be built up from systematic investigation.

The third factor — accessibility — refers to the ability of a company to direct its marketing efforts at a particular segment which may, for example, require special technical selling expertise.

The final factor — appropriateness — relates to the suitability of specific segments for an individual company's resources and overall objectives.

Bases for Market Segmentation

Various bases for segmenting markets have been adopted. In consumer markets, these have included socio-economic groupings, geographical location, personality characteristics, usage rate, brand loyalty, buying motives and attitudes, family life cycle, ethnic/religious influences, professional mobility, etc. Aspects of these diverse methods of analysing consumer buying behaviour are discussed in detail elsewhere.[6]

In organisational supplies and services, the policy of market segmentation may be related to factors such as customer size, location, industry classification, usage rate, nature of operations (commercial firm or public sector), etc.

An interesting example of effective market segmentation relates to the UK car market. A particularly vital sector of this market for UK producers concerns the demand for company cars which now represents 70% of new car registrations; in 1960 the figure was 20%.

Another instance of profitable segmentation is given by the UK paint industry which is dominated by a few relatively large firms, although many small and medium firms still exist. This concentration has increased over the past two decades or so: in 1963 there were 411 enterprises engaged in the manufacture of paint; by 1979 there were 327. Only seven companies employed 750 or more staff, yet they accounted for 64% of the gross output and 44% of total employment in the UK industry in 1979.

The UK market for paint can be segmented thus: decorative paints, used mainly on buildings, and industrial paints used in manufactured products. The former segment has various subsectors according to the types of paint which, while sharing common raw materials, differ significantly in their chemical make-up, related to specific market needs. In 1982, general industrial paint, by volume, represented 24%, automobile 14%, professional decorative 42% and DIY decorative 22% of total market sales in the UK. Four major manufacturers dominated the retail market in 1982: ICI (30% market share); Crown (18%); Berger (7%) and Macpherson (9%); the balance was taken by own label (15%) and 'other' (21%).

Demand for vehicle paints relates to automobile sales and to refinishing. Demand follows closely the levels of activity of the car and commercial vehicles markets.

General industrial paints have many applications; for example, coatings for drums and cans; aircraft finishes; rolling stock, etc. A specialised sector is concerned with marine coatings; these can again be divided into several subsectors, such as deck finishes, hull coatings, etc.

The paint industry could be clearly segmented, therefore, both by size of firm and by type of paint related to specific end-uses.

Segmentation by usage was also applied some years ago by the Massey Ferguson[7] group of companies to their earth-moving equipment.

Service markets can also be segmented, as is shown by an investigation[8] of the building society market which revealed that at the primary level, segmentation covered three distinct categories of people: (1) a building society's existing investors) (2) investors with accounts in other building societies, and (3) people who did not hold any building society investments. Within these primary segments, it was possible to identify a secondary stage of segmentation as follows:

1. 'Bankers' — People who use the building society more or less as a bank; these have relatively low average value accounts and also high rates of withdrawals to deposits.
2. 'Savers' — These represent an increasing number of more affluent customers who switch funds for differential gains; they tend to have larger accounts than the other categories, and relatively few transactions, either withdrawal or deposit.
3. 'Investors' — These represent an increasing number of more affluent customers who switch funds for differential gains; they tend to have larger accounts than the other categories, and relatively few transactions, either withdrawal or deposit.

In order to gain an 'even clearer picture', however, a tertiary segmentation is required.[8] This involves socio-economic analyses of the primary and secondary segments; for example, husband/wife role in savings and the selection of savings medium; decision criteria for savings; age and economic profile of key investor groups, etc.

Segmentation may also be applied to international marketing; one proposed method of analysing world markets classified countries according to their gross national product per capita. (Refer to Chapter 8.)

Segmentation of markets by industrial classification is quite widely used by marketing management. In Britain, the Standard Industrial Classification (SIC) forms the basic approach. (Refer to Chapter 4 for detailed discussion of this official system of industrial classification.)

A similar SIC of industrial activitiy in the US may also assist in specific market analyses and strategies (see Chapter 4).

Because of individual variations in classification, it is, unfortunately, difficult to make direct comparisons between the SICs of individual countries.

As noted in Chapter 4, analyses of industrial activities based on SICs need to be approached with care. Despite the limitations arising from some degree of arbitrary classification, the SICs provide useful bases for market analyses. Further analyses of UK SIC data may, in some cases, be available from the Business Statistics Office.

New market sectors may develop as a product matures; new uses may be found for the same basic material. For example, nylon was first used industrially as warp knits in 1945; by 1948 it had been adopted for tyre cords; it was used in textured yarns by 1955; and by 1959 it had extended to carpet yarns. Pharmaceutical compounds have tended to extend from being used in personal medical care to veterinary medicine.

Some manufacturers, such as those producing motor components or carpets, may segment their markets at the primary level according to the method of purchase, *viz.* derived demand customers (see Chapter 2), wholesale distributors, retail stockists, mail order business, etc. Further segmentation may occur because of customer size, location, or other significant variables.

But it should be remembered that the objective of market segmentation is not to complicate operations. The essence of an effective marketing segmentation strategy is that it should result in increased market penetration, more efficient use of corporate resources, and, at the same time, customers' needs should be more fully satisfied.

PRODUCT LIFE CYCLE (PLC)

The concept of product life cycle and innovation strategy are directly associated; products, in general, have limited lives during which they retain profit-earning capacity. The span of useful life varies considerably, according to the nature of products, the rate of technological developments, the nature of demand and marketing management decisions.

Despite its many critics, the PLC concept has much to contribute towards the development of effective marketing strategies. Basically, the PLC theory states that products tend to follow a pattern similar to biological development; from birth to growth, maturity, and then to eventual decline and death. This well known cycle of finite life is, therefore, applied to the study of the demand for specific types of products: the number of phases suggested by various researchers has ranged between four and six. In Figure 6.1, five phases are given to represent the generalised concept of product life stages.

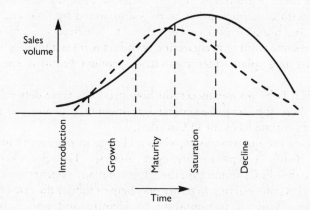

Figure 6.1   Generalised concept of product life cycle showing five sequential
                stages (Dotted line refers to general trend of unit profits).

The pattern of growth and development reflected by the curve in Figure 6.1 is, of course, only a *general* tendency; individual products will tend to have characteristic market profiles over time. The period of growth will vary — some products, particularly in fast-moving consumer markets such as pop records or fashion clothing, will experience volatile patterns of demand.

The length of profitable life as well as the duration of each stage of the demand curve will tend to vary significantly according to the types of products/services involved. Further, some markets are now experiencing more rapid change leading to product obsolescence, because of technological developments and the introduction of new competitive activities. Plastics, for example, have been widely adopted in furniture manufacture, encouraging the development of new moulded designs, upholstery coverings, etc.

Associated with the product life cycle concept is that of the profit cycle (refer to Figure 6.1, dotted line). It will be observed that the profit cycle of a product does not follow the same curve as the sales volume trend. No profit may be earned in the introductory stage because of high development and promotion costs. Unit profits will tend to attain their peak performance during the growth stage, until competition starts in earnest, when they may then start to decline, although total profits may still be rising because of rising sales volume. Eventually, in the later stages of the product life cycle, the declining volume of sales, increased costs and heavy competition are likely to cut deeply into profit margins and overall profit targets. In the final stage of product obsolescence and decline, profits may be entirely eliminated. (Refer to Chapter 5 — 'Marketing Audit'.)

The validity of the PLC and, in particular, the trend of the bell-shaped curve have been challenged by many researchers while, at the same time, enthusiastic supporters of the theory have promoted it as a powerful management tool. Intuitively, the concept has almost immediate appeal; rationally, it is more difficult to accept it without considerable qualification.

Of the several problems associated with PLC, that of product definition is one of the more formidable. Three levels of product identification in connection with consumer goods were distinguished by Polli and Cook[10]: class, form, and brand. Product class referred to substitutes that may be used to satisfy the same want (e.g. cigarettes); product form is a finer definition of product class (e.g. plain filter cigarettes); product brand is specific and unique.

Although it is by no means certain how products were defined in some researches, there appears to be general agreement that 'product form' offers the most appropriate basis for PLC studies.

Day[11] poses the question as to when a change in product is sufficiently distinct to justify a separate life cycle analysis. He cites examples to demonstrate that PLCs summarise the effects of many concurrent forces in a product market; those acting together may help or hinder the rate of product sales growth. While it is important to identify and understand these influences, they may not dictate an entirely new PLC.

What exactly constitutes a new product has proved a rather difficult hurdle for researchers to overcome satisfactorily. 'Newness' appears to be largely subjective and depends on customers' perceptions. Perhaps, as Rink and Swan[10] and others suggest, new products could be classified into several degrees of newness, and they offer the following four-way classification of new products: the unquestionably new product; the partially new product; the major product change; and the minor product change. (Also see Chapter 7 on categories of innovation.)

Another problem of the PLC concept is the difficulty of establishing the various stages of the life cycle, since these are, in practice, not clear cut at a particular time. Distinguishing, for example, between the introduction and growth stages seems to rest largely on marketing decisions which influence diffusion. 'Whether the growth process is slow or rapid is not determined by some absolute principle, but is partially dependent upon specific circumstances, the marketing strategy adopted and the resources allocated to the product'.[13] It is suggested that, in this case, the simple solution would be to merge the first and second stages into a single 'growth' stage. The elusive nature of the boundaries[11] between stages frequently mars the value of PLC as a reliable analytical tool.

A further problem of the PLC theory relates, as mentioned earlier, to the nature of the trend curve. While a considerable number of researches with consumer products (mostly food) have supported the existence of the classical bell-shaped curve, Cox's research[14] into ethical pharmaceuticals found that six different types of curve were necessary to explain sales trends. On the other hand, Cunningham[15] found that the sales of automobile components, chemicals and general engineering products in the UK usually followed the general PLC trend. However, research[16] focusing on about 100 industrial components marketed by a large mid-western manufacturer in the US to the heavy-duty truck and farm equipment industries over the period 1967–1973, revealed that three types of PLC curves appeared to exist: Type I related to products perceived to be highly innovative (see Chapter 7 on discontinuous innovations) — diffusion is fairly slow at first, indicating that a learning process is an important factor. Type II tend to conform to the more traditional PLC curve — growth is fairly rapid while decline is quite short (Robertson's dynamically continuous innovations in Chapter 7). Type III trend curve reflects very rapid growth followed by a long maturity phase which includes a decline prior to the eventual decline stage ('continuous innovations'). These curves are shown in Figure 6.2.

Projections from PLC historical data may also be problematical; for instance, what adjustments should be made where demand for some consumer durables and industrial materials may be particularly sensitive to economic conditions (as in derived demand — see Chapter 2). More sophisticated approaches than mere extrapolations are obviously imperative; the present state of knowledge suggests that caution and common sense would be advisable qualities when markets are exposed to many variables, some of which cannot be controlled.

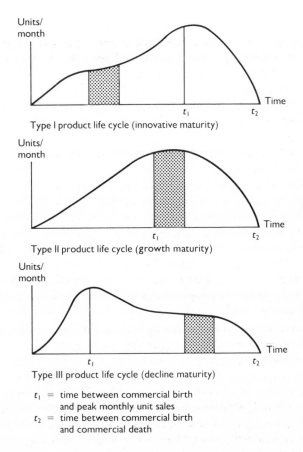

Type I product life cycle (innovative maturity)

Type II product life cycle (growth maturity)

Type III product life cycle (decline maturity)

t_1 = time between commercial birth and peak monthly unit sales
t_2 = time between commercial birth and commercial death

Figure 6.2 Three types of product life cycles for industrial components.

Source: See de Kluyver.[16] © 1977 by the Regents of the University of California. Reprinted by permission.

Using Life Cycle Creatively

Life cycle theory is particularly valuable in reminding management that innovation strategies are important to business survival and growth (see Chapter 7).

It is possible to extend the life cycle of a product by carefully planned improvements, as Rank Xerox did with their photocopying machines. Their policy of product improvement 'is really no more than the application of standard product life extension techniques ... [to] equipment whose basic design is now several years old'.[9]

Other methods of extending the profitable life of products could be; (1) new uses for the product; (2) extended use by existing customers; (3) increased consumption (in present use), by existing customers; (4) new customers. (See product/market matrix discussed in the preceding chapter.)

Although technical products, in general, do not have the volatility of consumer products, the concept of product life cycle should not be ignored. Sophisticated electronic control equipment, for instance, tends to experience rapid obsolescence. 'Not only are products maturing more rapidly, but product life cycles generally are growing shorter. For more than 15 years ... the DC-3 held its place as the leading commericial airliner. But the DC-7, and later the turbo-prop Electra, were obsoleted in less than five years by the pure jet DC-8, the 707 and others like them. Today's complex military weapons systems, unlike the weapons of World War II, are obsolete almost before they leave the drawing board ...'.[17]

In the textiles markets, natural fibres such as wool and cotton suffered a heavy setback when synthetic fibres were popularised. The decline in natural fibre clothing, for example, was partially halted by subsequent technical developments which resulted in satisfactory mixed fibres used, for example, in wool-mix and cotton-mix outerwear. New technology has, in fact, developed another product life cycle for these traditional products. Unfortunately, many textile companies underestimated the original challenge of synthetic fibres, and were unwilling to change their production and marketing policies. Inevitably, those which failed to respond to the new market needs, were either absorbed by more enterprising competitors or were forced out of business.

Product Life Cycle Analysis

Companies could make more effective marketing decisions if they analysed the performance of their products/services against the concept of the life cycle. This would enable them to plan a balanced product mix, and guide in the allocation of marketing efforts. Often, companies continue to spend heavily on promotion when the product featured is in the decline stage and should have been replaced by an improved model some time ago.

Marketing management has two fundamental tasks[17] related to product life cycle theory:

1. to reshape and control the life cycles of individual products/services
2. to improve corporate profitability by ensuring that products are at different stages of development so that the overall product mix is well balanced.

Life cycle management matches corporate objectives with the projected market performance of products.

The following *programme in life cycle analysis* (see Figure 6.3) has been proposed[17]:

1. *Develop trend data* over a period of time sufficiently long enough to indicate trends (perhaps 3–5 years). These data should cover unit and value sales, profit margins, total profit contribution, return on invested capital, market share and price.

Figure 6.3 Typical steps in product life cycle analysis.

Source: Based on Clifford.[22]

2. *Trace recent trends* in the number and nature of competitors; market shares of competitive products should be analysed and objective evaluations made of competitors' activities, such as distribution strategies, promotional policies, pricing policies, design, etc. These analyses should refer to specific market segments, as discussed earlier in this chapter.

3. *Analyse developments in short-term competitive strategies,* e.g. new products introduced; plans for expanded production; promotional plans announced.

4. *Develop, or update historical information on life cycles of similar or related products* as a guide to likely trend of particular products now under survey.

5. *Project sales for the product over the next 3–5 years, based on the data collected.*

6. *Estimate an incremental profit ratio for the product during each of the projected years' sales.* Incremental profit ratio refers to the ratio of total direct costs (manufacturing, advertising, product development, sales, etc.) to pre-tax profits. This is expressed as a ratio, e.g. 4.8 : 1 or 6.3 : 1 and measures the number of £s required to generate each additional £ of profit. The ratio improves (i.e. becomes lower) as the product enters its growth period; it begins to deteriorate (i.e. to rise) as the maturity stage is approached; and as obsolescence is reached, the ratio climbs more steeply.

7. *Estimate number of profitable years remaining in the product's life cycle.* On the basis of all the information available, allocate the product's position in its life cycle curve.

Developing Product Life Cycle Profiles

When the analytical processes outlined above have been applied to the various products which make up a company's product range, the next task of marketing management is to develop a life cycle profile of the total product line.

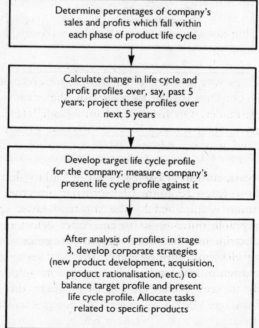

Figure 6.4   Typical steps in life cycle profile of total product line.

Source: Based on Clifford.[22]

The four stages involved in this analysis, given in Figure 6.4, are as follows:

1. *Determine percentage of company's sales and profits* which fall within each phase of product life cycle.
2. *Calculate change in life cycle and profit profiles* over, say, past 5 years; project these profiles over next 5 years.
3. *Develop target life cycle profile* for the company; measure company's present life cycle profile against it. This target profile will guide marketing strategies. Factors affecting it will be industry trends — rate of technological development and product innovation; the average length of product life cycles in the company's ranges; and corporate expansion and profitability objectives. If life cycles tend to be fairly short, clearly it will be necessary to have a high proportion of profitable products in the early stages of the sales curve.
4. *Develop corporate strategies* (new product programme, acquisition, product line rationalisation, etc.) to balance target profile and present life cycle profile. Allocate tasks related to specific products.

Relevance of Product Life Cycle Analysis to Organisational Marketing

As observed earlier, the concept of product life cycle has tended to be viewed as relevant to consumer products but to have limited, if any, validity for organisational marketing decisions. Obviously, theoretical concepts of this nature tend to deal in generalities and application of their principles inevitably calls for an appreciation of the characteristics of specific markets. That the profitability of industrial companies is affected by changes in market needs, technological invention and innovation, and factors such as high labour costs, etc., is clearly demonstrable. For instance, an electronics company whose products typically have limited life spans of about two years 'suddenly found itself within two products late in the growth phase, nine in the maturity or obsolescence phases — and none in introduction or early growth'.[17] Fortunately, the company realised its predicament in time, and managed to survive by a crash programme of rapid product development and through acquisition. A packaging company also found, through product life cycle analysis, that only 6% of current sales were represented by products in the growth stage, compared with 25% required in the target profile projected by the company planners. Two products were identified as obsolescent and were eliminated, reducing the total share of business represented by declining products from 15% to 11% — 'close to the 10% the target profile called for'.[17] At the same time, new product and acquisition programmes were given priority in the overall corporate strategy'.

Businesses of all kinds depend on an infusion of new products or services for corporate growth. Market strategies should be guided by the findings from analytical processes such as the product life cycle profile. New products should not be introduced indiscriminately; the total product range should be evaluated and related to marketing profitability and market share. (Refer to discussion in preceding chapter.) Otherwise, there is the danger that new products could merely end up competing with existing profitable products in a company's range while total market share is not expanded. Production and marketing costs will have been increased to no real corporate advantage.

MARKETING PORTFOLIO APPROACH

In the preceding chapter, a brief reference was made to product portfolio planning which, it was noted, derived from investment portfolio planning. Financial investment and product/market investment have much in common: both deal with finite resources that may be used in alternative ways to achieve agreed objectives. These goals may well vary over different types of investment and kinds of products/markets. Capital appreciation may be the guiding principle with a particular stock or share holding; market share growth may be the dominant factor in management decisions in a specific product market.

In both financial investment and product marketing, certain criteria will determine the objectives of management. These criteria will largely determine the overall nature of the resultant mix of investments or product markets.

Companies rarely make and sell just a single product to one market; the general tendency is to manufacture and market a range of products of various types and to offer them to a variety of markets. Complexity rather than simplicity characterises the majority of businesses; as a result, companies have to make key decisions related to the 'portfolio' of products and markets with which they are involved or plan to deal with. The objective is to attain an optimal mix of products and markets.

Factors to be considered will include the modification or deletion of existing products, the addition of new products, the allocation of marketing resources to develop new markets, the rationalisation of customer lists, etc. Unless marketing management evaluates its product and market activities as a *whole,* it is very likely that resources may be allocated in such ways that suboptimisations in performance occur. (See preceding chapter: marketing audit.)

Portfolio planning can be of particular help to diversified businesses with interests over several industries and markets. It can be used primarily as an analytical tool or, with greater benefit, extended to be a decisive factor in strategic management.

Steps in Portfolio Planning

The following stages in implementing portfolio planning can be usefully identified as:

1 Definition of SBU

Firms need to be redefined as strategic business units (SBUs); these may or may not coincide with operating units. The different businesses operated by a firm should be identified as economically distinct product/market segments; the resources used in these sectors should also be identified.

One of the difficulties of putting portfolio planning into practice is in definition of SBUs or product/market groups. To some extent, judgement appears to be involved. Linneman and Thomas[18] state that the key to successful portfolio planning is proper SBU definition, and they give the following guidelines in determining classifications of SBUs: (a) the SBU should be (or capable of becoming) a 'stand alone' business; (b) one manager should have accountability and control of the SBU's resources; (c) the SBU should have a distinct corporate role; (d) the SBU should have a clear market focus; (e) the SBU's businesses should be technologically related; (f) the SBU should be large enough to allow for scale and/or experience effects; (g) the SBU should make sense from a geographic standpoint.

As these authors[18] wisely observe, there must be a compromise between a too broad and a too narrow interpretation of an SBU. Fragmentation only results in an unwieldy and unmanageable number of SBUs. Aggregating business activities crudely may, on the other hand, be equally counter-productive: a cardinal principle of the SBU concept is to focus on strategies for discrete businesses.

2 Evaluation of each SBU against matrix criteria

The various product portfolio models (discussed on pp. 182–198) depend on a matrix or grid which basically classifies businesses by product/market attractiveness on one axis and by competitive position on the other. More sophisticated measurements are also associated with certain of these models, and rather ingenious descriptions are attached to individual cells of matrices.

The dimensions used in portfolio matrices can, for example, be based on market share and growth; or sector profitability and competitive position; or more complicated criteria such as brand (firm) and product category (industry) sales growth, market share and profitability.

Determination of valid and relevant criteria are clearly important if the portfolio analysis is to be useful to management. Whenever terms such as 'sales' are used, it is vital to define what is being measured; for instance, 'sales' could refer to the absolute level of a product's performance, to the rate of growth of those sales, to product *class* sales, to overall industry growth, to sales valued at current or constant prices, etc.

3 Development of SBU strategy

An effective marketing strategy is devised for each SBU, and progress is monitored regularly to ensure that corporate objectives are being achieved.

The three steps briefly outlined are by no means easy to ascend. While the theory of portfolio development is attractive, the more difficult task is to decide on the allocation of corporate resources that will result in an optimal, overall result. Like investment portfolio development, knowledge, insight, experience, judgement and luck seem to contribute towards success (or failure). Many factors lie outside the control of both the financial investor and the professional marketer: risk is usually related to the prospects of attractive rewards. According to Wind[19] it is more difficult to estimate the risk associated with most product portfolios than in the case of portfolios of securities. Also, 'whenever considering the product portfolio, the *sources of risk* (and their correlation) are also of considerable importance'.[19] He cites a product portfolio in which all products are subject to strong regulatory constraints as being generally less desirable than one with similar expected return but with diverse sources of risk (e.g. government and competitors).

Product Portfolio Models

At least four product portfolio models have been widely discussed and have attracted varying levels of support. These will now be described and compared.

Boston Consulting Group (BCG) Growth/Share Matrix
This popular matrix (see Figure 6.5) is based on the generation of cash flow as a measure of success and the allocation of cash to particular product groups.

Relative market share (cash generation)

Note: Circle area is proportional to size of business concerned, e.g. turnover or assets.

Figure 6.5   BCG portfolio model.

Source: See Hedley.[20] Reprinted by permission of Pergamon Press Ltd.

It uses market growth (vertical axis) and relative market share (horizontal axis) as the two definitive parameters. Relative market share measures individual market share relative to that of the largest competitor in a specific industry. Descriptive tags are attached to each sector of the matrix.

The 2 × 2 matrix in Figure 6.5 shows relative competitive positions plotted on a logarithmic scale 'in order to be consistent with the experience curve effect, which implies that profit margin or rate of cash generation differences between competitors will tend to be related to the *ratio* of their relative competitive positions (market shares)'.[20]

The experience curve effect, just mentioned, was noted by the Boston Consulting Group in research[21] into firms' activities over 1968–1970, and was studied over several countries. As a function of accumulated experience, a process of learning takes place over time. According to BCG, value added costs tend to decrease by 20–30% each time accumulated production doubles.

Enis[22] points out that BCG's experience analysis has two aspects: scale and learning. The first refers to the traditional concept of economies of scale which can result in lower costs per unit of production because fixed costs can be spread over more units. The second aspect of experience analysis is 'the fact that costs fall in a systematic relationship to cumulative production, i.e. the so-called learning curve'.[22]

As a firm gains experience over the various stages of developing, producing and marketing its products, many opportunities are presented for improving its performance, such as reducing costs, improving its technology, etc. These benefits accrue from experience, though clearly firms in an industry tend to exploit their opportunities differently. A successful company competing in a given market segment will, as a result of experience effectively applied, have lower costs and still sell at the going price; it should, therefore, be able to enjoy a higher profitability than its competitors. However, the contribution which experience can make to the profitability of a firm is governed by an important factor, *viz.* the transferability of such experience. In other words, where knowledge and technological skills are readily available in an industry, a new entrant may be able to outpace existing, experienced firms by rapidly acquiring and utilising these resources.

BCG Portfolio Strategy

Four principal strategies are related to the quadrants of the BCG matrix (see Figure 6.5).

1 Stars: high market share, high market growth
These products are market leaders and growing fast, but needing substantial amounts of cash to maintain their position. Eventually their rate of growth will slow down and they will become 'cash cows' and major earners supporting other SBUs. Star businesses 'are frequently roughly in balance on

net cash flow, and can be self-sustaining in growth terms'.[20] Sometimes, they may need heavy investment beyond their own cash generation potential and low margins may also be necessary at times to disengage competition. These products hold the company's future prosperity, so BCG advise an aggressive marketing strategy should be adopted.

2   Cash cows: high market share, low market growth

These products and businesses generate larger amounts of cash than are needed for their low growth market sector. They provide vital funds for investment elsewhere in the firm. Management should avoid expensive share-building activities, and carefully protect the profitability of these products.

3   Dogs: low market share, low market growth

Their poor competitive position results in poor profits, while, at the same time, they frequently demand cash in excess of what they can earn just to keep a competitive position. Hence these types of product are also known as 'cash traps'. Although their investment may be relatively low, there is little hope that they will earn satisfactory levels of profit.

4   Question marks/problem children: low market share, high market growth

These products and businesses demand a great deal of cash just to survive; they generate little themselves because of low market shares. Management has to decide whether to spend a lot more and build these products into leaders, or withdraw them from the market.

Wind[19] comments that companies may well find themselves with products or businesses in all four BCG categories, and so the portfolio concept calls for transfer of cash from cash cows to problem children, while the product or business flow is from problem children to stars and from stars to cash cows. These portfolio dynamics 'are based on the premise that high growth products require cash, while low growth products should provide cash'.[19]

Since discussion of the BCG portfolio approach involves market share as one of its parameters, a brief review of research into market share profitability would seem to be appropriate.

Profit Impact of Marketing Strategies (PIMS)

During 1973, the Marketing Science Institute and the Harvard Business School researched[23] the profitability of 57 major North American corporations involving 620 individual businesses for the three-year period 1970–1972. Their research focused 'primarily on RoI because this is the performance measure most often used in strategic planning'. It was recognised, however, that RoI results are often not entirely compatible between businesses because, for example, of variations between depreciation policies.

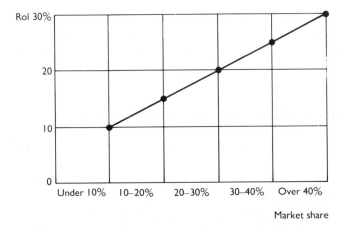

Figure 6.6   Relationship between market share and pre-tax RoI.

Source: Buzzell *et al.*[31]

The research findings were that a positive correlation existed between market share and RoI. (Refer to Figure 6.6.)

On average, it was found that 'a difference of 10% in market share is accompanied by a difference of about 5 points in pre-tax RoI'.

Explanations which were advanced for this included the impact of economies of scale, market power, and the quality of management. 'Specifically, as market share increases, a business is likely to have a higher profit margin, a declining purchase-to-sales ratio, a decline in marketing costs as a percentage of sales, higher quality and higher priced products'. Research data also showed that the advantages of large market shares are more significant for businesses which sell products that are 'purchased infrequently by a fragmented customer group'. (See Figure 6.7.)

Infrequently purchased products are generally durable, involve considerable expenditure, are frequently complex and often difficult for buyers to evaluate. (See discussion in Chapter 3 on the risk factor in buying.) Buyers may, therefore, be willing 'to pay a premium for assured quality'.

Frequently purchased products (typically bought at least once a month) tend to be of low unit value where the element of risk in buying from a relatively unknown supplier is not perceived to be great. This may encourage 'shopping-around'.

A strong relationship was established between companies which had strong competitive positions in their primary product markets and high profitability. These companies included IBM, Gillette, Eastman Kodak and Xerox, 'as well as smaller more specialised corporations like Dr Scholl and Hartz Mountain (pet foods and accessories)'.

Figure 6.7   Industry variations in market share/RoI relationship.

Source: See Buzzell *et al.*[23]

Why market share is profitable

The PIMS researchers advanced three 'possible reasons' why market share is profitable:

1. *Economies of scale* — In buying, manufacturing, marketing and other cost components. 'A business with 40% share of a given market is simply twice as big as one with 20% of the same market ...'.

   This statement reflects the experience curve which was discussed earlier.

2. *Market power* — Economies of scale, as many economists have postulated, may be less important than the actual bargaining power of large-scale enterprises. Powerful concentrated buying strengthens bargaining against suppliers. (See Chapter 2.)

   Size, as Drucker[21] has cogently argued, 'has a major impact on strategy, and strategy, in turn, has major impact on size'. While the simplicity and size of a small organisation enable it to respond with ability to opportunities, the larger organisation, because of its resources, is able to undertake, for example, long-term research projects or promotional schemes which are outside the scope of smaller companies.

3. *Quality of management* — It was suggested that the 'simplest of all explanations' accounting for the market share/profitability relationship lies in the quality of management which is generally characteristic of market leaders.

These three explanations are not mutually exclusive: PIMS stress the need to analyse and identify the relationship and impact of these variables on particular businesses.

Why do profit margins on sales increase so sharply with market share?
PIMS research discovered three significant factors influenced profitability related to market shares.

The biggest single difference in costs, as related to market share, referred to purchase-to-sales ratio. Research showed that for large-scale businesses (over 40% market share) purchases represent only 33% of sales, compared with 45% for businesses with market shares under 10%. Low purchases–sales ratio goes hand-in-hand with a high level of vertical integration. Although a greater extent of vertical integration 'ought to result in a rising level of manufacturing costs',[23] research did not show this, perhaps 'because, despite the increase in vertical integration, costs are offset by increased efficiency'.[23] But, in addition, economies of scale in buying may be effective. There was no evidence that large-scale firms charge higher prices, although it was admitted that the measures adopted were 'rather crude'.

The second contributory factor referred to the tendency, as market share increased, for the marketing costs-to-sales ratio to decline. Research indicated an average 2% saving in marketing costs to sales between the smallest and largest firms surveyed. This reflects the ability of larger undertakings to spread fixed marketing costs more widely, to use more efficient promotional media, and to adopt more effective selling tactics.

The third factor affecting profitability was observed to depend on the ability of market leaders 'to develop unique marketing strategies and to have higher prices for their higher quality products' than their smaller competitors. Market leaders tended to market 'significantly higher quality products and services' than those with lower market shares. They also spend considerably higher sums on R & D relative to sales (2.60% for market share under 10%; 3.55% for market share over 40%). Such firms as Eastman Kodak, IBM and Proctor and Gamble are typically market leaders whose marketing strategies are highly innovative.

PIMS researchers stressed that because of the strong relationship of market share to profitability, top management had the responsibility of establishing market share objectives.

The following broad groups of market share strategies were identified as:

1. building
2. holding
3. harvesting

to which Kotler[3] and others have added:

4. divesting

1. *Building strategies* are based on planned efforts to increase market share through new products and other systematic marketing schemes. Market-share building, as noted earlier, may be pursued in cases where the present market position and objective analysis of corporate resources suggest that potential for expansion exists. This aggressive share-building strategy, inevitably, carries risks which require expert evaluation.

Only about 20% of the businesses surveyed by PIMS enjoyed market-share gains of two points or more from 1970–1972; these successes were, as might be expected, mostly among new businesses.

Before launching an aggressive market share building strategy, PIMS propose that companies should be prepared to answer the following questions:

- Are there adequate financial resources?
- If the drive for market share is not successful, will the company remain viable?
- Will market targets be capable of being achieved within the constraints imposed, for example, monopoly?

2. *Holding strategies* are designed to maintain the existing market share held by a company: preserving the status quo. This cautious policy may be followed because further expansion of market share has been judged to be too costly. 'For established businesses in advanced economies — which is to say, for the majority of businesses in advanced economies — holding is undoubtedly the most common strategic goal with respect to market share'.

PIMS researchers acknowledged that because competitive conditions in markets vary so much, useful generalisations about methods of securing and maintaining profitable market shares are difficult to make. As observed earlier, however, some broad relationships were found to exist between RoI and competitive behaviour. Large market-share firms earn high rates of return when they charge premium prices — usually accompanied by premium quality. In addition, RoI is usually greater for large share businesses when they spend more than their major competitors on marketing and R & D. But for small-share firms, the most profitable holding strategy tends to be just the opposite: RoI is highest when prices are somewhat below the average of those charged by market leaders, and when marketing and R & D expenses are relatively low.

3. *Harvesting strategies* involve deliberate policies of allowing market shares to fall to secure higher short-term earnings and increased cash flows. This type of disinvestment decision is often dictated more by necessity than from strategic choice.

PIMS research reveals that only large firms are, in general, able to follow this strategy successfully. 'Market leaders enjoyed rates of return about ¾ point higher when they allowed market share to decline over 1970–1972'. It was not possible to measure definitively the profitability of harvesting, because in many cases market shares were reduced by intensified competition, rising costs, etc. Nevertheless, it is apparent that following a deliberate harvesting strategy 'affects profits diametrically differently from "building" ...'.

4. *Divesting strategies* are aimed at selling or liquidating the business because of other business opportunities offer prospects of better growth and profitability. In BCG matrix terms, this strategy might be applied to Dogs and Question marks/Problem children.

In addition to *divestment* or *harvest* strategies, Harrigan and Porter[25] propose that *leadership* and *niche* should be included among the strategies for decline, 'which vary greatly, not only in their goals but also in their implications for investment, and managers can pursue them individually or, in some cases, sequentially'.

Leadership strategy is followed by a firm which tries to reap above average profitability by remaining one of the few companies in a declining industry. Having obtained this position, the company will usually switch to a holding or controlled harvesting strategy. It is then, in theory, able to become more profitable (taking the investment into account) because it can exert more control over the process of decline. There are obvious risks attached to this policy.

Niche strategy in a declining industry involves identifying a segment that will either maintain stable demand or decay slowly, and which, at the same time, has market conditions allowing for high returns. A company choosing this exit strategy moves quickly and obtains a strong position in this segment and disinvests from other sectors.

It is reported[25] that the companies that are most objective about managing the decline process are also participants in the substitute industry: they view decline as a potential opportunity for profit.

Low market share strategies

The case for high market share has been so often emphasised that, as Woo and Cooper[26] assert, 'conventional wisdom has it that companies with low market shares are doomed to marginal profits, at best, while market share leaders show the best returns on investment'. If this view is accepted uncritically, the strategic alternatives facing those companies would seem to be either to fight hard and build up market shares or leave the market. However, it is contended that companies in industries with slow growth and few product changes, and those making frequently purchased products are among businesses that prosper with low market share. Likewise, low-share businesses that follow a specific focused competitive strategy, often emphasising quality and cost, appear to do best.

In 1978 Hammermesh and associates[27] researched three US companies which had low market shares: Burroughs Corporation, Crown Cork and Seal Co. Inc. and the Union Camp Corporation. All these earn 'quite respectable returns on their equity, have healthy profit margins and continue to maintain strong sales year after year'.[26] The only thing these companies had in common was low market share; their market environments were extremely different. But it was found that their strategies shared four characteristics: creative market segmentation, efficient use of R & D, strictly controlled growth: 'think small', and strong leadership.

Careful segmentation is vital for a low-share company which 'must compete in the segments where its own strengths will be most highly valued and where its large competitors will be most unlikely to compete'.[27] Crown Cork and Seal, for example, chose to concentrate on two product segments — metal cans for hard-to-hold products like beer and soft drinks, and aerosol cans. Because transport costs are a high proportion of total costs, Crown Cork built small, single-product plants near its customers instead of large and possible more efficient multi-product plants some distance away.

These two market segments have both shown disproportionate growth; they also need expert skills in container design and production. Crown Cork is also in a strong position because it is the largest supplier of filling equipment to the soft drink and brewing industries. Growth segments needing special expertise have resulted in profitable marketing opportunities for this low market share supplier.

An example of the efficient use of R & D is given by Union Camp, whose chairman declares that they do little basic research like Du Pont, but are good at improving processes, developing improved and some new products, and helping to build new manufacturing capabilities.

Burroughs' R & D is concentrated on 'truly innovative products'; its chairman is directly interested in this activity and 'exerts tremendous pressure on his engineers'.[27]

Low share companies also strictly control their expansion; Burroughs' growth is limited to 15% per annum. In the rapidly growing computer industry, where General Electric and RCA found the pursuit of market share too costly, Burroughs have been content with slowly gaining modest increases in market share.

Another important factor is that low-market share companies, unlike any of their larger competitors, are not, on the whole, diversified. If they diversify, they tend to enter closely related areas of business.

The final characteristic of these companies was the 'pervasive influence of the chief executive'.[27] For example, the chairman of Union Camp retains responsibility for sales and marketing.

Hammermesh[27] admits that low market share businesses face serious obstacles to success, such as small research budgets, few economies of scale in production, limited public and customer recognition and difficulties in attracting capital and ambitious employees. Also, previous research has indicated that, on average, the RoI in low share businesses is much less than in businesses with high market shares.

Extended research into low-market share firms was undertaken by Woo and Cooper,[26] who studied forty businesses taken from a total of 649 domestic manufacturing firms over the period 1972–1975. These low-share businesses were selected on the criteria of a pre-tax RoI of at least 20%, and market shares not exceeding 20% of the combined share of their three largest competitors. Because of the nature of the PIMS data base, from which these firms originated, most of them were divisions of large corporations, not 'free-standing' small businesses.

The findings of this research showed:

1. *Profitable low-market share businesses exist in low-growth markets* (the names of the companies and their industry segments could not be revealed, but the researchers were able to establish characteristics, as reflected by 13 different factors).
2. *Their products do not change often* — a stable market environment is the principal factor. 'Low market growth, infrequent product and process changes, high value added, and high purchase frequency all contribute to more predictable and less turbulent environments'.[26] Such markets are not likely to attract new entrants.
3. *Most products are standardised and few extra services are offered* — 'contrary to expectations, 72.5% of successful low-share performers competed in markets characterised by standard products'.
4. *Most make industrial components or supplies* — small businesses can forge strong links with their customers by understanding their needs in terms of performance, service and cost.
5. *More than half of the low-share businesses studied offered products and supplies that are frequently purchased,* and for which customers 'tend to rely more on experience and less on the brand name of market leaders for indications of reliability and performance'.[26] Such suppliers had comparatively low working capital ratios, because 'high purchase frequency, usually bends to faster turnover of inventory and receivables'[26]
6. *Over 80% of profitable low-share businesses studied were in industries with high value added products.* These industries are less prone to forward integration by suppliers or backward integration by customers. Also, many opportunities exist for product differentiation.

In summary, low-market share businesses that are well managed may well be profitable, provided they have carefully thought through their market opportunities related to their limited resources. Selective focus is the leading feature for a successful strategy: particular market segments are identified and customer needs closely studied — product quality, price and service are crucial factors. Strict control is kept over R & D and marketing costs and width of product line.

The various basic market-share strategies which have been reviewed do not offer ready-made solutions to specific marketing problems. Instead, they point to possible alternative ways of approaching particular market situations, after carefully evaluating the costs and benefits which accompany them. Companies may vary their market-share strategies in line with market opportunities, the level of competitive activities, and the general economic environment. From time to time, firms will probably find it necessary to modify their market posture; in today's business conditions a flexible policy may be advisable.

Critics of market share concept

The concept of market share is theorectically tidy and impressive, but it has attracted critics who point out that markets can be defined in many ways and the resultant market share measurements can be quite different. It is not always easy to measure a firm's market share, because information on a specific market is inadequate or unobtainable.

In other cases, as Majaro[28] points out, all the variables measured indicate a constant market share, as is distinctly observable in oligopolistic industries, such as cement, where a very small number of manufacturers dominate the market and where price leadership is strong.

Also, markets should be described in 'a marketing orientated way'; a high quality producer of, say, carpets, should not be directly compared in market share terms with a firm marking lower quality products. Like must be compared with like, otherwise market share analysis loses credibility; so precise definitions of markets are important before PIMS becomes really useful to a company in a specific industry and market sector.

Day[29] has noted that the influence of market share is most apparent with high value-added products, where there are significant barriers to entry and the competition consists of a few, large, diversified firms with the attendant large overheads, e.g. plastics, major appliances, automobiles, and semiconductors. However, even in these industries, there are factors that may distort market behaviour, such as:

1. a competitor with significant, patented technology
2. where the principal component of a product is supplied by a firm with inherent cost advantage because of an integrated process
3. acquisitions or licensing can result in access to significant experience (learning curve) or the benefit of lower costs through off-shore production or component sourcing
4. where profitability is highly sensitive to the rate of capacity utilisation, irrespective of size of plant.

In Day's[29] opinion, there are many situations where the relationship between profitability and market share is very tenuous. He states that there is, however, specific evidence from PIMS research that the value of market share is not as significant for consumer goods as for industrial products. 'The reasons are not well understood, but probably reflect differences in buying behaviour, the importance of product differentiation and the tendency for proliferation or marginally different brands in these categories'.[29]

As noted earlier, care is needed with definitions of the measures used in portfolio analysis, particularly where market share is concerned. How is the product-market or market sector defined? What level of geographic division is exercised? 'What is meaningful for a manufacturer of industrial equipment facing dominant local competition in each of the national markets in the EEC? Because the company is in each market it has a 5% share of the total EEC market, while the larger regional competitor has 9%. In this case the choice of a regional rather than national market definition was dictated by the *trend* to similarity of product requirements throughout the EEC and the consequent feasibility of a single manufacturing facility to serve several countries'.[29]

Market share at *any* price is likely to lead to corporate suicide. Sooner or later, the sales curve will flatten out, while profit contributions will reach a maximum and then start to deteriorate. Gains in market share will be at increasingly heavy costs, so that to grab at an extra percentage of the total market demand may not be justifiable in profit terms.

Strategies to increase market shares should, therefore, take note of *all* the factors which will influence profitable development. An efficient system of costing is clearly demanded or the chase after increasing market share may end in frustration. Most companies, as Sevin[30] has pointed out, are multi-product firms which lack sophisticated analytical techniques in determining and allocating marketing costs and net profit contributions. In real-life market conditions, the complexity of business operations, compounded by the lack of really adequate management information, renders it difficult, if not impossible, to indicate precisely the relationships between market share and profitability. It should be borne in mind that developing a market share entails a long-term investment in time and money and may well cut back profits in the immediate and middle future.

Market share analysis is concerned with establishing the relative size of a firm's business in comparison with its competitors in a given market segment. This approach is the logical step forward from market segmentation analysis which is the foundation of an effective marketing strategy. The profitable exploitation of market opportunities stems from objective market research and the identification of potentially valuable market segments which are relevant to the resources of a particular company. In these selected market sectors a firm should plan to secure effective market shares, carefully monitoring its overall progress and profitability.

The McKinsey/GE Business Assessment Array

The McKinsey/GE Business Assessment Array is a nine-cell portfolio matrix with the vertical axis representing 'industry attractiveness' (market dimension), and the horizontal axis representing 'business strength' (product dimension), of the strategic business unit. (See Figure 6.8.)

Industry attractiveness is based on rating of factors such as market growth rate, market size, profit margin, competitive intensity, cyclicality, seasonability and scale economies. According to applied weighting, a particular industry is classified as high, medium, or low in overall industry attractiveness.

Business strength or the ability to compete in a specific industry recognises that certain competences will be necessary; these following factors are weighted: relative market share, price competitiveness, product quality, knowledge of customer/market, sales effectiveness and geography.

Three 'zones' — known as green (go), amber (caution) and red (stop) — indicate respectively: 'invest and grow'; amber warning — maintain share rather than increase or decrease it; danger signal — harvest or divest.

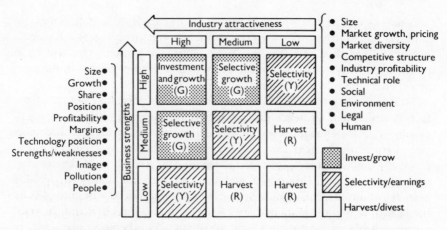

Figure 6.8   McKinsey/GE Business Screen.

This stop–caution–go screen would be helpful in guiding investment decisions and, obviously, requires regular review. Kotler[3] states that many companies first classify their business using the BCG approach and then go into greater detail with a GE screen.

AD Little Business Profile Matrix

The AD Little Business Profile Matrix has two basic dimensions: competitive position (vertical axis) and stage of industry maturity (horizontal axis). (See Figure 6.9.)

The four stages of 'industry maturity' follow a similar theme to the product life cycle stages. 'Competitive position' has five stages: weak, tentative, favourable, strong and dominant. Wind[19] points out that the data used are

		Stage of industry maturity			
		Embryonic	**Growth**	**Maturity**	**Ageing**
Competitive position	**Dominant**				
	Strong				
	Favourable				
	Tentative				
	Weak				

Figure 6.9   AD Little Business Profile Matrix.

primarily historical and, as with the BCG, the correlates of the dimensions are not explicit. It offers little advantage over the BCG, which it closely resembles.

The Shell International Directional Policy Matrix

The Shell International Directional Policy Matrix also has two basic dimensions: profitability prospects (horizontal axis); and competitive capabilities (vertical axis). (See Figure 6.10.)

The 'profitability' dimension has three classifications: unattractive, average and attractive. Profitability is determined by the market growth.

The 'competitive' dimension also has the same three classifications: it measures the relative competitive strength of the business or product. 'The prospects for a business can be evaluated for different scenarios and will establish a range of positions along the horizontal axis, the appraisal of its competitive ability will put it in a position along the vertical line. Between them, these assessments define a limited range of logical positions in the overall decision grid. These positions, in turn, can point to possible strategies for which more detailed study appears to be justified'.[31]

The strategy recommendations contained in the nine cells of the matrix and the categories of product are not dissimilar to the BCG approach.

Shell stress that whatever strategy is eventually selected, the aim is that it should be resilient, i.e. viable in a wide range of possible futures. Hence, each strategy ideally should be tested against all scenarios; the results in all of these should be acceptable — no disasters should result.

The Shell Portfolio of investments is analysed each year against the updated scenarios. 'The analysis tries to judge the mix of different businesses, the mix of countries, to examine where there are opportunities which one might be missing, when the business is unbalanced or vulnerable to risk, and what the internal strengths and weaknesses are'.[31]

Shell complete their analysis by a technique known as 'vulnerability analysis', developed from modern decision theory, and which is derived from the subjective, yet informed appraisal of a number of experts, whose estimates are quantified and the potential impact calculated.

		Prospects for sector profitability		
		Unattractive	Average	Attractive
Company's competitive capabilities	Weak	Disinvest	Phased withdrawal Custodial	Double or quit
	Average	Phased withdrawal	Custodial Growth	Try harder
	Strong	Cash generation	Growth Leader	Leader

Figure 6.10 The Shell International Directional Policy Matrix.

Source: See Seidl.[31] Reprinted with permission.

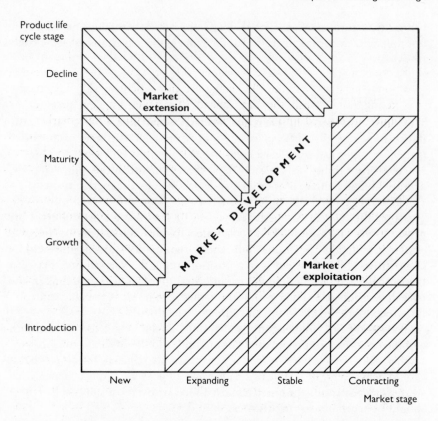

Figure 6.11   Product/market matching matrix.

Source: See Enis.[22] Reprinted by permission from *Business* Magazine.

In addition to the four basic product/market portfolio approaches, Wind[19] has developed a *model based on risk/return,* which is based on the two fundamental assumptions of portfolio analysis: expected return and degree of risk involved.

Other portfolio approaches have set the various stages of the product life cycle against stages of market development. For example, Enis[22] has designed a product/market matching matrix with four stages of the PLC on the vertical axis and four stages of market behaviour on the horizontal axis. (See Figure 6.11.)

It will be seen from Figure 6.11 that strategic guidance is given related to the nature of market development (new, expanding, stable and contracting) and the phase of product life (introduction, growth, maturity and decline). Also, there are three major areas of strategic activity: market development, market extension and market exploitation. As the result of various marketing-mix decisions, strategic decisions involving building, holding, or harvesting will be reflected in the relevant areas of the matrix.

Enis[22] observes that the traditional PLC discussion essentially assumes that PLC stage and market stage are synonymous. In this case, the position would be termed 'market development', and the trend indicated in Figure 6.11. However, marketers 'should consider the possibility that the market-development stage and the PLC stage are not synchronised'.[22] Aggressive marketing might push the PLC ahead of market stage; a product, for example, introduced into one market is brought into a new market, or a mature or even declining product is offered to an expanding or stable market. Enis instances the products of industrialised countries, such as chemical pesticides or jet aircraft, offered to developing countries. In such cases, 'market extension' occurs. (See Figure 6.11.)

Enis[22] says that a less admired but perhaps more common situation arises when a particular product lags behind the market stage. For example, a firm may introduce its brand of tyres, toothpaste, or turbine generators into markets already covered by competitors; this is referred to in Figure 6.11 as market exploitation.

Barksdale and Harris[13] have developed an integrated portfolio model incorporating the BCG and PLC approaches. (See Figure 6.12.)

These researchers[13] declare that the BCG matrix, as at present formulated, is incomplete for two reasons: it ignores products that are new to the world, and it overlooks products with negative rates of growth. 'In other words, the product portfolio matrix concentrates on the growth and maturity stages of the product life cycle'.

Following the practice of attaching names to identify products in different cells of the matrix, Barksdale and Harris[13] label pioneering products Infants, while products with high shares of declining markets are described as War Horses, and those with low shares of declining markets are called Dodos. (See Figures 6.12 and 6.13).

This 'extended hybrid model' recognises the importance of both the pioneering and decline stages of the PLC in strategic appraisals. The eight-cell matrix in Figure 6.12 is made up of the customary four BCG categories plus the new classifications mentioned above.

In a declining market, Cash Cows become War Horses; these successful veteran products still hold strong market positions and, if efficiently managed, can be significant cash generators. General Foods' Maxwell House Coffee is given as an excellent example of a War Horse. For years it has been a leading brand of instand coffee; although the market is declining, Maxwell House remains a viable successful brand.

Dodos are products with low shares of declining markets and offer little prospect of growth or cash generation; normally, they are removed from the product portfolio, but there are occasions when, as the result of competitors' withdrawal, it may be profitable for a firm to remain in a declining market. Nuclear reactors are given as an example of this type of product. The US market is rapidly declining because of government regulations, public opinion and accelerating costs.

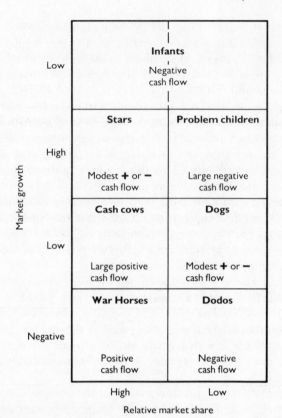

Figure 6.12   Product life cycle portfolio matrix.

Source: See Barksdale and Harris.[13] Reprinted by permission of Pegamon Press Ltd.

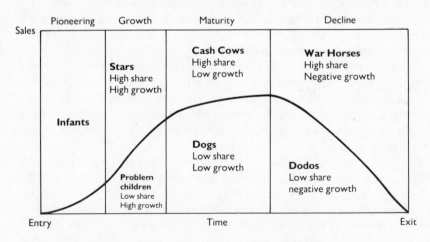

Figure 6.13   Combined PLC/product porfolio concepts.

Source: See Barksdale and Harris.[13] Reprinted by permission of Pergamon Press Ltd.

Infants are innovative products that must be marketed expertly. They do not generate profits for some time if, indeed, ever; meanwhile they consume large amounts of cash. The British Post Office electronic home information system, Prestel, is a typical example of this type of pioneering market activity.

Barksdale and Harris[13] admit that their expanded matrix does not overcome the problems involved in defining products and markets, or eliminate the ambiguity encountered in defining rates of growth. But their approach does offer, it is claimed, a stronger and more comprehensive framework for strategic decision making.

A further interesting and creative approach to product/market analysis is given by Campbell and Cunningham[32] who conducted a two-year study involving 63 customers of a leading company in the packaging industry. Data covering 167 trading relationships in ten market segments were collected. The analyses involved three stages: (1) a life cycle classification of customer relationships; only customers for one product or relatively homogeneous product group should be entered in the same analysis chart. Separate analyses are necessary where several different products are involved (see Figure 6.14).

Criteria for classification of customers	Customer categories			
	Tomorrow's customers	Today's special customer	Today's regular customers	Yesterday's customers
Sales volume	Low	High	Average	Low
Use of strategic resources*	High	High	Average	Low
Age of relationship	New	Old	Average	Old
Supplier's share of customer's purchases	Low	High	Average	Low
Profitability of customer to supplier	Low	High	Average	Low

   * The technical, marketing and production resources devoted to developing future business rather than maintaining existing business

Figure 6.14 Life cycle classification of customer relationships.

Source: See Campbell and Cunningham.[32] Reprinted by permission of John Wiley & Sons, Ltd.

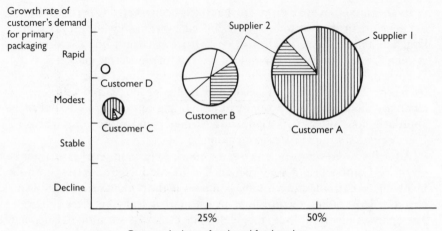

Figure 6.15   Customer/competitor analysis.

Source: See Campbell and Cunningham.[32] Reprinted by permission of John Wiley & Sons, Ltd.

(2) A customer/competitor chart which allows management to evaluate its competitive position in each market segment (see Figure 6.15). Separate charts should be prepared for different products. Examination of competitors' trading activities should be useful in designing effective strategies. (3) Key customers are identified and the most important ones are individually analysed. These are then grouped into a customer portfolio similar to the growth/share matrix (see Figure 6.16). The horizontal axis refers to the competitive position of the supplier company; the vertical axis relates to the growth rate of the customer's market. 'Competitive position is measured by the share the supplier holds of the customer's purchases relative to the share held by the largest competitor'.[33] Examination of Figure 6.16 reveals, for instance, that the company has one key customer in cell 4 whose market is growing steadily and where the company's share of purchases is relatively high. But there are some less optimistic business situations, such as cell 3, which require further investigation.

In cases where a very large customer represents a high proportion of sales, a more detailed breakdown splits the customer into a 'series of subcustomers'. As Figure 6.17 shows, the largest customer is made up of four separate businesses; these have been classified along the horizontal axis using the same categories as Figure 6.14. On the vertical axis, the growth rate of purchases has the same dimensions as in Figure 6.16. Analysis of Figure 6.17 shows that there is a small but developing business for product 1; a slow growing but specialised business for product 2; a large and steadily developing business for product 3; while product 4 experiences a slightly declining demand.

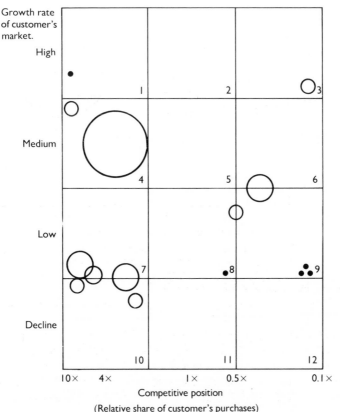

Competitive position
(Relative share of customer's purchases)

Note: Size of circles represents sales volume to each customer.

Figure 6.16   Key customers portfolio.

Source: See Campbell and Cunningham.[32] Reprinted by permission of John Wiley & Sons, Ltd.

This three-stage customer analysis applied to a specific industrial market sequentially refines and focuses the market evaluation. It adapts the well known marketing concepts of PLC, segmentation and portfolio analysis.

Portfolio frameworks are intended to supplement, not supplant, managerial judgement. They should be used sensitively and with an understanding of their limitations. Wind[33] and others have warned against viewing portfolio analyses, 'despite their attractiveness, as a ready cure for any ailment ... If a prescription ignores any relevant dimensions or the projected position of the business under alternative scenarios, it will be quite misleading'.

The four principal portfolio models that have been discussed are based on a matrix, one axis of which represents the relative market share or similar characteristic of a firm's strength, while the other axis relates to industry or market attractiveness. Some of these models use composite dimensions (e.g. McKinsey/GE) consisting of several objective and subjective factors to

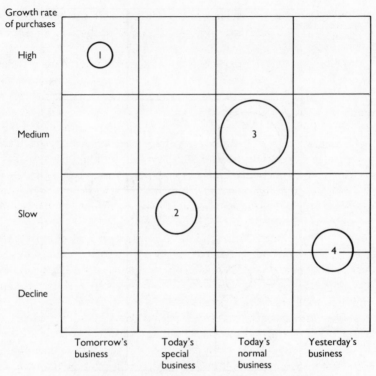

Note: Size of circles' represents the volume of customer's purchases. Numbers refer to the different products of the supplier company sold to the customer.

Figure 6.17   Analysis of a key customer.

Source: See Campbell and Cunningham. Reprinted by permission of John Wiley & Sons, Ltd.

describe each axis. Others, like the BCG, have a single measurable criterion for each axis. Because managerial judgement largely forms the basis for the inclusion of many factors in composite dimensions attached to portfolio analyses, considerable care is needed in interpreting the resultant information. Before portfolio dimensions are imposed, a company's trading environment and resources should be thoroughly studied. As Wind[33] suggests, a tailor-made approach may be desirable.

HBR Survey of Portfolio Planning

In 1979, a survey[34] of *Fortune's* '1000' companies was sponsored by the *Harvard Business Review* to evaluate strategic portfolio planning practices. It was found that portfolio models help managers to strengthen their planning processes and solve the problems of managing diversified industrial organisations. However, it was also found that the secret to success was not just in the analytical techniques that make up portfolio planning theory, but was to be found in meeting the administrative challenges of incorporating the theory into management practice.

The more serious limitations of portfolio planning were identified as: (1) portfolio planning takes a great deal of time and companies 'often get stuck'[34] trying to implement it; (2) if portfolio planning is regarded merely as an analytical planning tool, a company will fail to reap benefits; (3) in implementing portfolio planning, companies often focus on inappropriate factors, e.g. cost efficiency instead of organisational responsiveness; and (4) portfolio planning seems unable to 'successfully address the issue of new business generation'.

Despite the above difficulties, corporate managers supported portfolio planning largely because the approach: (1) promotes significant improvements in the quality of both business and corporate strategies; (2) results in selective allocation of resources; (3) provides a framework for adapting overall planning to needs of each business; and (4) greatly increases companies' strategic control.

In most companies, portfolio planning is 'triggered by a performance crisis and the need to allocate resources selectively in a capital-constrained environment'.[34] In major companies, the theory has been rapidly accepted as a useful management tool, although a great deal of 'ill focused' debate has been centred around the analytical techniques — which grid to use — and not enough attention has been given to the core issue of how a company can best 'define an SBU and assign a strategic mission to it'.[34]

In 1979, 36% of Fortune's '1000' and 45% of Fortune's '500' industrial companies had introduced portfolio planning to some extent, and each year during the last five years, another twenty-five to thrity firms used this approach.

According to the survey, 70% of all organisations commenced portfolio planning by comprehensively re-examining the definition of each of their businesses. 'In 75% of these, the re-evaluation led to the classification of SBUs as sometimes or usually different from operating units. The larger the company, the more likely it is to have SBUs that do not coincide with operating units'.[34] However, the resultant SBUs are usually aggregations of existing operating units or segment of single units.

Some of the companies surveyed were found to have reached the process portfolio planning stage very quickly: others had many attempts without success.

Portfolio planning 'is here to stay', because it can provide these critical benefits to management: (1) the generation of good strategies because of analysis of competitive activities; (2) promotion of more selective resource allocation trade-offs; and (3) the major contribution is the management process. 'The essence of managing diversity is the creation in each business, its competitive position and its strategic mission'.

Finally, portfolio planning should not be left as 'an elegant theory'; it must be implemented, and the findings of this survey indicate that this is widely happening.

SUMMARY

Specific features of strategic market planning are: market segmentation, product life cycle analysis, and marketing portfolio approach.

Market segmentation recognises that nearly every main market can be divided into several micro- or submarkets, according to certain characteristics of demand and supply. Effective segmentation is influenced by four factors: (1) identification; (2) measurability; (3) accessibility and (4) appropriateness.

Organisational markets may be segmented by customer size, location, industry classification, usage rate, nature of operation, etc.

Product life cycle theory and innovative strategy are closely linked. Despite many critics, PLC has much to contribute: it emphasises that products have limited lives in which to earn profits. More than one PLC curve may be evident in certain markets. Marketing strategies should use PLC analytically and creatively by developing PLC profiles of the various products in their product ranges, and plan, in good time, for 'new blood' products.

Marketing portfolio analysis, as noted in the preceding chapter, is critical to ensure that a balanced range of products and markets is achieved. Portfolio planning entails identification of strategic business units (SBUs). Four popular portfolio models have been developed: Boston Consulting Group (BCG); McKinsey/GE; AD Little, and Shell.

Four broad groups of market share strategies are: building, holding, harvesting and divesting.

Low market shares may be profitable in certain cases; expert handling is needed to ensure profitability.

Barksdale and Harris developed an integrated PLC/portfolio matrix.

Portfolio frameworks supplement managerial judgement: they do not supplant it. Before portfolio dimensions are imposed, thorough study of a firm's trading environment and resources must be done.

REFERENCES

1. Levitt, Theodore, *Marketing for Business Growth*, McGraw-Hill, New York, 1974.
2. Smith, Wendell R., 'Product Differentiation and Market Segmentation as Alternative Marketing Strategies', *Journal of Marketing*, Vol. XXI, July 1956.
3. Kotler, Philip, *Marketing Management: Analysis, Planning and Control*, Prentice-Hall, Englewood Cliff, NJ, 1980.
4. Smith, Lee, 'The Lures and Limits of Innovation', *Fortune*, 20 October 1980.
5. Price, Roy, 'How BRS Segments its Markets', *Industrial Marketing Digest*, Vol. 9, No. 1, 1984.
6. Chisnall, Peter M., *Marketing — A Behavioural Analysis*, 2nd edn, McGraw-Hill, Maidenhead, 1985.
7. Huston, John, 'Expansion into an Allied Market — Massey Ferguson', *Long Range Planning*, Vol. 2, No. 3, 1970.

8. Doyle, Peter and Newbould, Gerald D., 'Advertising Management for Building Societies', *Advertising Quarterly*, No. 42, Winter 1974/5.
9. Hughes, Michael, 'Increasing Penetration in Industrial Markets', in *Long Range Planning for Marketing and Diversification*, Taylor, Bernard and Wills, Gordon (eds), Bradford University Press/Crosby Lockwood, 1971.
10. Polli, Rolando and Cook, Victor, 'Validity of the Product Life Cycle', *Journal of Business*, Vol. 42, No. 4, 1969.
11. Day, George S., 'The Product Life Cycle: Analysis and Applications Issues', *Journal of Marketing*, No. 45, Fall 1981.
12. Rink, David R. and Swan, John E., 'Product Life Cycle Research: A Literature Review', *Journal of Business Research*, Vol. 7, No. 3, 1979.
13. Barksdale, Hiram C. and Harris, Clyde E. Jnr, 'Portfolio Analysis and the Product Life Cycle', *Long Range Planning*, Vol. 15, No. 6, 1982.
14. Cox, E.W., 'Product Life Cycles as Marketing Models', *Journal of Business*, October 1967.
15. Cunningham, M.T., 'The Application of Product Life Cycles to Corporate Strategy: Some Research Findings', *Marketing*, Spring 1969.
16. De Kluyver, Cornelius A., 'Innovation and Industrial Product Life Cycles', *California Management Review*, Vol. XX, No. 1, 1977.
17. Clifford, Donald K. Jnr., 'Managing the Product Life Cycle', *European Business*, July 1969.
18. Linneman, Robert E. and Thomas, Michael J., 'A Commonsense Approach to Portfolio Planning', *Long Range Planning*, Vol. 15, No. 2, 1982.
19. Wind, Yoram J., *Product Policy: Concepts, Methods and Strategy*, Addison-Wesley, Reading, Mass., 1982.
20. Hedley, Barry, 'Strategy and the "Business Portfolio"', *Long Range Planning*, Vol. 10, No. 1, 1977.
21. Boston Consulting Group, *Perspectives on Experience*, Boston, US, 1972.
22. Enis, Ben M., GE, PIMS, BCG and the PLC, *Business* Vol. 30, No. 3, 1980.
23. Buzzell, Robert D., Bradley, T. Gate and Sutton, Ralph GM, 'Market Share — A Key to Profitability', *Harvard Business Review*, Jan./Feb. 1975.
24. Drucker, Peter F., *Management: Tasks, Responsibilities, Practices*, Harper and Row, New York, 1974.
25. Harrigan, Kathryn Rudic and Porter, Michael E., 'End-Game Strategies for Declining Industries', *Harvard Business Review*, July/Aug. 1983.
26. Woo, Carolyn Y. and Cooper, Arnold C., 'The Surprising Case for Low Market Share', *Harvard Business Review*, Nov./Dec. 1982.
27. Hammermesh, R.G., Anderson, M.J. Jnr. and Harris, J.E., 'Strategies for Low Market Share Businesses', *Harvard Business Review*, May/June 1978.
28. Majaro, Simon, 'Market Share: Deception or Diagnosis?', *Marketing*, March 1977.
29. Day, George S., 'Diagnosing the Product Portfolio', *Journal of Marketing*, Vol. 41, No. 2, 1977.
30. Sevin, Charles H., *Marketing Productivity Analysis*, McGraw-Hill, New York, 1965.
31. Seidl, RL, 'How Useful is Corporate Planning Today?', Corporate Finance Conference, 10 October 1979, Shell Group Planning Division, Shell International Petroleum Co.
32. Campbell, NCG and Cunningham, MT, 'Customer Analysis for Strategy Development in Industrial Markets', *Strategic Management Journal*, Vol. 4, Oct./Dec. 1983.
33. Wind, Yoram and Mahajan, Vijay, 'Designing Products and Business Portfolios', *Harvard Business Review*, Vol. 59, No. 1, 1981.
34. Haspeslagh, Philippe, 'Portfolio Planning: Uses and Limits', *Harvard Business Review*, Jan/Feb. 1982.

Chapter Seven
INNOVATION STRATEGY

Successful innovation is one of the most challenging problems facing business management, and marketing in particular. Innovation is not just one action; it is a complex process of interrelated actions requiring expert integration and control. Many contributions are made to a successful programme of innovation related to products or services. These inputs originate from research and development, production, personnel services, purchasing and financial areas of management which, allied to the marketing function, take an organisation along the road to a profitable innovation. The interface relationships of marketing were reviewed in the opening chapter of this book. To succeed in innovation, communications and close working arrangements between the various functional management areas are essential. Innovation is risky enough without its problems being magnified by internal misunderstandings and inefficiencies. Ingenious ideas are not enough in themselves to generate new life in an organisation; they need to be translated into products and services that will be sought after because of the benefits conferred on people who adopt them. The management of innovation cannot be shirked; without effective team work even a stimulating concept can result in commercial disaster.

RELATIONSHIP BETWEEN INNOVATION AND INVENTION

The theoretical distinction between innovation and invention has been discussed by various leading management writers. Schumpeter[1] regarded the process of innovation as quite distinct from that of invention. He maintained that invention could exist either independently of, or combined with, innovation. In his view, although most innovations can be traced to some conquest in the realm of either theoretical or practical knowledge that has occurred in the immediate or the remote past, there are many which cannot. It is possible to innovate 'without anything we should identify as invention, and invention does not necessarily enhance innovation, but produces of itself ... no economically relevant effect at all ...'

Mansfield[2] applied the term 'innovation' to applied invention, and stated that economists have traditionally argued that an invention has little or no economic significance until it is applied commercially. He felt that successful innovation lay in exploiting fully an invention. To Rogers[3] innovation was 'an idea perceived as new by the individual. It really matters little so far as human behaviour is concerned, whether or not an idea is "objectively" new as measured by the amount of time elapsed since its first use or discovery. It is the newness of the idea to the individual that determines his reactions to it'.

The Report of the Central Advisory Council for Science and Technology (1968),[4] while acknowledging that technological innovation could be variously defined, confined its use in the Report to denote generally 'the technical, industrial and commercial steps which lead to the marketing of new manufactured products and to the commercial use of new technical processes and equipment. At one extreme, innovation can imply simply investment in new manufacturing equipment or any technical measures to improve methods of production; at the other it might mean the whole sequence of scientific research, market research, invention, development, design, tooling, first productions and marketing of a new product'.

Project Sappho[5], the study of industrial innovation conducted at the University of Sussex, qualified innovation as 'a complex sequence of events, involving scientific research as well as technological development, management, production and selling'. Like the Central Advisory Council Report, Sappho researchers viewed innovation as involving 'the commercial application of previous inventive work and experimental development'.

Peter Carl Goldmark,[6] a Hungarian physicist who worked for CBS, had over 150 inventions to his credit, including the first practical long-playing record. He believed that too much basic technology went begging for want of someone to take the step towards innovation: an inventive idea without development is quite useless.

To summarise, innovation depends on invention, but invention needs to be harnessed to commercial activities before it can contribute to the growth of an organisation. Innovation may involve fundamentally new inventions, for example, those based on the petro-chemicals and electronic industries, or it could refer to improvements in existing methods of manufacture which result in new versions of existing products. The commercial objectives, however, are likely to be the same: increased profitability through improved market share, expanded market opportunities, greater competitive advantages, etc.

PRAGMATIC APPROACH OF EARLY INDUSTRIAL INNOVATION

Many of the historic innovations in Britain's textile, pottery and metal industries sprang, however, from the outstanding inventive genius of individuals, like Hargreaves, Arkwright, Trevithick, Maudslay and Spode. Through their forceful personalities, these industrial pioneers — some of whom had limited theoretical knowledge — finally won acceptance for their revolutionary new methods of production. Their successes depended less on formal scientific education than on persistent experimentation in practical working conditions. For example, Goodyear, who was successful in the vulcanisation of rubber, had no pretensions to chemical knowledge and found that chemists, who had failed to rid rubber of its stickiness, were unable to help him in his persistent efforts. However, as Jewkes[7] observed, he was encouraged by reflecting that what is hidden and unknown and cannot be discovered by scientific research, will most likely be discovered accidentally, if at all, through sheer persistent effort. This he did with so much success that the US Commissioner of Patents wrote in his report of 1858 that Goodyear had made himself so much a master of rubber that nothing escaped his attention.

Good fortune appears to influence research success from time to time: serendipity (a term originated in 1754 by Horace Walpole in his fairytale 'Three Princes of Serendip' who 'were always making discoveries, by accident or sagacity, of things they were not in quest of') has accounted for some remarkable scientific and technological discoveries, e.g. the discovery of penicillin, floating soap and aniline dyes. The latter were discovered in 1856 by W.H. Perkin when a student at the Royal College of Chemistry. He experimented with compounds discovered by Faraday and Hoffman and in trying to synthesise quinine, discovered mauve, the first aniline dye.

Thus fortuitous invention, as Jewkes[7] notes, seems almost the rule in chemistry, but rarely occurs in mechanical engineering. A chemist might well accidentally come upon some new and surprising property in a known compound. But it seems most unlikely that an engineer grouping together 'pieces of metal with one idea in mind ... discovers that he has stumbled upon a device of a kind that he had not been seeking'.

Invention, as Burns and Stalker[8] have observed in their penetrating analysis of the problems of managing innovation, 'was seen as the product of genius, wayward, uncontrollable, often amateurish; or if not of genius, then of accident and sudden inspiration ... In nineteenth century Britain the archetypal formula for the process of innovation was enshrined in the fantasy of Watt and the kettle'.

Indeed, as some American researchers[6] have vividly commented: 'A common conception of the inventor ... is that of a solitary drudge, perhaps a bit gone in the head, toiling away in a basement workshop. Living on dreams and borrowed capital, he produces gadgets of dubious worth and is fondly tolerated by society as a harmless and even entertaining aberration ... Like most stereotypes, this one has a grain of truth in it. The world of invention does have its eccentrics, its seekers after perpetual motion, antigravity, death rays, and the like ... But you will also meet inventors who don't remotely fit the mould.'

The originators of some of today's popular products are often surprising: Gillette was originally a travelling salesman in corks; the joint inventors of Kodachrome were musicians; Carlson, the inventor of Xerography, was a patent lawyer, and the automatic dialling system was invented by Almon B. Strowger, a Kansas City undertaker.

When industry was still largely craft-based and men and their masters worked closely together, this unorganised approach to invention and innovation seemed to be sufficient. Even then, business opportunities were not always seized. 'Swan, a chemist, made experimental incandescent lamps in 1860 which employed the same high-resistance conductor, carbonised paper, as was used in the first commercial lamps marketed twenty years later ... it was Edison who ... first developed the lamp and formed an independent concern to manufacture it'.[8]

The apathy of industrial firms towards new product concepts has been critically noted[7]: RCA resisted Armstrong's ideas of frequency modulation; the Sulzer loom was offered to and rejected by the leading European textile manufacturers; the established aircraft companies did not think that the retractable undercarriage had any future; in 1925 the Marconi Company told Baird that they had no interest at all in television, and the invention of the gyro compass failed to receive the backing of the navigational equipment manufacturers.

ORGANISATIONAL CONSTRAINTS ON INNOVATION

The institutional environment of modern industry and commerce has tended to impose new constraints on innovative strategies. The haphazard though often successful pursuit of new technologies and their derived products can no longer be tolerated, particularly when the survival and growth of large corporate undertakings are at stake.

In an economic and social environment which has changed, and is still changing radically, product and service innovation is an increasingly important competitive strategy. Technological obsolescence has taken its toll of many products, and the pace of competition has shortened lead time and the resulting pay-off period. Data[9] on five hundred innovations in major industrialised countries over the period 1953–1973, and across a broad spectrum of industry, show that 13% of these products had to be withdrawn from the market and less than two-thirds of these significant innovations achieved financial profitability. Only 46% of these products generated repeat business; 42% became standard products. It was found that, with the exception of the UK, these innovations were also helpful in attracting new customers (53%) and in penetrating new markets.

Innovation strategies clearly contain a strong degree of risk; this may be compounded of financial, physical, social, or psychological elements. Pressure of competition, the expectations of customers and society in general, and corporate growth spur entrepreneurial activities. The Institute of Mechanical Engineers[10] have noted that major factors detracting from a higher rate of innovation in the UK are: (1) lack of enterprise and motivation among senior management; (2) lack of appreciation of marketing techniques in middle and lower engineering management; (3) shortage of production engineers; (4) shortage of skilled workers. This strongly pragmatic view is reflected in this quotation from their report: 'Good design is characterised by simplicity, and innovation must not be confused with complication. The prime requirements in the product are quality, reliability and delivery on time. These considerations should take precedence over advanced products ... There is no lack in British industry of novel ideas, but industry does lack the environment and encouragement needed for their successful application'.

INDUSTRIAL GROWTH RELIES ON INNOVATION

With characteristic directness, Drucker[11] reminds management that innovation is a slow process. Many companies owe their present-day leadership to the 'activity of a generation that went to its reward twenty-five or so years ago. Many companies that are unknown to the public will be leaders in their industry tomorrow because of their innovations today'. The successful company, says Drucker, is in constant danger of reclining in smugness, living off the accumulated innovative activities of an earlier generation.

Products which are today commonplace were unknown[12] at the onset of this century: aeroplanes, radio and television equipment; navigational aids; radar; diesel engines for road, rail and sea transport; fork-lift trucks; gas turbines; combine harvesters; synthetic fibres; silicones; antibiotics; synthetic detergents; fluorescent lamps; radioactive isotopes for industrial use; electronic computers and other electronic devices, etc.

Mansfield,[2] in his notable investigations into technological innovation, observed that successful innovators in steel and petroleum grew more rapidly in the 5–10 year period after innovation occurred than the other firms of comparable initial size. The average growth rate was often more than twice that of the others: 'the average effect of a successful innovation was to raise a firm's annual growth rate by 4–13%, depending on the time interval and the industry'. As may be expected, the impact of a successful innovation on the growth of a small firm was much greater than on a large firm.

In industries such as electronics, new product opportunities have been exploited by successful companies which, like Philips, have grown consistently over a long period of time. But the dynamic technology which characterises these markets has meant that products are brought to maturity at a fast and ever-quickening rate. The rapid technological growth resulted from the two World Wars was developed even further by the 'race to the moon'. In its meteoric progress, the electronics industry has been responsible for a profusion of inventions starting with the unsophisticated radio sets of the early 1900s, then to radar detection systems and mirco-waves; to television, transistorised equipment, guided missiles, as well as electronic computers.

This breathless pace of innovation has had far-reaching effects in industrial, medical and social life. Perhaps that miniscule product, the transistor, has done more to revolutionise communications than any other single product of the past three decades. Invented in 1947 and commercially applied four years later, the transistor ousted the vacuum tube and resulted in more reliable and compact computers, televisions and radio. This advance was followed in 1961 by the first integrated circuit which was developed very rapidly; in 1965 one chip could accommodate ten transistors; fifteen years later the number of transistors on one chip had grown to the astronomic figure of 100,000. Today, many thousands of transistors, resistors and diodes can be put on to one miniscule, low-cost chip.

One of the world's largest makers of chips for Teletext (Ceefax, Oracle, etc.) — the Mullard subsidiary of Philips — has reflected on the dynamic nature of its industry: 'We're now involved in the bulk manufacture of something which is very clever, only it has to be in extremely high volume production — millions of chips a year. Development is so rapid that we have had to devise a new way of coordinating the various engineering functions. There has to be much closer coordination between the various specialists in design, development and production. It costs a minimum of £3–4 million to set up a production facility and its expected life-span is only four years. For such levels of risk, professional management skills are imperative'.[13]

This remorseless pressure on innovation and profit making is also evident in 3M's corporate plans which, as discussed in *Fortune*,[14] stipulate that 25% of sales must be derived from products that did not exist five years before. Each of 3M's ten divisions is expected to hit this ambitious target.

LEADERS AND FOLLOWERS

Strategic change in many industries, as Ansoff[15] has emphasised, is so rapid that firms must continually survey their markets in search of new opportunities. 'For firms which have no provisions for response to strategic challenges and which refuse to anticipate it, the awareness of the problem usually comes through a traumatic experience, such as a drastic drop in sales or earnings, a product breakthrough by competition, a continued failure to meet profit objectives or a "sweep of the new broom" triggered by change in top management'.

Firms, according to Ansoff,[15] may be classified as either reactors, planners, or entrepreneurs. 'Reactors' wait for problems to occur before trying to solve them; 'planners' attempt to anticipate problems; and 'entrepreneurs' deliberately anticipate both problems and opportunites. This latter and more enterprising type of management does not wait for a specific trigger but is constantly researching for strategic market opportunities so that profitable growth can be maintained. Mature industries appear to have an innate resistance to new technology and to the challenge and change it may bring with it. Often there appears to be an almost insuperable barrier of resistance and even hostility, which may at last be overcome by the persistence and apparent market success of innovating firms. Finally, and almost reluctantly, the majority of firms in such industries adopt the role of followers.

DIFFUSION OF INNOVATION

One of the astonishing things[16] about earlier innovations and the patterns of diffusion has been the extent of the gap which has sometimes extended between knowledge and action, between invention and innovation, between innovation as 'best practice' technique and the diffusion of innovation to become 'representative' technique. Coke and smelted iron, Mathias notes,[16] had a time lag between innovation and diffusion from 1709 to 1760 and later.

Mansfield's[2] researches into the diffusion of new industrial products led him to observe that the speed with which a particular firm adopted a new technique appeared to be directly related to the firm's size and the potential profitability it offered. In general, there appeared to be a definite 'bandwagon' or 'contagion' effect which influenced the spread of a new process or product through an industry. Perceived risk was reduced as more firms used the innovation, while the fact that a large proportion of a firm's competitors had now adopted it also significantly influenced individual decisions. (Also see Chapters 2 and 3.) However, Mansfield warned against the facile assumption that particular firms are consistently leaders or followers. 'According to our findings, there is a very good chance that these firms will be relatively slow to introduce the next innovation that comes along'.[2]

Ozanne and Churchill's study[17] of the industrial adoption process was based on the five stages of adoption outlined by Rogers[3], viz. awareness, interest, evaluation, trial and adoption/rejection. They surveyed 90 'decision makers' in 39 mid-western US industrial firms about the adoption of a new automatic machine tool ($35,000–$70,000) which, although not radically innovative, had certain readily observable improvements. Respondents were analysed across several criteria.

Five factors affecting adoption of an industrial innovation were identified: (1) activating factors — 'changes in a company's external or internal environment that may set in motion the industrial adoption process'; (2) purchase-directing factors — 'factors which influenced choice of a particular supplier of an innovation'; (3) duration of the industrial adoption process; (4) alternatives considered; (5) use of information.

The researchers concluded that the industrial adoption process is extremely complicated and far more complex than in individual buying behaviour.

Webster[18] has also emphasised that the communication and diffusion processes of industrial innovation are 'somewhat different' from consumer markets 'because of the unique features of industrial markets' (see extended discussion on the complexity of organisational buying behaviour in Chapters 2 and 3).

The acceptance and diffusion of some novel and technically advanced products may be impeded unless marketers ensure that potential customers receive adequate 'education' in the uses and technical features of such innovations. This task may be shared between a firm's technical design staff and marketing management.

Research[19] into the diffusion of new capital equipment focused on the British flour milling industry in a survey reported in 1972. 'This industry was chosen because it had undergone very many changes over the years and was the first industry to adopt any form of automation, when in 1785 the industry introduced the first fully integrated handling and processing scheme'. This receptivity to technological change had continued to characterise the flour milling industry which was also comparatively compact: 'the entire flour output of the UK and Eire is manufactured by approximately 140 mills covering a wide range of capacities'. Hence, low cost research was feasible.

Following a series of unstructured interviews, five innovations were selected as representing significant technological improvements in flour milling: pneumatic conveying; bulk flour outloading bins; bulk flour silos; short surface milling system; and reverse jet filter dust collector.

During the research study, the initial introduction of an innovation was checked by reference to the machine record books in the various companies surveyed. The sample was stratified according to ownership, *viz.:* 'group' mills and independent mills.

Table 7.1 UK flour milling industry's adoption of selected technological innovations

Innovation	Number of years taken to adopt innovations by 25% and 50% of sample					
	Group mills		Independent mills		Total mills	
	25%	50%	25%	50%	25%	50%
Pneumatics	12	–	12	18	12	19
Bulk outloading	8	16	11	15	9	15
Flour silo	6	16	15	20	11	16
Short surface	12	–	11	12	11	–
Reverse jet filter	4	7	6	9	4	8

Source: See Allen and Hayward.[19]

From Table 7.1 it will be observed that pneumatic conveying and short surface milling systems diffused through the independent mills at a faster rate than in the group mills. The researchers suggested that this quicker pace may be due to the urgent need of independent millers to adopt new processes which will ensure their survival. On the other hand, bulk flour outloading and bulk flour silos have been more readily adopted by the group mills, presumably because these innovations are connected with economies of scale and involve substantial capital outlays which they can sustain. The reversed jet filter also diffused more rapidly through the group mills, aided perhaps by production trials which could be arranged conveniently in one mill of a group.

The number of innovations adopted by each mill was surveyed, and it will be seen from Table 7.2 that the independent mills led in adoption of all five innovations. Smaller capacity mills clearly lagged in utilising innovative methods pf production.

Table 7.2 UK flour milling industry's adoption of five selected innovations

No. of innovations	Group mills adopted	Independent mills	Total mills
0 ⎱ Laggards	2	5	7[*]
1 ⎰	5	6[*]	11
2 ⎱ Medians	13	10	23
3 ⎰	21	6	27
4 ⎱ Innovators	9	10	19
5 ⎰	8	16	24
Total	58	53	111

[*] Up to 15 sacks capacity.

Source: See Allen and Hayward.[19]

The rate of diffusion of new technological ideas within an industry such as flour milling is affected, therefore, by the structure of the industry and by the level of competition within it. Processes of adoption are also likely to be accelerated by the simplified decision making of smaller companies, the management of which are probably more keenly aware of the pressing need to be responsive to production and marketing innovations.

MULTI-COUNTRY RESEARCH ON DIFFUSION

The National Institute of Economic and Social Research has studied[20] the diffusion of new technologies across several industrial companies. In 1982, the latest research covered six technologies: the basic oxygen process which, in the 1970s, became the dominant method of steel making; continuous casting; tunnel kilns for use in brick production; shuttleless looms in the cotton-type weaving industry; the float process of manufacturing flat glass; and numerically controlled machine tools.

Of the six technologies studied, the two steel technologies, as well as float glass, were characterised as 'revolutionary' and have changed entirely the respective manufacturing processes. While the tunnel kiln was a significant step in brick making, it did not have the same kind of fundamental effect which was observed in the three 'revolutionary' innovations.

An important factor in the diffusion of these innovations related to the opportunity of trying them out on a limited basis, i.e. divisibility. The four technologies based on steel, glass and brick manufacture are intrinsically indivisible and involve widespread changes in production techniques, so diffusion has been at a different rate from shuttleless looms and numerically controlled machine tools which, because of their divisibility, and consequent lower risk in trial and adoption, had not resulted in major industrial changes. Small scale trials can be undertaken without heavy investment and fundamental restructuring of manufacturing processes.

During this research, the validity of the belief that diffusion followed an S-curve was studied, and it was reported that 'the figures do not provide much concrete evidence for the exclusive validity of any very regular S-curves, but they definitely support the rational expectation of *some kind* of an S-curve'. Slopes were observed to be different for each technology, and the turning points in growth also differed. The researchers advised caution in the use of an S-curve assumption and proposed that 'an equally good, indeed better, representation is that the *whole* wave of the technology, from birth through maximum use to death, might follow the bell shape of a normal distribution curve, although the right-hand side of the curve may fall more steeply'.

Major innovations take a long time to diffuse: the basic oxygen process of steel-making took nearly twenty years to reach saturation level. However, in the same time period, continuous casting and tunnel kilns had achieved only 50% diffusion.

Cheaper technologies require even longer periods of diffusion: then adoption is not a question of survival to the same extent as the more capital-intensive, 'revolutionary' innovations. Hence, non-adoption generally carries a lower risk to the firms involved; their investment costs are relatively modest, trial does not entail wide-scale disruption, and replacement machines can gradually be introduced, alongside the existing older plant.

The process of technological advance is inherently dynamic: the barriers of today may be swept away by radical innovations, such as electronic technology which has had far-reaching effects in electro-mechanical product markets.

BEHAVIOURAL FACTORS INFLUENCE INNOVATION

Detailed discussion of the behavioural factors which influence the diffusion of innovations has been given in another text[21] which is particularly concerned with the psychological and sociological aspects of marketing. In marketing or organisational supplies and services, management would benefit from acquiring an understanding of the non-economic factors that affect buying behaviour. Adoption of innovations is not confined to commercial goods or services, so management in the public sector involved, perhaps, in health, education, or other social services should also base their strategies on an appreciation of the fundamentals of human behaviour which considerably influence decisions to try innovatory products or services. Myths, fears and fables often inhibit the adoption of new ideas, as an attitude study which was concerned with the fluoridation of water revealed some years ago in the United States. 'Some people voted against it for a variety of bizarre reasons which they had persuaded themselves were facts. Fluoridation was said to be "rat poison", to cause hardening of the arteries, premature ageing, loss of memory and nymphomania; it also ruined batteries, radiators and lawns'.[8]

Diffusion, as an American researcher[22] has noted, is a complex social phenomenon involving both economic and non-economic factors. The latter cannot be ignored if successful marketing is to be the outcome of, perhaps, years of research and development. Mansfield[2] has proposed that economic variables may, in fact, be 'less important than the more elusive and essentially non-economic factors, such as the personality attributes, interest, training and other features of top and middle management, which will play a deciding role in determining how quickly a firm introduces an innovation'.

A practical example of the need to take note of non-economic factors to ensure acceptance and diffusion of new technologies and products was experienced by ICI[23], which designed a laser detector to give early warning of any escape of inflammable or toxic gases from process plants. This sophisticated device was mounted in a tower, forty metres from the ground, and continuously swept an area a little larger than a football pitch with its beams. ICI reported that not the least of the problems they encountered was to convince plant operators that they could pass safely through the laser beams, as well as assuring safety officers that there was no danger of the lasers igniting a leak of gas.

Those who are the first to adopt new products or services deserve the special interest of marketing management. Cultural, social and psychological factors may not always be immediately apparent, but they may, nevertheless, exercise very profound influences on buying preferences.

CATEGORIES OF INNOVATIONS

The nature of innovations was briefly referred to earlier; some methods of classifying innovations will now be considered. Difficulties immediately arise in defining what is meant by innovation and its related prior activity, invention. 'We speak of the development of some revolutionary idea, such as the jet engine or the Wankel rotary piston engine, meaning the building of one machine which established the fact that results can be obtained by the new principle. At the other extreme we speak of the development of a new aircraft design, which of itself embodies no radical innovation, meaning the systematic testing and modifying in numerous minor ways of the design to satisfy standards of performance and safety for the special conditions which the aircraft will encounter, and between the extremes, of course, there are to be found innumerable intermediate conditions'.[7]

Radical, earth-shattering innovations are rather rare events: the Polaroid camera or the Xerox dry-copying process are unique examples of inventive genius linked with shrewd marketing policies. Generally, however, inventive advance and technological change are built up from a number of small, incremental improvements. These do not usually attract the headlines, but the contribution to commercial success of many of these modest innovations may be substantial. The managing director of Philips Electrical Ltd has commented 'innovations are a continuing occurrence in our everyday business life — and they are mostly minor in nature ... all these changes are ongoing, and they are vital to the continued success of one business. Each minor innovation may have only a minor impact on its own, but if we put these innovations together over time, they are very important for an industry and for the position of an individual company within it'.[24]

The vital contribution of what may be termed 'sequential innovation' is supported by several researchers and writers, including Mathias[16] who notes that every major innovation is developed not only on basic advances by the famous but also on innumerable smaller developments made by the unknown. Also, the distinction between new products and product enhancements is often so small that it is rare for something entirely new to be developed without the idea, at least, originating in some earlier product. It has been noted[25] that even the pocket calculators of almost a generation ago. However, microtechnology has radically transformed the product, so that it bears little resemblance to its forebears.

Profit-earning products sometimes originate from an idea picked up almost at random, developed and improved, and then expertly marketed.

In his fascinating study of industrial innovation, *Langrish*[26] *produced four models of the innovation process* based on the linear sequence of events which 'most writers on innovation have either clearly stated or implicitly assumed'. These start either with a discovery or, at the other extreme, with some kind of need that requires to be satisfied. Langrish identified within each of these two subdivisions two types of model:

1. *Discovery push*
    (a) 'science discovers, technology applies' model
    (b) 'technological discovery' model, e.g. Pilkington's float glass process

2. *Need pull*
    (a) 'customer need' model — this may emanate from the direct request of a customer or result from systematic marketing research
    (b) 'management by objective' model, e.g. the need to lower manufacturing costs may encourage research into new and more economic processes

Langrish's research, based on a sample of 51 innovations, established that an average of three new ideas was necessary for each innovation. However, in some fields, such as high magnetic solenoid superconductors, the number was actually very much higher: 18. According to Ferrari[27], successful technical innovation is almost always the result of a synthesis between interpretation of market requirements ('market pull') and recognition of technical possibilities ('technology push').

However, Langrish confessed the difficulty he and his associates experienced in fitting innovations which had attracted the Queen's Award into any one of these models in 'a clear and unambiguous manner'.[26]

Major innovations, in the view of Philips Electrical[24], 'arise more from technological push than consumer pull'. There is the danger that such innovations may result in systems or products that have no easily developed market.

Philips emphasise that companies must avoid situations where R & D develop products without reference to marketing feasibility. This can be achieved only by developing strong links between R & D, production and marketing. Successful innovation is essentially a team job. (See Chapter 1: Interface Relationships of Management.)

In Stonier's view[28], market pull 'is being displaced by "technology push": there has been a shift from empirical knowledge (often derived from developing technology) leading science to theoretical science shaping technology. Advances in chemistry lead to the synthesis of new compounds in search of a use. Solid-state physics sets the stage for the transistor which then evolves into the microprocessor. The "miracle chip" looks for new markets. In 1971, the first pocket calculator, costing \$240, appeared in the US. Before the end of the decade, pocket calculators jumped across the Atlantic so that in Britain on average each household possessed one'.[28]

Another researcher, Rothwell,[29] has typified innovations as along a continuum: at one end are *evolutionary* innovations which are incremental in nature; at the opposite end are *revolutionary* innovations which are radical in their culture and impact. In his research which focused on the textile machinery market, Rothwell concluded that while the short-term prosperity of textile machinery companies can often be assured through 'product improvement' innovation (evolutionary), in most markets more radical innovation (revolutionary) has been necessary to ensure firms' long-term survival.

Myers and Marquis's[30] report of factors affecting technological innovation in the US over the period 1963–1967, classified innovations in manufacturing firms as *either defensive or offensive*.

Defensive innovation is aimed to preserve market share and the present rate of corporate growth. 'It may be in response to competition, or to changes in market demands for quality, reliability, design, safety, etc., or to price erosion of its products or to increased costs of materials, or labour, or to changes in government regulatory actions and tariffs'. Offensive innovation is a deliberate policy of opening up new markets or enlarging existing markets by a planned series of new products/services.

It is likely, of course, that individual companies may be engaged in a mix of innovation strategies across particular markets.

Another method[31] of categorising 'fundamental innovations' is as follows: (1) characteristic — these give rise to new socio-economic activities or industries, and (2) generic — these not only lay the basis of new socio-economic activities but also cut across several new and old industries. For example, 'both the catalytic cracking process and internal combustion engine were fundamental technical breakthroughs but the former was a characteristic innovation, whereas the latter was generic'. Although these types of innovation clearly overlap, they are, neverthess, conceptually distinct. What distinguishes them is the magnitude of the ripple effect; generic innovations tend to have more of a global effect while characteristic ones are more local in their effects. Generic innovations give rise to a cluster of interrelated innovations, e.g. steam power led to numerous other innovations.

A further classification[32] of innovations places them in three basic groups: continuous, dynamically continuous, and discontinuous.

1. A continuous innovation involves merely the modification of a product rather than the dramatic introduction of a totally new product. As noted earlier, incremental improvements form a very considerable part of innovation strategies. These products are so similar to existing products that consumers' behaviour does not need to be changed if these new products are to be adopted.

2. A dynamically continuous innovation involves more disruption than the first category, although not fundamentally changing established patterns of behaviour.

3. A discontinuous innovation refers to new products which have led to significant changes in ways of living and production processes: radio and television, long playing records, ballpoint pens, the jet engine, synthetic fibres, stainless steel, antibiotics, tungsten carbide tools, photo typesetting, etc.

These types of product innovation result in significant alterations in consumers' behaviour as and when adopted; they diffuse slowly because their use generally requires changes in values and habits, e.g. dehydrated foods were relatively slow in becoming widely accepted because of original concern about their nutritional value.

It may be possible to collate these basic groups of innovations with Langrish's models. Pilkington's float-glass process, for instance, would probably fall into the category of a 'discontinuous' innovation; Langrish classified this particular product as related to 'discovery push' and as a 'technological discovery'. Stainless steel would also follow this pattern of classification.

In this category of innovation, high risk appears to be inevitable. Float-glass, an invention which has been commercially exploited with great success, experienced several crises in its development. The first production plant, set up in May 1957, 'continued to turn out nothing but unsatisfactory glass for a period of 14 months'.[7] Pilkington persisted, and in July 1958, 'the first square foot of good glass was produced'.[7] Even then, difficulties were not at an end, and it was only after many more months of intensive work and enormous investment, that the float-glass process became commercially viable.

Jewkes[9] makes the salient point that the basic concept of floating molten glass over molten tin had, in fact, been patented in the early 1900s, but it had never been exploited. Commercialisation waited for a company with substantial resources, whose top management were willing to take high risks in the belief that market opportunities were now waiting to be seized.

Another example[23] of astute commercialisation of invention relates to Alfred Nobel who was not only a successful inventor but also an astute businessman. In 1863 he improved on Sobrero's invention of nitro-glycerine so that it could be detonated in a controlled way by means of a percussion cap. Later inventions led to dynamite and gelignite. Nobel perceived that lucrative industrial applications were ready for exploration in blasting for railways, roads, bridges, etc., in the rapidly developing industrial countries. He took out foreign patents and established manufacturing operations which, in time, spread over five continents. To finance and manage this vast enterprise, he developed effective local partners. In essence, Nobel founded the first multinational, industrial business, and skilfully controlled the risks of developing new markets.

Entrepreneurial spirit was also displayed when the decision to market the Xerox 914 copier was taken. When this innovatory machine was first planned, Xerox invited 'the three most reputable consulting firms to make separate independent studies as to marked opportunities and potential'.[33] Two consultants advised against marketing it; the third saw some vague chance of success but limited market potential of about 8000 placements being achieved in about six years. Xerox's president and his associates refused to accept these dismal projections, because the forecasts took very little note of a consumer learning curve: that 'people would learn to want copies of written materials once quality copies became easily available'.[33] With this latent demand in mind, Xerox boldly launched the 914 copier in 1961; within three years over 80,000 units were marketed.

The dry-process photocopying method, as noted earlier, was originated by Chester Carlson, a patent laywer, whose ingenuity and persistence eventually resulted in the process which Xerox were able to develop so spectacularly. But Carlson's path to success was not easy; for three years he researched his ideas at the New York Technical Library until, in 1937, he filed his first patent. Production was delayed until 1946, when a small company, the Haloid Corporation (later to be known as Xerox) decided to commercialise the revolutionary process.

Marketing of new products frequently calls for imagination as is illustrated by the way in which General Motors overcame the American railways' reluctance to replace their steam locomotives by the newly developed diesel locomotives. These had been designed and produced in anticipation of a potential demand but without any guaranteed sales.

By lending a diesel locomotive to a railroad for use in its switching yard, the manufacturers eventually obtained widespread use for long distance trains.

New inventions offer industry new opportunities to develop, but, inevitably, there has to be a time for assimilation so that the resultant innovations can be turned into profit making products. This critical problem was cogently described by the chairman of Bayer AG, the third largest (by sales turnover) of Germany's chemical companies: 'It is true that thirty years ago there was a lot of innovation in some areas, such as fibres. In order to produce new fibres, new dyestuffs, new plastic materials, new machines were needed. New materials in one field cause innovation in other fields. But after a time, innovation halts. You have to digest what you have. It is possible at that stage for the smaller companies and, when your patents run out, companies in other countries, to start manufacturing the same products without the burden of research and development and other overhead costs ... Then the only solution is more innovation. This is more difficult each time because of the ever-increasing costs of research. But it is absolutely necessary'.[34]

MODEL OF TECHNOLOGICAL INNOVATION

The process of technological innovation has been formalised by Myers and Marquis[30] as a series of stages, although they, in common with other leading researchers, have stressed that the linear sequence shown in Figure 7.1 will not always occur.

The starting point for successful innovations recognises the interaction of market demand and the technical resources available at a particular time. The nature of demand requires to be identified as either existing or potential; the latter category may call for considerable effort in promoting a new method of production. 'The idea for an innovation consists of the fusion of a recognised demand and a recognised technical feasibility into a design concept ... If a technical advance alone is considered, it may or may not result in a solution for which there will be a demand'. Levitt[33] has argued 'Ideation is relatively abundant. It is implementation that is scarce'. Ideas, no matter how brilliant, must be brought down to earth and considered within the environmental constraints in which a company has to develop its marketing strategy. The design concept is, therefore, the point from which, having identified certain market needs, there should follow an intensive process of problem solving. This critical stage of innovation will, no doubt, unearth many problems and may even result in abandonment of the proposal. Information will be needed,

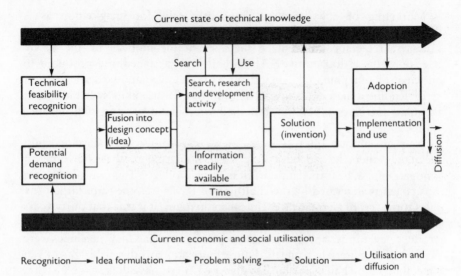

Figure 7.1   The process of technical innovation.

Source: See Myers and Marquis.[30]

some of which may be readily available, but, in some cases, special investigations into technical and commercial aspects will have to be initiated.

Eventually, a feasible technical solution may be forthcoming — or 'a solution to a modified problem with somewhat different objectives'.[30] But even then, the process of innovation is not complete: the final stage will decide the actual ability of a company to satisfy the needs of its customers. In this stage, considerable manufacturing start-up costs and marketing expenses will be incurred. The earlier technical uncertainties will now largely be replaced by the problems of marketing, including those involved in the vital processes of adoption and diffusion within periods of time which are commercially realistic.

The costs involved in this ultimate stage of the innovation process are typified by the estimates made by the US Department of Commerce, Panel on Innovation and Invention. (Refer to Figure 7.2.)

The data in Figure 7.2 indicate that start-up costs represent a major proportion of the development and implementation of costs of innovation. Jewkes[7] has pointed out that 'The more extensive the scale on which the new product must initially be manufactured, the more formidable may be the task of development'. Where both technical complexity and dynamic competition are present, a company is confronted with exceedingly difficult problems related to the scale of investment in innovative products.

NEW PRODUCT STRATEGIES

Johnson and Jones[35] have classified new products in terms of product

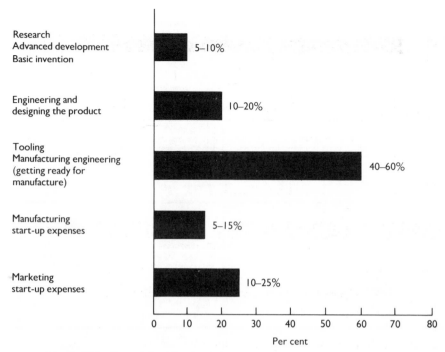

Figure 7.2 Typical distribution of costs in successful product innovations.

Source: Department of Commerce, *Technological Innovation,* 1967, quoted in Myers and Marquis.[30]

objectives defined in two dimensions: increasing market newness and increasing technological newness. (Refer to Figure 7.3.)

Although this matrix dates back to 1957, it still provides a very useful framework for analysing innovations and developing suitable marketing strategies. The choices open to a company may be noted from Figure 7.3 to involve:

1. no-change (sometimes referred to as 'masterly inactivity')
2. stay in the same market but endeavour to improve market share by policy of reformation (product modification) or replacement (product innovation)
3. stimulate demand for present products in existing markets by remerchandising, by planned improvements and by widening the line of products
4. identifying and expanding into new market segments, involving, perhaps, product modification and/or diversification.

The PIMS research identified three broad groups of market share strategies (building, holding, harvesting) which could usefully be considered in conjunction with the classifications of new product strategies outlined in Figure 7.3: a building strategy adopted by companies which seek to develop by planned innovation in design, production, marketing and distribution

←	Increasing technological newness	→	
Product objectives	**No technological change**	**Improved technology** To utilise more fully the company's present scientific knowledge and production skills.	**New technology** To acquire scientific knowledge and production skills new to the company.
No market change		**Reformulation** To maintain an optimum balance of cost, quality, and availability in the formulas of present company products. Examples use of oxidised microcystaline waxes in Glo-Coat (1946).	**Replacement** To seek new and better ingredients of formulation for present company products in technology not now employed by the company. Example: development of synthetic resin as a replacement for shellac in Glo-Coat (1950).
Strengthened market To exploit more fully the existing markets for the present company products.	**Remerchandising** To increase sales to consumers of types now served by the company. Example: use of dripless spout can for emulsion waxes (1955).	**Improved product** To improve present products for greater utility and merchandisability to consumers. Example: combination of auto paste wax and cleaner into one-step 'J.Wax' (1956)	**Product line extension** To broaden the line of products offered to present consumers through new technology. Example: development of a general purpose floor cleaner 'Emerel' in maintenance product line (1953)
New market To increase the number of types of consumers served by the company.	**New use** To find new classes of consumers that can utilize present company products. Example: sale of paste wax to furniture manufacturers for Coul Board wax (1945)	**Market extension** To reach new classes of consumers by modifying present products. Example: wax-based coolants and drawing compounds for industrial machining operations (1951).	**Diversification** To add to the classes of consumers served by developing new technical knowledge. Example: development of 'Raid'–dual purpose insecticide (1955).

↑ Increasing market newness →

Figure 7.3   New products classified by product objectives.

Source: See Johnson and Jones.[35]

methods. Such organisations aim to be industry leaders. This aggressive or 'offensive' marketing strategy, as observed earlier, carries with it risks which are frequently very substantial. (See Chapters 2, 3 and 6.)

Some firms prefer, however, a less adventurous programme of innovation; they adopt an imitative strategy as market followers who are content to 'wait and see'. They monitor the progress of new products marketed by 'leaders', and prepare to come quickly into a market when it begins to show symptoms of real growth. This follow-the-leader strategy may enable them to improve products and also to avoid some of the mistakes made by market pioneers. Although the initiative may have been taken by a more enterprising firm, some large concerns, because of their immense resources and experience, are able to catch up when, eventually, they decide to invade a market with a new product. This was certainly the case when Gillette finally decided that stainless steel razor blades pioneered by Wilkinsons were seriously challenging the market share held by their traditional type of blades. A sleeping giant, when finally aroused, has enormous muscle power in a market.

'Imitation is not only more abundant than innovation, but actually a much more prevalent road to business growth and profits. IBM got into computers as an imitator; Texas Instruments into transistors ... Holiday Inns into motels'.[37]

The imitative product strategy may well be associated with the PIMS 'holding' marketing share strategy which seeks to defend and preserve a company's position.

Being 'second to market' was seen by the National Institute Economic Review to have definite attractions in their report[36] on the electronic capital goods market: 'The performance of the first laboratory prototypes and early commercial deliveries almost always leaves a great deal to be desired, so that the scope for improvement is very great. For this reason, some entrepreneurs have followed a deliberate policy of being *second* with a new development rather than first. Success in such a policy often requires a greater capacity for moving fast with new developments once the time is considered ripe'.

Judgement is clearly a necessary attribute of successful business managers and this will rest on the assessment of risk associated with specific ventures.

Some companies may seek to extend their market opportunities through acquisition of firms which have complementary product ranges or special technological knowledge (refer to Figure 7.3). This strategy of innovation may be productive, but there are often considerable personal and organisational problems which tend to impede market progress.

An innovative strategy may be founded on developing new uses for a product (refer to bottom left-hand corner of Figure 7.3). For example, it has been noted[22] that Teflon[R] was originally developed as a corrosion-resistant material which could withstand high temperatures and was adopted, initially, for specific industrial purposes, such as low-friction bearings, rollers for desks and drawers, etc. Only later were the potentialities of this

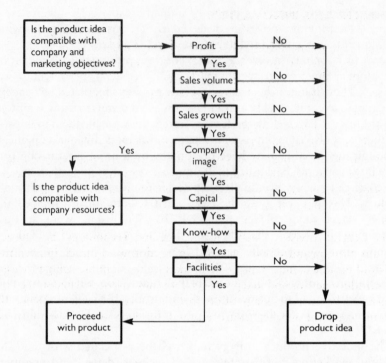

Figure 7.4   A simple decision model to assess the viability of a new product design.

Source: Derived from Design Council.

product recognised for consumer products; for example, Teflon-coated woodwork. This product now has diverse uses across industrial, commerical and consumer markets. (See also 'Market Segmentation Strategies' in Chapter 6.)

The innovative strategy to be followed by an individual company cannot be quoted like a set of rules. As with market share strategy (of which it is an intrinsic part), there are usually several alternative methods of 'innovation' open to careful evaluation. The most feasible solution may not necessarily be the ideal one, but at least it should have the virtues of realism.

Decision Model Approach to New Products

The viability of a new product could be analysed against the framework of a simple decision model[37], as shown in Figure 7.4. A checklist or logical decision model is often extremely useful in assessing potential marketing prospects for a new product or service. The example in Figure 7.4, may, of course, be further elaborated to meet specific corporate needs.

PLANNING AIDS INNOVATION

It is clear that innovation thrives where the managerial techniques of planning are applied in the various stages of developing new products/ services.

Pessemier[38] has proposed six steps (see Figure 7.5) in new product development.

Marketing research (refer to Chapters 4 and 8) *has an active part in new product development and commercialisation.* Ideas may be generated, for example, from observing people's behaviour, in the home market or in export markets, and both with consumer products and those used in factory processes. Markets of all types need to be closely monitored to ensure that trends are evuluted in time for corporate policies to be formed and put into effect.

The Central Advisory Council for Science and Technology[4] has stressed that 'any firm, or indeed any country, engaged in world trade in advanced industrial products, must repeatedly modernise its manufacturing processes and introduce new or updated products if it is not to lose markets and go out of business because of competition from advances elsewhere. Hence the constant need for market awareness and for technological innovation'.

Figure 7.5 Outline steps in new product programme.

Management should not only be effective technically but it should also be market orientated, and direct links should exist between R & D and the organisation as a whole. Realistic programmes of innovation should take account of production capacity and market size together with the costs involved in product development.

Project Sappho[5], which was concerned with investigating factors influencing successful industrial innovations, identified two marketing factors which directly affected the likelihood of success: 'successful innovators understood user needs better than less successful innovators, and, successful innovators pay more attention to marketing than less successful innovators'.

Four 'outstanding groups of success factors' were classified by Sappho in the following ranked order: the organisation and its market; the characteristics of the business innovator in the firm; the quality of research and development; and the efficiency of the firm's internal and external communication networks.

Andrew Robertson[39], has analysed the case studies in Sappho to see 'what had led the less successful innovating firms into error'. He found that four firms had made no enquiries of potential users, six had made too few enquiries, two had ignored the results of their enquiries, two had misinterpreted the answers they received, six were committed to preconceived designs, and three failed to understand the working environment to which their instrument (all three were instrument makers) would be subjected. These were all errors which successful innovators avoided by keeping closely in touch with their customers during the period of product development. For example, one instrument firm demonstrated working models of its new design to a select group of potential users with whom they maintained close contact, consulting them about cost estimates and pricing problems.

Eleven of the 34 firms had undertaken no marketing research or had neglected to apply the findings of any research done. Seven put too little effort into marketing, five largely neglected user education, while seven suffered from environmental factors which were beyond their control, such as the emergence of cheap substitute products. The need for educating users was reflected by the company which attempted to market an advanced analytical device which required skilled operation and maintenance. An adequate manual was not provided; 'in the words of one frustrated analytical chemist who could not get the results he wanted from the machine, the makers should have supplied an electronics engineer to keep it in working order'.[39]

Robertson[39] summarises the root causes of these failures as the neglect of marketing research and preconceived ideas about market needs.

Apart from the high rates of failure — between 60 and 90% — of industrial innovations, products that failed to achieve expected market share or profit projections overran cost estimates more than successful ones. It seems that 'there is no natural cut-off point in the failure sequence such as is provided by the break-even point in the successful sequence'.[39]

Project Teams and Successful Innovation

It was observed earlier that the days of the talented, sometimes amateurish, inventor who worked isolated from industrial and commercial pressures, seem to have gone for good.

After carefully studying the source of over eighty inventions made during the 19th and 20th centuries, Jewkes[7] concluded that more than one half of the cases can be ranked as individual inventions in the sense that much of the pioneering work was carried through by men working on their own behalf. Where inventors were employed in institutes, these organisations allowed the individuals to follow their own ideas without hindrance.

However, the fact that inventions require expensive development before they are commercially viable innovations has, inevitably, led to project teams whose members have a variety of talents, including managerial ability. According to a leading American source[6], independent inventors are giving way to scientist inventors who work for universities, companies and government. This trend has been accelerated by 'the remorseless advance of technology, and its high risks and need for substantial capital investment'.[6] Du Pont wistfully figures that it takes the lifetime of two highly paid researchers to yield a single major commercial development. But the pay-off from a single successful process or product may be worth lifetimes of work. 'A chemist named Wallace Carothers puttered fruitlessly in Du Pont labs for more than six years'.[6] He was trying to make fibre-forming polymers, and had experimented with polyesters but had given them up because of their low melting points. He then turned his attention to a different set of compounds — polyamides — and invented nylon. It took about 15 years, and involved the work of some 50 different scientists, before Du Pont were able to market Crolyn magnetic computer and video tape in June 1967.

As ICI[23] see it, 'inventors are individuals whose essential purpose is to create problems — by introducing something new'. These problems are then often solved by other innovators working as a group who have the task of developing the concept into a marketable product. Innovation, it is emphasised, 'is essentially about people, illogicality, climate, excitement; dull people cannot invent ... enthusiasm and personal attributes are linked with scientific logic and judgement — and more illogicality'.

The products which are successfully innovated today tend to be the result of team work in large, research-orientated organisations. Myers and Marquis[30] have emphasised: 'The management of innovation is a corporate-wide task, and is too important to be left to any one specialised functional department'.

Because of the danger that potentially good innovative ideas may never survive the built-in inertia or the devastating screening processes operated in some large organisations, some researchers, among them Schon[40], have proposed that 'product champions' should have the task of promoting feasible new ideas in their organisations. This role could be coupled with that of innovation manager or project team leader, who would have freedom of access to executives throughout the firm.

Sappho[5] found that a 'product champion' fulfilled a useful role where he was also the 'business innovator', but they did not subscribe to the 'somewhat romantic view that the product champion can overcome the defects of an unsuitable organisation or a weak business innovator'. Merely dispensing job titles is not enough to bring success; senior management should show their whole-hearted commitment to organised innovation by giving project leaders adequate authority to accomplish their difficult task. Sappho researchers observed that firms which modified their organisations and gave greater freedom to innovators performed 'slightly better'.[5]

After painstaking research, ICI[23] developed new alumina fibres into a marketable product, Saffil[R], capable of withstanding temperatures up to 1600°C and, unlike asbestos, biologically safe. A New Ventures Group was set up to conduct research and assess potential uses for this innovation and also organise marketing distribution.

Jewkes[7] has wisely observed that the working groups even in a large industrial research laboratory are normally small; the real moving spirits are few and the rest are pedestrian, although useful, of course, as team members. Because knowledge has become so specialised, researchers tend inevitably to focus on limited fields. Teamwork is essential, although it carries with it 'a countervailing loss of power'. Einstein, however, was said to have commented: 'I am a horse for single harness, and not cut out for landau or team work'.

Informality May Lead to Successful Innovations

Informal methods of working have, of course, had their successes, often outstanding, as in the case of the IBM disk memory unit which was developed secretly in one of the IBM laboratories without the sanction of management because of budget difficulties. Whittle, the jet engine pioneer, 'struggled along without any encouragement either from the Air Ministry or from aero-engineering firms and, in 1935, he actually allowed his patent to lapse. After 1935 he obtained limited backing from a London finance house and he was able to devote all his time to his research, although still an Air Force officer ... When the first jet aircraft flew successfully in Great Britain in May 1941, it could be said to be the product of Whittle's genius and the help of a small, but highly enthusiastic and extremely devoted group of collaborators'.[21]

BUYING-IN INNOVATIONS

Because of the enormously high cost of innovation, there is a growing trend by large organisations to buy-in feasible innovations. This may be effected by taking over a firm with a successful record of innovatory products; by merging with another company in the hope of achieving synergistic benefits;

by obtaining the rights of manufacture and marketing by licence deal; or by buying developed products or product ideas from inventors and/or product brokers.

Among the most successful product ideas bought by the Borg Warner Corporation were those that resulted in the automatic over-drive and the Schneider torque converter. The General Foods Corporation purchased from Birds Eye the rights to his invention of deep freezing methods.

Langrish and his colleagues[26] observe that analysis of the origins of twenty-five important process and product innovations by Du Pont, an American firm noted for its technical progressiveness, revealed that only ten of them were based on discoveries attributable to Du Pont's own staff.

As noted earlier, Du Pont[7] invented nylon and also developed it; they did not discover terylene but, as Dacron[R], they developed it. ICI developed both nylon and terylene but discovered neither, although they did discover and develop polyethylene.

British and American pharmaceutical companies were said[7] to have taken no part in the crucial discoveries connected with penicillin, and 'it was difficult enough to persuade them to take part at the pilot plant stage even when the chemotherapeutic virtues of penicillin had been placed beyond doubt'.

Conventional wisdom — or professional myopia — have proved difficult barriers for inventors to crash through. New scientific discoveries have frequently been ridiculed by those who have held the reins of power in research applications. Before the invention of the transistor, some scientists said[7] that there was nothing more to be discovered in that field.

LEAD TIME IS CRITICAL

Lead time is one of the most critical factors in innovation. The Central Advisory Council for Science and Technology[4] reported on the tendency for firms and countries to overcome long lead time and heavy development costs 'by buying-in other people's technological knowledge and by concentrating on the commercial application of important inventions and innovations'. Examples of significant innovations resulting from 'outside' inventors have just been given. Another notable example refers to ICI Plant Protection Division[23] which, in the mid-1970s, searched for a suitable post-emergence herbicide to control grass weeds, as part of their consistent research programme during which about 10,000 different chemical compounds active against major crop pests are screened each year. Work was stopped on a compound of its own when ICI's toxicological studies revealed that it might not meet the safety standards in crop protection. After 2½ years of complex negotiations, an agreement was reached with a Japanese chemical company for rights to a suitable compound which had been synthesised by them. This enabled ICI to produce Fusilade[R], which was first marketed in 1981 in

Central America and Rumania. Later, clearance was obtained virtually worldwide, and so within seven years of first hearing about a potential active ingredient, ICI had been able to launch a major new crop protection product. Success was achieved through the efficient cooperation of many innovative scientists and technologists.

The importance of the close working together of many specialists has already been discussed, but reiteration of this critical aspect of successful innovation is worthwhile. Not only must technical experts be of high calibre in their respective fields, but commercial management must also be equally effective. In the National Institute Economic Report[36] on the Electronic Capital Goods Market, particular stress was laid on the need for high quality management in all aspects of an innovating company's operations. 'Where this management talent was missing or where it did not obtain adequate finance, good inventors failed to make the transition to commercial success. This was the case with Forest in radio (and hundreds of other radio firms in the 1920s) with Farnsworth in television, and with Zuse and several other firms in computers. Good R & D is a necessary condition for success in this industry, but it is not a *sufficient* condition'.

'IN SEARCH OF EXCELLENCE'

Over the winter of 1979/80, two experienced American management consultants[41] set out to probe the secrets of successful business management and, supported mainly by McKinsey, they studied in depth the management techniques of a carefully selected sample of 62 companies in the US which had acknowledged reputations for innovativeness and excellent corporate performance. Although the sample was never intended to be perfectly representative of US industry as a whole, it was held to reflect a fairly broad spectrum and included: high technology, consumer goods, general industrial goods, services, project management and resource-based companies.

The research focused principally on big companies and was concerned to find out how they managed to survive, prosper, and keep an innovative edge. Specific financial criteria applicable to excellent performance were selected; these related to measures of growth and long-term wealth creation over 20 years; the other three were measures of return on capital and sales.

The findings of this extensive research, later published in the striking text, *In Search of Excellence[41]*, showed that successfully managed innovative companies were characterised by eight attributes. Although these are generally regarded as basic business skills and part of conventional wisdom, these outstanding companies were, 'above all, brilliant on the basics'. In other words, they fulfilled what are often described as the ordinary responsibilities of management, extraordinarily well.

These eight attributes were:

1. *Bias for action* — getting on with the job; tackling problems quickly in small, mixed groups.
2. *Close to the customer* — learning about customers' needs, and through regular contacts picking up ideas for new products.
3. *Autonomy and entrepreneurship* — innovation is fostered right through these highly successful companies; people are encouraged to be creative, to take risks and to give good ideas a chance.
4. *Productivity through people* — everyone in these outstanding companies is treated with respect: they are seen as important contributors to corporate success; managers are genuinely interested in helping members of their staffs to improve their performance through training, leadership and motivation.
5. *Hands-on, value driven* — companies that perform outstandingly well are clear about their corporate values: they know what they stand for, and their leaders are able to create 'exciting environments through personal attention, persistence and direct intervention — far down the line'. 'Excellent companies' have corporate leaders who demonstrate their total commitment to values that are clearly communicated; they are not content to leave these as abstract conceptions but make sure that detailed plans of action will ensure that ideas are put into practice.
6. *Stick to the knitting* — or, to use another homely expression, outstanding companies, like successful cobblers, stick to their lasts. Companies that expand by either acquisition or internal diversification are most successful when they stick close to their core skills, as 3M with coating and bonding technology. The next most likely to be successful are those companies that diversify into related fields; the least successful, generally, are those companies that diversify very widely. Growth in top performing companies has mostly been home grown; the few acquisitions made have been small businesses that could be easily assimilated without altering overall corporate values. Step-by-step diversification policies keep risks to manageable proportions.
7. *Simple form, lean staff* — the structures and systems of excellent companies are 'elegantly simple'; top-level corporate staff are frequently fewer than 100.
8. *Simultaneous loose–tight properties* — rigid control alongside corporate values of autonomy, entrepreneurship and innovation right down to the factory floor. Shared values include the need for disciplined feedback; customer problem solving is an obsession at all levels of these highly successful businesses.

The third factor — *autonomy and entrepreneurship* — demands extended discussion in a chapter dealing with innovation strategy. It is observed by these researchers that 'the most discouraging fact of big corporate life is the loss of what got them big in the first place: innovation'.[41] However, the companies with enviable track records had the ability 'to be big and yet to act small at the same time'. Many of them even encouraged 'skunk works' —

groups of eight of ten enthusiasts working more or less on their own in a kind of meaningful muddle.

For this fanatical activity to be productive, 'champions' are vital (see earlier notes on product champions and project teams). Such champions should essentially be volunteers who are fired by the prospects of developing a new product or process. In a review of its last fifty or so successful and unsuccessful new product introductions, Texas Instruments found that failures were *always* associated with the absence of a *volunteer* champion. The experiences of other large companies, such as IBM and GE also emphasised the importance of the role of champions.

Three primary roles in the 'championing system' were identified from this research study: (1) the *product champion* who *believes* in the project and who is likely to be a 'loner, egotistical, or cranky'; (2) the *executive champion*, invariably an ex-product-champion who knows all about the problems of husbanding an idea and protecting it from the corporate threat to smother it at birth; and (3) the *godfather*, likely to be 'an ageing leader who provides the model for championing'.

It is stressed that champions are pioneers and are, therefore, easily identifiable targets, particularly when innovations fail, as many inevitably do. But the companies that consistently support their champions reap rewards in successful innovation. Persistent effort must be encouraged; innovation has to work against very high odds (see earlier discussion), and the laws of probability clearly favour those companies which are prepared to make many attempts — 'innovation success is a numbers game'.

Regular experimentation, shared values, customer-orientation and quick and easy communication are constituents which helped to make the excellence of the companies surveyed.

SUMMARY

Innovation is vital for corporate growth; it is risky and, often, expensive, but without the systematic introduction of new products, a firm's future is imperilled.

Innovation and invention are not the same: the former applies the fruits of invention so that profits are earned. Innovation depends on invention, either inside the firm or through licensing and other arrangements. Many companies owe their present-day leadership to consistent programmes of invention and innovation. New dynamic technologies have accelerated the pace of change; products like electronics quickly become outdated.

Industrial innovation is frequently difficult due to internal organisational factors and also because of the complexity of buying behaviour. Methods of diffusion deserve special attention.

Various classifications of innovations have been applied, e.g. evolutionary, revolutionary, continuous, dynamically continuous and discontinuous. Incremental or sequential innovations often appear to be evident.

Behavioural factors influence the rate of adoption of innovations.

An imitative or follow-my-leader strategy is frequently attractive to firms; this reduces risk and may enable greatly improved versions of products to be marketed when the demand has been 'warmed up'.

A decision model approach to innovation (linked to market research) is helpful in assessing market prospects.

Project teams and product champions have contributed notably to innovations successes. On the other hand, informality and serendipity have also played quite significant roles in successful invention and innovation.

Lead time is critical: this encourages firms to 'buy-in' product concepts.

Successful firms are characterised by whole-hearted commitment of all who work in them to the development and commercialisation of new products.

REFERENCES

1. Schumpeter, Joesph A., *Business Cycles*, McGraw-Hill, New York, 1939
2. Mansfield, Edwin, *Industrial Research and Technological Innovation*, Longmans Green, London, 1969
3. Rogers, Everett M., *Diffusion of Innovation*, The Free Press, New York, 1962
4. Report of the Central Advisory Council for Science and Technology, Technological Innovation in Britain, HMSO, 1968.
5. Science Policy Research Unit, University of Sussex (Project Sappho) 'Success and Failure in Industrial Innovation', Centre for the Study of Industrial Innovation, London, February, 1972.
6. Blundell, William E. (ed.), *The Innovators: How Today's Inventors Shape Your Life Tomorrow*, Dow Jones, Princeton, NJ, 1968.
7. Jewkes, John, Sawers, David and Stillerman, Richard, *The Sources of Invention*, Macmillan, London, 1969.
8. Burns, Tom and Stalker, G.M., *The Management of Innovation*, Tavistock Publications, London, 1966.
9. Chakrabarti, Alok, K., 'Industrial Product Innovation: an International Comparison', *Industrial Marketing Management*, Vol. 7, No. 4, 1978.
10. Report to Advisory Council for Applied Research and Development 'Industrial Innovation', Institute of Mechanical Engineers, October 1979.
11. Drucker, Peter F., *The Practice of Management*, Heinemann, London, 1955.
12. Parsons, S.A.T., *The Framework of Innovation*, Macmillan, London, 1968.
13. Fennell, David, 'Racing Ahead with the Microchip', *Daily Telegraph*, 26 August 1982.
14. Smith, Lee, 'The Lures and Limits of Innovation', *Fortune*, 20 October 1980.
15. Ansoff, H. Igor, *Corporate Strategy*, Penguin, Harmondsworth, 1968.
16. Mathias, Peter, *The First Industrial Nation: An Economic History of Britain 1700–1914*, Methuen, London, 1983.
17. Ozanne, Urban B. and Churchill, Gilbert A. Jnr., 'Five Dimensions of the Industrial Buying Process', *Journal of Marketing Research*, Vol. 8, No.3, 1971.

18. Webster, Frederick. E. Jnr., 'Communication and Diffusion Processes in Industrial Markets', *European Journal of Marketing*, Vol. 5, No. 4, 1971.
19. Allen, D.H. and Hayward, George, 'Innovations in the Capital Equipment Area: Their Effects on Diffusion', *Business Graduate*, Vol. 2, No. 3, 1972.
20. Ray, George F., 'The Diffusion of Mature Technologies', *National Institute Economic Review*, No. 106, November 1983.
21. Chisnall, Peter M., *Marketing: A Behavioural Analysis*, McGraw-Hill, Maidenhead, 1985.
22. Warner, Kenneth E., 'The Need for Some Innovative Concepts of Innovation: An Examination of Research on the Diffusion of Innovations', *Policy Sciences*, Vol. 5, 1974.
23. Imperial Chemical Industries plc, *'The Innovators'*, ICI, London, 1983.
24. Stewart-Clark, Sir John, 'Market Assessment' in *Management of Innovation*, Bishop, Terry, (ed.) Design Council, London, 1975.
25. Jones, Trevor (ed.), *Micro Electronics and Society*, Open University Press, 1980.
26. Langrish, J., Gibbons, M., Evans, W.G., and Jevons, F.R., *Wealth from Knowledge — Studies of Innovation in Industry*, Macmillan, London, 1972.
27. Ferrari, Achille, 'Innovation: Myths and Realities', *Industrial Marketing Management*, Vol. 2, 1973.
28. Stonier, Tom, *The Wealth of Information: A Profile of the Post-Industrial Economy*, Thames, Methuen, London, 1983.
29. Rothwell, Roy, 'The Role of Technical Change in International Competitiveness: The Case of the Textile Machinery Industry', *Management Decisions*, Vol. 15, No. 6, 1980.
30. Myers, Summer and Marquis, Donald, G., 'Successful Industrial Innovations: A Study of Factors Underlying Innovations in Selected Firms', National Science Foundation (NSF 69–17), 1969.
31. Sahal, Devendra, 'Invention, Innovation and Economic Evaluation', *Technological Forecasting and Social Change*, Vol. 23, 1983.
32. Robertson, Thomas S., 'The Process of Innovations, and the Diffusion of Innovations', *Journal of Marketing*, Vol. 3, January 1967.
33. Levitt, Theodore, *Marketing for Business Growth*, McGraw-Hill, New York, 1974.
34. 'Bayers Formulation for Product Innovation', *International Management*, February, 1978.
35. Johnson, Samuel C. and Jones, Conrad, 'How to Organise for New Products', *Harvard Business Review*, May/June, 1957.
36. Freeman, C., 'Research and Development in Electronic Capital Goods', *National Institute Economic Review*, No. 34, November 1965.
37. Majaro, Simon, 'A Market Strategy for Europe', in *Designing for European Markets, A Management Guide*, Blake, John E., (ed.) Design Council, London, 1972.
38. Pessemier, Edgar, A., *New Product Decisions*, McGraw-Hill, New York, 1966.
39. Robertson, Andrew, 'The Marketing Factor in Successful Industrial Innovation', *Industrial Marketing Management*, Vol. 2, 1973.
40. Schon, Donald A., 'Champions for Radical New Inventions', *Harvard Business Review*, Mar./Apr. 1963.
41. Peters, Thomas J. and Waterman, Robert H. Jnr., *In Search of Excellence: Lessons from America's Best-Run Companies*, Harper and Row, New York, 1982.

Chapter Eight
INTERNATIONAL STRATEGY I

BRITAIN'S INDUSTRIAL SUPREMACY CHALLENGED

The close of the nineteenth century witnessed a fierce struggle for overseas trade between Britain, the United States and Germany. Aided by protectionist trading, the latter two countries had developed their basic industries, and were now challenging the long-held superiority of British industrialists in world markets.

Through the Edwardian period and down to the time of the Great War, British products and services were behind the strength of the gold sovereign in trading exchanges. But the inevitable depredations of two World Wars have radically changed the pattern of world trading.

The pattern of British export trade underwent a radical change from the First World War; textiles such as cotton piece goods halved their market share, while vehicles and machinery increased their market shares two-fold; chemicals also experienced a significant increase — about $\frac{1}{3}$ — although coal exports fell.

For generations, Britain — the first nation in the world to experience large-scale industrialisation — has pioneered production processes in ship-building, coal-mining, textiles and the metal industries. British industrial leadership was virtually unchallenged for many generations, but these days were in eclipse and have now gone forever.

Today, technologies are widely dispersed over the world. Competition is worldwide and increasing in intensity as countries which were formerly important export markets for British goods have developed politically and economically, and have largely adopted policies of self-sufficiency. The British Empire has dissolved into thin air, and with it have gone the trading privileges which were held to be the prerogatives of British industrialists and merchants. British goods and services are now exposed to the harsh climate of 'open' markets; old trading loyalties have been affected by the abrasive atmosphere of world economic conditions.

Technological expertise has contributed significantly to the growth of international business. 'Relatively small countries have indeed been able to establish very important positions in specific technologies which are of great importance to *all* countries ... The most important post-War advance in steel-making occurred in Austria; Switzerland leads in pharmaceuticals and pesticides; Japan in some branches of electrical technology ... The most recent studies appear to point clearly to a strong trend towards the fast development of trade in high technology products than in conventional products, showing that the newest trends are indeed the strongest'.[1]

For many years after the Second World War, British industrialists had not troubled to develop their market overseas — they had slipped into the easy habit of trading principally in the home market, where a 'sellers' market was in full swing. Production could be disposed of profitably and without undue effort.

In a report[2] dated May 1950, PEP stated quite bluntly: 'For most exporters overseas trading is a residual interest, of much less importance to the company's progress than the home market. In addition, the standard of export marketing practice is rudimentary'. This attitude contrasts strongly with business activities in these difficult trading times; more and more companies are finding that exporting has become vital for their continued prosperity.

Twenty-five years later, despite the acknowledged urgency, the Royal Society of Arts issued a research report[3] on the export performance of 122 British companies, the findings of which closely echoed the PEP Report. The research studied the export performance of 122 British companies with annual turnovers ranging from just under £5million to over £50million and accounting for about 25% of total UK exports of manufactured products.

The findings are disconcerting: the general lack of a professional marketing approach to overseas markets; a curious lack of managerial logic in planning marketing strategies: one company exported to a total of 164 countries, but 90% of export sales were with only 10 of these countries; the rest were expensive to service, but because the export sales director had spent 25 years in developing them, he would not consider rationalising his marketing efforts by axing some of these peripheral markets.

Most of the companies researched were surprised to discover that a remarkably large proportion of their exports were derived from a very limited number of countries, often fewer than six. The lowest overall return of profits on capital[3] appeared to be earned by companies which exported to the largest number of countries. Concentration on selected markets leads to increased opportunities and builds up market share.

Half the companies surveyed reported that exports were more profitable than home sales. About 40% obtained higher prices in most overseas markets, 45% occasionally were able to secure higher prices overseas and about 10% could not.

PRINCIPLE OF CRITICAL MASS

The principle of critical mass is often advanced as vital to the profitable exploitation of markets, wherever they may be. Briefly, a company needs to attain a minimum level of size — achieve critical mass — if it is to be effective in competitive environments. Instead of dissipating limited resources (as the BETRO report[3] observed of many British companies), companies should aim to obtain a significant position in carefully targeted markets. This view is also supported by a NEDO paper[4] on Britain's export performance which recommended concentration on key markets: exporters tended to spread their efforts too widely and hence failed to build competitive strength in such scattered markets.

This lack of critical mass has also been observed of 'many US manufacturers [who] still try to find shortcuts around the evaluations and management attention that profitable business necessitates. For example, one communications equipment manufacturer took the approach of trying to sell its products through agents in fifty countries, rather than perform the analyses required to determine which handful of markets offered the best long-term potential and warranted more significant investment. As a result, the company never developed a really strong position in any of these markets and eventually lost out to more targeted competitors ...'[5]

Selective targeting enables small companies, in particular, to build up really worthwhile export business; there is no sense in trying to be the world's supplier if corporate resources cannot sustain the efforts needed for this herculean task.

INTERNATIONAL MARKETING

International marketing is not merely a sophisticated way of describing export selling — it is far more fundamental and reflects attitudes, orientation and behaviour towards securing profitable business overseas.

'International marketing is the performance of business activities that direct the flow of a company's goods and services to consumers or users in more than one nation. The only difference between domestic marketing and international marketing is that the activities that take place are in more than one country ...'.[6] Wherever companies seek to transact business, the principles of marketing apply, although the techniques may vary.

Need for Integrated Planning

The specific needs of identified types of customers should be analysed and related to the resources (financial, productive, marketing and administrative) of the prospective supplying firm. This calls for systematic marketing research in order to obtain objective and reliable data, both qualitative and quantitative. (Discussed in Chapter 9.)

Marketing, therefore, is essentially strategic in nature compared with selling which is intrinsically concerned with tactical operations. The widespread responsibilities of the marketing function were cogently analysed in a NEDO report[7]: 'Marketing ... concerns market research, product planning, market planning, sales promotion, selling, customer service, the promotion of company and product image and equally the strategies and organisational systems needed to tie the market operations of the Company, for example, guiding R & D or providing essential information for decisions on the location, size and timing of new investment'.

In an unfamiliar environment, marketing does not lose its value as a vital management activity. The overseas market of a particular company remains, of course, the home market of national and competing firms. Successful operations by a foreign supplier will depend on his attitudes towards his customers, wherever they may be living: 'in a growing number of companies the concept of *foreign* is breaking down because of the growing involvement of the corporate headquarters in the company's marketing programs regardless of location ... to International Telephone and Telegraph there is no such thing as a "foreign" market in the psychological sense — there are markets in different parts of the world, at different stages of development with different characteristics ... ITT know as much about the French market for telecommunications as it knows about the US market'.[8]

The mechanics of marketing can be adapted to the particular environmental differences of overseas markets. Involvement with customers' problems, wherever they may arise, is a function of successful marketing. In organisational markets, this will largely depend on the ability of suppliers to offer feasible solutions to problems such as the quality of alloy steels used in production. Solutions are being sought not just from home-based firms; competition is now across the continents of the world.

MOTIVATIONS INFLUENCING INTERNATIONAL TRADING

The Principle of Comparative Advantage or Comparative Cost was developed in the nineteenth century by some of the leading British classical economists as an explanation of international trading. This theory postulated that each nation tends to specialise in the production of these goods and services in which it is comparatively most efficient, exporting them, and importing those goods which they could produce less advantageously. At the macro level of economic activity, this theory of international business maximises, it is claimed, output from world resources. It is related to the basic economic techniques of mass production, specialisation of output and division of labour. Without such concentration of resources and specialisation of efforts, the rapid industrialisation of the western economies would not have been feasible.

The Principle of Absolute Cost Advantage referred to the situation where a product could be produced distinctly more cheaply in a specific country than in another country. The first country was described as having an absolute cost advantage. This differential could be eroded by technological developments and the industrialisation of countries which formerly depended, for example, on Britain for supplies of certain kinds of machine tools. These theories do not, however, fully explain the pattern of contemporary world trade. Other motivations exist at the micro level which cause companies to seek business overseas.

BUSINESS MOTIVATIONS

An individual company is not directly affected by the theory of comparative advantage: self-interest is the prime motivation of individuals and trading organisations — direct conflict with national interests may well arise. Businessmen may consider, in fact, that they suffer from some of the trading policies laid down by governments. Perhaps it is only to be expected 'that the attitudes of governments on the one hand and businessmen on the other should, at times, be strongly ambivalent. Governments are under numerous pressures, internal and external, while businessmen can hardly be expected to support with enthusiasm measures which do not benefit them fairly directly ...'.[1]

Motivations such as economies of scale are likely to influence business decisions to expand markets overseas. As a Unilever Chairman observed:

> 'The economics of scale in research and specialised central services owe their importance to a very simple principle. Knowledge has no marginal cost. It costs no more to use it in the 70 countries in which we operate than in one. It is this principle which makes Unilever economically viable'.[9]

The opportunity to increase profitability, particularly when home market prices are depressed or controlled by government intervention, has forced many managements increasingly to look overseas for continued profitability and growth.

A manufacturer considering export business for the first time should carefully evaluate several factors before committing himself. He will need to know, for example, the nature of the demand for his kind of products in specific overseas markets — is it likely to be regular and progressive? Does he have the resources (financial, production, etc.) to meet the anticipated extra demand generated from export activities. Pricing policy will be of significant importance. Could prices in export markets be fixed to equal those obtainable in the home market after allowing for the extra costs involved in overseas selling? Alternatively, would export sales, even at prices somewhat below home market prices, be of value in contributing to overall profitability?

Although motivations at the macro and at the micro levels may differ to some extent, in the multinational business organisations the theory of comparative advantage tends to become more evident.

Kotler[10] states that two factors draw a firm towards a strategy of international market development: (1) *push* — because of the lack of home market opportunities, and (2) *pull* — by increasing opportunities for its products abroad.

Companies which are contemplating exporting might well find the sequential approach given in Figure 8.1 a useful guide; this develops logically from identification of basic motivations to audit of resources and then to analyses of specific market opportunities. These steps follow the general guidelines given in Chapter 6 on overall market planning.

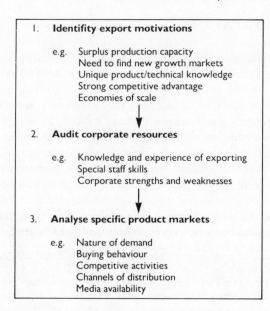

1. **Identifity export motivations**

    e.g. Surplus production capacity
          Need to find new growth markets
          Unique product/technical knowledge
          Strong competitive advantage
          Economies of scale

2. **Audit corporate resources**

    e.g. Knowledge and experience of exporting
          Special staff skills
          Corporate strengths and weaknesses

3. **Analyse specific product markets**

    e.g. Nature of demand
          Buying behaviour
          Competitive activities
          Channels of distribution
          Media availability

Figure 8.1   Steps in evaluation of export opportunities.

PHASES IN DEVELOPMENT OF OVERSEAS BUSINESS

Some companies almost stumble into exporting; much to their surprise, and even alarm, they suddenly find themselves faced with an unsolicited enquiry from abroad. Others have become involved through merging with a business that already had overseas activities. In some cases, personal links had resulted in business being developed with certain countries. From the accidental to the planned approach there are clearly many events which may trigger off overseas marketing, but even today many companies prefer to adopt a passive attitude, or if they go abroad they tend to take up a defensive posture. Positive dynamic marketing often appears to be sadly lacking in many firms which seem to have little real conception of the need to tackle market opportunities in a systematic, planned way. Their lack of success does not surprise experienced, professional export managers who know that infiltration and exploitation of overseas markets demand standards of management and personal qualities which are far from common.

Five phases (see Figure 8.2) in the evolutionary process affecting companies engaged in international business have been identified.[1] These range from accidental to planned market operations and reflect different levels of behaviour and commitment.

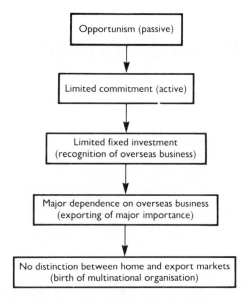

Figure 8.2 Phases in development of overseas business.

1. Opportunism is connected with the accidental entry into exporting just discussed. The opportunity presented by a chance enquiry could, perhaps, be developed by enterprising management; luck is really nothing more than being ready to seize suitable opportunities and turn them to advantage. Often a relatively small company dealing almost exclusively with home-market customers, receives an overseas enquiry about one of its products which has been noticed in the home market by an overseas business visitor. This may set in motion a whole series of policy and tactical decisions affecting product range, pricing, production policy etc.

   The alertness of management to new market opportunities does not depend on high technical competence: it calls for some of the instinctive flair for business without which corporate resources are sterile.

2. Limited commitment: the second stage of corporate commitment to exporting — reflects the willingness of management to consider particular overseas markets because of the success, perhaps, of the opportunistic policy. These markets may be chosen because they are geographically accessible; they appear to have cultural and social characteristics similar to existing markets, or because the degree of risk involved in entering them is acceptable. At this stage of exporting, products and pricing are likely to be the same as with 'opportunistic'

exporting; there will be no long-term fixed investment, production will be limited to marginal capacity. This stage is important, however, because it marks the transition from 'passive' to 'active' exporting.

3. Limited fixed investment: the promise of increased export business leads to greater commitment by the exporter — extra capacity is allocated to export orders which are increasingly recognised as an important contribution to the overall trading policy.

    Products are developed and pricing policies carefully devised to secure effective penetration of selected markets. There is a tendency to follow marginal pricing, and, in general, an increasing commitment to overseas trade.

4. Major dependence for overseas business: this fourth sequential stage of exporting reflects top management's whole-hearted commitment to exporting. Board level directives will now activate management to concentrate more of their time to overseas trading problems. Pricing and product policies will tend to rank equal with domestic business. An overseas division may be set up which will quickly assume significance in corporate activities. Such a firm is not in exporting for fun, but to earn specific rates of return on its capital and other resources. There are likely to be some management casualties during this period of dynamic re-orientation.

5. No distinction between home and export markets: this final evolutionary stage heralds the birth of the multinational organisation which views the world as its oyster. Strategic business opportunities are assessed across entire continents and involving diverse cultures. It is the birth of the multinational organisation involving global strategy.

    'Capital may be held outside the country of origin, the shares may be quoted on all the principal stock exchanges and dividends declared in a currency not that of the country of origin ..'[1]. Many companies are heavily dependent on foreign revenues: Nestlé about 97%, IBM over 50%. Shell and Unilever are effectively binational in capital, management, and domicile. Terpstra[11] has observed that General Electric (US) owns several manufacturing plants in overseas countries, as well as joint ventures, licensing and a large export operation from the US.

This ultimate stage in the transition from 'accidental' overseas involvement to long-term corporate commitment has had a significant influence on the pattern of world trading. It has affected not just economic policies, but has extended into social, political and other environmental factors. More large organisations are becoming international both in philosophy and in scope of operations. For a continually growing number of firms, the entire world is considered a market place for their products. Rather than ask "Where in our country should a new plant be built or a new market developed?" more firms are asking: "Where in the *world* should a new product be made or sold?"[6] Trading horizons have developed far beyond the traditional perspectives held for many years by business firms. This more enterprising view of world markets ('The world is our oyster') influenced the supply side as well as the marketing policy. Firms may seek suppliers from regions which have not traditionally been regarded as sources for particular kinds of goods. This liberalising of trading attitudes and behaviour should not be overlooked by firms which have tended to regard access to certain markets, and to some customers, as almost a trading right.

Of 78 North American companies studied[12], 58 indicated that international business had grown faster than domestic business over the previous five years; there was a general realisation that business outside the US was of critical importance and 'that it should have an important influence on shaping the strategy, policy and actions of the entire corporation'.[12] The trend towards operating corporate and nationally based companies under local management was widely accepted policy. Only eleven of the multinationals surveyed reserved key posts in their foreign subsidiaries and affiliates for personnel sent from head office. In line with greater local autonomy, there may well develop an increasing emphasis on management control information and reporting to corporate headquarters.

MULTINATIONAL TRADING

Large overseas trading corporations are not, of course, exclusive phenomena of this century. Chartered companies such as the Hudson Bay Company and the East India Company originally governed as well as commercially exploited the then new lands of Africa and Asia, and large tracts of North America.

Ulrich Wiechmann[13] has defined a multinational company as one that operates subsidiaries in a number of different nation states which often have vastly differing political, cultural, economic and legal environments. He identified the key problem of top management as that of 'tying together the business activities of the far-flung subsidiaries'. This central task had to be undertaken actively so that a multinational marketing policy was developed.

Three factors have been noted[14] as accounting for the rapid increase in multinational trading:

1. It has been the norm rather than otherwise for a firm to manufacture in more than one country
2. Foreign investment is no longer exclusively or even principally of European origin
3. The multinational company is acquiring a cosmopolitan appearance

Multinational companies are very large and have extensive corporate resources; these significant resources are available, often at no or low cost, to

Table 8.1 The world's top fifty industrial groupings

Rank	Company	Headquarters	Main activity	Sales £m	Year end
1	Exxon Corpn.	USA	Oil industry	66,705.2	31.12.82
2	Shell Transport & Trading Royal Dutch Petroleum	UK/Netherlands	Oil industry	54,776.0	31.12.82
3	American Telephone & Telegraph	USA	Telephone system operators	42,544.4	31.12.82
4	Mobil Corpn.	USA	Oil industry	41,251.0	31.12.82
5	Mitsubishi Corpn.	Japan	sogo shosha	40,182.1	31.03.82
6	General Motors Corpn.	USA	Motor vehicles	39,232.4	31.12.82
7	Mitsui & Co.	Japan	sogo shosha	36,183.3	31.03.82
8	British Petroleum	UK	Oil industry	34,583.0	31.12.82
9	C. Itoh & Co.	Japan	sogo shosha	33,750.1	31.03.82
10	Marubeni	Japan	sogo shosha	31,593.6	31.03.82
11	Texaco	USA	Oil industry	30,710.0	31.12.82
12	Sumitomo Corpn.	Japan	sogo shosha	29,998.2	31.03.82
13	Ford Motor	USA	Motor vehicles	24,226.9	31.12.82
14	Standard Oil Co. of California	USA	Oil industry	23,018.3	31.12.82
15	International Business Machines	USA	Business machine manufacturers	22,460.1	31.12.82
16	De Pont (E.I.) de Nemours	USA	Chemical and oil industries	21,785.0	31.12.82
17	Nissho Iwai	Japan	sogo shosha	20,334.3	31.03.82
18	Gulf Oil Corpn.	USA	Oil industry	20,020.0	31.12.82
19	Sears, Roebuck	USA	General merchandise retailers	19,620.8	31.12.82
20	Standard Oil (Indiana)	USA	Oil industry	18,348.4	31.12.82
21	Atlantic Richfield	USA	Oil industry	17,640.9	31.12.82
22	General Electric	USA	Consumer product & power system manufacturers	17,320.3	31.12.82
23	ENI	Italy	Oil and chemical industries, etc.	16,092.6	31.12.81
24	Shell Oil	USA	Oil and gas industries	13,585.6	31.12.82
25	Unilever PLC/Unilever NV	UK/Netherlands	Food, detergents, animal foods, toiletries	13,215.7	31.12.82

26	Veba	West Germany	Electricity, oil, chemicals	13,023.7	31.12.82
27	United States Steel	USA	Steel and oil & gas producers	12,357.5	31.12.82
28	Occidental Petroleum	USA	Energy resources co.	11,903.4	31.12.82
29	Safeway Stores	USA	Supermarket operators	11,524.7	01.01.83
30	BAT Industries	UK	Tobacco, retailing, paper, packaging, etc.	11,318.0	31.12.82
31	Française des Petroles	France	Oil industry	11,310.8	31.12.82
32	K Mart Corpn.	USA	Discount store operators	10,962.2	26.01.83
33	Petróleos de Venezuela	Venezuela	Oil industry	10,762.5	31.12.82
34	Toyota Motor	Japan	Motor vehicles	10,532.3	31.03.83
35	Sun Co., Inc.	USA	Oil industry	10,482.4	31.12.82
36	International Telephone & Telegraph	USA	Telecommunication & electronic equipment manufactuers	10,430.4	31.12.82
37	Siemens	West Germany	Electrical & general engineering	10,336.6	31.12.82
38	Philips Petroleum	USA	Oil industry	10,260.1	31.12.82
39	Toyo Menka	Japan	sogo shosha*	10,164.5	31.03.82
40	Daimler-Benz	West Germany	Motor vehicles	10,027.1	31.12.82
41	Philips' Lamps Holding	Netherlands	Electrical & electronic products	9,883.0	31.12.82
42	Elf Aquitaine (Sté National)—SNEA	France	Oil industry	9,859.0	31.12.82
43	Tenneco	USA	Oil industry, etc.	9,790.2	31.12.82
44	Volkswagenwerk	West Germany	Motor vehicles	9,647.9	31.12.82
45	Nippon Oil	Japan	Oil industry	9,637.7	31.03.83
46	Tokyo Electric Power	Japan	Electric utility	9,531.6	31.03.83
47	Fiat	Italy	Motor vehicles	9,019.8	31.12.82
48	Hoechst	West Germany	Chemicals, dyes & plastics	9,017.0	31.12.82
49	Bayer	West Germany	Chemicals	8,977.8	31.12.82
50	Renault	France	Motor vehicles	8,943.3	31.12.82

Exchange rates used at 30.6.83 France 11.645 Francs to £1, Italy 2300.5 Lira to £1, Japan 365.5 Yen to £1, Netherlands 4.35 Guilders to £1, USA $1.53 to £1, Venezuela 6.57 Bolivar to £1 and West Germany 3.88 Dm to £1.

* 'sogo shosha' means a 'general' or 'integrated' trading company, covering marketing, development and general organisation.

Source: Times 1000, 1983/84. Reprinted by permission of Times Books Ltd.

their subsidiaries which, as a result, are able to behave extremely competitively in their respective markets.

Table 8.1 lists the world's top fifty industrial groupings, from which it will be noted that petroleum companies figure prominently among the multinationals. Their significance in the world economy has grown substantially over the past decade; it has also earned them some harsh criticism. The oil companies' activities are closely linked with the political power exercised by countries which have emerged to challenge the whole structure of western economic and social life. Their operations involve networks of commercial, technological and political commitments which have developed in complexity, particularly since the dramatic emergence of OPEC. Wherever international companies exploit indigeneous basic raw materials, political and cultural reactions become highly sensitive.

Many of the large food and household consumer goods firms have developed multinationally 'as the tastes of industrial societies grow more alike and personal incomes are high enough'.[15] Unilever, Corn products and Nestlé are typical of companies which originated from exploiting a particular process related to specific new materials. From this base, they then extended their product ranges and markets until they have become large, transnational organisations.

International business negotiations are affected considerably by the relationships between the multinational firms and governments of the countries in which they operate. Developing countries are benefitting from the immense investment programmes of these giant organisations; there is often an uneasy balance between the demands of commercial policies and the expectancies of governments in host countries. Political events may sometimes radically change, if not entirely destroy, the functioning of multinationals in certain countries.

Although multinational corporations may be able to enjoy the benefits of economies of scale, the ability to raise funds at most advantageous rates and to shift funds to secure most favourable rates of return, they are also particularly prone to risk, compounded of many variables, several of which will lie outside their control. This may encourage them to pursue a policy of risk-minimising; this cautious approach to trading is likely to inhibit managerial initiative and corporate innovativeness. (See preceding chapter.)

Third World Multinationals

An arresting article in the *Harvard Business Review* entitled 'Rise of the Third World Multinationals'[16] drew attention to this fast-growing phenomenon in world trading. Thirty-four of *Fortune's* 'Overseas 500 companies' had headquarters in the developing countries during 1979. It is time to reconsider the prevailing image of the developing countries; while Third World multinationalism is still in its early days, the potential for growth is impressive. There are, it is alleged, *three kinds of economic soil in which*

Third World multinational operations are taking root: (1) *resource-rich* developing countries, mostly OPEC; (2) *labour-rich* industrialising countries, of limited natural resources and narrow domestic markets, e.g. Singapore, Hong Kong, China and Korea. These countries 'have evolved from basic trading nations to more complex, production-based economies'. In the 1960s, many satellite plants from developed countries were set up in these distant parts of the world: Hewlett Packard, Fairchild, Philips, etc. However, by the 1970s, the more enterprising developing countries 'became net exporters of labour, products and ideas'; (3) *market-rich,* rapidly expanding industrialising countries, such as Brazil, Mexico, the Phillippines, Argentina, Venezuela and Turkey.

Although significant differences exist between these three broad categories of Third World multinationals, they have a common advantage: 'governments that are manifestly pro-business and committed to enterprise growth'. Two other factors are also seen to be effective in helping to accelerate the growth of business: Third World solidarity and access to technology.

On the other hand, there are certain impediments to expansion. These are perceived to be: (1) low level of demand in general in developed countries which are essential customers of the Third World; (2) rising protectionism; (3) growing public debt, and (4) the widening gap between rich and poor.

The growth of Third World multinational business is also the focus of a research article[17] in *Multinational Info.* The authors state that, by and large, the Third World multinational companies (MNCs) specialise in more mature technologies, are well behind the frontiers of technological advance and are weak in marketing skills. Joint ventures offer them opportunities of extending their production and other skills. The newly industrialised countries (NICs) which have developed a new version of multinational trading will grow to 'challenge traditional MNCs in some areas'.

MANAGERIAL IMPLICATIONS OF OVERSEAS BUSINESS

Risk Policies

The five sequential stages of exporting which have been outlined are necessarily associated with varying degrees of risk.

The development of organisations brings management face to face with new problems as well as extending the area of existing problems. Decision making becomes more complex, and is likely to take more time; the effects of these decisions are likely to be felt more widely, and their implementation is likely to take longer. Exporting generally involves management in higher risks than their home-market trading. A paradoxical situation exists in that one of the fundamental reasons for exporting is to spread corporate risks across diverse markets, and yet, inevitably, a considerable degree of risk is involved in operating in overseas markets. Decision making — a basic activity of management — entails acceptance of risk of some kind.

Aspects of risk in industrial buying behaviour were discussed in Chapter 3, when perception was observed to be effective in evaluating the nature of specific types of risk. The ability to tolerate risk has been seen to be related to a firm's size and liquidity, and to the degree of self-confidence of its management. The extent of 'tolerable' risk is also affected by the nature of a business; some are intrinsically high-risk, others are low-risk enterprises. Research-intensive businesses such as aeronautics or pharmaceuticals, or the extractive industries such as oil-drilling have a 'natural' acceptance of high-risk. Nut and bolt manufacturers, on the other hand, do not operate in these parameters of risk; demand for their products may fluctuate, but the rate of innovation is low, plant is unlikely to become rapidly obsolescent, and vast sums are not at risk in research and development.

Attractive overseas opportunities should, therefore, be objectively assessed against the risks inherent in specific markets. Douglas and Craig[18] suggest that risks might be assessed on factors such as the number of expropriations, rates of inflation and foreign exchange risk; opportunities could be based on indicators such as GNP per capita, growth of GNP and population size and density. In addition, cost of market entry and development require expert attention; costs of energy, labour, distribution and media are likely to vary over different territories. Many companies, accustomed to home trading for many years and then faced with developing export markets should accept that they need to learn almost from scratch about the factors affecting profitable operations overseas, otherwise they may become involved in ventures of distinctly unacceptable risk. Management need to have up-to-date information and exercise judgement based on evaluation of these facts, bearing in mind the complexity of factors, such as economic, socio-cultural and politico-legal, which will most certainly affect business development.

Successful overseas operations will depend considerably on the development of a carefully conceived risk policy. Marketing is a profit-earning function: it is not concerned merely with booking impressive orders, as the Rolls Royce RB211 debacle unmistakably showed some years ago.

In formulating marketing strategies — for home or overseas activities — companies should *develop an articulated risk policy*. Three kinds of risk policy have been classified:[2]

1. Risk avoidance (reduction of vulnerability)
2. Risk minimising (draw up 'risk profiles' of market opportunities)
3. Risk bearing (planned dispersion of risk through licensing, joint ventures, consortia, etc.)

Risk policies need to be established to control the element of risk involved in marketing goods and services overseas.

MARKET ENTRY: PRODUCT/COMMUNICATION STRATEGIES

Companies planning to enter overseas markets have to decide on the nature of the products to be offered. Will these be standard versions of existing ranges already sold in the home market?; will they be adapted versions of such products?; or will specially designed products have to be developed in order to compete successfully? (See Chapters 5 and 6: product policy and portfolio planning.)

Clearly, products identical or similar to those already in production for the home market will result in economies of scale, and also allow for rapid entry into chosen export markets. However, the likelihood of acceptance by foreign customers requires careful research; standard products may, of course, be acceptable provided certain modifications are incorporated to comply with specific national and industrial specifications. Again, market research should be undertaken to give guidance about the type of adaptation that may be necessary.

There may be other attractive overseas opportunities that can only be catered for by specially designed products. Such opportunities should be expertly assessed both in terms of potential business and also the costs involved, such as research and development, start-up production costs, marketing skills, etc.

Apart from matching products to markets, communication methods will also need to be appropriate to specific market environments. The decisions involved are shown schematically in Figure 8.3.

The top left cell of the matrix (straight extension) is obviously the simplest strategy and the lowest immediate risk to the marketer; a typical successful example has been Pepsi Cola.

The lower left cell (communication adaptation) is also a fairly low-risk venture, where only the methods of promotion, e.g. advertising copy, are modified to suit national markets.

The top middle (product adaptation) and the lower middle cells (dual adaptation) entail more fundamental changes than those just considered.

Products

	No product change	Adapt product	Develop new product
No communication change	Straight extension	Product adaptation	Product invention
Communications			Product invention
Adapt communications	Communication adaptation	Dual adaptation	

Figure 8.3 Product/communications strategies.

Source: See Keegan.[19] Reprinted by permission of the American Marketing Association.

SIM-I*

Petrol, for example, may require reformulation for different altitudes; engineering products may be modified to comply, for example, with safety standards in particular countries. The extra costs will have to be set against the prospects of profit; in any case, modifications are likely to be significantly less than developing entirely new products, such as indicated in the far right cell of the matrix (product invention). On the other hand, this latter strategy, although costly, may well pay off provided that the market is thoroughly investigated and the company has resources suitable for this innovative strategy.

The various product/communications strategies are already associated with degrees of risk and, as discussed earlier, the nature and extent of such risks should be identified and appropriate strategies developed so the markets can be exploited profitably.

LOGISTICS OF OVERSEAS OPERATIONS

Two vital areas of management are involved in the logistic planning of overseas operations: production and distribution.

Production can be arranged in several ways; the most effective method will depend on several factors, e.g. the type of product, accessibility of raw materials, sources of supply of component parts, type of labour required for successful operation, amount of capital demanded for production facilities, degree of technical and other expert knowledge available at head office and the state of development of the organisation.

Cars produced by the large multinational firms, mostly Amercian-owned, are designed for global sales, and are made in regional factories, drawing components and supplies from the most economical sources of specialised production, thus ensuring economies of scale.

Production Strategies

The following methods of production may, therefore, be considered suitable under particular conditions, dependent on the nature and resources of the trading organisation and the environment of the market overseas. Various strategies may be effective over different markets, so an exporting company may well have a variety of strategic approaches over world markets (refer to Figure 8.4):

1. direct export, e.g. production at home-based factory from which overseas markets are directly supplied
2. licensing arrangements, e.g. Pilkington's float-glass, is made under licence by many foreign glass manufacturers
3. build new factory overseas and develop strong national coverage, e.g. Philips' electronic equipment

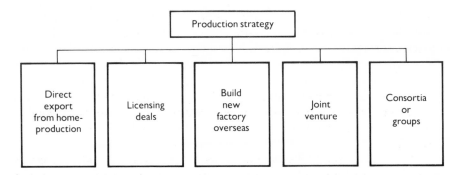

Figure 8.4   Production strategies for overseas trading.

4. joint venture with a foreign company, e.g. Du Pont
5. consortia or groups

Home-based Production

The type of product may largely determine its place of production. Large items of capital equipment demanding expert technical knowledge and manufacturing skills may be bought fairly infrequently and it would tend to be uneconomic to set up highly specialised plant in more than one major area. Where direct exporting is adopted, manufacturers have the advantage of being able to have full control of the product eventually marketed. Specifications, qualities and service remain the prerogative and responsibility of the home-based organisations. Apart from home-based production of completely finished products, some manufacturers, for example British car producers, export their products in kit form for assembly abroad. This substantial trade is to accommodate foreign insistence on incorporating locally made parts in cars sold in their countries, and to overcome trade barriers against fully assembled vehicles.

Licensing may be attractive to some manufacturers as an overseas production and marketing strategy; it may be very effective in minimising risks by avoiding the need to make heavy investment in capital and labour. Many licensing arrangements tend to be found among smaller companies which lack resources to exploit markets by themselves. Exceptions such as Pilkingtons occur, and it is possible only to generalise. Pilkingtons, whose float-glass process had 100 relevant UK patents by 1972, and corresponding patents in fifty other countries is an outstanding example of successful licensing. All the world's major glass manufacturers had taken licences to be processed by 1969: twenty-three manufacturers in over thirteen countries were involved.

In their race to 'catch up' with the western economies, Japanese companies obtained over 2500 licences to exploit foreign technologies.[20] A similar pattern is being followed by the Eastern Bloc countries. In the Middle East, imported technologies are significantly simpler, while in the developing countries as a whole, there are opportunities for licensing 'often almost forgotten' technologies.

A licence deal is usually a strategy adopted to gain time, compared with the time normally taken to plan and to develop a product apart from the risks involved in starting from scratch. In addition, some existing products may already be protected by patents in specific markets, and the only effective method of marketing in these areas would be to acquire a manufacturing or patent licence. It would be advisable to enquire fully into territorial restrictions, degree of exclusive use in specific markets, access to technical services of sponsoring company, precise financial commitment involved, i.e. initial down-payments and subsequent royalties, and options relating to future developments affecting the products now under licence. With a view to long-term development, a company may refuse to license in a market which is regarded as having important potential opportunities.

The plastics and petrochemical industries have been developed over the world through effective international licensing agreements. 'In the manufacture of low-density polyethylene about 40–45% of the world's capacity is based on the original ICI development ... Half of the total capacity is thought to have been installed via licence agreements'.[14]

A particularly interesting example of effective licensing arrangements related to Associated Engineering (now called the AE Group), the largest manufacturer of engine components in the world, which negotiated a licensing agreement with the Lippon Piston Ring Company, enabling the Japanese to manufacture piston rings and valve seat inserts for car engines by the powdered metal (sintering) process. Brico Engineering, a subsidiary of Associated Engineering, had been successfully manufacturing these components by this method for some years, whereas their international competitors were, at that time, still in the prototype stage of development. The improved technical performance of sintered parts is demonstrated in the ability to withstand increasing wear and tear.

This was the second licensing agreement which AE had negotiated with a Japanese company. Some time previously, another group subsidiary, Glacier Metals, entered into a licensing arrangement relating to the production of thin wall bearings in Japan.

Licence deals may involve service industries as well as tangible products. Franchising is like licensing, but is generally discussed in connection with the service industries.

For example, the Hilton Hotels Corporation has developed a new strategy to combat increasing competition from rivals such as Holiday Inns, Sheraton, etc. In a deal with the Prudential Assurance Company of America, Hilton sold off their hotels in Los Angeles, San Francisco, Dallas, Washington and New

York State, and now take half the profits plus a fixed 3% of the gross revenues in management fees. The ready cash from this large scale deal has been used to reduce Hilton's long-term debt.

It was reported[22] that although the Hilton flag identifies more than 200 hotels around the world, the company actually ownes (or leases and operates) only about 20 of these. The preferred policy is to operate franchises or to enter into joint ventures. An initial franchise fee of between $10,000 and $50,000 is charged, and Hilton supply the know-how in exchange for 5% share of room revenues.

As with licensing, franchising calls for careful research to identify suitable potential franchisees, while marketing plans should consider that adequate control is exercised over this fast-growing trading development. Franchising has spread rapidly from the US; well known names such as Hertz, Avis, and McDonalds typify this form of business activity.

Licensing entails, however, risks of its own; for example, royalties may be withheld or not paid at all for various reasons, often dubious; the territorial constraints may be disregarded and enforcement of the original licence terms may not be feasible. Clearly, the granting of licences requires expert legal and commercial advice.

Apart from direct licensing, a company may make arrangements, known as contract manufacturing, for the manufacture of some of its products by an overseas firm, but retain marketing responsibilities themselves. Kotler[10] notes that this strategy has been used by Sears Roebuck in opening up department stores in Mexico and Spain, and arranging for approved local manufacturers to produce some of the products it sells. Proctor and Gamble have adopted contract manufacturing of soap in order to enter the Italian market; this strategy enabled them to challenge Colgate and Unilever, who were already firmly established with their own production resources. One of the drawbacks of contract manufacturing is control over the quality and efficiency of the production processes undertaken by a local manufacturer.

Build New Factory Overseas

To set up manufacturing facilities in an overseas market requires considerable capital expenditure and long-term investment; these risks should only be undertaken after very thorough research into all the factors affecting production, e.g. recruitment and training of a suitable workforce, employment policies and those countries under study, political and other constraints on development by non-national organisations, etc. Leading industrial groups such as ICI, Philips Electrical and Michelin, have supplied, for several years, many overseas markets from factories in those countries.

In some instances, the national origin of the trading organisation has tended to become of minor interest to customers, and the products made in these satellite factories are accepted as belonging entirely to the countries in which they are produced. As a matter of business policy, large international organisations frequently prefer to emphasise their national links in order to build up strong brand loyalty amongst their overseas customers.

Some types of products attract custom by virtue of the fact that they originate from specific regions. Scotch whisky, English bone china and Sheffield cutlery are held by many to be superior to indigenous products, and manufacturers need to reflect carefully on the effect on their sales if they were to supply certain markets from internal sources.

It is unlikely that factories will be dispersed over several overseas markets by relatively young companies. This phase in overseas production/marketing strategy tends to be confined to mature organisations with substantial experience in export trading, and who possess technical and commercial expertise of unusual quality. A *Financial Times* report[23] noted that 'Companies rarely have a straight choice between putting up a plant at home and abroad. Most manufacturing investment overseas is related to where the market is. ICI built a polythene plant in the South of France because, in its view, that was the only way to gain a substantial share of the market.

The inviting prospect of new business or the threat of losing a valuable market may be powerful motivations for companies to set up manufacturing plants overseas. In addition, of course, factors such as lower labour costs, transport charges, ease of recruiting suitable types of labour skills, etc., are likely to be influential. The cost of transporting liquid ammonia 'was such as to preclude its export to distant countries, and it was necessary to manufacture it locally if a place in the market was sought'.[1]

Probably the world's most highly organised multinational food company is Nestlé, the Swiss controlled organisation with 300 factories dispersed over 70 countries. From its headquarters at Vevey, on the shores of Lake Geneva, Nestlé top management continuously monitor their global commercial strategies. The enlargement of the Common Market, worldwide realignments of currencies, together with the growing pressure on large corporations by their financial institutions and their investors to reveal more information about their trading operations, have all contributed to Nestlé's strategic appraisals. In furthering a policy of diversification away from milk-based foods, Nestlé have had to abandon another of its corporate faiths — 100% ownership of operating subsidiaries, and they are increasingly becoming involved in partial take-overs; this in turn has led to the need for increased disclosure about their financial affairs. As Nestlé continue their strategy of diversification and part-ownership, it will be interesting to study the repercussions of this new strategy on their traditional methods of capital structure and management.

Joint ventures, as mentioned in Chapter 2, often involve large organisations in the belief that their substantial combined resources may result in more effective infiltration and expansion in chosen markets. Equity held by a company can range from 10 to 90%, but most fall within 25–75%. In certain overseas markets, such as Mexico, India, or Sri Lanka, joint venture operations are the only permissible entry strategy.[18]

Firms may have complementary resources; specialised technology plus marketing skills may result from effective joint venture operations. This was the reason why 'the 170 US companies with widest international spread chose the joint venture form for nearly one-third of their 3400 entries into foreign manufacturing between 1900 and 1967'.[24]

The three most important contributions made by overseas joint venture partners, as perceived by the managers of 80 out of 170 US companies surveyed, were: (1) general knowledge about the local environment; (2) local general managers; (3) marketing personnel. Other advantages were related to the provision of local capital, access to local raw materials and production and technical research and development skills.

Joint ventures may, in general, benefit both parties but there is sometimes a clash of policies, which is inclined to be particularly felt by minority interests. This had tended to make companies rather cautious in their attitudes towards joint working arrangements. The problems of joint ventures are reflected in the fact that 'nearly 35% of all the joint ventures that American companies have entered into with European companies in Europe have ended either in divorce, usually with the American company taking over, or in a significant shift of power, to a majority holding in favour of the American partner'.[24] It has also been established that one-third of the 30 joint ventures in America entered into by 45 European companies no longer exist; they are now fully owned European subsidiaries. For instance, Smith's Food Group was eventually taken over completely by General Mills; the Chrysler Corporation's joint venture with the Rootes British Motor Group ended with outright purchase.

Research[24] has identified the following predictors of the probable viability of joint ventures:

1. the strategies of the enterprises concerned, particularly related to the degree to which their product lines may be diversified or not
2. the organisational structure of the companies involved, particularly of the company from the investing country
3. the degree to which the investing partner feels its head office staff are able to predict and, therefore, plan and control, the outcome of the marketing and production activities of the joint venture subsidiary

The following variables were not regarded as significant by the companies surveyed:

1. the 'cultural distance' between the US firm and the country of its European partners
2. the industry of either the parent or foreign joint-venture subsidiary
3. the degree to which conflicts or problems in joint ventures were over such matters as slowness of decision making, or desire to integrate accounting systems, etc.

The terms of a joint venture should be carefully drafted. As with licensing arrangements, it is clearly advisable to have expert legal and commercial consultations before joint venture commitments are undertaken. Division of ownership may create conflicting loyalites among individual executives in member companies constituting the joint venture.

Du Pont, the mammoth US chemical group, announced in 1974 a major investment programme on worldwide expansion, of which Europe was to receive a substantial share. 'An $80m joint venture with Société des Usines Chemiques Rhone–Poulenc to build and operate a 100,000 tons a year adiponitrile plant in France'.[25] This first European joint venture for Du Pont has encouraged further links of this nature. The Chairman of Du Pont acknowledged the dangers of diversification: 'We have learned that being good in the chemical business does not necessarily mean you are good in the pharmaceuticals business. To put it bluntly, we have laid an egg.'[25]

Matsushita made a joint venture agreement with General Electric in order to introduce its new video disc system into the US. This helped them to face the strong competition from RCA and Philips of North America. Fujitsu teamed up with TRW so that they could break into the US computer market.[11]

In 1983, AT & T formed a joint company with Philips in Europe to market public telephone exchanges internationally. It has also agreed to buy a 25% interest in Olivetti. GTE of the US has formed a UK subsidiary with Ferranti in Manchester. LM Ericsson has a joint venture with the American oil company, Atlantic Richfield, and is also collaborating closely with Honeywell, the US computer firm.[26]

Rank Xerox was set up as the 50/50 jointly owned subsidiary of the British Rank Organisation and the American Xerox Corporation. McVitie (United Biscuits Group) established in the early 1970s, a 50/50 joint venture with Meiji, the largest Japanese bakery and confectionery firm. This has enabled them to infiltrate successfully into the Japanese market. The British firm is reported to have spent over £100,000 on market research, working through a list of 26 possible candidates presented by the Boston Consulting Group for joint venture operations, before eventually drawing up an agreement with Meiji which offered the considerable attraction of an extremely effective distribution network of 1500 'primary' wholesalers covering the four main Japanese islands.

Metal Box, Britain's largest can manufacturing group, teamed up with Toyo Glass, the biggest makers of glass containers in Japan, to develop a glass-making industry in Nigeria. Metal Box took 51% of the equity; Toyo, which provided the technical know-how, had 9%. The balance of the equity was distributed over the Nigerian Industrial Development Bank, National Insurance Corporation of Nigeria and the Ibru Group of Companies (25%), the residual shares were taken up by twenty Nigerian citizens who included senior Nigerian management of Metal Box. This enterprising deal has enabled Nigeria to reduce its import bill and has also provided work for its labour force; among the objectives laid down by the Nigerian Government was that this manufacturing venture should not result merely in the production of glass containers at minimum cost but to produce them at less cost than *imported* bottles. At the same time, the social and economic aspects of employment in this developing country were to be borne in mind when deciding on production techniques.

Consortia or Groups

A consortium or group of companies involved in multinational business operations may be effective in certain industries. Some large civil engineering contracts (as noted in Chapter 2) are often won by an association of construction companies; these may be entirely British or include foreign companies. Some contracts are of such scale that they demand resources beyond the scope of even the largest contractors, so companies like Costain and Taylor Woodrow team up on multi-million pound projects such as civil engineering contracts in the Middle East. In 1976 Tarmac, a leading British construction group, was reported[27] to have secured, in conjunction with Asman Ahmed Osman & Co., the Arab contractors, a contract for a tunnel under the Suez Canal.

Consortia are likely to develop as effective methods of securing valuable export business, particularly where political factors may be significant in the allocation of large-scale contracts. The provision of project management services is developing fast to meet the increasing trend towards consortia working. Clearly, the overall design and coordination of the various inputs into a large civil engineering contract calls for expert project management involving not only technical problems but diverse cultural reactions. As an American management consultant has observed: 'Ramadan is a month-long Arab fasting period. Although employees are required to come to work, (construction) output historically falls to under 25% of US levels during that month'.[28]

Distribution Strategies

There are several alternative, and sometimes complementary, methods of distribution in overseas markets. The general principles of these various methods will be reviewed, but individual arrangements will obviously be made after thorough market knowledge has been obtained.

Methods of distribution may be one or a mix of the following (see Figure 8.5):

1. direct marketing
2. stockist–distributor network
3. agencies
   (a) exclusive
   (b) shared

Figure 8.5 Distribution strategies for overseas trading.

Direct production and direct marketing strategies frequently go hand-in-hand. They tend to give greater effective control over export operations, but the costs involved should always be assessed carefully. Many medium and smaller companies would be unable to absorb the extra overheads involved in setting up, for example, a specialised staff to deal with export orders and enquiries. The alternative may be to use the services of export merchants who will supply, on a professional basis, expert knowledge and administrative facilities to exporters. With consumer products, direct selling operations may include setting up an exclusive network of retail distributors in large stores situated in major cities and towns. This type of selective marketing has been adopted for many years by some leading manufacturers of furniture, tableware and textiles.

An alternative distribution strategy may involve appointing local distributors who would be expected to hold reasonable stocks of a range of products for quick local delivery.

It is important for exporters to appreciate the status and role of distributors. Normally, they would buy the products which are specified in their agreements with the exporting firms, import these goods, pay all import charges and duties, warehouse expenses and selling costs. Commission is usually not included in their remuneration which is based on the difference between the gross costs of the goods imported and the prices at which these goods are sold to their customers. In certain cases, a distributor may have to sell at schedule prices approved by the principal and the commission may then be paid. Distributors are normally concerned with consumer products including durables such as cars; capital investment products and industrial supplies are generally too costly and bulky for distributive stock-holding purposes.

A commission agent, as distinct from a distributor, obtains orders for his principal who ships and invoices direct to the customers involved. For this service, the agent receives an agreed rate of commission. In some cases, an agent may buy on his own behalf as a distributor, but this option would need to be agreed.

The appointment of agents, exclusive or shared, should not be undertaken casually. Exhaustive enquiries should be made about the commercial standing of prospective agents, and their terms of appointment require very careful drafting regarding details such as remuneration, products to be sold, prices and discount structure, methods of promotion, provision of after-sales service, where applicable, and other significant aspects of satisfactory commercial operations. Where agents are also selling products made by other companies, the agreement normally excludes them from selling goods which may reduce the likelihood of success with the products mentioned in the agreement.

The territory covered should be defined clearly, particularly where an extensive national area may be divided between several agents. It is also necessary to obtain agreement about the method of dealing with the commission payable, enquiries and orders which may emanate from the agents' territory without his active intervention, as in the case of visiting foreign buyers, trade buying missions, etc.

The duration of an agency agreement should be mutually agreed; also the method of determination which is acceptable to both parties. Certain events such as bankruptcy, liquidation or merger may be held to give either party a right to determine an agency agreement. It is important, therefore, to stipulate the nature of such events, and the system of law to which the contract is to be subject. There may be cases where an agency agreement has to recognise the law of a particular overseas country, so exporters would be advised to examine the legal implications very carefully before committing themselves.

The British Overseas Trade Board and the Department of Trade offer British firms assistance in identifying suitable agents, and may provide a shortlist of prospects. However, it is the responsibility of companies to meet these potential agents, preferably in their own territories, and to assess their suitability for the specific marketing tasks to be undertaken.

Manufacturers may prefer to open up their own sales offices in major centres to control the marketing operation. Sometimes, companies may find it advantageous to 'buy their way in' to a market by purchasing one or more distributors. However, this strategy needs careful handling as it could build up general trade resistance. Some industrial companies, such as Massey-Ferguson and the various motor vehicle manufacturers, have worldwide networks of dealers with exclusive selling rights in defined geographical areas.

Barter — An Old System in a New Environment

Barter, one of the oldest kinds of trading known to man, was widespread in the 1920s, when war-stricken Europe was trying to revive international trade. Again, in the depression years of the 1930s, barter deals were popular; Hitler's Germany was a notable user.

Nowadays, barter deals are tending to increase because of the market opportunities they offer which, otherwise, would be closed to traditional methods of financing deals.

Some countries with chronic balance of payments deficits and consequent shortages of foreign exchange, impose priorities on the imports allowed into their countries. Would-be importers face these alternatives: manufacturing within the market, abandoning the prospective market, or evolving some suitable scheme of barter with products which are in excess supply. The barter transaction rests on the fact that the prospective importing nation cannot sell the excess goods itself for hard currencies. The bartering firm has to sell or use profitably the goods acquired by barter.

Barter has been widely used by Communist countries, but it is not limited to them, or even to the less developed countries with balance of payments deficits. For example, Ford of Britain has bartered cars for coffee (Columbia), cranes (Norway), toilet seats (Finland), potatoes (Spain) and cotton (Sudan). Companies which are not generally accustomed to the complexities of bartering often rely on specialised intermediaries to sell the goods they receive in exchange for their exports.

In order to sell their products in the USSR, the Pepsi Company made a barter agreement which involved them in becoming the sole agent for Russian Vodka in the US.

The British subsidiary of Gillette has extended its sales in eastern Europe by extensive bartering arrangements made through a special London agency.

General Motors fixed up a multi-million dollar deal by agreeing to barter its earth-moving equipment for Russian timber.[11]

Barter, or counter trading, as it is often called, appears to be growing in trade with Latin American countries, particularly Brazil. Some deals can become unusually complex. A London-based agency arranged for the sale of British pharmaceuticals and vehicles to Ecuador in exchange for bananas, which had to be transhipped via a Mediterranean port for eventual sale in Egypt. It was discovered that Western Shipping Lines would not handle the fruit, and a Soviet fleet had to be signed up; all this resulted in a month's intensive work for the agency involved.[29]

Because bartering is different from normal trading, and also owing to its complexity, it may well be less profitable than regular export sales, which leads most firms to regard it as a necessary evil or a last resort. In tackling contemporary problems in overseas markets, a firm should, however, adopt a more positive approach. If a company has unlimited market opportunities in non-barter transactions, it would be advisable to pursue these without getting involved in barter deals. But if the firm has more productive capacity than market opportunities, and if the future pattern of trading is likely to have to extend to numerous countries with balance of payments deficits and exchange restrictions, there will be the need for the top management to decide how to optimise its profits.

In reacting positively to barter opportunities, a firm should evaluate the costs and benefits of the operation, and set up and effective method of dealing with this new-style trading.

Some of the factors to be carefully evaluated are: (1) possibility of a lower return on some barter deals than normal trading; (2) risk in handling unfamiliar products; (3) payment time will most likely be extended; (4) conflict with firm's hard-currency markets may arise; and (5) long and complex negotiations with buying countries, many of whom may lack business expertise.

Barter can also offer benefits, some of which could be: (1) the use of excess productive capacity to cover variable costs and to make a contribution towards fixed costs and total profits; (2) maintenance of exports and employment when these are important both to the firm and to the national economy (these factors affected Ford of Britain); (3) entry into otherwise closed markets; (4) attracting goodwill of overseas governments which could lead to extended business later in normal trading terms; and (5) possible development of new and economic sources of supply for raw materials or component parts.

Barter dealing requires a systematic approach. The first step would be to establish a market intelligence system to identify and evaluate opportunities. (Export marketing research is discussed later.) Special negotiating expertise would have to be developed or acquired from professional agencies. Instead of relying entirely on intermediaries, a firm may develop its own barter organisation, authorised by top management to deal in a wide range of exchange commodities. Ford of Britain, for example, appointed an executive as Special Transactions Manager.

Chrysler has been involved in barter deals on numerous occasions. In one instance, a Middle Eastern country had no foreign exchange but had a surplus of hazelnuts. The government wanted to exchange trucks for hazelnuts. Chrylser were able to locate an import house that would buy 100 tons at a discount. The nuts were shipped to the import house; on receipt, the importer paid the money into an account against which several trucks were sold. Another case involved Columbia which, at that time, was experiencing low coffee prices and a serious shortage of foreign exchange. A farm group had a surplus potato crop and wanted to buy trucks. Chrysler contacted several American brokers, and then learned that the existence of a potato disease in Latin America meant that the US Department of Agriculture would not allow the potatoes to be imported. Not daunted, Chrylser turned to Europe and finally located a buyer in France who, in turn, sold the potatoes to a manufacturer of industrial alcohol.

Kaiser Industries accepted from Columbia a bulk consignment of coffee in exchange for 1000 jeeps. The coffee 'was traded in Europe for sugar, then the sugar for pig iron, and finally, the pig iron for US dollars'.[6]

Switch Trading

This is a more complex method of accomplishing similar results to barter trading. Many countries have bilateral trade and payment agreements. Because the bilateral trade seldom balances exactly, these accounts usually contain a supply of non-convertible currencies. The nation with these balances does not need them to buy more goods from the bilateral trading partner, and it cannot use them elsewhere because they are inconvertible. Thus the nation may be quite willing to transfer these credits to a third country, even at a discount, to obtain useful goods.

An international firm may be able to sell its exports to such a third country through a specialist in switch trading. These specialists are located primarily in Austria and Switzerland. The criteria for evaluation switch trading are generally the same as apply to barter transactions.

Switch trading is complicated and usually involves three or more parties, one from each of the countries with bilateral trading agreements with one or more of the other countries involved in a particular transaction. Clearly, this exporting strategy requires extremely careful planning and execution.

Leasing in International Markets

Aspects of leasing equipment were considered in Chapter 2, when it was noted that leasing is an important marketing strategy which is developing considerably. Although more prevalent in the US than elsewhere, leasing is growing rapidly in foreign markets. It is offsetting the immediate impact of escalating prices of capital equipment which, together with the problems of generating sufficient profits to invest in new machinery, have made this marketing strategy remarkably effective.

Clark Equipment Company in the US has a subsidiary, Clark Rental Corporation, which leases fork-lift trucks with marked success. The Prudential Insurance Co. of America has invested $7 million as part owner of a new venture, TAW International Leasing, which plans to operate across the African continent, leasing industrial equipment.[6] In Britain, equipment used in civil engineering contracts is often obtained through leasing agreements; this is particularly attractive to small firms.

In Europe, leasing has become popular and is growing at a fast pace. Expensive equipment can be used without capital investment and for a low annual cost. Under leasing contracts, service and maintenance clauses may be further benefits to the lessee. In countries with shortages of skilled mechanics and technicians, this back-up service is a strong inducement to negotiate a lease.

Leasing opens up new opportunities in world markets. It also encourages the use of new types of equipment, the adoption of which may be slow because of the perceived risk in innovation.

When inflation is rife in a particular overseas market, leasing agreements need to be drafted with special care, or, as the contract period extends, heavy losses could be incurred by the supplying company. Another hazard could be in the entire loss of leased equipment because of political upheavals in some areas.

Many leasing arrangements provide users with the option of purchase after a period of time and on agreed terms. This flexible policy allows users to generate funds from the equipment before they are faced with an investment option.

Leasing as an overseas marketing strategy is likely to represent an increasing proportion of the income from export activities to industrial firms. Since it involves industrial exporters in substantial investment in equipment and in the logistics of servicing, very thorough evaluation of market opportunities is strongly advisable before making this necessarily long-term commitment in specific market areas.

SPAN OF INTERNATIONAL MARKETING STRATEGIES

International marketing strategies range, therefore, across a continuum from direct exporting from a home-based factory to sophisticated systems of supranational marketing by which large international undertakings, such as Ford, divide their marketing activities into 'zones', with a distribution network controlled by the zone company. This global approach to marketing, frequently involving zoned production of specific types or variations of products, is the ultimate expression of highly specialised mass production and distribution strategies.

Need for Flexibility in an Organisation

The determination of strategies suitable for companies to adopt is the crucial responsibility of senior management. Within industries, companies operate to secure advantage over their competitors in chosen markets. It follows that the dynamics of those industries and the nature of the business environment affect the style of individual company's operational strategies. (Refer to Porter's model: Chapter 5.)

The types of organisation — production and marketing — should not be regarded as fixed for all time. As markets and technologies develop, new organisational structures may be advisable to enable companies to take advantage of changing environments in world markets. Further, it is unlikely that a standard strategy would be acceptable and successful in all markets. Whatever approach is used, rigidity should be avoided and remote control should not be allowed to frustrate marketing opportunties.

Companies marketing over many countries face a variety of problems, some of which will be complex, particularly where political, fiscal and social variables appear to be in a state of almost continuous change. Reappraisals may be necessary of particular marketing strategies because of these changes. Marketing management decisions are likely to be taken nearer to the actual area of operations, where the advantage of close working knowledge of the environment will be of enormous help maintaining a flexible marketing posture.

BASIC BEHAVIOURAL PATTERNS OF INTERNATIONAL COMPANIES

Two basic approaches adopted by companies with international sales organisations were identified in the *Harvard Business Review*.[30] These organisational features may be viewed as extremes of a continuum, as shown in Figure 8.6

These two extreme approaches to the management of international sales have their distinctive attractions and also disadvantages.

The 'centrist' approach allows head office to continue to have strong control over management policies, methods of operation, costs, etc., but it weakens management initiative in overseas areas which are modelled on the home-based organisation. It tends to breed inflexibility and, eventually, inability to respond effectivly to the needs of different markets. Hostility between local management and head office staff may also be a danger of this rigid system of management.

Figure 8.6   Basic behavioural patterns of international companies.

Source: See Gestetner.[30]

The 'non-centrist' management philosphy recognises the need for flexibility in dealing with the diverse problems encountered in international trading. Immediate on-the-spot management decisions can be taken to take advantage of changes in local conditions. Of course, there are some drawbacks: lack of centralised control could lead to wasted managerial time in 're-inventing the wheel', when central policy could have dictated solutions based on other areas. Local management may grow to resent any type of head office intervention, and locally evolved decisions may lack the perspective vantage of a less personally involved evaluation made at head office.

'In general, controlling a non-centrist company is a much more contradictory procedure than controlling a centrist company. Whereas the centrist's whole being is bound up with control mechanisms, the non-centrist constantly walks a tightrope between allowing the local office freedom of action within certain bounds and safeguarding a financial investment from which a fair return must come — between avoiding corporate anarchy and giving the freedom to develop, create and relate to local circumstances'.[30]

In general, companies with a large home market tend to adopt a centrist policy, largely because management assumes that policies which have been successful domestically will be equally effective in other areas. Where companies have only a limited home market, management tends to be more alert to opportunities in other markets and is more willing to adapt its strategy.

International trading 'is more in the blood of businessmen in the small countries', which often based their trade on the old colonial markets. Until recently, however, 'there has been no tradition of international trading in the United States'[30] because of its self-sufficiency in raw materials and internal development. Although this self-sufficiency no longer exists, the huge American home market generally encourages the development of a centrist policy, whereas European organisations tend to be non-centrist.

Permutter's view[31] is that an organisation's policy is determined by the attitudes of its managers. He has suggested three models of international managemenet: *ethnocentric, polycentric* and *geocentric*. The first two relate to the typical development observable in large companies which have substantial overseas business. In ethnocentric organisations, decision making is highly centralised and detailed, day-to-day control is exercised from head office in London, New York or elsewhere. The polycentric style evolves from realising that there are sound reasons why many management decisions should be taken in the actual markets; local personnel are acknowledged to be more likely to know at first hand about the effects of certain management decisions than executives in distant headquarters. The needs of local communities may, for example, be given more attention, and hostile reactions avoided. This loosening of direct, central authority will tend to be offset by greater attention to systematic financial reporting. The major automobile groups have various degrees of polycentricity, which is occasionally modified by direct intervention from corporate headquarters.

Geocentrism means having a truly worldwide approach; staff regardless of nationality are moved freely across international subsidiaries.

In this idealised concept of transglobal trading, research and development would be organised on an international basis, the resultant findings would be made freely available to all subsidiary companies. The corporate creed is 'internationalism' built in the foundations of the free movement of staff and knowledge within constituent companies of a multinational group. Whether this idealistic approach would earn the whole-hearted support of some senior management is open to some doubt.

Critics[32] of this typology, while conceding it is conceptually useful, comment that it is difficult to distinguish accurately between the various types of corporate behaviour patterns. There may be far more than just the three basic typologies and, in any case, structures and systems are dynamic in international firms.

Stopford[33] states that the attitudes and assumptions of the senior executives greatly influence styles of management which vary considerably. However, there are 'certain common denominators' which distinguish Americans from their European colleagues, and these reflect the divergent cultures and philosophies. Foreign nationals may not share the attitudes and assumptions of senior executives in the parent company. Recently, there have been major changes in the domestic and foreign structures of many European firms, and subsidiaries have been adapting the American techniques to suit their particular way of doing business.

Rigid criteria of organisational behaviour may have had more chance of success some years ago when market environments were less competitive; more flexible and innovative structures seem to be evident.

Some middle path may be the most effective international management policy which, whilst encouraging local initiative and developing managerial talent, safeguards the overall profitability of the organisation by a degree of intervention necessitating, for example, head office sanction of structural changes to local companies or the appointment of key personnel.

Three types of personality among national managers have been identified[15]: the *strategist* who is best able to grasp the issues and put forward an integrated planning proposal; the *politician* who has particular ability to influence people; and the *executive* who is the highly motivated decision taker. How far these attributes are necessary or desirable in overseas marketing positions is not clear; but it would seem that managers would generally be more effective if they were to develop a balanced blend of these distinct qualities. In particular, the need to be responsive to market changes — which are social as well as economic — should be a prime managerial objective. A new type of international manager needs to be developed who can move easily across cultural and national boundaries and develop his company's business activities without offending sensitive areas of human behaviour.

NEED FOR EXECUTIVE FREEDOM

Although modern travel encourages head office staff to visit overseas markets regularly, and on special missions, constant intervention will not develop in local marketing staff their personal responsibility for the success of the agreed marketing strategy in their area. Overseas staff should be selected not only for their technical knowledge but also for their commercial abilities. If the right people are appointed, they should be given the opportunity of developing management judgement in their particular sphere of operations. Tactical decisions should largely be left to them within, of course, the framework of the company's policy.

The need for a degree of executive freedom at local levels of operation has been commented upon by Hussey[34]: 'I believe that a sound approach to long range planning requires that the talents of these managers be used in a broader sense to help the chief executive of the total group to identify and select the strategies open to him. It is possible to gain considerable benefit by allowing a measure of subsidiary participation in the shaping of the future of the group. This is a process which, for example, is well developed in the Swiss based pharmaceutical and chemical company, Sandoz A.G. of Basle.

'All strategic planning systems should be designed to encourage flair, an acceptance of the challenge of change and to nurture that all too scarce commodity, management talent.'

A programme of corporate acculturation may be a creative approach which some multinational companies would find fruitful. 'Corporate acculturation generally requires a firm to select carefully and train subsidiary managers extensively in order to make them deeply ingrained with corporate objectives and philosophy ... As a parallel, Antony Jay cites the example of the Roman governor and the British Colonial Officer who ruled far from home with virtually no supervision or policy guidance'.[13]

It will be seen, therefore, that exporting calls for a flexible approach to marketing strategy and tactics. Although a manufacturer may enjoy a strong brand image in his home market, when he ventures abroad he may suddenly find himself trading not only in a different environment but without the benefit of an acceptable brand name. It may be necessary to pioneer sales abroad — and this calls for an entirely different orientation towards the potential customer. Some marketing executives seem to find difficulty in changing their personal attitudes which have been formed from years of brand leadership, perhaps, in the home market. Unless they are willing to face this problem honestly, success is unlikely.

BETRO RESEARCH

Research[3] undertaken under the auspices of the Royal Society of Arts identified specific determinants of export success. The need to concentrate on fewer markets and to develop these in depth has been referred to earlier in the section headed 'The Principle of Critical Mass'.

Another critical factor related to staffing, and it was found that British companies' export staffs are small in relation to the numbers employed on home sales and are also small in comparison with the number of countries they have to cover. But the Japanese, in fact, appear to be far more realistic and to reverse the ratio of home and export salesmen.

BETRO considered that two historic reasons may have led to the low staffing ratios in export selling:

1. the relatively low level of interest in exports (until 1965, British exports of manufactured goods never exceeded 12%)
2. export was largely on a 'residual' basis after home market needs had been satisfied. A further cause could relate to the general tendency for overseas countries to be handled *en bloc*, whereas the home market would be subdivided into individual sales territories enabling sales efforts to be directed more effectively.

Although over recent years there has been a higher priority given by most companies to export marketing, sales personnel have increased by only about a quarter, and a disproportionate allocation of selling resources over home and export markets is apparent.

BETRO reported that there are 'many companies where almost the entire export effort revolves around one man (including a number exporting 50–80% of their production)'.[3] The physical task of keeping in touch with customers was clearly extremely difficult and the report emphasised that regular personal contracts with overseas customers were vital to success in competitive markets. BETRO found that 'even the giant companies are short of adequate manpower to deploy in the most profitable markets'.[3]

Another important factor contributing to exporting success related to the selection of agents. British companies placed more stress on sound financial status and adequate technical qualifications than marketing strength; the Germans and French tended to reverse the order of these criteria.

Only about a third of British companies set targets for their agents, but those which did achieved higher sales. There was also some feeling that French and German companies demanded a higher performance from their agents than British companies which often failed to integrate agents into their marketing strategies. Close working arrangements between companies and agents generally proved to be very successful.

BETRO also studied the impact of methods of costing and pricing policy on export performance. It was recommended that the professional expertise of accountants could be improved by a keener awareness of and closer involvement in problems of exporting, particularly price determination. Marketing management should be prepared to discuss fully these problems with their financial colleagues and should acquire, for example, knowledge of the cost structure of their products. The allocation of these costs over home and export markets should be carefully examined for its effect on total corporate profitability.

NEDO RESEARCH

In the earlier discussions in concentrating on key markets, the NEDO paper[4] identified significant factors affecting the UK's export performance. In addition to market targeting, other significant factors were isolated and are briefly: many companies devote insufficient effort to increasing competitiveness in non-price terms (e.g. design, development of new products, after-sales service, etc.); many companies treat exporting as a marginal activity; there is a tendency to lose share more rapidly in fast-growing, large markets; products made are not those required by large, faster growing economies — the UK is being forced into smaller, slower growing markets; inability to supply the goods when needed.

Another NEDO report[35] had also emphasised the need for the UK to produce higher added value products, and to get away from mere price-comparison products. 'Price is one of a number of characteristics of manufactured products upon which market share depends; and firms often find competition less easily matched when it extends to non-price factors'. The report stated that the British engineering industry tended to turn out products of lower unit value than Germany or France, and to import relatively higher added value products.

SUMMARY

International marketing demands systematic planning, starting with well designed marketing research. Companies should identify their export motivations, audit corporate resources, and relate these to identified market opportunities.

Five phases in entry to international marketing have been noted as: opportunism; limited commitment; limited fixed investment, major dependence on overseas business; and no distinction between home and export markets.

Multinational corporations operate subsidiaries in a number of different nation states; oil companies figure prominently. International business negotiations are affected considerably by relationships between multinational firms and the governments of the countries concerned. Third World multinationals are growing fast.

Risk policies in relation to export opportunities should be drawn up. Three kinds of risk policy have been classified thus: risk avoidance, risk minimising, and risk bearing.

Product/communication strategies should be devised according to specific market conditions.

Production and distribution strategies should also be related to market opportunities: options for production include direct exporting, licensing, overseas manufacture, joint venture, consortia or groups; methods of distribution may involve direct marketing, stockist–distributor network or agencies (exclusive, or shared).

Barter, switch-trading, and leasing are other options which may be suitable for certain deals.

The style of control of international sales may be across a continuum: centrist–non-centrist. Another approach suggests three models of international management: ethnocentric, polycentric, and geocentric. How far it is possible in practice to distinguish accurately between these various models is unclear.

A programme of corporate acculturation may be helpful to some multinational companies to ensure that managers are so knowledgeable about corporate objectives and philosophy that they can operate successfully wherever their sphere of activities takes them.

BETRO research identified exporting success as specifically related to concentration on key markets, the ratio of home and export sales staff, the selection and management of agents, and the need for accountants and marketers to work closely together, particularly in price determination.

NEDO emphasised that exporting success was also linked to 'non-price competitiveness' and the development of higher added value products.

REFERENCES

1. Wormald, Avison, *International Business,* Pan Books, London, 1973.
2. Political and Economic Planning, 'Sample Surveys — Part One', PEP Report No. 313, Vol. XVI, May 1950.
3. Royal Society of Arts, 'Concentration on Key Markets', BETRO Report, 1975.
4. Cornell, David, National Economic Development Office, Discussion Paper No. 6: 'UK's Performance in Export Markets', January 1980.
5. Attiyeh, Robert S. and Wenner, David L., 'Critical Mass: key to Export Profits', *Business Horizons,* December 1979.
6. Cateora, Philip R. and Hess, John M., *International Marketing,* Richard D. Irwin, Homewood, Illinois, 1975.
7. National Economic Development Office, 'The Plastics Industry and Its Prospects', Report of the Plastics Working Party of the Chemicals EDC, HMSO, London, 1972.
8. Keegan, Warren J., *Multinational Marketing Management,* Prentice-Hall, Englewood Cliffs, N.J., 1974.
9. Unilever Company Report, 1972.
10. Kotler, Philip, *Marketing Management: Analysis, Planning and Control,* Prentice-Hall, Englewood Cliffs, N.J., 1980.
11. Terpstra, Vern, *International Marketing* (3rd edn), The Dryden Press, New York, 1983.

12. Duerr, Michael G., 'Trends in Multinational Operations', *The Conference Board Record*, September 1973.
13. Wiechmann, Ulrich, 'Integrating Multinational Marketing Activities', *Columbia Journal of World Business*, Vol. IX, No. 4, 1974.
14. Brooke, Michael Z. and Remmers, H. Lee, *The Strategy of Multinational Enterprise*, Longman, London, 1972.
15. Barto, Roig, 'The Role of the National Manager in a Multinational Company', in *The Multinational Company in Europe*, Brooke, Michael Z. and Rommers, H. Lee (eds), Longman, London, 1972.
16. Heenan, David A. and Keegan, Warren J., 'Rise of the Third World Multinationals', *Harvard Business Review*, Vol. 57, Jan./Feb. 1979.
17. Lall, Sanjaya, Chen, Edward, Katz, Jorge, Kosacoff, Bernado and Villela, Annibal, 'The New Multinationals: the Spread of the Third World Enterprises', *Multinational Info.*, No. 4, February 1984.
18. Douglas, Susan P. and Craig, C. Samuel, *International Marketing Research*, Prentice-Hall, Englewood Cliffs, NJ, 1983.
19. Keegan, Warren J., 'Multinational Product Planning: Strategic Alternatives', *Journal of Marketing*, January 1983.
20. Ford, David and Ryan, Chris, 'The Marketing of Technology', *European Journal of Marketing*, Vol. 11, No. 6, 1980.
21. Charlesworth, P.L., 'Crucial Role of Licensing Deals', *Financial Times*, 17 May 1971.
22. Irvine Maurice, 'Hilton Owns Less, Manages More', *Financial Times*, 11 June 1975.
23. 'At Long Last, Exporting Really Does Seem Fun', *Financial Times*, 28 May 1974.
24. Franko, Lawrence G., 'The Art of Choosing an American Joint-Venture Partner', in *The Multi-National Company in Europe*, Brooke, Michael Z. and Remmers, H. Lee (eds.), Longman, London, 1972.
25. Dafter, Ray, 'Du Pont in $1000m. Europe Sales Plan', *Financial Times*, 29 April 1974.
26. De Jonquieres, Guy, 'Multinational Trends in the Telecommunications Industry', *Multinational Info.*, No. 4 February 1984.
27. Harris, Derek, 'Tarmac in £50m. Deal for Suez Canal', *The Times*, 17 March 1976.
28. Rand, Edward J., 'Learning to do Business in the Middle East', *Conference Board Record*, Vol. XIII, No. 2, 1976.
29. Vines, Steven, 'Trading Minus the Money', *Observer*, 18 December 1983.
30. Gestetner, David, 'Strategy in Managing International Sales', *Harvard Business Review*, Sept./Oct. 1974.
31. Permutter, Howard, 'The Tortuous Evolution of the Multinational Corporation', *Columbia Journal of World Business*, Vol. IV, January 1969.
32. Froggatt, J. David, 'Problems of Resource Allocation in an International Corporation', in *The Multinational Company in Europe*, Brooke, Michael Z. and Remmers, H. Lee (eds), Longman, London, 1972.
33. Stopford, John R., 'Organising the Multinational Firm: Can the Americans Learn from the Europeans?', in *The Multinational Company in Europe*, Brooke, Michael Z. and Remmers, H. Lee (eds), Longman, London, 1972.
34. Hussey, D.E., 'Strategic Planning for International Business', *Long Range Planning*, Vol. 5, No. 2, 1972.
35. Stout, David, 'International Price Competitiveness, Non-Price Factors and Export Performance', National Economic Development Office, London, 1977.

Chapter Nine

INTERNATIONAL STRATEGY 2

RESEARCHING OVERSEAS MARKETS

Manufacturers are likely to know less about overseas markets than their own home markets where they may have been in business for many years. There are likely to be areas of uncertainty — 'grey' areas of undetermined risk that require evaluation before viable management decisions can be made.

Marketing research in the home market (see Chapters 4, 5 and 6) was seen to be fulfilling an important role in developing marketing strategies. The need for objective information is even more urgent for overseas marketing programmes. Basically, the type of information needed is similar, although it is often more difficult to obtain reliable data about certain export markets. A multi-stage market research operation seeks to obtain general guides and then to proceed to isolate and investigate significant market behaviour and trends. The first step involves, therefore, a macro-analysis to identify countries or areas which appear to offer potentially attractive opportunities for market development. (Refer to Figure 9.1.)

This initial screening will be undertaken by means of desk research. It will entail examination of environmental factors, political and legal constraints to entry and operation, and trading blocs; broad estimates will be made of total market size, past trends and probable future developments; figures relating to per capita income, GNP, and similar economic data will also be collected.

As a result of this preliminary analysis and appraisal, it should be possible to obtain some general guides as to the areas which are most likely to be of interest to a prospective exporting company. It may be feasible to classify market opportunities by groupings or clusterings suitable for commercial operations. These may be ranked according to their prospects of market cultivation. The degree of homogeneity existing within identified clusters or groups of markets needs careful investigation. It would be naïve to assume that national boundaries are necessarily the controlling factors in the adoption and popularity of some products. Asa Briggs[1] referred to the Common Market and future trends: 'The younger generation are already far more "integrated" than any generation before — through fashion, through entertainment, through education, above all through travel. Yet there will remain differences, some of which will not correspond to national boundaries and will rather reflect subcultures and economic subgroups — with religion continuing in some sense to influence the first and with the latter including not only pockets of poverty but occupational groupings. There is room for more long-term studies of constants and variables which would add a

Figure 9.1 Multi-phase research for international markets.

different dimension to market research. Europe may be integrated, but it will never in my view become completely "homogenised". It will always have variety, which is the essence of its inheritance, and the variety will be expressed in attitudes as much as in local circumstances'.

The second step consists of intensive research into the areas which the earlier filtering process had indicated to be of potential value. Depth knowledge will be sought of buying behaviour and all those factors affecting purchase of the products under survey. This is where the application of segmentation analysis proves to be of vital interest to marketers.

Data collected during this multi-stage research are analysed, interpreted and related to the resources and objectives of prospective exporters. Specialised segments of national markets may be revealed that will offer manufacturers profitable outlets for their production capacities.

International marketing strategy will be based on the systematic research programme outlined. How far it may be possible to use a standardised strategy will depend on the type of product and the characteristics of the markets involved, and the availability, for instance, of comparable advertising media. Products may have a strong international appeal to certain age groups, e.g. Pepsi Cola — the promoting of which has deliberately fostered an international image. But it would be dangerous to assume that standardisation of products and methods of presentation across world markets is the answer to successful exporting.

Graham Turner[2], in his penetrating analysis of British industry, referred to the increasing tendency of big American corporations to take more heed of what their overseas executives say about new products. He instanced IBM which, for several years, was content to design its computers for the American market, and if by chance these also suited European needs, they were delighted. As the result of past mistakes, IBM now pays attention to what Europe says. In Kodak, much the same process has been taking place. In the past, products were developed to suit the needs of the US market; the overseas companies commonly took parts from the American model and it was launched in Europe six months later. 'Although the Instamatic was developed in the US, the European companies were closely consulted and the camera was manufactured simultaneously in Rochester, London and Stuttgart'.[2]

DECISIONS FOR PROSPECTIVE EXPORTERS

Marketing management wishing to enter or extend the sales of their products or services overseas are faced with these questions:

1. Whether — overseas markets should be developed?
2. Where   — markets should be selected for development?
3. When   — should these markets be tackled?
4. How   — should these markets be tackled? I.e., what market strategy or strategies should be adopted?

These points should be considered in relation to the company's overall marketing strategy, and opportunities (and attendant risks) should be studied. It is sound policy for a company to spread its risks, so that it does not become too dependent on one or two large markets which could, through political or economic upheavals, suddenly decline, e.g. the American protectionist policy of 1971 placed some British firms in difficult stituations almost overnight. (Also see Chapter 6: Product Portfolio Planning.)

All this points to the fact that would-be exporters should not be content with a few superficial ideas about the markets they propose to enter. Systematic research thoroughly planned and carried out by experts, will provide factual data relating to the economic, social, psychological and cultural factors which are likely to effect the acceptance of a new product and the progressive sales planned.

SCOPE OF INVESTIGATIONS FOR OVERSEAS MARKETING

The theory of market segmentation underlies successful marketing, wherever it is practised. Market segmentation analysis provides data about buyers which enable products to be developed and offered to satisfy identified needs, economic, physical, social or psychological, or a mix of all these variables. In home markets, popular methods of market segmentation (see Chapter 6) are based on age, sex, social class, personality, brand loyalty, attitudes towards products and the extent of use of particular products. International market analayses may also take note of these demographic and other data, but, in addition, special attention would be given to environmental factors, such as cultural and social patterns, and the state of technological development (see Figure 9.2), which analyses in the home market tend to treat as basic, everyday knowledge. Different patterns of behaviour in some overseas markets may mean that products which are perfectly acceptable in a different environment may not be successful when offered without any attempt at modifying the flavouring, consistency, packaging or, perhaps, the method of distribution to suit national preferences and habits. For instance, an American recipe of condensed soup was not successful when introduced to British housewives because they were unaccustomed to diluting the contents of prepared soups and, at first sight, the new product compared unfavourably in price. In addition, the colour and flavour differed strongly from their established buying habits and expectations. The golden rule for success is to take nothing for granted.

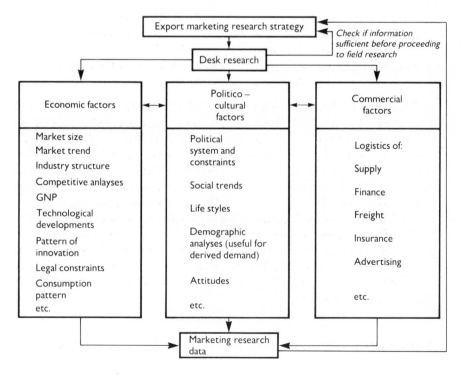

Figure 9.2 Scope of export marketing research.

Size and Extent of Market

Although population size is obviously of interest it may not necessarily indicate the potential value of a particular export market. Some countries, though small, like Switzerland or Sweden, have high purchasing power and are likely to be good customers for luxury products or those having strong design appeal. The ranges of products and services demanded in 'economies of affluence' are likely to be more sophisticated and complex than in less developed countries. Transport, entertainment and educational services will be highly organised and, in turn, will generate demands for supplies. Housing will be of a better standard in developed economies, and there will be greater opportunities for investment and the creation of further wealth.

The social and demographic structure of the population may be significant, e.g. population trends, available educational facilities, welfare services, etc. may affect the adoption of certain types of products. A growing community with increased spending power and rising standards of living will be likely to offer valuable opportunities to enterprising marketers.

Countries could be ranked for market opportunities by gross national products per capita. It was suggested[3] that by adopting this method of classification three main segments or world markets emerge:

industrialised countries (ICs)
developing countries (DCs)
less developed countries (LDCs)

It was proposed that multinational corporations should direct their marketing efforts towards the DC segment 'which covers 19% of the world's population and accounts for 32% of the world's income'.[2] Countries in this sector also 'have a high growth rate of income (7.2%) and limited population growth (1.5%)'. Income per capita has, therefore, increased at a net rate of 5.7% per year, compared with a growth rate of income per capita for ICs of under 3.5% during the same period of time. It is claimed that total world income is experiencing a fundamental change in its dispersion; the developing countries are claiming a greater share of global income.

The LDCs also deserve special consideration by marketing strategists; in these countries live about two-thirds of the world's population, but at present, they account for less than 15% of the world's income. However, LDCs offer enormously valuable potential markets because many of these countries are experiencing rapid economic development. 'During the UN's development decade of the 1960s, no fewer than twelve LDCs began to emerge from stagnation'.[2] Growth of per capita income is at least 4.5% per capita in Korea, the Republic of China, Thailand, Iran, Saudi Arabia, Zambia and the Ivory Coast. Per capita GNP of the Latin American countries as a whole increased at an annual rate of 3.5% over 1968–1971. Population growth has slowed down in the LDCs; this trend is likely to become more marked as industrialisation increases and control methods are more widely practised.

The highly developed and long established economies of the ICs do not, in general, reflect the same dynamic growth as the less mature economies. 'The average annual real growth of GNP (3.2%) experienced by the US between 1967 and 1972 was the lowest of all OECD countries except Britain'.[2] It is suggested that the market growth in the future lies with the DCs and, in the longer term, the LDCs. These growing economies will surge forward in the world league eventually to attain the comparative affluence which the older economies achieved only after many generations of industrialised activities.

Cultural Influences

Research in international marketing operations should provide cultural guidelines. Without this fundamental appreciation, marketers are ill-equipped, despite an imposing portfolio of economic data, to attract overseas business. Superficially, modern cities over the world tend to look alike — the modern "Superculture" ... built upon the culture of airports, throughways, skyscrapers and artificial fertilisers, birth control and universities'[4] — but beneath the surface, cultural shackles may not be loosened as easily as old buildings are demolished.

Cultural development within markets deserves special attention. It has been argued that there is nothing common about the Common Market, for example. The EC is not a cultural entitiy which has identical patterns of thought, attitudes and behaviour throughout. Mark Abrams has described, in fact, three Europes: the 'new Europe' of big cities like Paris, London, Hamburg, Stockholm and their conurbations, together with areas of high density population such as Switzerland and north-west Italy. The 'emerging Europe' of his second classification, is composed of areas as the semi-urbanised hinterlands of southern France, northern Italy and south-west Germany. His third grouping, termed 'old Europe' refers to the 'marginal' farming lands to be found in parts of Spain, Portugal and the north-west of Scotland.

Despite the EC, there are vast cultural differences throughout Europe, reflected in traditional behaviour and attitudes, and in at least eleven languages — without noting local or regional variations of which many exist expressing subcultural value systems.

A market analysis of countries based purely on geographical contiguity is arbitrary and misleading. For example, the Middle East is defined geographically in many ways; it includes very different cultures, economies, and market prospects. In popular terms, this vast area is considered to be synonymous with 'Arab', but Iran, for example, 'one of the most dynamically growing industrial countries in the Middle East is non-Arab with the Farsi language'.[5] It is also important, though, to realise that Arab countries extend far into Africa and include Sudan and Somalia; and that Israel also comes within this developing region. It is necessary to distinguish between the countries still predominantly agricultural and possessing natural resources other than oil (e.g. Egypt), countries not so endowed but also producing oil (Iran), countries producing oil but with few other resources (Abu Dhabi), and finally those countries endowed with poor resources of any description where the pattern of life still has changed very little (South Yemen)'.[6]

Prospective exporters need to differentiate the trading orientations of countries, like Saudi Arabia, which encourage private sector activities from the socialist states, notably Iraq, Algeria and Syria, where major developments are in the public sector, and private sector activities are not regarded favourably. For example, almost 90% of Iraq's imports are in the hands of State trading organisations which buy direct from foreign manufacturers; 90% of Algeria's exports and 75% of her imports are handled by the public sector; 70% of Syria's imports are controlled by State agencies.

McKinsey[7] have drawn attention to the classification of OPEC countries made by Hollis Chenery of the World Bank. He identified the three groups within the OPEC countries based on their absorptive capacities, resources, and likely future policies.

Group 1 consists of five countries that have only 4% of the population but 50% of the output of the OPEC group. Of these, Saudi Arabia, Kuwait and Abu Dhabi could continue to produce at today's level for the next 50 years, but they find it hard to absorb all their oil revenues for internal economic development.

Group 2 — Algeria, Iran, Iraq and Venezuela — represent about 25% of total OPEC population and 30% of total output. Their oil reserves are definitely limited and they are likely to run out before the year 2000. Their policies are based on maximising present revenues which are taken up by massive productive investment internally.

Group 3 — Nigeria and Indonesia — account for only 10% of total output but 70% of OPEC population. Their oil revenues will be easily absorbed; there will be no problems of accumulating significant financial surpluses.

This comparative analysis again illustrates the dangers of superficial classification; the OPEC classification itself is an insufficient guide to marketing strategies.

International Flavours and Fragrances Inc. produces flavours and fragrances which are marketed internationally to industries for use in their own consumer products such as goods and drinks, soaps and cosmetics.[8]

The Chairman of IFF emphasised the need for exporters to developing countries to understand human motivation and behaviour: 'that value systems change with cultures'.[8] The 'small luxury of a flavoured drink or smoke, bright colour, or a perfumed soap or detergent' is attractive even where malnutrition may be evident. 'People in the developing countries are not automatons who will follow motivations to do what is best for them by someone else's value system'. Marketers should not attempt to impose their own sets of values; they must be sensitively aware of the cultural differences which affect consumption habits. Small details can affect sales: in many developing countries the best packaging is the kind that can be re-used as a household countainer. 'Added value, not throwaway, is what people in these countries prefer'.

Purchase decisions are clearly influenced by cultural patterns of behaviour. The status of women in society will be of significant interest, for instance, to manufacturers of domestic labour-saving equipment. A few years ago, Singer found that in selling sewing machines in Middle Eastern countries, the husband rather than the wife had to be approached with the argument that the ownership of a sewing machine would make his wife more efficient and useful, and not merely save her personal trouble and time.

In a report[9] to shareholders, the Unilever Chairman commented that the price of success in multinational trading is 'endless readiness to adapt. We must recognise that the Irish like a different flavour in margarine from the English, that in the UK we can build up our own distribution of frozen food direct to the shop but in Germany we also use the existing wholesaler distribution, that in Switzerland fabrics may be washed in an automatic washing machine at 85°C which in Portugal will be washed by hand at 40°C. The price of ignorance is loss. In Spain, for instance, we did not appreciate the role of the barman in the beer market, or the difference between the requirements of the small farmer in north-west Spain for animal feed and those of the very much bigger farmer in England. For each country, for each segment of the market, we must formulate our package of knowledge afresh'.

Small things often account for disturbing variations in sales, particularly in overseas markets. A British company which had exported successfully to New Zealand for several years found that a substantial fall in sales was not attributable to any fundamental dissatisfaction with his products, but was caused by an accidental change in the legend from 'Made in England' to 'British made' on a newly designed package. 'The New Zealand consumer had thought that he was buying something produced in Hong Kong, since some products made in the Crown Colony are labelled "British Made"'.[8]

An article in the *Harvard Business Review*[10] has emphasised the 'widely differing assumptions' which affect the management behaviour of Japanese and Americans; these diverge particularly in their attitudes toward individuality and self-sufficiency. In the American culture, a rugged sense of the pioneer spirit which opened up new territories has been tempered by, and often appears to be in conflict with, the other strong cultural factor — the emphasis of the American Constitution on the equality of man. 'But in a large American organisation, the consequence of equality can be impersonalisation; in the effort to treat all men equally, all men are often treated the same. As one Japanese executive observed, "You Americans treat each other like IBM cards — the only difference is where the punch holes are".

'But the Japanese, on the other hand, views himself far less as an individual than he does as a part of his family or work group. His achievements as an independent are not as important to him as his role in furthering the well-being of people associated with him ... The Japanese are interested in fitting in with the group; in achieving harmonious relationships.'

These observations, based on a research study at Stanford University, were reflected in several work-situations. The growth of Japanese banks was considered to be only partly due to patronage by the subsidiaries of Japanese companies on the West Coast. It was thought to be attributable more to the 'aggressiveness and *esprit de corps* that the Japanese staff instils in fellow managers and workers'. This sense of corporate responsibility is fostered by the systematic training of staff in a diverse range of duties, which gives the bank unusual flexibility in staffing arrangements, and also relieves employees of the tedium of being restricted solely to one function of banking.

The fact that the basic psychological processes such as cognitions, learning, motivation, or attitudes are experienced by everyone could, it is argued,[11] lead to the supposition that customer response over different countries will tend to be similar. But this simplistic approach does not explain, for example, why a Frenchman does not satisfy his hunger with a hamburger just as an American tends to, or 'why should use of a status appeal in Africa not be equally as effective as in Europe?'

Although basic drives and psychological needs are universal, environmental factors, such as cultural or subcultural inhibitions, affect the responses made, for example, to advertising campaigns.

Commercial Factors

Feasibility studies need to be undertaken to evaluate the most efficient methods of transporting products to overseas markets (container shipments; roll on-roll off; air freight).

Air freight of exports has increased significantly and is particularly important for goods of high value and low bulk. Speed of delivery may be a very important factor in dynamic markets such as fashion clothing. Costs of stock-holding overseas can be reduced; equipment can be installed and be productive within a very short time from leaving suppliers' premises. The use of capital is economised because air freight speeds up delivery. For instance, 'a manufacturer shipping parts to a factory abroad for use on his assembly line or as spares for existing equipment. On a straight comparison of air versus surface charges, he would pay say £10,000 more for air freight than for sea every year. But because the surface journey might take several weeks he has to commit perhaps £130,000 of his capital to stock in transit. If he used air freight he could invest this money, and even at 10% this would earn £13,000 a year. By using air freight he would thus save something of the order of £3000 on his real distribution costs'.[12]

Other benefits include lower costs of packing (an important factor with some sophisticated and fragile products), and, generally, more favourable insurance premiums because of the shorter transit times.

Marketing researchers should, therefore, examine thoroughly the alternative methods of transport available. Evaluation of costs should be comprehensive, and bear in mind some of the points just discussed. This 'total distribution cost' approach may suggest a more flexible freight strategy which balances up the needs of individual customers with the full costs of using specific means of transport.

Commercial investigations should also cover the availability of media for advertising purposes and the costs involved. Present methods used by competitors should be identified and assessed for effectiveness.

In the UK, people are avid newspaper readers; they are well served by a variety of national 'dailies', Sunday newspapers, and regional morning and evening papers, as well as hundreds of special interest magazines. This market saturation makes Britain unique in press media: the same intensive pattern should not be assumed in overseas countries.

In the US for instance, only the Wall St. Journal can claim to have any sort of national distribution as a newspaper; a national press, as known in Britain, does not exist — there are about 1750 daily newspapers but they have restricted circulation areas — although some of the larger newspapers, e.g. *Washington Post*, have extensive syndication services.

There are striking differences also in Europe: France has no national newspapers on the British model; Belgian papers have small circulations and several would have to be used for a national coverage; in West Germany only three papers could be classified as national.

Consumer and technical journals are widely available in most western countries. In addition, there is a growing range of 'international' journals such as *The Economist*, or *Time*. The Readers' Digest publishes thirty local editions.

Rank Xerox[13] recognises the need to maintain an awareness of the international media; 'customers particularly in the major account areas no longer sit still within the confines of a national boundary'. Rank estimates that an average 60% of businesspeople in most major markets can be covered by a modest schedule of five publications; national media, like businesspeople, readily cross boundaries.

Commercial television is widespread in overseas markets, though some countries still do not allow it to operate. 'Intermittent' advertising on the British systems with the television company supplying the programme, is more customary in the Commonwealth. Sponsored programmes, after the American pattern, are evident in many Far East markets and in South American countries. Most major countries have some form of sponsored radio programmes.

Cinema advertising has declined in advanced economies, but in some remote markets, where the cinema continues to provide mass entertainment on the scale which was customary in the western countries, advertising in this medium may be very effective.

Poster advertising campaigns have been affected by various legislatory constraints in western countries.

The media available in an overseas market should, therefore, be carefully analysed for its effectiveness in selling specific types of products or services. Campaigns would probably be linked to special export events sponsored by overseas trade missions, and involve local agents and distributors.

A survey of top businessmen in Europe, conducted by Research Services Ltd., identified two groups: those who read only national publications and those who also read international magazines as well. 'The readers of the multinationals showed a 10% advantage in willingness to consider non-national capital goods and equipment for their company, and a 33% advantage in usage of other than just the local bank. These multinational readers also showed a 57% higher travel incidence and a 10% greater personal car purchase factor when compared with those who only read national media.'[14]

Multinational media are applicable not just to advertise consumer products, but are widely adopted for promoting business equipment and services. Research should, therefore, evaluate the effect of multinational media across, for example, several national boundaries in Europe. Local advertising campaigns could be effectively complemented by multinational advertising which is particularly effective in reaching those in higher management.

The languages which are in commercial use in particular markets need identification, e.g. in Switzerland, where French, German and Italian are spoken, and Belgium, where French and Flemish are in daily use. In South Africa, when it is necessary to use Afrikaans, the wording of research questions will be affected by the limited vocabulary of that language. It cannot be assumed that the Spanish and Portuguese spoken in the Americas, and the French and Dutch spoken in Mauritius and Indonesia are necessarily the same as those spoken in the mother country. Differences exist even between the precise meanings of some English words as used by Americans and as understood by English people. Margaret Mead[15] has commented upon different meanings which the word 'compromise' carries for an English person and an American. 'For Britain the word "compromise" is a good word, and one may speak approvingly of any arrangement which has been termed a compromise, including, very often, one in which the other side has gained more than 50% of the points at issue ... Where, in Britain, to compromise means to work out a good solution, in America it usually means to work out a bad one, a solution in which all the points of importance (to both sides) are lost.'

An American researcher[16] who interviewed textile workers on strike, found that 'arbitration' had come to mean in the workers' vocabulary the same as 'surrender'. Hence the question: 'Are you in favour of arbitration?' was interpreted as: 'Are you in favour of giving in completely to the employers?'

Linguistic differences occur inside national boundaries. Regional variations are largely appreciated in the home market, but they tend to be overlooked in overseas markets. Subcultural influences may be important factors in certain regions, so research should include an examination of these related to particular types of supplies.

Political Influences

Careful examination should be made of the likely impact on trade of political developments in countries envisaged as export markets. Trade is more likely to develop where political stability is evident. Economic and political factors are often inextricably linked; devaluation, floating rates of exchange, political strategies aimed at maintaining balances of power, etc.: all these are sophisticated influences which make international trading complex, difficult and exciting.

As discussed earlier, the growth of mammoth trading organisations — the multinationals — has focused attention, some of it harshly critical, on the influence of big business on the political, social and economic environment in many countries. Multinational companies have injected vast sums in technological development and have contributed to the growth of national economies, not only directly but through the multiplier effect which has generated substantial wealth. Critics of multinational companies draw attention to the power they are alleged to have to transfer production across national borders; the economic and social consequences of such disinvestment is particularly disliked by the trade unions. But this freedom is largely mythical as any radical business move of this nature would be in collision with government policies and would alienate public opinion. The multinational firms tend to develop highly sensitive political antennae which are even more vital in the expanding economic and political structures such as the European Economic Community. The liberalisation of industry and trade and the opportunities for employment which are embodied in the Treaty of Rome, depend on the most effective use of the resources of several countries. Within member countries, national business firms, while retaining a considerable degree of managerial autonomy, frequently have the backing of the immense financial and other resources that are available to subsidiaries of multinational corporations.

Political intervention in business affairs will emanate from national governments and increasingly be at a federal level in Europe. Industrial activities will take place within a far more complex environment. Regulations concerning safety, food and drugs, packaging, etc., should be included in a marketing research study.

'Intermediate Technology'

Marketing research enquiries may not always be concerned with sophisticated market behaviour; customers have different needs. 'Backward invention' may be the answer to supply certain markets. 'There are an estimated 600 million women in the world who still scrub their clothes by hand. These women have been served by soap and detergent companies for decades, yet only last year (1969) did one of these companies attempt to develop an inexpensive *manual* washing device'.[17]

Colgate Palmolive invited the 'leading inventor of modern mechanical washing processes' to design a much better manual device. He did so at a price below $10, and test market reports from Mexico were very favourable.

Intermediate Technology Development Group, a non-profit making British enterprise which publishes a catalogue of equipment for small firms in developing countries, has acted as a catalyst in marketing unsophisticated equipment to satisfy urgent overseas needs. 'Esso Petroleum contacted ITDG with an enquiry about 1000 animal-drawn reapers and mowers for Turkey. Tanzania and Pakistan wanted them too'.[18] A small Yorkshire firm, which had virtually ceased making this simple equipment, sold a licence to a company in Pakistan to produce this equipment which had seemed obsolete over ten years ago.

Combine-harvesters may not be the answer to agricultural problems in some developing countries; hand or animal-hauled machinery may, as was found in Nigeria, be far more useful. Marketing researchers should remember that products and services are useful only if they solve customers' problems; simple technology may not be inappropriate in some markets.

The capital intensive, sophisticated production methods of developed economies cannot be translated to a totally different economic and social environment without fundamental side effects. Development programmes should not be planned in isolation; a comprehensive appreciation of problems should avoid the social and cultural tragedies which have arisen from premature and indiscriminate mechanisation.

Companies may find that valuable markets exist in developing countries for products for which home demand has fallen because of the introduction of radical technological innovations. Product life cycle theory, discussed in Chapter 3, could be applied to export opportunities. In some cases, cheaper, relatively simple machinery which is near the 'decline' stage of the product life cycle, may be just right for the needs of certain overseas markets. Where labour is plentiful, low machine productivity may not be disadvantageous: 'horses for courses' seems to be a relevant guide when evaluating potential markets.

RESEARCH METHODS OF OVERSEAS MARKETING

Desk Research

Desk research is particularly important in export research; this type of research should be fully exploited before considering field research. It may well provide sufficient information for the particular decision which has to be made. It saves time and money, and is particularly valuable in giving a deep knowledge of markets. A good grasp of statistical data concerning overseas economies is essential; clearly, in some areas there is a shortage of reliable and readily available information. A great deal of desk research can be done in the UK, where extremely valuable information is freely available from governmental and other sources.

Useful references can be made to statistics, directories and catalogues available from: The British Overseas Trade Board, Statistics and Market Intelligence Library, 1 Victoria Street, London SW1, where there are:

- over 85,000 statistical volumes giving trade, production and other economic data on overseas countries;
- foreign trade and telephone directories, covering about 200 countries;
- over 12,000 catalogues published by overseas firms. New ones are constantly being added and attempts will be made, through Government officers overseas, to obtain catalogues not already in stock.

A document-copying service is available at a charge; the Statistics Division will also extract figures from publications in the Library on payment of the cost of the staff time involved.

Export and import statistics, as summarised in the monthly overseas trade statistics of the UK, can be obtained from: Statistical Office (Bill of Entry Section), HM Customs and Excise, 27 Victoria Avenue, Southend-on-Sea, Essex.

Market assessments can be made through information from the BOTB.

Manufacturers are helped to identify export prospects by information regularly received from British Commercial Officers in overseas countries. Background data can be supplied on markets, including assessments of economic and commercial conditions, consumer tastes, trading methods, strength of local and other competition.

The 'Daily Export Service Bulletin', issued by the Board of Trade for several years, was superseded in 1970 by a computerised export intelligence scheme. This advanced new system of market intelligence is fed with up-to-the-minute information from British Commercial Officers in 120 countries. The data are immediately processed by computer and matched with the individual export needs of companies subscribing to the service. Matched notices, printed on punched cards, are posted to subscribing companies the day after the information is received from abroad.

Companies interested in this efficient service complete a questionnaire which is fed into the computer. Data given indicate the countries from which intelligence is required, the type of intelligence, and the product groups of interest; projects of interest, e.g. new power stations, and opportunities for consultancy and other services can also be covered. For a fee of £25, companies will be supplied over a period with 500 matched notices on every country/subject/market for which they have registered.

The Department of Trade and Industry also uses a computerised matching system to distribute to overseas offices a Source of Supply List for each product which, it is claimed, will bring registered subscribing companies valuable export inquiries.

British Business (formerly *Trade and Industry Journal*), published weekly, gives a wealth of information covering overseas markets, tariff charges, import regulations, overseas trade missions. Special market surveys, details of trade fairs and exhibitions, and other vital export data are given. It is a remarkable source of reliable and up-to-date information over world markets.

Hints to Businessmen is published by the Department of Trade and Industry. This series of booklets, covering almost every export market, gives a quick overall view of countries, their trading customs, travel facilities, economic conditions, etc.

Economic surveys, published by HMSO on behalf of the Export Credits Guarantee Department, give detailed appraisals of local economic conditions in overseas markets.

Economic surveys and reports published by the United Nations and foreign governments are available through HMSO.

Other useful publications include the *Overseas Trade Bulletin,* issued fortnightly by the Confederation of British Industries. The *Overseas Directorate of CBI* is divided into special geographical areas with a network of overseas representatives and contacts.

Valuable information on export markets can also be obtained from the following:

European Community Information Office, 20 Kensington Palace Gardens, London W8

which maintains an information service and library, including a catalogue of all published literature on the EC.

EC Information Unit, Department of Industry, 11th Floor, Millbank Tower, London SW1
National Economic Development Office (NEDO)
Central Office of Information (CoI), Hercules Road, London SE1 (publicity unit working jointly with BOTB to promote British exports)
Embassies
British Export Houses Association
London World Trade Centre, St. Katherine's Dock, London E1
Institute of Export — which publishes *Export*
Institute of Packaging
Institute of Directors

Institute of Marketing — Special Information Service
Institute of Practitioners in Advertising (IPA)
Banks; British joint stock banks, merchant banks and special overseas
    banks with London offices
The Press: *The Economist, The Times, The Guardian, The Financial
    Times, The Daily Telegraph* and the quality Sunday papers
Various publishing houses
Chambers of Commerce, particularly the London Chamber of Commerce
Trade associations
Academic institutions
UN Publications
OECD Publications
IMF Financial Statistics

When the examination of the basic data suggests that a particular market
may be of value to a marketer, the next step is to make a personal visit to that
market. Discussions can be held with potential buyers and distributors, and
with embassy officials.

Sampling tends to be more complicated in overseas marketing research. It
may be difficult, or even impossible, to obtain reliable sampling frames for
random sampling techniques. The quality of statistical sources varies greatly,
and it is advisable to examine data for validity and reliability. Experienced
judgement may have to be the basis for constructing a sample in countries
where social and economic data are sparse. The accepted practice of
marketing research cannot always be directly transferred to some overseas
markets, and data may have to be collected by less formalised methods. Free
samples, small gifts and free lottery tickets have been used to attract
cooperation in some economically underdeveloped countries.

Questionnaires for overseas research need particular care in drafting.
Literal translation would obviously be totally wrong, and expert local
knowledge in drafting questionnaires is vital to ensure that they will be
acceptable and effective. In some cases, pictorial methods, e.g. the barometer,
have been particularly valuable in assessing consumer response, and some
ingenuity should be used in designing suitable diagrams.

Principal Methods of Organising Research

Research for export marketing can be undertaken in various ways, and a brief
outline of the principal methods will now be considered.

1. **Using own staff or importing agents**
    (a) The first objection to this method is probably lack of objectivity;
        sales staff are usually incapable of giving an unbiased estimate of
        their products' likelihood of success.

(b) The second objection is that the agents may have other interests which prevent them from giving an objective assessment of the market.

(c) Research is a specialist's job which requires particular training and experience .

(d) This method, may, perhaps, be the only feasible way of researching in some 'backward' markets.

2. **Using research agencies in overseas markets**
    (a) Selection of these can be difficult and risky.
    (b) Where several markets are involved, multiple agencies may have to be used to cover the whole export programme.
    (c) A big advantage is that national research organisations should possess intimate knowledge of their own home market.

3. **Using a marketing research organisation based in the UK plus the services of a locally based research firm**
    (a) This method is rather cumbersome and offers few advantages over method 2.
    (b) It could be useful where manufacturers had no trained research staff (often the case in smaller companies).

4. **Using the services of a consortium of research agencies**
    (a) Superficially attractive, but member firms may vary considerably in the quality of their services.
    (b) Closely related to this method is that of an international research organisation linked with advertising agencies over principal markets. This is generally effective.

It is largely a matter of policy whether marketing research is centrally controlled or otherwise. Large companies may have central direction of research with localised research units reporting back at regular intervals. Some systematic 'monitoring' of market movements is obviously desirable, and continous research at an agreed level should be practised. Deeper research is undertaken on particular projects as the need arises, and as the monitoring system reveals potential market opportunities.

Leading research agenices offer special facilites for overseas research. For example, Gallup Poll's London office will organise multicountry research 'irrespective of the number of countries involved'. The inquiry is piloted in the UK, and the revised final questionnaire is then sent to the other interested countries for translation and further piloting if this is considered desirable. Translated questionnaires, together with any comments, are returned to London where re-translation into English takes place. These are then checked against the original questionnaire and if any divergenices have occurred, corrections are made. Any changes to take account of local conditions in particular markets are made at this stage, and the translations are then agreed with clients.

The analysis required by clients is compared with the questionnaire to ensure that the correct type of data results.

Coding instructions, to agreed standards, are given by London to affiliate research companies. Punching and tabulation are also controlled by London and processing is by computer in the UK.

Whatever system is used, sponsors and researchers must work closely together. As with research in the home market, objectives of the survey must be clearly defined and agreed, particular attention being given to geographical limitations or other market boundaries. Instructions to investigate the European market might refer solely, for example, to the EEC countries. Europe is not, as observed earlier, merely one community; parts of it are highly industrialised with large populations and substantial spending power. Other parts are still developing, and in some areas the level of economic activity is low. Research into these markets should be objective and thorough; broad generalisations about national characteristics are not enough to identify valuable marketing opportunities.

Because marketing is concerned with fitting products and services to identified needs, specific products or services should be carefully examined in relation to the special requirements of individual overseas markets. Some commercial factors will require special attention: the impact of duties and taxes, trade quotas, food and drugs legislation, safety regulations (electrical appliance safety standards or American car safety regulations), labelling and packaging regulations. Special packaging may be necessary because of climatic conditions.

Selective List of Research Organisations

Professional advice on export marketing research is obtainable from the following organisations:

- The European Association for Industrial Marketing (EVAF), which can supply a comprehensive list of consultants or companies in western Europe who are able to undertake industrial marketing research.
- The Market Research Society, 15 Belgrave Square, London, W1, which can provide a list of members qualified in overseas marketing research.
- The Industrial Marketing Research Association, 28 Bore Street, Lichfield.
- The British Standards Institution, Hemel Hempstead, Herts., which provides British exporters with information about technical requirements related to specific engineering, industrial and technological products. It publishes 'Technical Help to Exporters' at regular intervals, listing standards, regulations, codes of practice and approval systems.
- The International Trade Centre, UNCTAD GATT, United Nations CH 1211 Geneva 10, Switzerland.
- The International Chamber of Commerce, 38 Cours Albert, 75, Paris.

- The London Chamber of Commerce and Industry, 69 Cannon Street, London, EC4N 5AB.

GOVERNMENT ASSISTANCE IN THE UK

The British Overseas Trade Board

Initially known as the British Export Board, this was formed in January 1972 to take over the work of the British National Export Council and also some of the activities formerly carried out by the export services branch of the Department of Trade and Industry. The BOTB is concerned with giving directions for the development of British export activities and establishing priorities in those areas.

The *Export Marketing Research Scheme* was introduced by the Department of Trade and Industry (at that time the Board of Trade) in July 1969 to assist British industry, on a selective basis, in overseas marketing research, and is now operated by the BOTB.

This service provided exporters with consultancy advice on the planning of marketing research, engaging of marketing research firms, and related matters. In approved cases a proportion of the cost involved in a marketing research project in an overseas market may be met by the BOTB.

In April 1972, the scheme was revised to include support for research by Trade Associations and firms' own qualified marketing research staff and for the purchase of multi-client researches. In addition, the BOTB sponsors research to help identify suitable overseas opportunities for British firms.

The Overseas Projects Group's policy is to concentrate on a limited number of important projects which indicate valuable potential for future business for British exporters. To assist firms in developing such markets, the BOTB has an Overseas Project Fund which will give financial support.

The BOTB issues a quarterly newsletter and other publications to encourage the promotion of interest in overseas markets. In cooperation with the Central Office of Information (COI) and other official bodies, the BOTB endeavours to publicise British goods and services in overseas markets. The BBC External Services and the London-based overseas press correspondents are kept closely informed of British industrial and commercial achievements.

The BOTB also operates an *Overseas Visitors' Bureau* which organises and funds the visits of overseas buyers to Britain; in addition, the BOTB assists business visitors who come to Britain in the normal course of their own business.

Commercial Officers of the BOTB study, in depth, particular sectors of industry, so that overseas visitors can be given reliable information about sources of supply. The regional offices of the BOTB ensure that close personal contacts are maintained with local industries.

Export Credits Guarantee Department (ECGD)

This government department provides extremely valuable assistance to British exporters through insurance against the major financial risks involved in exporting. Policies are far-reaching and give exporters a substantial measure of financial protection against losses arising from insolvency or protracted default of buyers, import licensing and exchange control restrictions, war and civil war in the buyer's country. Rates vary according to individual markets and the risks involved. Details are obtainable from: Export Credits Guarantee Department, Aldermanbury House, Aldermanbury, London EC2, and also from Regional Offices.

EXPORT MARKETING CHECK LIST

Note: Answers to the following questions should be based on objective analyses, and should be stated in quantitative terms wherever possible Qualitative assessments should not be neglected and should be used to qualify and give depth to analyses.

Questions

1. What are your exporting objectives?
2. Have you formally investigated overseas markets?
3. Which market or markets appear to be most promising?
4. What is the basis of your evaluation of market opportunities?
5. Have you researched these particular markets *in depth?*
6. What is the state of competition within those markets?
   (Prepare comparative data giving *your* anticipated market position)
7. What strategy do you plan to adopt in order to enter these markets?
8. How do you intend to   (a)   sell
                                (b)   promote
                                (c)   package
                                (d)   transport
                                (e)   finance
   your operations?
9. Have you carefully drawn up forecasts of prospective sales in these specific markets?
10. Have you adequate production facilities to meet anticipated demand?
11. How will these anticipated sales contribute to your overall profitability
    (a) in the short term?
    (b) in the long term?
12. Have you the right type of staff to market successfully overseas?

SUMMARY

Like home markets, export markets need to be professionally researched: the need is even greater, since market knowledge is likely to be rather less complete.

Multi-phased research, starting with desk research, will assist in screening markets for further detailed investigation. Economic, political, cultural, social and commercial factors should be included in this organised research.

Desk research facilities are extensive and should be fully exploited; there are many sources of export knowledge and assistance.

Groups or clusters of markets may be identified; these might be ranked for their prospective market opportunities.

Intensive research into selected areas or market clusters may suggest that specialised segments exist which are worth cultivation.

Prospective exporters have to find sound answers to the following questions: whether, where, when and how? Hence the need for systematic market research. Finding effective commercial answers to these apparently simple questions is by no means easy. Sampling, for instance, tends to be more difficult than in the UK; the quality of published statistical data is likely to vary considerably; questionnaires require expert drafting, bearing in mind that literal translation would clearly be quite wrong.

Professional advice is obtainable from the Market Research Society, EVAF, IMRA, BSI, ITC, and other bodies.

REFERENCES

1. Briggs, Asa, *Advertising Quarterly*, No. 33, Autumn, 1972.
2. Turner, Graham, *Business in Britain*, Pelican, London, 1971.
3. Weber, John G., 'Worldwide Strategies for Market Segmentation', *Columbia Journal of World Business*, Vol. IX, No. 4, 1974.
4. Limerick, Lord, 'A Mecca for Exporters', *Industrial Management*, March, 1975.
5. Upshaw, Douglas N., 'Organising to Sell Middle East Markets', *Conference Board Record*, Vol. XIII, No. 2, 1976.
6. Walter, Henry G. Jnr., 'Marketing in Developing Countries', *Columbia Journal of World Business*, Vol. IX, No. 4, 1974.
7. Strange, Henry M. and Wood, Peter M., 'Facts Behind the Middle East Myths', *The Mckinsey Quarterly*, Summer, 1975.
8. Hillman, Dan, 'Designs on the Market', *The Guardian*, 20 May 1974.
9. Unilever Company Report, 1972.
10. Johnson, Richard Tanner, and Duchi, Wilbain G., 'Made in America (under Japanese Management)', *Harvard Business Review*, Sept./Oct. 1974.
11. Sinclair, Craig, 'Technological Change = Social Change', *Industrial Marketing Management*, Vol. 2, 1973.
12. Martin, Frank, 'Air Freight for Exports', *Trade and Industry*, 30 January 1975.
13. O'Neill, Harry J., 'More on Multi-National Marketing', *Admap*, May 1976.
14. Elliman, Don and Cox, Tim (eds), 'The Multi-National Media Market in Europe', *Admap*, February, 1973.
15. Mead, Margaret, 'The Application of Anthropological Techniques to Cross-National Communication', *Trans. New York Academy of Science*, Series II, 9, No. 4, 1947.
16. Bingham, Walter Van Dyke and Moore, Bruce Victor, *How to interview*, Harper, New York, 1941.
17. Keegan, W.J., 'Five Strategies for Multi-National Marketing', *European Business*, January 1970.
18. Stone, P., 'The Massive Market for Simplicity', *British Industry Week*, 25 April 1969.

Chapter Ten
COMMUNICATIONS STRATEGY

The theoretical concept of the perfect market, at one time popular with classical economists, was based on certain assumptions. It was postulated, for example, that products and services of a type were homogeneous so buying preferences could not be based on differentiation in design or quality; large numbers of buyers and sellers were involved, hence no one firm could influence market prices and no discrimination existed; close and easy contact existed between suppliers and their customers; new firms were able, without difficulty, to enter an industry; and everyone had access to the same level of ideal information on market supplies. In these Utopian conditions that fictional character, 'Economic Man', was held to be motivated in all his activities by purely economic considerations. This curious, completely rational being fitted in neatly to the artificial environment projected by the early classical economists.

In such an 'ideal' economic situation, advertising was not needed, because 'perfect' information was shared equally, and no differences existed between generic products or services. It was the age of reason, not of emotion: rational choice determined buying behaviour.

Of course, the absurdity of these oversimplified and distorted economic theories is clear today. Modern business environments are complex and far removed from those primitive projections of economic life. Competitive activities involving product design, price, promotion, servicing, etc., characterise industrial economies. The market place is a riotous assembly of suppliers shoving hard against each other to attract the attention of customers.

GROWTH OF MASS COMMUNICATIONS

The dissemination of information about the availability, and desirability, of particular kinds of products and services is not, of course, new. It has been practised in rudimentary form from the earliest days of civilisation. By the Middle Ages, town criers and pedlars competed for the populace's attention. Gutenberg's invention of movable type in the fifteenth century laid the foundation of modern advertising. From the early seventeenth century, 'mercuries', the forerunners of newspapers, began to appear on the streets of London. In 1702, the first daily newspaper — The Daily Courant — heralded the massive printed media industry which has had such a profound effect on social, cultural and political life. The omniscient Doctor Johnson complained in 1758 that advertisements had grown 'so numerous that they were very negligently perused', and therefore extravagant language was used to attract the fitful reader's attention. By 1833 the 'Penny Press' was a reality: Priestley's Admass Culture was in its infancy.

Mass communication was aided by the growth of literacy and by technological developments in the printing industry. By the end of the nineteenth century, there were over 3000 newspapers published in Britain. The availability of mass media enabled Victorian entrepreneurs to expand their scales of production and sales to hitherto undreamed of levels. During this period of unprecedented growth, famous brand names like Hovis, Bovril, Pears and Dunlop were born.

This exponential growth of mass communications continued in the present century with the advent of radio and television. The advertising industry acquired sophisticated skills in presentation while also attracting the unfavourable attention of economists who, like Alfred Marshall, distinguished between 'constructive' or informative advertising and 'combative' or competitive advertising. The former was considered to be useful, whereas the latter was held to be a wasteful use of resources, even though output may have been increased and costs reduced. Marshall contended that these economies would have occurred without advertising. The debate about the economics of advertising continues; it is an area in which opinions are more plentiful than facts.

Advertising ratios vary considerably over industries with particularly strong relationships between sales and advertising in fast-moving consumer goods, such as toiletries (about 15%) and detergents (over 10%). In industrial products and services markets, however, much lower ratios are apparent — the overall industrial ratio is just over 1%. Considerable advertising expenditures relate to the public sector services covering health, social welfare and education; other campaigns are aimed to save energy, recruit for the armed forces, etc.; apart from government aid to industry and commerce through various marketing schemes in overseas countries.

ORGANISATIONS OF ALL TYPES NEED TO COMMUNICATE

In the real world of industrial and commerical competition, organisations of all types and sizes attempt to communicate with their customers, past, present, and potential. Not only profit-orientated organisations are engaged in the process of communication. Organisations are diverse with their activities ranging over commerical, cultural, political and social objectives. But, whatever their motivation, organisations must establish links with those they seek to serve; and they do this by some form of communication.

Organisations can choose to communicate with their customers and clients in several ways: through personal selling, public relations campaigns, exhibitions and various kinds of advertising. The promotional mix is to be determined according to criteria such as the nature of the product, relative market share, nature of the market environment, etc. The responsibilities of communicating with present and potential customers should be carefully considered against available resources, such as the size of the salesforce, frequency of sales calls, competitive behaviour and advertising budget. Advertising should help to make the salesforce more effective, and it should, therefore, be planned in an integrated way, i.e. making sure that advertising efforts are closely linked with sales objectives and the activities of the salesforce. Unless advertising plans are fully meshed with the other elements of marketing strategy, frustration and wastage are almost inevitable. Sometimes, it seems as if companies develop their advertising schemes in virtual isolation from their selling operations; it should be remembered that advertising is primarily an alternative and complementary method of selling products and services. It seldom, if ever, does the whole of this task, particularly in industrial markets. Market communications, whether personal or otherwise demand clear thinking and expert planning. (See Chapter 5: Marketing Strategy and Promotional Input.)

CORPORATE PERSONALITY

'An organisation is an entity, with a personality which it has acquired as the result of past behaviour and of the messages which it has given to those it serves, and also to members of its staff'.[1] This corporate image and reputation will influence the reactions of customers, potential as well as existing, and affect its development and prosperity. Further, this corporate personality may be based on subjective beliefs and attitudes which may appear to management to be biased and irrational.

Image is how others — customers, present and potential, suppliers and also government agencies — see an organisation. They may not necessarily have had direct experience of that company or its products, but, from hearsay as well as special knowledge, perhaps, they have gained an impression — formed a mental picture or image — of that company.

Those who have such opinions and attitudes will consider them to be valid; perception is rarely objective. People tend to distort information through a process of selective attention, perception and recall. 'Not all marketing communications will be significant for all individuals; people tend to select from the myriad stimuli to which they are exposed those which appear to be relevant to their needs. Information, for example, will be filtered through the mesh of personal interests, attitudes, motivational structure, social background, and cultural influences'.[1] With organisational buying, the relevance of information will also be concerned with specific needs, such as equipping a new warehouse or factory. Favourable or helpful communications are more likely to be perceived than neutral or hostile messages. 'And the more interested people are in the subject, the more likely is such selective attention'.[2]

Organisations, like individuals, are not islands: they need the support of their customers and the backing of their workpeople. They also prosper when they attract favourable public attitudes, as the enlightened communication policies of firms like ICI and Marks and Spencer have shown over several years.

There are several target audiences for corporate communications; these are likely to need different kinds of information. The tasks of communicating corporate policies should be drawn up with the needs of particular audiences firmly in mind. These will range from organisational buyers (and other members of the 'buying team') to trade distributors or agents, to raw materials and component suppliers, to 'opinion leaders' in industrial, financial and governmental circles, to members of staff (at all levels), and perhaps through eventually to the final consumers of the product. Additionally, staff recruitment will be affected by the 'visibility' of an organisation.

'A strong corporate image, influences the predisposition to buy a company's products, speak favourably of it, believe its statements, apply for a job with it, and the like. It is important for industrial goods companies with listed shares. It is important to companies ... and other organisations ... seeking highly technical staff in a tight staff availability situation'.[3]

David Lowe Watson[4], supporting Bauer's concept[5] of communications as 'a transactional process in which both audience and communicator take important initiative', has suggested that the advertising process should be viewed as 'part of a network of relationships, linking the buyer, the seller and the product advertised'.[4] This concept of total communication and interrelationship should motivate transmitters to give reliable and useful information which, in turn, would attract receivers to give their messages more favourable attention. These are indications that this more professional attitude to communication is influencing the publicity programmes of some large organisations. (The trend towards greater corporate responsibility in advertising and other functions of management is reviewed in Chapter 11.)

THE FAMILIARITY PRINCIPLE

The Familiarity Principle ('Something that is known inspires more confidence than something that is unknown') enunciated by Alfred Politz[6] about consumer product branding, is not without significance in organisational supplies and services markets. Uncertainty about the quality of products offered by a relatively unknown supplier will deter buyers who will, as the discussion in Chapter 4 suggests, adopt, consciously or otherwise, risk-policies in selecting sources of supply. Consistent and well devised promotional compaigns will help to break down the barrier or suspicion which frequently makes it extremely difficult to enter new markets.

An illustration of the effect of familiarity on public opinion has been given by Robert Worcester[3]. (Refer to Figure 10.1.)

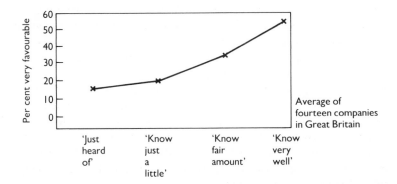

Figure 10.1   Effect of personal knowledge on attitudes to British companies.

Source: See Worcester,[3] Market & Opinion Research International, 1991 interviews. 'National probability sample of all adults in Great Britain, cooperative corporate image study', Autumn 1969.

MODEL OF MARKETING COMMUNICATIONS

Communications are, therefore, influenced by several factors which lie outside the direct control of those who project messages for various reasons to target audiences. A more detailed appreciation of these behavioural influences is presented in another text[1]; a general understanding would, however, assist in developing insight into the complexities of strategic communications.

Figure 10.2 outlines the four principal phases of marketing communications; briefly these concern four aspects: *Who; What; How; To whom.*

The communication process is originated by the sender; in marketing terms, the supplier of a product or service of some kind. From this source, messages are directed to selected markets through media of various types; these may be personal or impersonal. The final phase of the model refers to the customers or consumers (personal or corporate) with whom it is intended to communicate.

But, as already noted, the sequential flow of communications outlined in Figure 10.1, is not a simple process. Apart from the influence of personal factors such as subjective perception, a 'noise' factor affects communications (refer to Figure 10.2). This may modify or even radically change the whole nature of specific messages. Sources of external 'noise' may relate to the activities of competitors who launch a special version of their equipment which directly challenges the product at present being promoted. Customers' attention will probably be diverted; the reception of the advertising campaign is likely to be distorted. Other sources of 'noise' could originate from political, social, or economic disturbances which may lead to fundamental changes in organisational behaviour. Investment plans, for example, may be

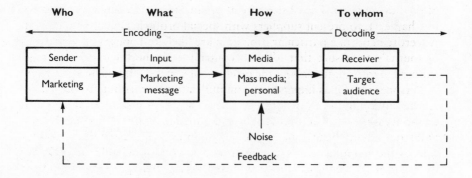

Figure 10.2   Outline model of marketing communications.

severely curtailed because of a sudden downfall in world demand for the raw materials or finished products marketed by certain sectors of industry. Stringent financial measures will supervene in management decisions. Many of these factors will not be controllable by the communicator whose messages may, in a changed environment, be discarded or given very marginal attention.

Occasionally, the 'noise' factor may act to the communicator's advantage, as in the case of rumoured shortages of certain basic materials. Buyers may be alerted by these rumours to stock up; they may, therefore, deliberately scan the technical press for sources of supply, and be particularly receptive to advertising messages.

Two other factors influence the flow of communications between transmitters and receivers: these are 'encoding' and 'decoding'. The former relates to the communicator's message which he has designed to give, in his opinion, certain information to his audience (customers in the case of marketing management). A marketer may, unfortunately, misunderstand the needs of his market; his messages may be unhelpful because they are not relevant or only partially so. The encoding factor reflects the sensitivity which a marketer has developed to the changing needs of his customers.

The decoding factor concerns the reception of communication by the target audience. As discussed earlier, perception is seldom objective.

Because communication involves many factors, some of which cannot be governed by the communicator, a feedback mechanism is vital in order to monitor the effectiveness of, for example, particular advertisements so that maximum advantage can be taken of the various opportunities available for marketing communications. Often, the feedback system is neglected; vast sums are spent on advertising campaigns, but comparatively little expenditure or effort is directed towards measuring the effectiveness of particular promotions.

Feedback information may indicate that advertising, for example, is being misdirected, because the medium used is not influential with certain members of the buying team. The complexity of organisational buying was observed, in Chapter 4, to present suppliers with special problems in communication. Advertisements in a particular campaign are likely to appear in several types of journals to ensure that *all* who contribute to the buying decision are exposed to information about the products or services offered by a company.

Personal as well as impersonal communications contribute to the overall marketing communications strategy. Hence, feedback should not be confined to the messages transmitted via the mass media. Webster's research[7] into industrial buying behaviour (quoted in Chapter 3) indicated the important role of the manufacturer's salesman as a source of reliable and relevant information. It would seem logical for marketing management to train their representatives to be effective communicators, and to assess their performance in this critical function of negotiation.

Communication is a social process; people are both transmitters and receivers of messages of various kinds. Interaction takes place which develops attitudes and may lead to positive behaviour, for example, the purchase of a promoted product. Feedback information may include: volume of sales in specific industries or areas; changes in buying attitudes; competitive strategies; or the perceived efficiency of the sales-servicing arrangements. There are many aspects of marketing which, as discussed in Chapter 5, call for a systematic flow of information to guide management decisions. Marketing research techniques may be most usefully applied to the evaluation of promotional efforts. (Refer to Chapters 4 and 5.)

Word-of-mouth Communication and Opinion Leadership

Not all communication is direct or dependent solely upon advertising personally viewed. Word-of-mouth communication — informal communication — may be an effective, though largely covert, method of influencing attitudes and behaviour. Personal influence may modify or even entirely frustrate the persuasive effects of advertising campaigns. This type of subtle communication embodies group affiliations and opinion leadership.

> 'When we speak of studying communications, we must immediately face up to the transmission of ideas. We have, in the past, tended to think of idea communication as primarily a function of the printed word — or certainly of the formal mass and selective media, since radio and television have become so important. Perhaps we have given an over-emphasis to this formal mode of transmission of ideas — or at least not understood the level at which it works ...'.[8]

This quotation is from the foreword[8] to *Personal Influence* in which Eliha Katz and Paul Lazarsfeld[9] presented their pioneer studies of how ideas are transmitted through the various levels of society. The buying behaviour of 800 women in Decatur, Illinois, was researched in the areas of movies, fashion, public affairs and food shopping. Personal influence was found to be a significant factor; 'although the fact that a woman is a leader in one area has no bearing on the likelihood that she will be a leader in another'.

The concept of opinion leadership to a 'two-step flow of communication' was first formulated by Lazarsfeld, Berelson and Gaudet[10] in their researches in connection with the 1940 American elections. They hypothesised that: 'ideas often flow *from* radio and print to the opinion leaders and *from* them to the less active sections of the population'. Lazarsfeld and his associates found that friends, co-workers and relatives influenced personal voting decisions. 'Common observations and many community studies show that in every area and for every public issue there are certain people who are most concerned about the issue as well as most articulate about it. We call them the "opinion leaders"'.[10]

Katz and Lazarsfeld, in their Decatur study, showed that opinion leaders are more likely to be exposed to the mass media than those they later influence. Opinion leaders are seen as vital links in the chain of communication; they mediate between primary sources of information and the mass audience. Figure 10.3 is a radically simplified model fo the gradual dissemination of information based on a 'trickle down' theory of communication. The identification of opinion leaders in specific areas of human activity, including the buying of goods and services, presents practical problems. It may be possible, through marketing research, to identify particular firms and individuals in certain industries whose managerial behaviour suggests that they regard themselves as innovators (refer to Chapter 7). As mentioned in Chapter 5, it is often possible, when researching industrial markets, to locate recognised experts who will be regarded within their industries as leading sources of information.

Reference Groups

Herbert Hyman[11] originated the term 'reference group' in 1942: 'the concept says in effect that man's behaviour is influenced in different ways and in varying degrees by other people ... an unrealised truism which has long been recognised'.[12] Later, Hyman[13] felt that more attention should be given 'to the reference *individual* who had tended to be overlooked in the development of the group theory. He stressed that *both* concepts were influential; in buying certain products, 'influentials' or 'opinion leadership' were active'.

Opinion leadership and communications strategy

Since 1968 the Continental Can Company of US has undertaken regular research into the characteristics of opinion leaders in developing its communications strategy. It found that leaders were 'involved to a greater degree in organisations';[14] they had higher levels of aspiration, and were of higher socio-economic groups than non-leaders.

Opinion leadership is a phenomenon which appears to be well established, although, in practice, the nature and extent of the influence wielded by industrial and community leaders is not easy to assess. Opinion leaders are not generalised; specific spheres of influence seem to fall within the scope of

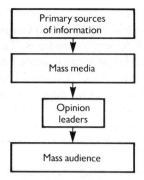

Figure 10.3 Simplified model of filtered communications.

certain individuals. The diffusion of innovations — political, social, or involving the choice of new products and services — was observed in Chapter 7 to depend on a small proportion of people who are early adopters. In the field of communications such individuals, acting through their social and professional contacts, may act as catalysts in developing public opinion. (For further discussion see bibliography.[1])

Communications Strategy

In Chapter 5 a methodical approach to achieving organisational objectives was recommended; this entails developing a strategy. A marketing strategy was seen to have several components, to be combined in different 'mixes' according to the needs of specific markets. Of these various inputs to the overall marketing strategy, the promotional or communications strategy is an essential element. Communication objectives should be devised which are directly related to the general marketing objectives.

This strategic plan of communications should be comprehensive, and should exploit fully the diversity of media available in modern communities. These, as mentioned earlier, will include media advertising, editorial publicity, public relations campaigns, personal selling and 'word-of-mouth' informal communication.

MAJOR DECISIONS IN MARKETING COMMUNICATIONS

Four main areas of decisions in developing an effective scheme of communications may be summarised as:

1. Whom to say it to
2. What to say
3. How to say it
4. Where to say it

The first stage is to define, as accurately as possible, the target audience: Whom to say it to. Senders aim to transmit messages to particular people — target audiences. The extent to which all potential buyers of a particular product or service are reached depends on the accuracy with which they were originally defined and on the effectiveness with which certain media cover these markets.

The next step — What to say — is termed communications policy; it is the primary stage which is advisably related to objective data from marketing research. Organisations will have diverse objectives and different needs for communicating with their public. At various stages in corporate growth, messages may change in their content or style. Whatever variation occurs, it is crucially important that these messages should reflect the overall corporate objectives, and form an integral part of the marketing strategy.

The third step — How to say it — refers to the creative presentations of communications, particularly advertising. Ideas have to be translated into effective copy. Research will aid in identifying the nature of particular audiences and their communication needs. With industrial and commercial supplies, the complexity of buying has added to the problems of effective communication. In overseas markets in particular, research will give guidance about the influence of cultural factors in communication.

The final stage — Where to say it — involves the selection of suitable media of communications, the timing of specific messages, the frequency of communication with specific audiences, and the relative costs of alternative methods. If advertising, for example, fails to project the right message to the intended audience and at the desired time, then it is badly conceived and planned.

These four areas of decision making in communications are, of course, interrelated. They have been separately discussed merely to identify the elements of an effective scheme of communications.

PLANNING COMMUNICATIONS STRATEGIES

That systematic planning contributes to marketing success was discussed at some length in Chapter 5; the benefits of planning apply also to communications strategy and tactics. Figure 10.4 outlines a planned approach which should encourage management to develop expertise in this function of marketing.

The sequential processes shown in Figure 10.4 should be considered in conjunction with the areas of decision making just discussed, when the need for marketing research data became clear. As Berelson and Steiner[2] have observed: 'Communications that are thought to represent some particular interest or characteristic of the audience are more influential on opinion than general undifferentiated sources. Thus, communications directed to particular audiences are more effective than those directed to the public at

Figure 10.4 Planned sequence of communications strategy.

large'.[2] Communications designed with particular kinds of people in mind are more likely to appeal than those which are so general that no one feels personally involved. Communications aimed at some vague stereotype customer or client are hardly likely to stimulate strong personal interest.

Specific types of communications strategies and tactics should be related to the significant characteristics of submarkets, which were reviewed in Chapter 6 in the section dealing with market segmentation.

Communication objectives, like general corporate objectives, may be classified as long-term or short-term. In organisational markets, immediate reaction to advertising, for example, is most unlikely. Companies generally have several objectives in mind when communicating with their markets; these should be articulated because this will help in planning an effective communications strategy.

SUPPORTING THE SALES EFFORT

A significant function of advertising of industrial products is to support the selling effort. Some years ago McGraw-Hill, in promotional campaigns for their business publications, featured a rather belligerent buyer who greeted some salesmen as follows:

I don't know who you are
I don't know your company's product
I don't know what your company stands for
I don't know your company's customers
I don't know your company's record
I don't know your company's reputation
Now — what is it you wanted to sell me?

This rather discouraging reception is not just a copywriter's fertile imagination let loose, as Morrill's intensive research[15] into the effectiveness of advertising of industrial products clearly showed. Reporting his findings in the *Harvard Business Review*, Morrill's extended study covers 1000 advertising schedules for 26 different product lines in 90 product markets at 30,000 different buying locations. The products included 'a basic chemical sold in quantity to a tight market of 500 processors'; of the three major manufacturers, only the leader advertised. Also covered, were three manufacturers who all made a low-priced electrical device used in all kinds of industrial plants[15] (where competition is very keen).

Morrill admitted that two particular difficulties arose when researching the impact of industrial advertising: (1) 'it is impossible to assume the familiar principle that "what is recalled is effective" and then question buyers about what advertising they remember'.[15] Buyers may recall advertisements, for example, that were not relevant to buying decisions which are, in any case, complex. Recall may also be biased because 'a company executive tends to continue to read the advertising'[15] of his present suppliers rather than of competing suppliers; (2) 'it is difficult to isolate the creative qualities of an advertising campaign from all the other elements that go into it ...'.[15]

For these reasons, Morrill and his associates concentrated research on the *extent* of advertising in a particular campaign and the buyer's exposure to it. 'If we can show that these correlate with levels of sales — if more advertising and more exposure mean more sales, and less of both mean fewer sales — then we shall score a base hit ...'.[15]

Morrill's research indicated that industrial advertising effects 'are profound — and profoundly useful to know about'; they can be summarised as follows:

1. The buyer's opinion of the manufacturer who advertises is improved: 'this means a larger share of the market for the manufacturer'.
2. Advertising acts as a valuable introduction to prospective customers; costs of selling are reduced.
3. Lack of frequency of advertising is the single most common cause of promotional failure. Of several hundred failures studied, more than 90% ran fewer than five pages of advertising in one magazine over twelve months. In general, five pages per year were needed to render a programme effective.
4. With adequate frequency, most industrial advertising appears extremely worthwhile. Total costs of selling to target audiences often falls by 10%–30%.
5. In a well advertised market, the non-advertiser selling costs may actually increase 20%–40%.
6. Companies can certainly sell without advertising, but planned advertising increases profitability.
7. Salespeople are made more effective; costs of advertising are outweighed by increased sales and profitability.

That there are plenty of industrial firms experiencing the value of advertising is well documented by the lively American journal, *Sales Management*.[16]

Scriptomatic ran an advertising campaign totalling $14,248 in business publications and estimated that 'immediate sales' of $444,000 resulted. The sales to inquiry ratio was 31 : 16; the year before it had been 8 : 12.

Rather than employ more salesmen, the Bird Machine Co. of South Walpole, Mass., which planned to enter the mining and metallurgical market with a horizontal vacuum filter, decided to start this new marketing venture by a series of strategically-targeted advertisements, the replies to which would be screened before being passed to their salesforce.

Caterpillar Tractor's promotional strategy emphasised the cost benefits of their equipment; its initial costs are more than compensated for by low maintenance costs and high trade-in value. They provided dealers with direct mail shots based on the consistent advertising theme; 'Total cost evaluation', so that full value is obtained from the various media used.

Webster's research[7], detailed in Chapter 3, supported the important role of the trade press at the 'awareness' stage of the industrial buying process.

A market study[17] of machine tool buyers in Chicago was contacted by telephone; a total of 159 calls resulted in 92 completed interviews. Chicago was chosen as offering a representative sample because of its high concentration of machine tools and a large number of firms in the four SICs selected for coverage. Following this initial phase of research, a mail survey among manufacturers and marketers of machine tools in the US was carried out; 144 usable questionnaries were returned, representing 55.6% of the membership of the National Machine Tool Builders' Association.

The objective of the study was to assess the degree to which industrial buyers and marketers have the same perception of the relative usefulness of alternative channels of market communication.

Buyers of machine tools regarded advertising in trade magazines as the most important source of information about products and services (37%); salespeople followed in second ranking (27%). Although statistical tests indicated a relatively low significant difference, the results showed that buyers consider advertising at *least* as important as personal salespeople in keeping them well informed.

Industrial marketers of machine tools considered that salespeople were by far the most important sources of communication with customers and prospects. This appears to reinforce the generally held view of the prime importance of personal selling in industrial marketing strategies.

INDUSTRIAL SELLING EXPERTISE

Although personal selling is regarded as a vital input into industrial marketing, the ever-increasing costs of maintaining a direct salesforce demand that selling effectiveness should be ensured. Costs per call — which include prospective as well as actual customers — continue to rise sharply. Greater attention should be given to identifying target markets and firms within those markets. In the UK, Market Location of Royal Leamington Spa offer a research-based service that is aimed to provide specific target clusters of user industries.

Professional selling skills should be developed in industrial salesforces. Elements of such skill include thorough knowledge of products and their applications in specific industries; the ability to diagnose customers' problems and to offer acceptable solutions in terms of the products being offered for sale; sound grasp of the essential nature of customers' technologies and business operations; perceptive and sensitive insights into human behaviour (see Chapter 3); and highly developed negotiating skills, including knowledge of the buying practices of specific companies.

Such a demanding set of criteria would seem to call for a paragon, not just a salesperson!

For their part, companies should stimulate and direct their salesforces through effective motivation (pay and promotional prospects, training programmes, job satisfaction, etc.), and by setting sales quotas or targets that bear realistic relationships to the prospects of given territories. In some large industrial organisations, representatives virtually assume the role and responsibilities of area marketing managers; they should be fully briefed about the overall objectives of their organisation.

ADVERTISING MEDIA FOR ORGANISATIONAL COMMUNICATIONS

Most industrial and commercial publicity (as well as that undertaken by official organisations) is through printed media of various kinds. In Britain, there is a highly diversified range of publications, from the mass dailies through to esoteric quarterly journals, catering for the information needs of people at all levels of society. Details of these journals are contained in directories such as *British Rate and Data* (BRAD), *Willings Press Guide,* and the *Newspaper Press Directory.*

Three Types of Circulation of Trade Press

Trade and technical publications use three general methods of circulation: paid circulation (by post to subscribers, or over the counter); controlled circulation (mailed free to selected individuals); professional circulation (to members of an institute).

Some controversial views have been expressed on the value of controlled circulation publications, although these have tended to grow considerably and now represent a major proportion of British trade publishing. They usually operate a readership reply service, and are produced to high professional standards. Their proliferation and the fact that they involve no personal commitment or cost, may reduce their effectiveness.

Professionally-circulated journals tend to be read with a degree of personal identification and involvement which adds significance to their announcements, including advertisements.

The relatively small circulations of some trade publications may involve advertisers in costs out of balance with the benefits likely to accrue.

Preferably, circulation figures should be authenticated, as with ABC (Audit Bureau of Circulations) independent checks. Audited circulation figures are now quoted by certain leading technical journals. It may be more advantageous for industrial advertisers to use the national press on some occasions. 'A manufacturer of automatic vending machines wanted to appeal directly to top management and create an awareness at that level of its automatic catering service. The media list included the *Financial Times* as well as management and industrial journals. The manufacturers discovered subsequently that 75% of the enquiries received came from the *Financial Times*. Part of this response, furthermore, may have uncovered market areas unsuspected by the advertiser, thanks to the breadth of coverage'.[18]

Two Major Categories of Trade Press

Two major categories of trade and technical journals can be identified: horizontal and vertical.

Horizontal journals have a broad approach to the industry or profession they cater for. *Management Today,* for example spans the problems of business management at a senior level. It features advertisements offering manageral services applicable to industry in general, travel, finance, insurance, credit cards, etc.

Vertical journals have a narrower field of operations; they aim to serve specific industries or professions, and narrowing even to particular functions within those areas. These journals may be particularly useful in communicating with highly segmented markets. Some, like *Farmers' Weekly* have six-figure circulations, whereas *Optics and Laser Technology* has a specialised circulation of just over one thousand.

Expert Advice Needed for Effective Media Selection

The nature of technical publications is clearly significant is selecting effective media. Organisational suppliers should make themselves aware of the different publications which cover their markets, and assess the value of individual journals. Specialist advertising agencies can offer expert advice in the selection of media, timing of advertisements, and the integration of national press and trade press publicity. To ensure that industrial or technical advertising is seen by as many buyers as possible, copies of the publication (or 'pulls' of the advertisements) could be mailed to a selected list of customers and prospects. A reply-paid card could be included with a covering letter inviting attention to the products or services featured.

As noted in Chapter 9, the Central Office of Information (COI), the British Overseas Trade Board (BOTB) and the BBC External Services, offer exporters expert advice and opportunities for publicising British products and services in overseas markets.

Editorial Comment

In designing a communications strategy, the influence of editorial comment should never be ignored. Press releases, giving adequate information on new products, mergers, export achievements, etc., should be systematically organised either within companies or by professional public relations agencies. Many companies prepare 'press kits' which contain, for example, relevant statistics, photographs suitable for reproduction, news about policies and specific achievements, etc. Some distribute these after formal press conferences addressed by a senior member of the board of directors. Details of forthcoming promotional plans may be revealed. Members of the press may be invited to visit the production plant and, at the company's expense, may obtain first-hand knowledge of overseas operations.

Integrated Scheme of Corporate Communications

All these activities are part of the scheme of corporate communications; they require careful planning and direction to ensure that publicity efforts are synchronised. Individual corporate communication problems should be analysed, so that the most effective combination of communication media may be devised. A favourable corporate image is developed only by systematic and sustained effort in the expert management of communications.

BUDGETING FOR EFFECTIVE COMMUNICATIONS

Like all products or services, costs are incurred in corporate communications. In commercial practice, there are five main methods of estimating expenditure on publicity:

1. what can be afforded
2. percentage of sales, current or anticipated
3. comparative parity
4. objective and task
5. residual

Usually, companies tend to be influenced by a mixture of these approaches to budgeting.

'Objective and task' is the most logical way of dealing with the problem, although it is not as widely practised as it deserves to be. Several large American firms now use this method. The first method rests on a subjective estimate of the value of publicity; it is arbitrary. It disregards the long-range investment of corporate communications. Essentially a play-safe strategy, it can lead to wasteful spending.

The 'percentage of sales' method is widely used; this leads to heavy advertising when sales are high and light advertising when sales fall, which, it could be argued, is just the reverse of what should actually happen. Boom demands tends to be intensified while a slump may become even more pronounced. Fixed advertising/sales ratios may mean that too much or too little is being spent over particular time periods.

'Comparative parity' — or taking note of what comparable organisations spend on publicity — could equally lead to wasteful expenditure. This method assumes that competitors, for example, allocate their funds in an effective manner, and there may be no proof that they are more successful in their efforts. The costs of securing increased market share, as noted in Chapter 6, may be out of all proportion to the benefits to the organisation. It is clearly useful to know what competitors are spending on their corporate communications, but more sophisticated analyses are necessary before decisions to follow them are taken. For example, the distribution of market shares related to promotional expenditures should be carefully researched. Further, the 'promotional mix' of leading competitors should be identified, and some assessment made of their overall marketing strategies.

'Objective and task' entails defining clearly the objectives of corporate communications. (See Chapter 5, and earlier discussion in this chapter.) These tasks should relate to specific targets, such as market share growth, levels of awareness, change of attitudes, percentage increase in sales, distribution coverage, etc. With new products in particular, it is obviously important to make sure that promotional plans are carefully devised so that, for example, the right level and amount of information is provided to decision makers to encourage the adoption of these innovations.

The costs of achieving certain objectives should, of course, be realistic. This approach encourages the development of managerial responsibility in the allocation of promotional funds, as well as acting as a useful framework of analysis on which to build the overall budget. In general, it is the recommended route to effective budgeting.

The residual method of funding promotional activities is the least satisfactory approach because it takes no account of the objectives of the communications strategy. It suggests a half-hearted interest in corporate communications, and could frustrate the development of effective long-term plans.

RESEARCH ON ADVERTISING OBJECTIVES

To obtain a clearer picture of how UK and Continental companies developed their advertising strategies, and particularly of how they set and evaluated their objectives, Urwick Orr and Partners researched[19] leading firms. The number of companies using fairly sophisticated mathematical models was small, 'and even these companies were not entirely clear about what precisely they were trying to measure'.[19] Although most consumer-product firms declared that they practised advertising-by-objectives, such objectives were frequently expressed in elementary terms. The majority of companies marketing industrial goods admitted to having no advertising objectives at all. Banks and hire-purchase companies' advertising budgets were increasing, 'but none could point to clearly defined goals'.[19]

Even 'progressive' firms which had formulated clear advertising objectives, tended to measure the effectiveness of their campaigns by irrelevant methods. One company, for instance, used psychological depth interviews to measure attitude changes, although their survey response stated their advertising objective to be 'informing the public of a product's availability'.

In general, the findings of this professional survey are not very reassuring. It is time that advertising objectives were more rigorously set, and that relevant and effective methods of assessing the impact of campaigns were developed.

Some years ago, Donald Marschner[20] investigated and analysed the advertising policies and practices of nine major oil companies in the US which were all marketing nationally-branded petroleum products. His purpose was to review the extent to which this sector of industry had adopted the practices recommended by the DAGMAR concept[21].

'Traditionally, oil companies have been huge advertisers. Several of them spend between $10 and $25 million annually on advertising and sales promotion ... nevertheless, advertising is a relatively unimportant ingredient in the typical gasoline marketing mix, simply because successful marketing depends upon doing a lot of other jobs well, too. The typical large oil company ploughs back only 1% or 1½% of its sales dollars into advertising'.[20]

Nine major oil companies answered a lengthy questionnaire covering all aspects of advertising management. Marschner reported that the companies 'which accepted the DAGMAR theory in the early 1960s appear to be more successful than those which did not ...'.[20] Eight criteria were used in this assessment: adequacy of research funds; isolation of advertising goals; goal-determination in measurable terms; establishment of bench-marks in advance; advance agreement to use objective judgement; adequacy of survey methods; advertising director's attitude; and top management's attitude.

Marschner noted that there was some evidence 'to support the observation that usually advertising management seems to take its cue from top management, and that where the proper climate for objectivity has been decreed by the powers-to-be, better advertising is frequently the outcome'.[20] Perhaps there is scope for more communication, *within* organisations, so that the benefits of managerial functions like financial budgeting are more widely known and appreciated.

SYNCHRONISING ADVERTISING AND PRODUCT LIFE CYCLE STRATEGIES

Products and services, as noted earlier, pass through a process of market development until, eventually, diminishing returns set in: the terminal stage of decline has been reached. This phenomenon appears to relate particularly to consumer products, although technological developments have resulted in many industrial products ageing, perhaps, prematurely.

Communications strategies should be linked closely with the various phases at which specific products are identified in their life cycles. (Refer to Figure 10.5.) In the early stages of introduction and growth, relatively heavy promotional costs may be incurred. These may be viewed as part of the development costs of new products, and as an investment recoverable over a period of one to five years. If products are protected by patents, it may be possible to spread promotional costs over several years, but, with the high attrition rate which affects so many new products, the temptation to take too optimistic a view of a free run should be resisted. Patents can often be circumvented, and, in any case, other innovations are likely to be marketed before long.

As a product or service approaches maturity, promotional expenditures tend to fall, and advertising is generally held at a level sufficient to extract full value (profit) as the decline stage is reached. 'Milking' the product entails maintaining demand at a level which does not tie up corporate resources that could be deployed more profitably elsewhere, for example, in the development and marketing of new products. Overall corporate profitability is likely to be increased if the rate of decline is slowed down by carefully controlling promotional efforts.

In general, therefore, the intensity and content of advertising will differ according to the stage reached in a product's life cycle. Content, for example, will be likely to change its principal emphasis from information to persuasion and finally to 'reminder', as a product matures.

If, during the life cycle, it is decided to restyle a product, then extra promotional efforts are likely to be involved to stimulate demand. This frequently occurs with household products, superficially little changed from a generation or more ago, but which, in fact, have passed through several metamorphoses. The demand curve is then lifted, and the product life may be

Figure 10.5   General relationship of product life cycle and promotional costs.

extended, in some cases, for some years. (See Chapters 5 and 6: Strategic Planning, particularly PLC and Portfolio Analysis.)

LIMITED POWER OF ADVERTISING

Advertising is popularly thought to have almost unlimited power; to be some kind of brainwashing activity in which the viewer is a helpless captive. By the sheer brute force of heavy promotion, it is claimed that people can be 'forced to buy almost anything'. These fallacies are refuted by briefly examining a few classic examples of extensive promotional campaigns which failed to achieve their targets.

On 18 March 1971, Du Pont announced the withdrawal of Corfam[R] after losses amounting to $250 million had been incurred. This shoe-leather substitute had been developed in the 1930s, but further activities were postponed because of the Second World War. By 1953, three departments of Du Pont were again involved in Corfam, and in 1962 a venture manager was appointed. In 1964, after extensive research and market tests, this novel product was launched and over one million pairs of shoes were sold. By 1968, over 40 million pairs of shoes were being sold in the US alone; sales growth doubled each year, until 1969 when it seemed as if a plateau had been reached.

The European Corfam campaign was not as successful as had been planned, and the Belgian finishing plant was closed down. Despite Du Pont's colossal expenditure on research and development, and marketing (including heavy advertising), Corfam did not recover its investment costs in the six years it was on sale.

Significant factors which accounted for this marketing failure were partly technological and partly behavioural. During the period of Corfam's market growth, PVC became extremely popular on account of its cheapness. Corfam was very durable but relatively expensive. Younger consumers increasingly preferred cheap 'throw-away' shoes, regardless of comfort, permeability and other quality attributes which Du Pont's researchers had painstakingly analysed.

Another example of the restricted power of advertising relates to part-works' publications (magazines which are published in a planned series to form a comprehensive treatment of a particular subject). In 1975 Marshall Cavendish, one of the leading firms in part-works publishing, wrote-off a projected 98-part weekly colour magazine about modern history, *Post-War World*, after only three issues. About £100,000 had been spent on Press, television and radio advertising, as well as £50,000 in production costs. Projected sales had been estimated at 250,000 but fewer than 10,000 copies were actually bought. The publishers ordered an immediate investigation into this 'extraordinary and unprecedented' failure ... investigators are expected to find that there is little interest in that 'depressed period of history' among the British public.[22]

The British Eggs Authority once spent £150,000 (more than 10% of its annual budget) on a special advertising campaign featuring National Egg Week. 'Hardly any extra eggs were sold, producers believe'.[23] People are not likely to change their consumption habits, particularly those related to food, in direct response to advertisements no matter how ingenious the promotional bombardment.

Advertising is only part of the marketing effort; it cannot force people to buy. A generation ago, tea bags were promoted widely in Britain, but no significant sales resulted. Today, this product is very successful because of changed social habits, increased disposable incomes, etc. Slowly, the product overcame its original 'American' image and infiltrated into the supermarkets through being widely adopted in the catering trade.

Advertising is not a solo performer in corporate communications, nor can it for long sustain inferior products or poor service. Many advertising campaigns have been ineffectual because either the goods have not been up to expectations or they have not been delivered in time.

FUNDAMENTAL QUESTIONS BEFORE ADVERTISING

Before advertising or any other form of promotion is considered, some very fundamental questions should be asked: these can be slotted into the phases of developing a communications strategy as outlined in Figure 10.4. One simple question could well be the first to be asked: 'Why advertise?'. If a logical and coherent answer is not forthcoming, then no commitments should be made. The use of corporate funds, whether in the public or private sectors of the economy, carries with it the managerial responsibility for careful investigation and allocation of scarce resources. Production managers are expected to put forward factual information about the improved qualities or increased rates of production which could result from investing large sums of money in new equipment. Marketing managers should be prepared to state an equally sound case for the heavy costs incurred in their sphere of operations, particularly those related to promotional expenditure.

THE CHALLENGE OF CORPORATE COMMUNICATIONS

Business, particularly big business, is the target today for almost incessant criticism. It is the sitting duck at which politicians, economists, sociologists, and the public at large delight to snipe.

Some of this criticism has been earned but, in many cases, it is founded more on ignorance and fear than fact.

Multinational firms, in particular, have attracted unfavourable attention; they have been viewed as the bogey-men of modern industry and commerce. Their mammoth size and multifarious activities have appeared to many spectators to be threats to society itself, apart from suspicions about the vast economic power which they exercise across the world. Earlier it was observed that in certain countries an uneasy relationship tended to exist between some mammoth businesses and the governments of those lands.

Organisations of many kinds are getting bigger and on a scale which seems to be limitless. Asa Briggs[24] has observed that because the organisations are so big and seem so powerful that dissent can be so strident, rebellion so prevalent and so contagious. Reactions are often articulate and well organised, as with the consumerist movement which, in a few years, has grown from the level of a cottage industry to a sophisticated system of highly organised lobbying.

Infiltration of the policies of large institutions into the personal lives of millions has aroused public antipathy on a scale previously unknown. More enlightened management have correctly interpreted these trends and taken steps to improve, among other things, their processes of communication both within their organisations and with the environment in which they operate.

Companies should not wait for some corporate misbehaviour (either real or imaginary) before they communicate with their customers and with the public at large. If they fail to give facts about their activities, then the field is wide open for conjecture, rumour and even hostile reaction. Perception, so discussed earlier, is seldom objective: fragments of information are often put together in a fairly haphazard manner, while the gaps in knowledge tend to be filled in by a mix of past experience, hearsay and, most likely, prejudice. Time is limited; the search for complete, objective knowledge is unlikely to be conducted by most people, including industrial buyers. Perhaps it would be well to recall Schumacher's[25] wise words: 'We often notice the existence of more or less fixed ideas in other people's minds — ideas *with which* they think without being aware of doing so. We then call them prejudices, which is logically quite correct because they have merely seeped into the mind and are in no way the result of judgement ... .'

Experienced marketers like ICI know full well the advantages of keeping a favourable market image. Their famous 'Pathfinders' campaign, consistently run over years, has significantly affected public attitudes, as research has established.

In an era of well organised and articulate lobbying against perceived industrial and commercial malpractices, no company can afford to neglect the quality and quantity of its communications with customers and people at large. But clever promotional campaigns will not cover up an unattractive public face if this has devolved from unacceptable corporate behaviour.

It might be as well to close with some penetrating observations by Enoch Powell[26] about public reaction to advertising: 'The professional politician can sympathise with the professional advertiser. They inhabit similar dog-houses. In the public mind advertising stands suspect of deception, and fearless loyalty to the unvarnished truth is not generally supposed to be the first qualification for success in it. I suppose the practitioner in advertising comes to accept, as one of the inconveniences incident to his profession, this low public estimation of his veracity and sincerity'.

SUMMARY

A well devised communications strategy contributes significantly to marketing success. Corporate personality attaches to all types of organisations; they need the support of their customers, work people, suppliers, and the public at large. The Familiarity Principle applies to organisations as well as product brands.

An outline communication model has four aspects: *Who; What; How; To whom.* Encoding, decoding, and noise factors affect the transmission and reception of market messages. Word-of-mouth and opinion leadership may help or hinder a firm's marketing communications.

Major decisions to take: whom to say it to; what to say; how to say it; and where to say it. Planning is necessary at each stage, and feedback should be organised to check that communication objectives have been achieved.

Market communications should be linked with sales efforts to ensure economic use of marketing resources. Advertising expenditure, for example, should be related to PLC stages.

REFERENCES

1. Chisnall, Peter M., *Marketing — A Behavioural Analysis,* 2nd edn, McGraw-Hill, Maidenhead, 1985.
2. Berelson, Bernard and Steiner, Gary A., *Human Behaviour: An Inventory of Scientific Findings,* Harcourt, Brace and World, New York, 1964.
3. Worcester, Robert, 'Corporate Image Research', in *Consumer Market Research Handbook,* McGraw-Hill, Maidenhead, 1973.
4. Watson, David Lowe, 'Advertising and the Buyer/Seller Relationship', *Admap,* August 1968.
5. Bauer, R.A., 'The Initiative of the Audience', *Journal of Advertising Research,* Vol. 3, No. 2, 1963.
6. Politz, Alfred, 'The Dilemma of Creative Advertising', *Journal of Marketing,* Vol. 25, No. 2, 1960.
7. Webster, Frederick E. Jnr., 'Informal Communications in Industrial Markets', *Journal of Marketing Research,* Vol. VII, No. 2, 1970.
8. Roper, Elmo, Foreword to: *Personal Influence,* by Katz, Elihu and Lazarsfield, Paul, F., The Free Press, New York, 1955.
9. Katz, Elihu and Lazarsfeld, Paul, *Personal Influence,* The Free Press, New York, 1955.
10. Lazarsfeld, Paul F., Berelson, Bernard and Gaudet, Hazel, *The People's Choice,* Columbia, New York, 1948.
11. Hyman, Herbert, H., 'The Psychology of Status', *Archives of Psychology,* No. 269, 1942.

12. Bourne, Francis S., 'Group Influence in Marketing and Public Relations', in *Some Applications of Behavioural Research*, Likert, Rensis and Hayes, Samuel, P. Jnr. (eds), UNESCO, 1959.
13. Hyman, Herbert H., 'Reflections on Reference Groups', *Public Opinion Quarterly*, Fall, 1960.
14. Fenton, James S. and Leggatt, Thomas R., 'A New Way to Find Opinion Leaders', *Journal of Advertising Research*, Vol. II No. 2, 1971.
15. Morrill, John E., 'Industrial Advertising Pays Off', *Harvard Business Review*, March/April 1970.
16. 'Business Publications: How to Make Them Work Harder for You', *Sales Management*, 2 June 1975.
17. Patti, Charles H., 'Buyer Information Sources in the Capital Equipment Industry', *Industrial Marketing Management*, Vol. 6, 1977.
18. Dening, James, *Marketing of Industrial Goods*, Business Publications Ltd., London, 1968.
19. Majaro, Simon, 'Advertising by Objectives', *Management Today*, January 1970.
20. Marschner, Donald C., 'DAGMAR Revisited — 8 Years Later', *Journal of Advertising Research*, Vol. II, No. 2, 1971.
21. Colley, Russell H., *Defining Advertising Goals for Measured Advertising Results*, Association of National Advertisers Inc., New York, 1961.
22. 'Magazine — "A Monumental Failure"', *Daily Telegraph*, 25 March 1975.
23. 'Egg Week a "Fiasco"', *Sunday Telegraph*, 17 March 1974.
24. Briggs, Asa, 'What Kind of Europe — Old or New?', *Advertising Quarterly*, No. 33, Autumn 1972.
25. Schumacher, *Small is Beautiful: As if People Mattered*, Harper and Row, London, 1973.
26. Powell, Enoch, 'Truth, Politics and Persuasion', *Advertising*, No. 67, Spring 1981.

Chapter Eleven
STRATEGIC CHALLENGES

DYNAMIC ENVIRONMENT

As never before, business management — and marketing managers in particular — are immersed in a restless, dynamic environment in which complex problems arise with unfailing regularity. Almost everything seems to have changed, sometimes profoundly and with deep-rooted effects on patterns of consumption, lifestyles, attitudes and motivations. New norms of behaviour, both personal and corporate, have arisen. Many new factors have radically altered the nature of the buyer–seller relationship. Some of these changes are not palatable; for example, the erosion of loyalty, increased 'shopping around', sharper bargaining practices, etc.

New ideas and experiences are ruthlessly discarded if they fail to satisfy the rising expectations of those who have become accustomed to buying an amazing variety of goods and services from across the world.

It is virtually a cliché to say that the world is a global village, but it is certainly true. Modern methods of transport and communications have shrunk continents; satellites now serve the business and entertainment needs of millions. Computers are commonplace; jet travel is not novel; the man on the moon is no longer science fiction. Meanwhile, biotechnology is opening up exciting new prospects for people and industry.

Priorities and values are endlessly debated in the mass media as well as in private discussions. The spontaneous optimism generated by what appeared to be the unlimited growth of industry and technological innovation over most of the western world has been shattered by the growing realisation of the problems which rapid expansion has inevitably brought with it. Some people feel that the whole system of modern technology, for instance, 'is like an uncontrollable and unpredictable juggernaut which is sweeping society along in its wake. Instead of technology serving human beings it sometimes seems to be the other way about'.[1]

Disillusioned and dismayed, many are observing the appalling side effects of scientific and technological ingenuity: overpopulation, endemic pollution, the prospect of exhausting natural resources, corrosive rates of inflation, the diabolical pace of obsolescence, and the recurrent threat of nuclear holocaust.

Paradoxically, in some ways, living is safer but in other directions it is more precarious. Medical science has helped to prolong life and has overcome many of its illnesses; but psychological disorders have proliferated. Modern systems of transport have made the world a much smaller place, yet, at the same time, have brought once-distant threats alarmingly near. 'It is only comparatively recently that most of us have been made aware of the fact that we live in a world of finite size and limited resources. Hitherto we have expected this finite world to provide an increasing population with an adequate supply of food and to satisfy its insatiable material wants in a never-ending spiral of growth'.[2] Dissident voices were few a decade ago; there was no 'market' for views about the disamenities of modern industrial society. Economic growth was widely believed to contain the solutions to mankind's problems: material prosperity would lead to 'the greatest happiness of the greatest number'.[2] This myth has been dismissed by many who are now beginning to count the costs of attaining some of the dubious benefits of economic progress. Mishan[3] has acidly commented that men are unable to enjoy the present because they are restlessly pursuing 'with greed the rewards of the future'. He thought that men cannot escape feeling that they are but units of exploitation geared to the economic machine which grinds relentlessly on, devoid of conscience or human feeling. They are caught up in the 'whirling-dervish economy' characterised by Dennis Gabor[4] as largely dependent upon 'the continual consumption of rapidly wearing articles'.

People, in general, live in a more sophisticated style than even a generation ago, let alone a hundred years. But they have largely exchanged their personal freedom and initiative for the security of social welfare schemes of various kinds which anaesthetise them against the pains of modern life. Large, impersonal organisations have replaced the intimate family firms which had strong ties with their customers and workpeople. Industry has become concentrated into a small number of gigantic corporations whose policies often appear to be misunderstood or mismanaged. Powerful élites in government, the trade unions and the public administration are increasingly influencing, and limiting, the personal lives of millions. Intervention in practically every aspect of industrial and personal activity by 'interested' authorities has become the norm in the mixed, controlled economy. From Government ministries and town halls flows an incessant stream of exhortations, guides and threats aimed to direct and control the diverse activities of modern life.

Society itself is far from stable; old standards of behaviour have largely been declared outmoded. The relative roles of men and women are endlessly debated; campaigns for equality of opportunity have met with measurable success. Equal pay, which has existed in the professions for some years, has now rapidly extended to commerce and industry. Discrimination against the employment of women is now a statutory offence in Britain. In addition to personal emancipation, women have largely gained economic independence. Improved educational opportunities, the wide acceptance of birth control practices, smaller families and better health care have all helped to give women a new role in society where, as equals, they can compete with men in professional and business careers.

Lifestyles have been revolutionised by the advent of electronic entertainment and communication. Cultural values are disseminated widely and swiftly; consumption of many goods and services is no longer dictated by social class membership. Rigid social stratification is not so apparent, although clearly inequalities of income, power and prestige still exist. Differences tend to rely less on money than a generation ago; better educational opportunities have given birth to the 'meritocracy' who occupy positions of influence in both the private and public sectors of the economy.

Within the short span of two generations, a new industrial state has evolved in many western countries. In Britain, socialisation of the economy has been extended on a far wider scale than would have been tolerated or even envisaged a few years ago. The 'technological revolution' of the post-War era has had significant social and political impacts as well as economic consequences. Industry and commerce now operate in an environment which is overtly critical and even hostile. The parameters of management are vastly different from those which have been traditionally accepted by business and society for many years.

Challenege to Management

The turbulence of modern society and of industry in general presents a direct challenge to management. Societal and economic pressures are forcing organisations to rethink their corporate strategies.

Marketing strategists, in particular, should be aware of the changes which have taken place in both general and specific terms: these are likely to include economic, technological, social and psychological factors. As Ansoff has observed: 'The accelerated pace of product and market change will require that tomorrow's firms have wide-open "windows of perception" on the surrounding business scene'.[5] Success will depend on the willingness and ability of organisations to adjust their corporate behaviour so that it (and hence their products/services) is acceptable to their customers.

ECONOMIC USE OF NATURAL RESOURCES

The dire prospect that at present rates of consumption the world's supply of several vital natural resources, such as minerals or oil, will soon be exhausted has become the focus of attention to scientists, technologists and a diverse range of professional experts, apart from catching the headlines of the mass media. Various estimates have been published of the likely life of available resources; the period of time during which basic metals like copper, lead or zinc will be available has been projected[6] as less than fifty years. Controversy exists about the methods by which some of these statistics have been computed, although there is general alarm about the contemporary rates of extraction and the reserves which are known to exist at the present time.

Even if mining exploration and extraction techniques can add substantially to the world's supply of strategic raw materials, political and economic factors have intervened dramatically and prices have soared.

Recycling of Materials

Reclamation and recycling of many materials has developed to a level hitherto unknown. Ferrous metals have consistently relied on reclamation, with recycled material representing about 50% of new production. Also, almost half of the non-ferrous metals used in Britain are now derived from recycled scrap. In the paper industry, recycling is now an important activity which is expected to develop still further as wood pulp prices continue to spiral. Lubricating oils are now being reprocessed after use, and although so far representing a miniscule proportion of total oil sales, there are indications that this commercial activity will extend significantly. Because the raw materials in glass represent only about 13% of the finished product, there is no great economic incentive for the manufacturers to reclaim glass containers, etc. However, recycled glass accounts for about 22% of new production of glass containers. 'Bottle banks' are evident in some towns and, presumably, apart from their economic purpose, also fulfil a valuable public relations role for the glass industry.

Substitution of Scarce Supplies

High prices and the difficulty of obtaining regular supplies of basic natural materials have encouraged many manufacturers to use substitute materials that are cheaper and readily available. Plastic mouldings, for example, have replaced brass fittings; chipboard is widely used in place of wood. In some cases it is not technically feasible to replace natural materials, e.g. silver for photographic emulsions. With some kinds of substitution, problems tend to be compounded because a new level of demand is created for materials such as plastics, products of the petrochemicals industry, which derive from limited world reserves of oil or natural gas.

Some of these problems may be solved by a more intelligent and integrated approach to product design including the application of value analysis (see later discussion pp.338–339.)

SOME SPECIFIC MARKETING SOLUTIONS

In common with other expenses, costs of selling have risen alarmingly over the past decade. More productive use of salespeople's time is obviously vital; this is one of the most important tasks of modern marketing management. Increasing competition, more sophisticated specifications, environmental pressures affecting, for example, safety standards, or tougher levels of negotiation have all made the function of selling more complicated and, therefore, more costly. (See Chapters 2, 3, 5 and 10.)

In Chapter 5, the overall marketing strategic plan was noted to have four elements: product, price, promotion, and selling and distribution. This last factor is particularly important in industrial markets which are frequently complex in the products and services offered and also in the customary buying arrangements (see Chapters 2 and 3). High professional competence is necessary for success in markets where competition has greatly increased. In this kind of negotiation, the interaction between buyer and seller contributes significantly to the overall marketing strategy; Hakansson's[7] researches have emphasised the need to develop long term, satisfactory relationships. Industrial negotiation is not just a matter of booking orders but of building up, often over years, trust and mutual respect related to both the organisations and the people engaged in the vital commercial processes of buying and selling.

Companies should examine critically their selling and distribution arrangements. Usually, they were designed many years ago when trading conditions were vastly different from those experienced today.

In 1972, McKinsey[8] probed the selling activities of the American giant telecommunications group, AT&T. They found that AT&T salespeople spent too much time in non-selling activities, and that marketing efforts were dissipated because of splintered responsibilities.

AT&T salespeople's time was split between selling and servicing; as a result they gave only about a third of their time to actual selling. To correct this unsatisfactory situation, the service function was made the responsibility of sales assistants. Also, relatively simple sales enquiries were handled by trained service representatives working district offices. Paperwork was also rationalised.

Direct mail and telephone selling were also adopted for smaller volume business, while a two-tier salesforce handled larger accounts.

McKinsey's second major recommendation resulted in AT&T reorganising their marketing department into four divisions: marketing management; product management; sales development and marketing services.

By market segmentation, AT&T identified about fifty sectors of industrial markets of significance to their business. These industrial markets fall into three broad divisions: manufacturing, services and government-education-medical (GEM). These major groups are subdivided: services, for example, include transportation, utilities, financial institutions and hotels/motels. Further analyses refine these subsectors: hotels/motels, for instance, are divided into resort, convention and transient types (see Chapter 6: Segmentation Strategies).

Special task forces were organised to probe each industry in depth. Investigations covered all aspects of buying, and the nature of specific communication problems — both present and anticipated — within specific industries. This detailed information is then studied by the Product Management Division; the needs of customers become the generators of product strategy. 'That in itself represents a dramatic turning point in AT&T's new product programming, because it had been content to take the latest Bell marvel and find customers for it'.[7]

AT&T also gave attention to innovation, and arranged for the speedier development of new products which, in the past, had taken up to six years from design concept to marketing. (See extended discussion of innovation in Chapter 7.)

The Product Management Division was given a wide range of responsibilities. These included estimating production requirements and ensuring that products perform satisfactorily; arranging availability of products to meet market needs, updating products as necessary; and finally deciding when a product should be withdrawn from sale (see Chapter 6: Product Life Cycle Analysis). Product managers also had the authority to operate two-tier pricing wherever market analyses indicated that it could be an effective method of attracting business. A higher monthly lease is charged for an initial period, after which charges 'drop sharply to a level that covers ongoing expenses of maintenance, administration and the sacred "reasonable contribution to earnings"'.[8] Corporate product managers work closely with their counterparts in the operating companies of AT&T to ensure the close integration and execution of marketing strategies.

An industry orientated salesforce was developed in order to offer expert advice to customers in telecommunication services. To ensure the efficiency of this new sales strategy, AT&T organised a large-scale sales training programme with special courses related to particular industries.

This major realignment of the marketing strategy of a large-scale American industrial group follows the well trodden path which was laid down some years ago by IBM and other highly successful market orientated companies.

Special Trading Practices

In Chapter 2, some of the more sophisticated methods of tackling specific industrial markets were discussed. For example, consortia, leasing, project (turn-key) operations, licensing and systems selling. These flexible approaches typify effective marketing strategies, which aim to attract business by studying the needs of specific customers and their industrial environments, and then providing them with goods and services in a form most likely to be acceptable. Marketing is then perceived as a problem solving activity for particular industries and customers.

International Harvester's Product Support Centre

In the Agricultural Industrial Equipment Division of International Harvester, a radical reappraisal of the value of efficient servicing resulted in a Product

Support Centre which consolidated spare parts, servicing and reliability operations. Dealer servicemen were trained to repair IH's newest tractors; warranty cards were processed by computer; technical editorial staff prepare service manuals to guide IH's 3000 dealers to estimate repair costs and schedule their shop operations; and engineers carefully inspected components that had failed during the warranty period.

Earlier, IH viewed themselves as 'purely a sales organisation. We gave the dealer a product and told him to sell it. The serviceman was just a fireman. He had no authority to settle claims and no way to generate ideas for better servicing procedures'.[9] This orientation was influenced by IH's field organisation. Before the reorganisation, there had been twenty sales districts, with district service managers reporting to sales managers; service representatives worked from district sales offices. Generally, at a time when equipment was becoming more sophisticated, IH's dealer service was deteriorating.

Following a severe fall in agricultural equipment sales and profits in the late 1960s, IH realised that they would have to improve their service operations and give better support to their dealers. The original twenty sales districts were consolidated into nine regions with individual managers responsible for sales, marketing, parts, service and retail operations in each region. Regional service training supervisors and service supervisors were also appointed. Local service representatives were relocated within easy travelling distance of the thirty or so dealers each serves.

In addition to this restructuring, IH instituted a 'certified dealer programme', designed to upgrade service to the end-user. Dealers were carefully checked for the quality of their staff, tools, etc. 'Service has to be on a completely different level from what it used to be: 'you don't take someone off the street to work on a tractor worth $30,000'.[9] As an incentive to dealers to obtain 'certification', IH decided to allow them to sell service maintenance contracts for its equipment and to charge IH their list price for the components used in maintenance work.

IH regarded the potential benefits from good servicing operations to extend to opportunities to collect data from service contracts, parts sales, and warranty claims which will enable them to estimate the effective life of components and the causes, perhaps, of premature ageing.

Service training was regarded as an important element of IH's comprehensive marketing strategy. Courses ranged from special five-day programmes concerned with new products to one-day 'refresher' events for dealers and their customers organised by local service representatives. Representatives were set training quotas, measured in training hours (one training hour represents one hour spent with one dealer or his customer).

THE CREATIVE ROLE OF SERVICING

In Chapter 2, the growth of the modern service economy was traced, and the dependence of the national economy on non-tangibles was seen to be of major importance. The concept of the augmented product was also discussed: that a business deal may often mean far more than a tangible product. Surrounding the core product may be 'added values' created by skilful marketing that provides customers with many benefits, such as technical training, after-sales service, comprehensive warranties, etc. The tendency to integrate the servicing function, and to improve its status within the firm, is a step towards greater efficiency. For too long the service side of many organisations has been regarded rather as a nuisance than as offering management unique opportunities to back up their products and secure further profitable business. Today, efficient marketing should include first-class servicing arrangements. Before VW developed their British marketing operations, several regional warehouses, strategically based, were organised to ensure that spare parts could be obtained with minimum delay. A similar strategy was followed some years later by Renault, which built a huge new parts distribution centre at Reading to feed component supplies to regional stores throughout the UK.

KEEPING CUSTOMERS INFORMED

One of the most irritating feelings which people tend to have from time to time is that what they are, or what they think, is of little concern to the faceless organisations — public or private — with which they are 'forced' to transact business. No *person* seems to be interested in them and their problems; they are about as significant as a flea on an elephant. Even if they manage to secure a listener, their complaints seem to be little heeded, or they are met with stunning indifference or crass rudeness. Eventually, even the 'silent majority' grow tired of such malpractice and seek, wherever possible, alternative sources of supply. In many markets, these replacement products will attract others to change their buying preferences.

Marketers should, therefore, improve their communications with distributors and with end-users. Some American companies are reported[9] to have set up 'hot-lines' (toll-free direct telephone calling) which are growing in popularity. Callers can receive accurate information about, for example, parts and equipment from specially trained service consultants who have access to microfilmed data. This creative approach to servicing customers illustrates how astute firms can add to the satisfactions offered to their customers, especially if they are experiencing difficulties in obtaining supplies for vital equipment. Customer loyalty is worth a great deal of thought and effort.

Complaints often arise from bad communication or the entire absence of it. For instance, customers should be advised, in good time, of possible delays in shipment of certain products or in the execution of some services. Goodwill can be fostered by keeping customers informed about likely shortages of raw materials or components, often outside the control of individual firms.

During the paper industry's difficulties in 1973 and 1974, a leading American company instructed their salesmen to tell customers the actual nature of the problems, and then cooperated with them in working out new schedules. This positive approach strengthened customer loyalty as well as boosting the morale of their salespeople.

An American business consultant examined the Civil Aeronautics Board records of passenger complaints and noticed that three airlines — Continental, Delta and Western — 'consistently showed the smallest number of complaints and were usually among the leaders in profit margins. On the other hand, Pan American and Eastern had both a high level of complaints and financial difficulties in recent years'.[10]

By improving servicing arrangements to complaints, a whole new era of marketing prospects can be opened up. Customers will respond to genuine efforts to provide them with greater benefits. New products are more likely to be adopted if those used at present have been backed up by satisfactory service. With some products, especially where intrinsic differences among competitive lines are small, the quality of service back-up may be the deciding factor in placing business. (Also refer to Chapter 3: Post-decisional Dissonance).

PLANNING CUSTOMER SERVICE

Maintaining a high level of customer service clearly entails costs; these have to be justified. In profit-orientated organisations, success will, in the final issue, be measured by the higher level of profitability achieved by adopting more comprehensive sales-servicing policies. Sometimes, immediate results may not be spectacular; it may take time to win back lost customers and to reassure those who were on the brink of departure.

An article in the *Harvard Business Review*[11] gave three examples of where customer service had proved really effective: a supplier to the oil industry attributed a 5% increase in sales directly to the improved delivery service and reduced number of stock shortages which they had achieved several months ago; a tool manufacturer's use of air freight had enabled them to enter a new market; a food manufacturer evaluated their customer's real service needs, redesigned their entire distribution system, and thereby saved $2 million annually.

Although the companies quoted had applied different solutions to their problems, each had evaluated the contribution of the service element to marketing success, and had followed a six-step programme for customer service management. This phased plan is as follows:

1. Define the elements of service
2. Determine the customer's viewpoint
3. Design a competitive service 'package'
4. Develop a programme to sell service

5. Market-test the programme
6. Establish performance controls

The first stage requires marketers to identify the precise nature of the service to be supplied to their customers. In the case of industrial products, aspects of service could range from order processing time through to efficient maintenance calls. Other elements could include delivery time for spares, consistent quality, etc. This preparatory analysis should be undertaken thoroughly and as objectively as possible, perhaps by an independent consultant.

The next stage should take note of three important aspects of the customer's view of service: (1) additional elements of service perceived by customers to be important (more information about products; more convenient invoicing, etc.); (2) economic significance of each element of service to the customer (these reasons require careful checking); (3) rating of competitors' service levels by the customer (clues may be given to help in designing more attractive services).

Designing a competitive service 'package' follows the same principles as in the development of tangible products (refer to earlier chapters on marketing research principles). Customers' service needs should be analysed and the effects, for example, of certain delivery periods should be assessed: 'if failure to deliver the product within ten days after receipt of a customer's order will shut down his plant, the minimum service level required is obvious. Similarly, if all competitors are meeting a seven-day delivery schedule, there is a strong indication that the company should do at least as well'.[11] If additional levels of service are planned, the likely impact on customers' businesses should be carefully assessed. 'Sometimes better service can even be provided at lower cost — for example, by shipping parts of a product line by air freight rather than use field warehouses'.[11]

Operational research techniques may usefully be employed in assessing the most effective methods of providing specific types of service.

The fourth phase — selling the service — is critical. An ingenious service is of no real value until it is used by those for whom it was planned. Like new products, novel services require expert marketing. This includes planned selling, good publicity, and all other elements of an effective marketing mix.

The fifth phase — market testing — applies to services some of the valuable techniques used for several years with products. Pilot marketing schemes, suitably controlled and researched, may be extremely useful in assessing total market demand and in amending certain elements of a service before it is launched nationally.

The final phase relates to the establishment of quantitative standards of performance for each service element. Causes of variance should be analysed and corrective action taken. Often, of course, services present special problems because some elements, for example, delivery, are outside the direct control of the marketer. But alternative methods may be devised to overcome some of these handicaps to good service.

The importance of objective enquiry is illustrated by a company which 'established a nationwide network of thirty warehouses which was capable of delivering products to most customers in one-day transit time. However, the investment was wasted because the company spent an average of six days on order processing ...'.[10] The need for accurate management information is just as crucial in the service area as it is with goods which rely heavily on the quality of clerical as well as technical services. (It would be useful to refer again to Chapters 5 and 6 dealing with strategic planning.)

Research[11] into customer service by a large American company which sold two major product lines — one to institutional customers and one to retail outlets ranging from individual stores to large chains, revealed the following principal general findings:

1. Retailers were inclined to be indifferent to delivery service time compared with the other factors that influenced their relationship with suppliers, provided a minimum level of service was constantly given.
2. Institutional buyers, however, considered reliable delivery service as important as any other commercial factor.
3. Both classes of customers regarded the frequency of the salesperson's calls as a major element of customer service.
4. Supplier inventory reliability — having all items in stock – was held to be just as important as delivery time.

The customers' view of service was noted to have 'many complex and interrelated dimensions' — delivery time, order placement convenience, availability of goods ordered, etc.

It is important for marketing managers to observe that 'the overall image the customer had of the supplier from salesman contacts, trade advertising and relations, and product quality affected his reaction to delivery time'.[10] Suppliers who enjoyed a good overall reputation were likely to be tolerated if delivery times were not always favourable. On the other hand, customers who were displeased with some aspect of the company — pricing policy, for instance — also tended to complain about service'.[10]

It should be borne in mind by recruitment and training departments that sales representatives were viewed by both types of customers as contributing a major element of customer service. It was noted in Chapter 3, for instance, that the manufacturer's salesman was regarded as a source of highly useful and reliable information. Despite technological advances, the human factor in business is still highly significant.

PRODUCT DESIGN: CREATIVE CONTRIBUTION TO MARKETING SUCCESS

Costs of labour, raw materials and overheads are rising inexorably; competition is keener than ever experienced and is truly global in its effects;

buyers are more demanding and knowledgeable; and supplies of essential materials and components are often at peril. Every weapon in the management armoury should be mobilised in the counter-attack; among the most valuable of these is product design.

No firm can ignore the function of design and still expect to survive and prosper, especially when competitors from distant parts of the world are prepared to make design a significant marketing attraction. Design is an integral part of a product; it is the fusion of utility and beauty so that maximum motivation to buy is created. But even an ideal design is not likely to be successful without the support of the other factors in the marketing mix, e.g. sensitive pricing, effective distribution and expert promotion. A carefully planned marketing strategy integrates design policy with the other factors which contribute to profitable business. There is a reciprocal relationship between design and price, methods of distribution, etc. Only if these various factors are closely coordinated and organised can marketing strategies really achieve corporate objectives. Design policies must be drawn up within the overall marketing plan, to which it should make a distinctive and carefully integrated contribution. (See Chapters 5 and 6; Product Policy.)

Aesthetic Appeals *are* Relevant to Industrial Products

The aesthetics of design are not restricted to consumer products, as Theodore Levitt[12] has indicated. A testing machine was shown to a panel of highly experiencd technical directors, one version of which had a front panel designed by the engineers who had developed the equipment; the alternative machine, intrinsically identical, was fitted with a control panel designed by professional industrial designers. This latter version attracted twice the purchase intention compared with the engineers' design.

Another insight into the influence of design in technical products concerns a Canadian pump manufacturer who was asked why he thought it necessary to have their range of machines redesigned because, after all, they were only used underground. His reply reflected commercial acumen 'May be, but they are not bought underground'.[13]

The added values of good styling have been shown to influence buying decisions, even though the effects may not be at a conscious level or openly admitted.

Other striking examples[14] of the contribution to profitability made by effective design related to the driver's cab of an excavator which was redesigned to give all-round vision. This not only made the driver's job easier and safer, but also resulted in a significant reduction in the time taken to train drivers. In another case, a spectrometer proved difficult to demonstrate because it could not be carried easily in a representative's car and was too bulky to take inside a laboratory. Professional designers were able to reduce the size by half through rearranging the components, thus directly helping the sales campaign.

Product design is playing an increasingly important part in buying decisions; better educated, more widely travelled and experienced buyers are assessing products far more critically than a few years ago. Some domestic products, e.g. vacuum cleaners, floor polishers or spin dryers, are fundamentally the same mechanically as their predecessors of over a generation ago. But in many cases, by clever restyling, designers have been able to extend the life cycle of these products.

Innovation — one of the prime responsibilities of marketing management (see Chapter 7) — is closely linked to design; indeed, the two are working partners in the task of attracting a flow of new business to a firm. Although it is widely recognised that successsful innovation is one of the most difficult areas of business, the role of the designer is frequently limited to his or her professional specialism. But market-orientated design is unlikely unless designers and marketing executives work in partnership, sharing their respective individual expertise. Industrial design has a purpose: to attract and keep customers in competitive markets.

Industrial design, it is said[15], should be related not only to the invention as such, but to the wider innovative scene that involves materials, systems, principles of statics, kinetics and thermodynamics, the relevant scientific and engineering specialisms, calculation, drafting and experience; it takes account of collateral forces — the environment, market conditions, conservation, fashion, obsolescence, etc.

Planning Product Benefits

Experienced marketers plan their products so that they offer a 'package of benefits' to their customers. This creative approach acknowledges that people, whether they are buying for their individual needs or for organisations, are influenced by many motivations: economic, social, cultural and psychological. To assume that price is always the dominant buying influence, reflects too narrow a conception of buying behaviour. Products may be acquired because of the desire to own something of unusual beauty or exclusivity; too low a price may, in fact, be a deterrent. Rarely does one motive alone influence human behaviour; motivations interact and modify the effects of single motives, for example, consumers may be motivated by economy to choose the lowest-priced brand of a product, but, at the same time, they will also be motivated by safety, security or risk factors. So they tend to select well known brands, even though lower-priced alternatives may be available'.[16]

Design Is Not Just a Pretty Face

Product design should not be merely cosmetic or some kind of face-lift; apart from aesthetic appeal, products should function well: they should provide the fundamenal satisfactions which buyers expect. In designing furniture, for example, problems of ergonomics arise. Chairs should be shaped so that they are comfortable to sit in and support areas of the body such as the spine. With tools, it is essential that they work efficiently and are safe to use; integrated design ensures that components, such as handles, are styled for ease in holding, reducing muscular fatigue and improving safety in use.

In a NEDO report[17] concentrating on manufacturing industry, product design was defined as 'both engineering design and aesthetic design. Both are important. Too often industrial design considerations predominate in consumer goods, to the detriment of engineering design, and the reverse is true of engineering capital goods. Good design is perceived to increase the value added to the resources of a business; it is not just a peripheral activity, but plays a core role in the development of markets. Unfortunately, however, as the NEDO report observes, products tend to be designed 'in isolation from all the other key functions'. At a relatively late stage of development, product designs are often modified to meet market needs which were inadequately identified earlier. In other cases, designs are changed at a late stage because of production problems or cost constraints that are suddenly brought into discussions. Such wasteful behaviour could be avoided if the design function was integrated into the early planning stages, and adequate market information was available and shared among designers, marketers, production and finance specialists.

The NEDO report recommends that companies 'should designate an appropriate member of their boards to take on the design function as a prime responsibility'. Design should be regarded as part of the investment decisions made by companies. (This point should be considered in relation to innovation strategies: Chapter 7.)

Design can make a direct contribution to the development of high added value products, which are essential for the development of UK industrial output, especially in overseas markets. But the design function must accept the disciplines of commercial management, and accept that design specifications should only be drawn up after objective market enquiries have been made.

In 1983, a report[18] was commissioned by the Department of Education and Science in association with the Design Council to identify what skills, knowledge and attitudes industry requires from industrial designers and how far these requirements are being fulfilled.

A survey covered about 300 individuals in 130 manufacturing and other companies in the UK, France, Germany, Italy, Scandinavia and the Netherlands. Eighty-five UK manufacturing companies were interviewed, of which 78 gave information about their designers.

Among the principal findings of this systematic survey are the following: 23 UK companies had a separate design budget; 20 UK companies had a designer at board or equivalent level (these companies generally made products heavily dependent on design); it was felt that designers were not sufficiently willing to offer alternative solutions to a design problem, and did not sufficiently appreciate the value of seeing the product in its market context; there was general agreement that basic design skills were the most important, followed by those needed to adapt to a corporate environment — about 20% of respondents regarded the latter as a particular cause of dissatisfaction, and cited designers' inability to work to deadlines and also to communicate effectively with other management; there was an above-average shortfall in industrial designers' awareness of commercial realities; designers were perceived to be insufficiently aware of market needs, and seemed to want to educate public taste rather than respond to it.

In continental Europe, the percentage of companies with separate design budgets was about twice that of the UK. In general, European companies rated highly the contribution of design to commercial success, and it was judged likely to become even more important; Italian, Scandinavian and West German companies were far more aware of the importance of industrial design to market success than French or UK companies. 'Adapting to the corporate environment' was rated rather lower by European companies than UK ones, but foreign language proficiency and the ability to assess customer feedback were rated more important in Europe than in the UK.

There was overall agreement in the UK and abroad that more emphasis on corporate skills in design education would improve company competitiveness. It was interesting to note that design education abroad is no better in this respect than in the UK; moreover, European firms regard British design education as superior in general.

Successful companies appeared to combine an *excellent* performance in one of the following five perceived criteria — identification of market opportunity, competitive pricing, quality and performance, delivery and aesthetic appeal — with *adequate* performance in all the others.

Profitable Design is a Team Effort

Product design depends on effective team work; the complexity of modern equipment increasingly demands a synthesis of skills.

McKinsey (see Holland[19]) studied the manufacturing operations of UK firms and their foreign competitors. They found, for instance, that overseas companies tend to spend a 'much greater proportion of overheads on engineering and marketing but considerably less on functions related to production'. In other words, they 'spend more on getting the design right and much less subsequently on getting the product made'. What Britain lacks is competence at manufacturing engineering; there are not enough manufacturing engineers and they are not given sufficient status in their firms.

Product design largely dictates the processes of manufacture and the costs involved; it is central to the whole concept of profitability. Yet the simple principle of integrated design is 'missed by many British industries ... Too often British product design progresses from concept to finished product with little or none of this essential feedback. The gleam in the researcher's eye is converted into a prototype by a development engineer whose primary objective is to produce something that works as well as possible. Then, the manufacturing engineer creates the facilities and processes to make the protoype in quantity. Finally, others try to sell it and maintain it'.[19]

This uncoordinated approach to product design can result in severe diseconomies in production; costs of processing cheaper materials may outweigh the initial savings.

McKinsey emphasised that manufacturing engineers in overseas companies have considerable authority in the development of products. Instead of the widespread British practice of a *linear* approach to design, a *cyclical* one is adopted. Development prototypes are subject to critical commercial and technical evaluation. There is constant feedback from the various departments of a business — production, purchasing, marketing and costing — to eliminate snags: several redesigns may be necessary before a product is finally approved for production. (See Chapter 1: Corporate Performance Inputs.)

A major UK firm employs only six graduate engineers in product design, exclusively in development engineering. Their American competitors, whose output was only 50% greater, had nearly 400 graduates employed, mostly in manufacturing engineering. 'The American company's production overhead staff, however (schedulers, chasers, storeman, quality inspectors, and so on) are fewer by a factor of 30. And, not surprisingly, the US product is cheaper, more reliable, and can be delivered faster'.[19]

The case for including designers in corporate long-range planning teams has been well argued: 'a new type of engineer has begun to emerge who may eventually provide the element in the forward planning team which is still normally lacking. This engineering specialisation is sometimes called "industrial design", sometimes "design engineering"'. Engineering, technological and social sciences may be fused 'to produce a multi-discipline man, part scientist, part technologist, part artist'.[20] This type of industrial designer has an enormously important part to play in the profitable marketing of products, and also in the provision of amenities in the public sector. The Research Unit of the School of Industrial Design (Engineering) at the Royal College of Art has contributed most valuably to the public health services by designing many appliances for handicapped people. Professor Bruce Archer has underlined the need for design activities to be integrated within the area of strategic planning. In a project concerned with improving the design of a range of dental equipment, it was found that the policy of bringing the designer into the heart of business discussions resulted in more effective solutions. 'Time and again, the presence of the designer at the market researcher's elbow led to the formulation of vital secondary questions, and of the market researcher at the designer's elbow led to more valid interpretation of the answers'.[21]

It is essential to plan and control the development and design of products. The techniques of marketing research should be applied to testing new product designs, and in monitoring the market performance of existing products. The investment costs of new products are heavy, and it is vital for marketing management to have objective information about their product ranges; this includes an assessment of design trends. (See Chapters 4 and 5.)

Ideally, designers should work, as McKinsey has recommended, in partnership with other functional managers in companies. These cover all the diverse activities to be found in industrial organisations: costing, financial control, purchasing, production, marketing research, marketing, including promotional activities. These functions should be viewed as complementary rather than competitive. (See Chapter 1 for detailed discussion of the interfaces of marketing.)

Marketing executives and designers should exchange ideas about ways in which the design of existing products could be improved, as well as being closely involved in the design development stages of new products. James Pilditch[14], writing of consultant design services, referred to the misguided kindness which inhibits some clients from briefing designers thoroughly because 'we don't want to impose our ideas on you'. Designers, says Pilditch, need good briefing: 'Describe the problem and your objectives. Describe the market, customer, competition, cost targets and your production capability ... The more the designer knows of your problem and situation, the better'.

Designers might be encouraged to attend sales conferences; they would be able to learn about reactions of customers as well as the salesforce to product improvements and also new models. Designers might occasionally accompany selected members of the salesforce and meet customers at first hand. If a company is active in exporting, designers should visit these territories and see for themselves the conditions under which their products have to operate or be consumed. From these personal visits, designers' creative talents will be stimulated, and they will gain insight into the needs of those who actually use the products they design.

Designers, in turn, should be prepared to learn about the business techniques of costing, production planning, marketing and the related activities that are necessary for the profitable exploitation of their designs.

Professional designers accept that their skills have to be exercised within the resources of the companies for which they are working. To quote Bruce Archer again: 'If managements are going to achieve better vertical integration of the innovative effort, then there will certainly have to be much more management involvement on the part of designers than has been normal in the past. That is to say, designers must become more directly and more deeply involved in problems of investment, problems of the market place and problems of value, price and cost, as well as with the problems of function, production and aesthetics with which they are already familiar'.[21] Designers may, perhaps, profitably extend their knowledge to modern techniques such as those used in operational research management.

Obtaining Design Skills

The services of a skilled designer are not limited to large companies which are able to absorb the costs of relatively sophisticated management structures. Some consumer product companies, e.g. the larger firms in the textiles and pottery tableware industries, have traditionally had a staff of resident designers. Many companies, however, use the services of consultant designers; these may also contribute to, and complement, the work being undertaken by staff designers. The old commercial criterion of 'make-or-buy' may be applied. In complex areas of business activities such as law or taxation, many companies although having members of staff qualified as general practitioners, call in the services of specialists when expert knowledge in depth is required in connection with particular problems. Specialised design skills may likewise be acquired.

The Design Council, 28 Haymarket, London SW1, which has extended its interests to cover industrial products, can assist firms in the difficult task of finding the right designer for their particular range of products. The Design Selection Service maintains a detailed record of designers which enables them to match a firm's needs and an individual designer's skills and experience. For a nominal fee, the Design Council will discuss the design problems facing a firm and present them with a short list of suitable designers. The professional association for industrial designers is the Society of Industrial Artists and Designers, 12 Carlton House Terrace, London SW1. It offers manufacturers a Design Advisory Service, and will provide enquirers with full details of designers who are considered to have knowledge and experience relevant to specific design projects. The SIAD also maintains a central library of photoprints, proofs, specimens of design work, etc. which may be inspected by prospective clients. In addition, the SIAD keeps a register of qualified designers who are seeking staff appointments; these are matched against vacancies notified by client companies, and arrangements can be made to circulate specific vacancies to all members of SIAD.

Design fees are normally based on the time involved in fulfilling a commission; in addition, business expenses attributable to the work undertaken are also charged. Occasionally, designers prefer to accept minimum fees and recoup themselves largely on a royalty basis. One well known hardware manufacturer obtained by licensing arrangements access to a fundamental new design for their range of products. It proved to be a highly profitable negotiation.

Firms of *all* sizes, and over a wide spectrum of industry, can have access to the skills of professional designers; there is no valid argument for ignoring the design content of products of all kinds. An effective design policy should be developed as part of the overall marketing strategy of progressive companies. Britain once led the world in the excellence of her products; British manufacturers should regain their prestige by ensuring that the services of professional designers are used fully in the development and improvement of their products.

VALUE ANALYSIS AND VALUE ENGINEERING

Value analysis is defined by British Standards as 'a systematic interdisciplinary examination of design and other factors affecting the cost of a product or service in order to define means of achieving the specified purpose most economically at the required standards of quality and reliability'. It involves an analytical approach to the design and manufacture of products so that costs of production are rigidly controlled or reduced while efficient functioning is not impaired in any way. 'In an engineering sense VA is a technique used to examine ways of redesigning a product so that it costs less to build or functions more effectively, or both. Quality must not be sacrificed to cut costs'.[22]

Value engineering refers to the analytical approach, outlined above, applied to *new* products at the design stage, while value analysis is the term used to describe systematic investigation of *existing* products.

As with several other management techniques, value analysis originated during the Second World War when there were considerable problems in the availability and costs of manufacturing supplies. In the US, pioneering work in this area was undertaken by the General Electric Company, where value analysis was developed into a systematic and disciplined technique. Interest in this approach continued after the war and in 1959, the Society of American Value Engineers was founded in Washington DC. In the 1950s, the American Department of Defense adopted value analysis as a formal requirement for all government contracts.

Value analysis has now spread widely, although it has been adopted less enthusiastically in the UK than in the US.

The British Productivity Council[23] published sixteen case studies in value analysis; in seven of the cases it was advantageous for firms buying equipment to encourage suppliers to contribute their technical expertise in solving production problems. Again, the importance of the industrial salesperson in these negotiations is clear. Effective industrial selling entails considerable analytical and creative ability backed up by adequate technical knowledge, and also the skill to communicate ideas persuasively. (See Chapters 4 and 5.)

An American capital-goods company's policy was to sell the largest, highest powered, most maintenance-free units possible. Customers, however, began to request smaller, less costly units 'without the rugged engineering characteristics required for maintenance-free operation'.[24] Marketing management recommended that the product line should be radically redesigned, but the manufacturing and technical experts strongly opposed this, arguing that the current design and cost structure were superior to any competitors. What was needed, in their opinion, was more selling effort: their views were backed by top management. The company lost a substantial share of its market before the president ordered the whole range to be redesigned. 'Now that he has, things are looking up ... it is unrealistic, of course, to expect a dramatic turnaround'.[24]

Colt International Ltd are enthusiastic users of value analysis techniques which have solved many types of problems for them. One special application involved a huge oil-fired space heater which was technologically superb but too costly to attract business. By slightly varying the specifications, Colt were able to buy parts, such as fans, at much lower prices than they could produce them internally. The actual construction of the heater was also carefully analysed. It was found that by reinforcing the external panels, for instance, it was possible to eliminate the expensive steel framework which had supported them. Altogether, Colt reduced costs 50% without affecting technical performance.

From this pioneer application of VA, Colt then analysed its entire product range, and it is now standard practice to use VA at the design stage of new products. 'Since the company began using VA in 1964 its sales have increased eight-fold'.[22] The precise savings made by VA are not readily calculable, but estimates have placed it well over $500,000 a year. As observed in Chapter 1, Colt's VA policy has encouraged closer working between the different departments; managers are no longer considering problems in isolation.

SOCIAL RESPONSIBILITY OF BUSINESS

The concept and practice of business has been under searching scrutiny for some years. The activities of large corporations, in particular, have been ruthlessly examined by 'activist' groups which, for various motives, have energetically attacked some of the practices of industries and even individual firms.

Social Audit Ltd, a British non-profit making organisation, has the avowed intention of improving the general responsiveness of government and corporate bodies to the public. This independent body, an offshoot of the Public Interest Research Centre, has published in its quarterly journal *Social Audit*, detailed and critical reports of some British-based companies. It has also made an evaluation of the standards and practices of advertising in Britain. *Social Audit* and its parent organisation PIRC are substantially funded by the Joseph Rowntree Social Service Trust, and the Joseph Rowntree Charitable Trust respectively.

In America, Ralph Nader, who jumped to fame as the result of his highly successful 'consumerist' campaigns, has extended his range of missionary activities. Public Citizens Inc., which has the financial and active support of over 150,000 private citizens, aims to achieve greater freedom, justice and democracy in American society. Nader's sphere of interests has widened far beyond the testing of products for safety, and this new organisation includes political, economic and social issues. This highly organised lobby may well become as significant as the consumerist movement which developed from humble origins: it would be unwise to discount its growth potential. Consumerism is certainly no passing phenomenon as a survey[25] of US managers, subscribers to the *Harvard Business Review,* indicated some time ago. They viewed 'consumerism as permanent, and are optimistic about its effect on the market place ... by far the most dominant management view of consumerism is that it represents an opportunity for marketers rather than a threat ...'. The traditional 'buyer beware' philosophy of the market place is seen as fast eroding. The most constructive consumer-orientated programme that a company could undertake would be to improve the quality of its products and its commerical behaviour.

The concept of countervailing power in society has been noted in America, where the interplay of various value sources in farm life, small towns, churches, business, education and so on have shaped individual values and, in sum, the values of society. If business organisations have now reached a stage where they have unacceptable dominance in society 'then society must restore its *countervailing* influence and business leadership must increase its ability to discern the social consequences of decisions and develop the ability to set social goals'.[26]

Some large corporations are leading the way in accepting their responsibilities to society. Xerox has declared that its basic philosophy as a corporation is involvement in the problems of society. Employees are granted social and service leave up to twelve months, during which they may, without personal loss, 'make their contribution to a better society'.[26]

Participation in management decision making and in public affairs is increasingly demanded by those who live in democratic societies. As a society becomes more affluent and better educated, its members grow more sensitive to official and business policies.

Environmental pollution, for example, has been the subject of a Royal Commission; the Clean Air Act of 1956 has significantly reduced smoke pollution and has dramatically changed the appearance of Britain's industrial cities and towns. Large industrial firms, such as ICI have spent many millions of pounds on capital equipment to control effluents.

If three words could be said to mirror the mood of modern society they might well be: agitation, representation, and participation. People at virtually all levels of society have quickly learned how to make their voices heard in the market place; the mass media have frequently encouraged the trend towards organised and articulate criticism of trading practices. Company directors should accept that their responsibilities do not stop at the balance sheet; greater skill and sensitivity in communications should be developed (see Chapter 10).

In the past, technology and business have had some disastrous relationships with society. Smog, fumes, waste and dubious business behaviour have all added to the ammunition of opinion leaders who, in general, have been remarkably successful in their zealous campaigns. The growth of consumerism across countries has been viewed[27] as a social movement with four essential stages: crusading, popular movement, managerial, and bureaucratic. These four stages could offer guidelines for marketing strategies. 'The crusading and popular stage difference is analogous to the faddist–innovators vs. the activist–early majority. While growth to the managerial stage denotes the movement as a more formal activity, the bureaucratic stage is the complete institutionalisation of the cause'.[27] Firms should assess the nature of the particular 'consumerist' activity and respond effectively. To keep strictly within the present permissible legal limits of, for example, pollution, does not necessarily provide an acceptable answer to hostile and well informed critics. Inertia or insensitivity to public opinion could eventually lead to even greater official intervention in corporate affairs; the choice lies with top management.

CORPORATE PERCEPTIONS OF THE FUTURE

In 1982, a national survey in the US of the chief marketing officers of *Fortune's* 1000 top industrial firms and the 300 largest service organisations investigated the operating environment envisaged by these executives in the 1980s. (20% response to a mail survey was achieved.) The following general findings resulted: (1) the consumer movement will greatly increase its influence on business; (2) customers will be more eager to try new products, but will buy fewer but better products than in the last decade; (3) conspicuous consumption will be replaced by more sophisticated, critical buying; (4) banking will continue to experience increasing competition; (5) government regulations will continue to curtail the number of products offered by a company in a given category; (6) wage and price controls are a posssibility in the 1980s; (7) permanently high inflation will be present; (8) a steady supply of raw materials will become more of a major concern; (9) product life cycles will be shorter and fewer raw products will be successful; (10) despite regular media reports, there was disagreement that foreign firms will become world leaders in technology and new product development — but it was agreed that investment by foreign firms in US business posed a threat.

Overall, surveyed executives perceived foreign competition as an increasing threat; that consumers will become more sophisticated and demanding, and that greater intervention in business by government is to be expected during the 1980s.

Despite these constraints, executives were optimistic about opportunities, but felt the need for 'greater precision in marketing strategies to deal with the attendant high risks'.

Another US survey[29] covering 64 of the largest companies in eight major domestic manufacturing industries focused on their strategies 'for survival in a hostile environment'. The industries were over the following sectors: steel, tyre and rubber, automative, heavy duty truck and construction equipment, home appliances, beer and cigarette manufacture.

Research findings suggest that basic industries in mature hostile environments (lower growth, inflation, more regulatory constraints and sharpened competition) are moving through a structural evolution that is leading ultimately to four industry and performance subgroups: (1)leadership position; (2) next best position; (3) next worse position; and (4) marginal or failing position'.

Successful companies will be those which achieve either the lowest cost or the most differentiated market position. At the same time, survival is possible for other companies provided they identify suitable market niches and realign their resources so that they gain leadership in these submarkets. Weaker companies will suffer from the inability to achieve lowest cost or effective market positioning; they will be highly vulnerable in the abrasive conditions of the 1980s.

The research concludes that: 'The laws of the jungle change as maturity comes and hostility intensifies. In such a jungle, the range of strategic options narrows, requiring both an early warning of the coming hostility and an early strategic repositioning for a company to survive and prosper'.[29]

There are, as some other American researchers[30] point out, a number of ways to respond to what is termed 'the new global game'. The first, and perhaps most prevalent, is to wish for a return of 'the good old days', acting as if nothing had changed since the 1950s, or lobbying for various kinds of trade restrictions, import quotas, etc. The second response is basically emotional and often adopts a patriotic guise: 'buy home-produced goods'. However, the third response is proactive and creative: executives search for new opportunities suitable for their corporate resources (see Chapter 5, when firms were classified broadly as either reactive or proactive.)

In this dynamic environment, there are four questions[30] to be put to business executives:

1. Given your political assumptions about the world and your premises for change in the 1980s, how should your business strategy change?
2. Do your key managers understand that the global environment is changing, and are they developing a strategy for repositioning your business?
3. Does your organisation facilitate and encourage the identification and coordination of environmental trends?
4. In your strategic planning process, do your managers think through their assumptions about the environment, evaluate the risks and develop new alternatives?

The answers to these fundamental questions should indicate how well a company is responding to the changing global environment.

SUMMARY

Many factors have contributed to the dynamic nature of modern markets, some of these are technical and economic; others are political, social and behavioural. Organic growth is increasingly difficult, but opportunities still exist for proactive, creative management. High added value products incorporating attractive design features should be developed.

Selling and distribution strategies should be critically reviewed; new methods may be appropriate. Servicing of customers adds to the 'augmented product' value which helps companies to differentiate their products.

Value analysis and value engineering involve an analytical approach to the design and manufacture of products which can lead to improved product performance and profitability.

The social responsibilities of business are increasingly debated and 'action groups' encourage critical, and often hostile, attitudes to specific industries and firms. Agitation, representation, and participation seem to mirror the mood of modern society. Organisations of all kinds cannot ignore their newly perceived roles in society. To keep strictly within legal limits is a lamentably inadequate corporate policy.

The future operating environment will stretch the talents of corporate executives. Well devised strategic planning is more important than ever; but plans should be flexible — the global environment is inherently unstable. Risk policies should form an integral part of overall planning.

REFERENCES

1. Freeman, Christopher, *The Economics of Industrial Innovation*, Penguin, Harmondsworth, 1974.
2. Kempner, Thomas, Macmillan, Keith and Hawkins, Kevin, *Business and Society: Tradition and Change*, Allen Lane, London, 1974.
3. Mishan, E.J., *The Costs of Economic Growth*, Penguin, Harmondsworth, 1967.
4. Gabor, Dennis, *The Mature Society*, Secker and Warburg, London, 1972.
5. Ansoff, H. Igor, *Business Strategy*, Penguin, Harmondsworth, 1969.
6. Meadows, Dennis, *The Limits to Growth*, Universe Books, New York, 1972.
7. Hakansson, Hakan (ed.), *International Marketing and Purchasing of Industrial Goods*, Wiley, Chichester, 1982.
8. Taylor, Thayer C., 'AT & T is on the Line — At Last', *Sales Management*, 13 March 1975.
9. Scanlon, Sally, 'International Harvester Revs Up Service', *Sales Management*, 17 February 1975.
10. Korn, Don, 'Customer Service and the Bottom Line', *Sales Management*, 17 February 1975.
11. Hutchinson, William M. and Stolle, John F., 'How to Manage Customer Service', *Harvard Business Review*, Nov./Dec. 1968.
12. Levitt, Theodore, 'The Morality of Advertising', *Harvard Business Review*, July/Aug. 1970.
13. Pilditch, James, *Marketing*, November 1971.
14. Pilditch, James, 'Five Questions About Design', *The Director*, October, 1974.
15. Locke, H. Brian, 'Innovation by Design', *Long Range Planning*, August 1976.
16. Chisnall, Peter M., *Marketing — A Behavioural Analysis*, McGraw-Hill, Maidenhead, 1985.

17. Corfield, K.G., 'Product Design', NEDO, London, March 1979.
18. 'The Industrial Design Requirements of Industry', Design Council, London, September 1983.
19. Holland, Roger, 'Industrial Britain's Achilles Hell', *The Director*, May 1974.
20. Black, Misha, 'The Function of Design in Long Range Planning', *Long Range Planning*, June 1972.
21. Archer, Bruce, 'Design and Management for the 70s, *Design*, June 1969.
22. Tavernier, Gerard, 'Where Value Analysis is a Way of Life', *International Management*, February, 1975.
23. British Productivity Council, *Sixteen Case Studies in Value Analysis*, BPC, London, 1964.
24. Ames, Charles B., 'Trappings vs. Substance in Industrial Marketing', *Harvard Business Review*, Jul./Aug. 1970.
25. Greyser, Stephen A. and Diamond, Steven L., '"Probing Opinions"': Business is Adapting to Consumerism', *Harvard Business Review*, Sept./Oct. 1974.
26. Whitaker, John H., 'The Supremacy of the Business Ethic', *Business and Society Review*, No. 10, Summer 1975.
27. Kaufman, Ira and Channon, Derek, 'International Consumerism; A Threat or Opportunity', *Industrial Marketing Management*, Vol. 3, October 1973.
28. Mason, J. Barry and Resnik, Alan, 'Marketing: The Prospects for the 1980s', *Long Range Planning*, Vol. 15, No. 1, 1982.
29. Hall, William K., 'Survival Strategies in a Hostile Environment', *Harvard Business Review*, Sept./Oct. 1980.
30. Charan, Ram and Freeman, R. Edward, 'Planning for the Business Environment of the 1980s', *Journal of Business Strategy*, Vol. 1, No. 2, 1980.

INDEX